101 Projects for Your
Porsche 911

101 Projects for Your
Porsche 911

Wayne R. Dempsey

motorbooks

© 2001 Quarto Publishing Group USA Inc.
Text © 2001 Wayne R. Dempsey

First published in 2001 by Motorbooks, an imprint of The Quarto Group, 100 Cummings Center, Suite 265-D, Beverly, MA 01915, USA. T (978) 282-9590 F (978) 283-2742 www.QuartoKnows.com

All photographs are from the author's collection unless noted otherwise.

Motorbooks titles are also available at discount for retail, wholesale, promotional, and bulk purchase. For details, contact the Special Sales Manager by email at specialsales@quarto.com or by mail at The Quarto Group, Attn: Special Sales Manager, 100 Cummings Center, Suite 265-D, Beverly, MA 01915, USA.

ISBN-13: 978-0-7603-0853-0

Editor: John Adams-Graf
Design Manager: Jim Snyder
Additional photography by Tom Sharpes and Bob Tindel

About the Author:
Wayne R. Dempsey has been working and playing with machines all his life. At the Massachusetts Institute of Technology, he earned both B.S. and M.S. degrees in mechanical engineering, specializing in flexible manufacturing technology. His introduction to automobiles came when he raced with the MIT Solar Electric Vehicle Racing Team. After a few years of building communications satellites for Hughes Space and Communications, Wayne left to pursue an entrepreneurial calling. Literally starting in their garages, Wayne and his partner, Tom Gould, founded Pelican Part, an internet-based Porsche and BMW parts company. Today, Pelican Parts is thriving with the growth in the Internet technology. Wayne maintains the site and has written most of the technical articles that it features (www.pelicanparts.com). He currently owns a 1982 911 SC coupe (featured in this book), a 1960 356B coupe, a 1984 944, and a 1974 914-6 conversion with a 2.7-liter 911S engine under the hood.

On the front cover:
Main: A 1988 3.3 911 Turbo and a sunny day—what more could you ask for? *John Lamm*
Inset: photo by *Wayne R. Dempsey*
On the title page: Nothing quite beats the look of a 911 alloy wheel rim. *David Gooley*
On the back cover: One of the most popular styles for the 911 is the RS Replica. The 1973 911RS is one of the most-sought-after and most-replicated cars around. The conversions can range from the simple addition of fiberglass bodywork and famous lettering to the more complex task of installing a 2.7 RS-spec engine. Either way, replicating the look of the 911 RS is a very popular project for early 911 owners.

Printed in China

CONTENTS

SECTION IX   BODY

SECTION X   ELECTRICAL

SECTION XI   MISCELLANEOUS

ACKNOWLEDGMENTS

It's obvious that a book of this magnitude does not simply write itself, but needs a cooperative effort from many people in all walks of life. A lot of people helped me on this book, and joined in my enthusiastic vision of what I wanted it to be.

First I would like to dedicate this book to my wife Nori, for without her unending support and patience, this project would never have been finished. She has earned herself plenty of "Wayne-time" credit for both the near- and long-term future. Tom Woodford of Factory Tour and Tom Gould of Pelican Parts are primarily responsible for making sure that this book is correct and to the point. When dealing with the 30-year span of production of the 911, there were plenty of times when they kept me from filling in the blanks with information from the back of my mind that wasn't necessarily factual in nature. Tom Woodford, in particular, used his editing pen single-handedly to thrash the unnecessary and sometimes misleading BS out of the book. Tom Gould was especially helpful as my go-to answer man late at night when I was tearing apart my 911SC.

Also extremely helpful were James Bricken and Bob Tindel of Pelican Parts, and Gill Paszek. All three helped to edit multiple sections of the book, and gave me a unique perspective on both what content I should cover and what details I was missing. Special thanks also to Alex Wong of Precision Tech Motorsports in Marina Del Rey. Alex is probably the best professional mechanic I know, and the only one that I trust with the cars I'm too busy to fix myself.

Also special thanks to Bill Duncan and Dick Nuss of Engine Machine Service in Los Angeles for some great machine work, great advice, and the opportunity to take some great photos.

Special thanks are due to John Adams-Graf, my Motorbooks editor, for not cutting too much out of the book to meet our publishing quotas. John also deserves credit for withstanding all the trials and tribulations associated with converting the organization to digital photography. Thanks also to Scott Hanson, who in movie terms could be called my volunteer grip. Thanks are also appropriate for Don at Graphic Presentations for his tireless help with the slides, and the finicky slide machine. Thanks to Tom Sharpes, whose pictures are scattered throughout the book.

Of course, no good acknowledgments section would be complete without a note of thanks to my parents, Meg and Ed Dempsey. In the beginning, I'm certain they thought I was headed for trouble, but somehow they managed to turn the tide, and this book is one of many accomplishments that they have been proud of over the years.

Quite a few other people deserve thanks for their help. Bernard E. Jones for help rebuilding the 911 engine; Darren Bond of Pelican Parts for suggestions on topics and format; Patrick C. Paternie for turning me on to MBI Publishing Company; Don Haney of Pelican Parts, for quite a few pictures and jokes; Craig Stark for pictures of his 911; and Michael Russell for use of his 911 chassis.

INTRODUCTION

Over its 35-year lifespan, the Porsche 911 has earned itself a reputation as one of the world's greatest sports cars. Not only has the 911 been improved and refined over the years to a state of near perfection, it has also garnered a huge, loyal following of people who love to restore them. Porsche 911 owners tend to adore their cars and also enjoy restoring, modifying, and maintaining them to perfection. If you're one of these people, this book was written especially for you.

Information is the key to success in any project or endeavor. Without the proper knowledge, you can make costly mistakes and waste your time as you trudge through the learning process. The projects in this book aim to eliminate any guesswork that you may have while working on your 911. As principal technical writer for Pelican Parts, my slogan has always been, "Let us make the mistakes and warn you about them, so you won't do the same." Believe me, I've made many mistakes and learned the hard way the best and worst way to repair, restore, and modify these cars. My lessons, as well as the lessons learned by the expert mechanics I've consulted with, are compiled here for you.

The projects are written in a format and style that should empower anyone to work on his or her car. One of the principal drawbacks to owning a Porsche 911 is the high cost of maintaining it. You can literally save thousands of dollars in mechanic's costs simply by performing the work yourself. It is the goal of this book to get more people out working on their 911s— it's too much fun not to! Plus, when you personally complete a job on your 911, you get the added satisfaction of having done it yourself. Working on your own car can give you that emotional attachment to your 911 that is common with Porsche owners.

This book is divided into 11 sections, each focusing on a particular system of the Porsche 911. The "backyard" mechanic can perform almost any of the projects contained within these pages over a weekend or two. In an attempt to appeal to everyone, some of the projects are basic, and some are more advanced. Some of the projects are simply overviews of systems on the 911. For example, projects 12 through 14, which cover the 911 engine teardown and rebuild, are simply meant to give you an inside look into what happens when you take your engine in to be rebuilt. For those wanting to tackle this job themselves, keep a lookout for my upcoming book that focuses solely on the 911 engine

rebuilding process.

Most projects follow a distinct how-to format. Step-by-step instructions tell you how to perform the job, what tools to use, and what costly mistakes to avoid. The photos that accompany the projects tell a story of their own. I've spread hints and tips throughout each project, so make sure that you read all the text and captions in the photos before you start.

Please don't be afraid to get this book dirty! The factory workshop manuals are so expensive that most owners have an inherent desire to keep them immaculate and spotless. While keeping them clean is a good way to protect your investment, they aren't very useful sitting in your library when you're down in the garage. Don't treat this book that way—take it with you underneath the car. Get it greasy. Compare the pictures in the book to your own car. Follow along step by step as you tear into each project. If this book gets dirty, then I will sleep well at night knowing that it's being put to good use.

While this book is a great guide for determining what upgrades and maintenance you need to perform on your 911, it's not meant to be the only book for your car. Limited by a fixed page count, I can't provide the detailed diagrams, torque settings, and factory procedures that are documented in the original factory workshop manuals. If you are planning to work on your own car, I recommend that you invest as much as you can in books and information that will help you along the way. Make sure that you review the Information Resources section in the rear of this book for my recommendations of the best places to find additional technical information on the 911.

This book is not meant to be read from cover to cover, but is designed to be flipped through so that you can get an idea of what projects interest you for your 911. I've structured the projects so that you can simply open up the book and start working on your car. I do recommend, however, that you read the "Tools of the Trade" section in the first part of the book, and also Project 1, "Jacking Up Your Car," before you start working on any of the projects.

One of the features in this book that I have taken special care with is the index. I find it especially frustrating when a good book has a lousy index, where you can't find anything useful. For that reason, I've indexed the book according to project, and also listed each index item under multiple names. This way, if there are different names for a part or procedure, it will still be easy to locate it within the body of the text

For example, shocks are listed as both shock absorbers and inserts, as they are sometimes called. Please feel free to use the index as one of your primary guides to the book.

Finally, remember that safety should be your Number One concern. It's very easy to get so intimately involved with working on your 911 that you forget how fragile and vulnerable the human body can be. Have patience, and think about every action you make. Think ahead as to what might happen if you slip, or if something breaks. Using your head a little will go a long way toward protecting yourself.

I hope you enjoy the book, as I have spent a long time compiling this information and filtering it so that it's easy to understand and follow. If you have any feedback or questions for me, you can contact me at this book's dedicated website, http://www.101projects.com. Enjoy!

DECIPHERING THE INFORMATION BOXES

At the beginning of each project you'll find a list of topics keyed to picture icons. This is a guide to assist you in having all the "right stuff" to complete the project. It is sincerely hoped that you'll get a good idea of what you are facing and what you will need in the way of time, tools, talent, and money. Most of the list is self-explanatory, but in case you're curious, here is a break down:

"Time" is a rough estimate for a person who has basic car and tool skills. If you don't know your open-end 15mm from a Vise-Grip, you may want to add to the time estimate.

"Tools" lists what you need to the job at hand. For simple projects, every tool is listed by size and type. For more complex projects, the assumption is that the reader has the basics covered (see "Tools of the Trade" on page 11). In these advanced projects, tools may be listed by general categories (sets of combination wrenches, sockets, etc.) but not by size. Special tools, however, will always be listed specifically.

"Talent" is represented by a little mechanic. One mechanic means any warm body with the inkling to tinker can do the job. Two mechanics means the project requires some mechanical experience and ability. Three mechanics means you should be comfortable working on more complex assemblies, such as top ends, clutches, or exhaust replacement. Four mechanics means preparation, training, and practice are required—these projects are not for novices.

"Applicable Years" is an important box to note before beginning a project. All 911s are not created equally. Model variations may mean what works for one car won't work for another. Always check that your car falls within the year span listed.

"Tab" is a ballpark expense figure. Use it as a basic guideline, not as a firm figure.

"Tinware" lists the parts that you will have to acquire to accomplish this project. This is directly related to "Tab."

"Tip" lists a slick trick that will make the project easier. It might be a gem of knowledge that the shop manual doesn't include.

"Performance Gain" is self-explanatory. What you get for your money is answered right here.

"Complementary Modifications" will offer some trick bits and alterations to help you get the most out of the project. In some cases, these might be other projects that work well when performed with the current one.

Throughout this book, I will refer to the locations of various components. This nomenclature can be confusing at times, because the 911 engine is located in the rear of the car. Just keep in mind that when I refer to the rear of the engine compartment, I'm referring to the back of the car, near the bumper. Likewise, the front of the engine compartment abuts the rear passenger seats.

TOOLS OF THE TRADE

James Bricken of Pelican Parts, a man who might be described as having too many tools for his own good, and I teamed up to write this introduction to building your own tool collection. We've all heard the clichés about having the right to tool for the job. Most of us have heard stories about a botched repair or wasted hours because somebody attempted to save a few dollars by putting off buying the right tool. Here's the nuts and bolts of it: Even though all good mechanics will admit that there is no substitute for the correct tool, they will also admit that no matter how many tools you have, you will never have every tool you need.

THE BASIC TOOL SET

There are literally tens of thousands of tools available to perform an equal number of tasks. Fortunately, it's not likely you'll need all of them.

Everybody has to start somewhere, and for most people that means a small set or kit (often received as a gift). Sets are an excellent way to buy tools, since the discounts are pretty hefty, compared to buying each tool individually. Aside from the cost, one of your primary considerations when buying tools should be quality. The warranty and ease of replacement are other good considerations, but it does no good if you have to mail your broken tool back to Taiwan Province of China for replacement, or if your tool truck guy doesn't come around at 2 A.M. on Sunday when you need him the most. Ultimately, the best bet is to buy tools that don't break, or to carry the spares you need.

Two of the best and most economical places to purchase tools are Sears and Home Depot. They both offer good-quality tools that are American made, and seldom break. In addition, both the Sears Craftsman line and the Home Depot Husky line offer lifetime replacements. No matter how much damage is done to your tool, you can take it back to them, and they will give you a replacement free of charge. One thing to look out for, though, is to make sure that you purchase the brand that offers the warranty. For example, Sears sells both Craftsman tools and Sears brand tools—the latter is not covered under the lifetime replacement warranty.

The Craftsman and Husky lines are good-quality tools. It's human nature sometimes to "cheap-out" and attempt to purchase tools that are bargain basement. These will usually follow the rule that "you get what you pay for." It's advisable to stay away from tools made in China. The quality is usually very questionable.

One exception to the foreign tool rule can apply to what I call "disposable" tools. A few foreign-made socket sets that are cheaper than the American sets sometimes have socket walls that are much thinner than the American sets. This allows these sockets to be fitted onto nuts that the American thick-walled sets might not fit. In cases like these, it is nice to have a set of these sockets around, although after about three to four uses, they are usually worn out enough to be thrown away.

Your tool set should consist of some basic items:

Screwdrivers: You should have at least three flat-tip (3/32, 3/16, and 5/16), and two Phillips tip (Number 1 and Number 2) screwdrivers. Inspect the tips of your screwdrivers to be sure that they are not bent, broken, or otherwise worn. A damaged screwdriver is a quick way to strip the head of a fastener, causing an otherwise simple repair to turn into a nightmare. A ratcheting screwdriver is a useful tool as well. This allows you to unscrew fasteners without removing the tip from the fastener.

Adjustable wrench: Many mechanics won't admit to actually owning an adjustable wrench (sometimes known as an adjustable Crescent wrench), but usually will have a couple hidden for lapses of laziness. Quality is of the utmost importance when choosing an adjustable wrench. Less expensive wrenches have jaws that will stretch, mar, and otherwise fall apart when used; this is another very good way to damage a fastener and ruin your day. A good adjustable plumber's wrench can also come in handy when you need to remove large stubborn nuts.

Pliers: No tool set would be complete without a few sets of pliers. The three basic pliers are: slip-joint, adjustable (sometimes called Channel-Lock), and needle-nose. The important consideration when choosing most pliers is the teeth. The teeth should be sharp, and they should stay sharp, as pliers are generally used under less than ideal circumstances. Again, don't cheap-out on the pliers. The Vise-Grip brand is very good, and a set of multiple sizes will service you well over many years.

Sockets and Drivers: Aside from a variety of sizes, sockets come in either 12 point or 6 point, regular and deep versions. Twelve-point versions are more versa tile, but 6 point sockets are stronger and do less dam-

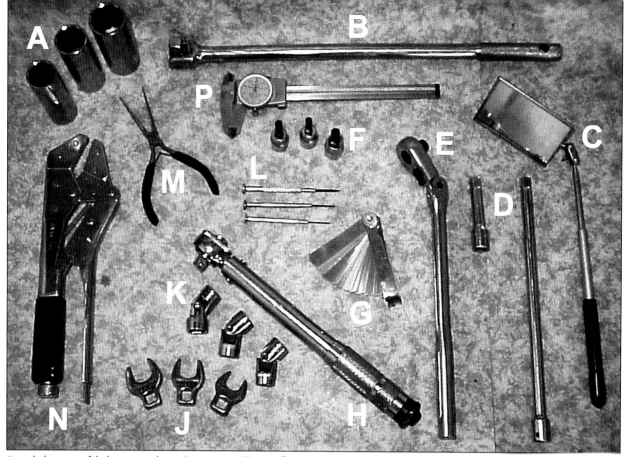

I've picked out some of the less commonplace tools for this photo. This is a collection of tools that you might not normally think to purchase, but ones that I would consider vital, and use on a daily basis:

A—Deep socket metric set. This is most useful for those large fasteners that you really need a socket for. Eventually, you will need one of the sockets in this set—might as well spring for the set all at once.

B—Breaker bar. In conjunction with the deep socket set, you will need a tool that will give you the amount of torque that you need to remove those troublesome fasteners.

C—Inspection mirror. Very useful when you just can't see into the rear of your engine compartment, or around blind corners.

D—Extension set. Extensions for your 3/8-inch drive are most useful, but other sizes can also come in handy. Some nuts are just impossible to reach with a standard-length socket and ratchet.

E—Flexible ratchet. I purchased this tool because it looked real cool—not because I could think of a unique purpose for it. However, it has become one of the most valuable tools in my collection. You don't realize the limitations of a standard ratchet until you've tried one of these.

F—Allen wrench socket set. Most of us have the standard set of right-angle Allen wrenches; however, the ability to use a socket driver increases your ability to get into tight places and apply greater torque.

G—Feeler gauges. You really can't get away without a set of these. Useful for setting valve clearances, or adjusting the clutch.

H—Torque wrench. A must-have in everyone's collection. Purchase a good-quality one, and make sure that its range covers the tasks that you need to accomplish.

J—Crowfoot wrenches. These are perfect for that one nut that you just can't get to. They are particularly good for removing those hard-to-reach nuts on the heat exchangers.

K—Swivel-foot sockets. These are great for using your sockets in hard-to-reach places, like the nuts on the CIS-injection intake manifolds. You can get away with a standard universal joint adapter for your socket driver as well.

L—Miniscrewdrivers. You don't know when you will need one, but when you do they're tremendously useful.

M—Needle-nose pliers. Very handy for grabbing lost screws or nuts, or for simply installing small snap rings. Get a good-quality pair that won't bend or break on you.

N—Locking pliers. These are sometimes called Vise-Grips, and are very good multipurpose tools as long as they are not abused. Don't get lazy and use them instead of the proper tool for the job.

age to fasteners. Socket drives normally come in 1/4-, 3/8-, 1/2-, 3/4-, and 1-inch sizes. If I had a choice of only one drive size it would be 3/8 inch. Not only is 3/8 inch most ideal for torque applications on cars (up to about 60 ft-lb), but it also has the greatest number of available accessories. Your socket set should also include a good ratchet (money well spent), a 2-inch extension, a 6-inch extension, and a universal joint.

The Sears Craftsman line offers a great 99-piece socket set for about $100 that is entirely metric. This is

a great starting point, and will likely be the cornerstone of your collection. This set contains three socket ratchet drivers in three different sizes, and the associated short and deep sockets. Also useful are a set of universal or swivel joints that allow you to reach difficult nuts. Start with the basic universal joint set, and then buy the one with the built-in sockets when you need it.

A deep-socket metric set is useful as well. Again, Craftsman has a good-quality set that you will find useful all the time. In general, if you find that you need an individual socket, it's wise to purchase a small set that has that size in it, rather than purchase the individual socket.

Wrenches: The combination wrench is the backbone of any good automotive tool set. Combination usually implies a wrench that is closed (boxed) at one end (like a socket), and open at the other end. There are also other varieties available, such as the double-open, double-boxed, deep-offset, and socket wrench. There have been a number recent innovations in wrench technology. These newcomers claim to have a special shape that will not damage fasteners; one-size wrench to fit many fasteners; or a wrench that works without having to be lifted from the fastener. In my opinion these are mostly gimmicks. Ideally you'll need a range of 7- to 19-millimeter for starters (and a spare 10- and 13-millimeter will always come in handy).

Hammers: Sounds easy enough, but choosing a hammer is as complex as choosing any other tool. There are hundreds of different types of hammers, each in a variety of different sizes. There are ball-peen hammers, claw hammers, soft blow hammers, nonmarring, welding hammers, and picks, just to name a few. The hammer you need to be concerned with is the 16-ounce ball-peen. This is a great all-purpose hammer, but you may desire a 32-ounce, if you really need to hit something hard. Buying a hammer shouldn't be rocket science, but there are some precautions. Aside from the weight and the quality of the head, the handle is an important consideration. There are now a variety of different handles: wood, fiberglass, steel, and reinforced plastic. I prefer a hardwood, like oak, for ball-peen hammers, but all my hammers have different handles, based on how I want the blow to strike certain objects. Regardless of which handle you choose, make sure it is capable of staying firmly attached to the head. A dislodged head will usually land safely on the hood or windshield of your car—or your face if no cars are close by. One trick with wood handles is to soak them in water, which causes the wood to swell to the shape of the head bore. Also useful is a rubber mallet for removing parts without inflicting damage.

Allen Wrenches: Available as a socket, or hex key, you will undoubtedly need a set. There are many variations of this tool: socket drive, T-handle, and multifunction. If you're only going to have one set, a basic right-angle hex key set will give you the most versatility and serve you best. I have found that having a spare 5- and 6-millimeter to be a necessity, as they do wear out at the least opportune times. The next step up is the socket set that fits on the end of a ratchet driver. These are very useful for applying more torque when you need it.

Torque Wrenches: No good mechanic or weekend warrior is complete without a torque wrench. The ultimate tool for assembly, the torque wrench is used to measure and restrict the amount of torque that is applied to a fastener. This is of the utmost importance, since too little torque can result in a nut falling off, or too much torque can damage a valuable part. Make sure that you get a torque wrench with both English and metric measurements labeled on it. I recommend purchasing two wrenches, one for small increments, 0–25 ft-lb, and one for larger tasks, above 25 ft-lb. Both Craftsman and Husky sell good-quality, adjustable torque wrenches for about $65.

Electrical Repair: You don't need a degree in physics to perform basic electrical repairs on cars, but you do need the right tools. At a minimum you'll need a test light, wire crimping pliers, wire strippers, an assortment of solder-less terminals, and a good multi-tester. Most parts stores carry inexpensive kits that are suitable for most jobs. Of course a soldering iron is the correct way to make electrical repairs, but often is not as convenient as solder-less terminals. The automotive electronics company SUN manufactures a great hand-held voltmeter, ammeter, tachometer, and dwell meter unit, and is available at most local auto parts stores. Wiring diagrams for your year car are also extremely valuable for the process of troubleshooting electrical problems.

Timing Light: A staple of your tool collection should be the adjustable timing lamp. Sears makes a decent timing light with degree angle adjustability built in. The small knob on the light allows you to set the offset in degrees and adjust the timing of the car even if your pulley is missing the required timing marks. A standard nonadjustable light will perform well, although having the option of adjustability is useful for fine tuning and troubleshooting.

Hydraulic Jack: Arguably the most important tool in your collection. It's wise not to cheap-out on this one. Although good-quality jacks are often expensive, they are definitely worth it, and they will last a long, long time. Purchase a large jack with a very large lifting throw. Weight capacity is not as important as how high you can lift with the jack. Purchase a 3- to 5-ton jack with the highest lift that you can find. Typical costs for these are in the $150–$200 range, but they are well worth it. Also necessary are jack stands. I like to have two different sizes around so that I can adjust the car to different heights. See Project 1 for more details.

Shop Lamp: Another extremely useful tool is the shop lamp. My favorite type of shop lamp is the fluorescent hand-held unit on a retractable cord. These allow the spring-loaded cord to be wound back into the main housing, similar to a vacuum cleaner. The only disadvantage to these lamps is that you have to replace the entire lamp and cord assembly if you break a part of the assembly (as has happened to me many times). A good alternative is the fluorescent hand-held lamps without the retractable cords. Stay away from the shop lamps that use a standard 60-watt incandescent light bulb. These get hot, and can burn you under the car, or even worse, start fires if oil or gasoline accidentally drips on them. Stick with the fluorescent lamps.

Another good lamp is the shop halogen lamp. These are extremely high-powered lamps that come with adjustable stands and metal grille covers. Although these lamps get very hot, they give out a lot of light, and are especially useful for lighting up engine compartments when you're working on them.

Safety Glasses: Anyone who has worked on cars for any length of time, or worked in a machine shop, knows the importance of wearing safety glasses whenever there is a chance that something might get in your eye. Never get underneath the car without them. Always make sure that you have three or four pairs around. You will undoubtedly misplace them, and you want to make sure that you have plenty of spares so that you don't avoid using them because you can't find them.

Miscellaneous: There are plenty of tools that fit into this category. Here are some that you should not be without: X-acto or craft knife, small pick, tape measure, scissors, a set of good feeler gauges, a hack saw, a set of files, and an inspection mirror.

THE ADVANCED COLLECTION

The upgraded tool set is simply an extension of basic set. As you perform more tasks, your skills and needs will be further defined and you'll want to extend your investment to meet your needs. A greater range of sockets, wrenches, screwdrivers, and pliers will become increasingly helpful. You should also begin purchasing diagnostic tools.

Some popular tools you might be quick to add are: snap ring pliers; socket drive Allen and Torx set; stubby wrenches; and swivel sockets.

The Dremel tool and angle grinder are two of the most destructive, yet useful, tools for working on older cars (see Project 96). When bolts are rusted solid, and there really isn't any alternative, the grinding tools play an important role. No one should be without a Dremel tool, as it is most useful for cutting off small bolts and other pieces of metal that are difficult to reach. The

Dremel tool with a flexible extension is particularly useful for reaching into tight places.

Everyone who works around the house probably has a good variable-speed electric hand drill. However, what are really important are the drill bits. Make sure that you have a good, clean set of drill bits at all times. Bargain-basement drill bits are fine for drilling through wood, but when it comes to metal, you need the best quality you can get. Make sure that you get a good-quality set; otherwise you may end up hurting yourself or your car.

One tool that is not commonly used but can save you many hours is the electric impact wrench. This tool is similar to the air compressor impact wrenches that are used in automotive shops everywhere, except that it runs on ordinary 120-volt current. The impact wrench is especially useful for removing nuts that can't be well secured, and tend to rotate when you are trying to remove them.

Diagnosis by use of a "vacuum gauge" is pretty much a lost art these days. This is a tool I still use frequently; in fact, some of my cars even have a vacuum gauge permanently mounted in the instrument panel. By monitoring the vacuum readings, a person can gain information on the condition of the valve train, as well as the overall tuning of the motor. Vacuum gauges can now be purchased with a hand pump attached. These are called "vacuum pumps" and can be used to test a variety of injection and emissions components.

When serious engine problems are suspected, the tool most people turn to first is the "compression tester." This is for good reason, as the compression tester will provide clues to such problems as bad rings, leaking valves, or even a hole in one of the pistons. A recent tool that is gaining more common acceptance is the "leakdown tester." The leakdown tester works by pressurizing the cylinder and measuring how much pressure the cylinder loses over time. Although some people consider the leakdown tester to be a more precise measurement, it should be used in conjunction with the compression tester to gain a more complete picture and better diagnosis of your engine.

Finally, nobody should be without the proper "fuel pressure tester." Most fuel pressure testers are not very expensive, and they are sometimes built into high-end vacuum gauges. If you have a fuel-injected car, you will need to purchase a tester specifically for your type of injection system. Although these can be pretty expensive, fuel-injected cars use very high pressure (sometimes up to 100 psi), and having the exact pressure is crucial to the system performing correctly.

SPECIALTY AND ENGINE BUILDING TOOLS

If you are to engage in the experience of rebuilding your own motor, there are a number of tools you'll be interested in. Again, many of these are expensive, but most can be rented for a small fee at your local parts store or machine shop. Caution should be used when renting tools, as they are often not used or maintained correctly. If a tool is not working as well as you believe it should be, take it back, or buy a good one if you have to. It's not worth the risk of damaging your project or injuring yourself.

Clutch Alignment Tool: A clutch alignment tool is used to center the clutch disk between the flywheel and pressure plate, allowing the input shaft of the transmission to be inserted onto the pilot bearing on the crankshaft. Every car uses a different clutch alignment tool, and they usually costs less than $10.

Ring Expander: A ring expander is used to install piston rings onto the pistons. There are some complicated and expensive versions of this tool, but my $8 version has served me well over the years. The thing to remember is not to expand the ring any more than necessary. Rings break easily and are expensive to replace.

Ring Compressor: Ring compressors are used when installing the pistons into the cylinders. They come in a variety of styles, ranging from $5 to $75. Most ring compressors are made to work with only a limited range of piston sizes, so be sure you know the diameter of your piston when shopping for a compressor. Use this tool with a liberal amount of motor oil to help the piston slide into the cylinder more easily.

PRECISION INSTRUMENTS

Unless you get into some serious engine building and blue printing, it's not likely you'll have much need for a lot of precision instruments. However, there are a couple I would recommend that everyone have in their toolbox. Precision and quality in a measurement instrument is far more important than most other tools. There is no point in measuring a tolerance to .0001 inch when the tool is only accurate to .0003 inch. If it says "Made in China" on it, keep looking.

Dial or vernier caliper: Dial calipers are general purpose and very versatile. They can be used for a variety of measurements related to bore, diameter, depth, or length when a precise measurement is needed. Typically they are offered with a 0–6-inch range, in .01-inch or .001-inch increments. Digital models often offer the versatility of being able to instantly convert from metric to SAE, hold measurements in memory, and compare dimensions. Prices can range from $5 to over $200. My personal recommendation would be to purchase one with a 0–6 inch

When working on my 911, I like to use a cover for the engine compartment. This cover protects the paint and finish from tools, fluids, and other accidents waiting to happen. No matter how careful you are, you will slip up one day and scratch your paint. A few dollars spent on a cover is a good investment in the long run.

range, .001 precision, and don't even consider looking at calipers that cost less than $50.

Dial Indicator: For anybody doing serious engine work, the dial indicator is an indispensable tool. The dial indicator is primarily used to measure backlash and runout on a variety of components. It's a must for any 911 owner who chooses to check or adjust the cam timing (see Project 15). There are several different styles available including the bottom plunger, back plunger, and dovetail. To further confuse the issue, there are also a variety of different mounting systems (backs) and hundreds of attachments, holders, and tips. Prices range from $20 to over $300, not including extras. I would recommend starting with an indicator with a 1-inch range, a 001-inch increment, a bottom plunger, a back mount, and a few attachments for positioning. A magnetic base will eventually come in handy.

Straight Edge: A straight edge is simply a flat piece of steel that has been precision ground to an exact tolerance. The straight edge is used whenever you need to verify a surface to be absolutely flat, such as a head or block, or it can even be used to check the alignment of pulleys (such as cam gears on a 911). Straight edges can be purchased in a variety of sizes, the most common being 18x1.5x.25 inches, which is what you'll most likely need. Prices for a good edge can be more than $100, but keep in mind this is a precision instrument. Even though it appears simple, special care should be taken when handling and storing your edge. If you drop it, it will probably be damaged beyond repair. You should oil the edge (it will rust quickly) and store it in its container, returning it immediately after each use.

SECTION ONE
BASICS

This section is a good place to start in this book. If you've just purchased your 911, and it lacks an owner's manual, Basics covers what you need to know. No special tools are required, and the projects here will give you a good idea of the format and tone of the rest of the book. If you've never worked on your 911 before—don't worry. These first few projects are very simple, and are a good introduction to your car.

BASICS
PROJECT 1 • JACKING UP YOUR CAR

 Time: 20 minutes

 Tools: 2-ton jack, jack stands, jack pad tool

 Talent:

 Applicable Years: All

 Tab: $0

 Tinware: None

 Tip: Check the condition of the transmission and motor mounts when lifting from underneath the motor.

PERFORMANCE GAIN: Starting point for all work underneath the car.

COMPLEMENTARY MODIFICATION: Check front suspension bushings.

Some projects cannot be performed without elevating the car. Surprisingly, the 911 is one of the few cars on which the procedure for raising the car is not completely obvious. Haphazard use of a floor jack can result in some pretty significant and expensive damage to your car. Before you begin raising the car, make sure to have the wheels of the car blocked so it can't roll. It's also wise to have your parking brake on, and the car placed in first gear. Always use the jack stands in pairs to support the car—not simply the floor jack. Even if you are only lifting the car up for a few minutes, make sure that you place a jack stand loosely underneath the transmission or the motor, just in case the floor jack fails.

If you would like to raise the rear of the car, there are a few methods you can use. The most common one is to lift the entire car by the bottom of the engine. This will not damage the engine, as it is very strong at this point. Do not lift the car at the rear seam where the floor meets the rear firewall. This is not a strong point, and the chassis can dent or buckle when the weight of the car is placed on this spot.

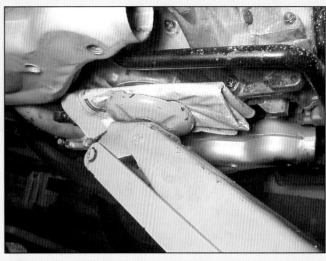

1 The bottom engine sump is one of the best places to jack up your 911. Use a rolled up newspaper or a small block of wood in order to avoid scratching or damaging the bottom sump plate. As you begin to lift the engine, check to make sure that the car chassis moves as soon as the engine is lifted. If the transmission mounts or motor mounts are worn out, the engine will lift up slightly before the rest of the car moves.

2 The best place to support the car is on the torsion bar covers. Instinct would tend to have you believe that this isn't a very strong spot, but people have been using this as a jack point for many years without a problem.

3 The jack pad tool is essential for anyone who is planning on working on their 911. Its design provides an excellent mounting point for lifting that won't damage the undercarriage. Using the factory jack can be dangerous, and should only be used in an emergency.

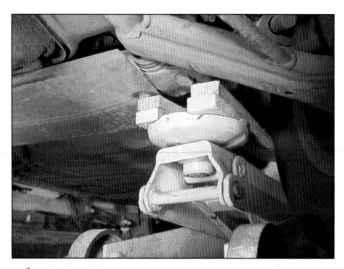

4 To jack up the front, make sure that you use a strong, supported point on the car. The mounting points for the A-arms are excellent points. Place a block of wood in between the jack and the A-arm mounting point to prevent any damage to your A-arms. If you have a front sway bar that runs along the bottom of the front suspension, make sure that you don't jack up the car on the bar.

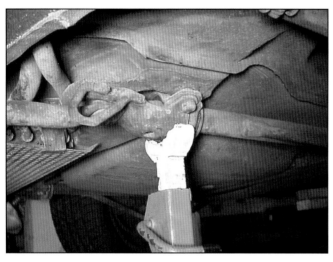

5 An excellent spot to place the jack stands is underneath the front torsion bar mounting points. Not only is this point very structurally sound, it also fits the top ends of most jack stands very well.

Another method of raising the car is to use a floor jack pad. This handy tool is placed in the factory jack holes on each side of the car. The car can be raised in small increments by jacking up one side of the car, supporting it, and then moving to the other side. The torsion bar covers are the ideal place for rear support. I don't recommend that you place the jack stands underneath the engine or transmission, as this can lead to instability. The torsion bar covers provide the most possible rigid support of the rear.

It is **not** recommended that you lift the car by placing your jack under the floor of the car. Oil lines and air conditioning hoses run below the floor of the car, making them easy targets for being crushed by a floor jack. Lifting the car from an unsupported section of the floor can also lead to a significant dent in your car's floor.

The front of the car can be lifted by either of the two mounting points of the A-arms. Use a block of wood when jacking the car up and be careful not to damage the A-arm when you are using it to lift the car. Also be aware that raising one side of the front of the car will most likely raise the car on the other side, creating a potentially unstable condition.

Once you have the car up in the air and supported on the jack stands, push on the car and see if it is unstable. If the car moves at all, you do not have it properly supported. It is far better for the car to fall off the jack stands while you are pushing on it, than when you are under it. Set the floor jack under the engine or transmission as yet another support; it's also a wise idea to set up a spare jack stand or two as a precautionary measure against one of them failing.

When you are ready to lower the car, take care in placing your floor jack. Sometimes you will not be able to remove the jack easily when the car is lowered, or the jack handle may crush or damage an oil line or tube on the way down. Proceed very slowly, and also be aware that some floor jacks release very quickly. Also be careful to place the car in gear, or to pull the parking brake before you lower it. The car may have a tendency to roll away right after it's back on the ground.

BASICS
PROJECT 2 • CHANGING ENGINE OIL

 Time: 1 hour

 Tools: 15- or 19-mm wrench, 10-mm Allen wrench on early cars, paper towels, oil pan bucket

 Talent:

 Applicable Years: All

 Tab: $30

 Tinware: Oil filter, motor oil (12 quarts), drain plug seals

 Tip: Make sure that you have a big enough bucket

 PERFORMANCE GAIN: Prolonged engine life and reliability

COMPLEMENTARY MODIFICATION: Install synthetic oil

One of the most common tasks to perform is replacing your engine oil. Frequent oil changes are supposedly the most important thing you can do to maintain and prolong the life of your engine. With the better oils that are available today, the requirement for frequent changes is diminishing. Even though Porsche now recommends oil changes every 15,000 miles or so, it's usually recommended to keep the changes under the 5,000-mile limit. If you don't drive your car too often, you should change the oil at least once a year to keep things fresh.

The first thing you need to do is to make sure that you have everything that is required for the job. Nothing is more frustrating than emptying your oil, only to find out that you don't have a replacement filter or enough oil. You will need an oil filter, a wrench, a roll of paper towels, a very large oil pan or bucket, and about 12 quarts of oil. Check the bottom of your oil tank for the appropriate-sized wrench that you need—it's not uncommon for the older cars to have different-sized drain plugs than were originally installed. Start by driving the car around, and letting it heat up to operating temperature. You want to empty your oil when it's hot, because the heat makes the oil

1 On all 911s, the oil filter is attached to the oil tank. Be sure to arm yourself with paper towels, as it is almost impossible to avoid spilling at least some oil when removing the filter. The oil tanks on all 911s are located in the rear of the car inside the right rear fender, except for 1972 cars, on which they were located toward the front of the car. The oil filler neck is also shown in this photo. The dipstick for measuring oil level is contained in a slot inside the filler neck.

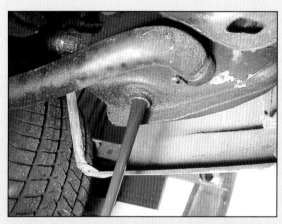

2 Make sure that you plan to have a very large container below the oil tank. Approximately 4 to 6 quarts of oil or more will empty out of the tank very quickly. It's also wise to have a drip pan underneath your container. It's very easy to underestimate the amount of oil that will empty out of the tank.

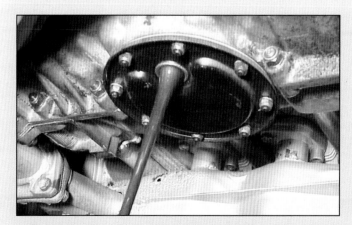

3 Approximately 3 to 4 quarts of oil will empty out of the bottom of the engine. Although not necessary during each oil change, removal and cleaning of the sump screen on 1965–1983 911s can help keep your engine oil cleaner. Remove the eight nuts that hold the sump plate on and clean the screen carefully. If you notice bits and pieces of metal or other debris in the screen, it may be a sign that it's time to rebuild your engine. Make sure that when you reinstall the screen, you don't place the drain plug under the oil pickup tube—it can interfere with the oil pickup and circulation.

flow a lot easier, and more particles of metal and dirt will come out when the oil is emptied.

Once you get the car parked, place the oil pan bucket underneath the oil tank of the car. The 911 uses a dry-sump system, which holds most of the oil in the oil tank instead of at the bottom of the engine. There is still plenty of oil at the bottom of the engine, but there isn't enough for the engine to run properly, so the oil tank holds the reserve. The oil tank for all 911s (except 1972) is located on the right side of the car, inside the rear fender just behind the wheel. At the bottom of the tank there is a plug that is used for draining oil. Remove this plug carefully, and make sure you have a very large oil pan—about 9-quart capacity—under it, with a drip pan under the oil pan in case you underestimate. The oil will be very hot, and will empty out extremely quickly, so be careful not to burn yourself. There will be no time to grab any more buckets or oil pans, so make sure that the one you choose is big enough.

This is a good time to remove the oil filter. You want to make sure that you remove the filter with the oil pan still under the oil tank because the oil filter is full of oil, and this oil will have a tendency to drip down out of the filter into the tank and out the drain hole. The filter should only be screwed on finger tight, but you may need a filter wrench to remove it. If the filter is really on tight, you may need to resort to more drastic measures. One sure-fire way to get the oil filter off is to poke a long screwdriver through it and use the handle of the screwdriver for leverage. It doesn't matter that you are destroying the filter, because you are going to install a new one. Be aware, though, that this method will leak oil out of the filter into your engine compartment, so have some paper towels handy.

After the oil tank is empty, proceed to the center of the bottom of the engine, where you will find a similar plug. Remove this plug, as you did on the oil tank, and empty the oil into your oil pan. The bottom of the engine sump will contain significantly less oil than in the oil tank. Starting in late 1983, Porsche moved the location of this drain plug from the bottom of the engine to the side of the case.

While all of your oil is draining, take the two plugs from the engine and the tank, and carefully clean them with a paper towel. The plug at the bottom of the engine is magnetic, and attracts all the little bits and pieces of metal that get trapped in the engine oil. Sometimes the plug on the bottom of the oil tank is magnetic as well, if the original has been replaced. When both plugs are clean, replace them in the car with new metal gaskets around the plugs.

If you don't use the gasket, they will leak oil. Torque the two plugs to 42 N-m (30.8 ft-lbs).

Now head back into the engine compartment, and install the new oil filter. Install the oil filter with the seal wet—wipe a small bit of oil on a paper towel, and use it to make sure there is oil on the seal all the way around the filter. Screw on the filter and make it snug tight. No need to use the iron grip of death when tightening the oil filter—these don't have a tendency to leak.

Now it's time to fill up your 911 with motor oil. A lot of people aren't really sure what motor oil to use in their car. Traditionally, the characteristics of motor oil were linked closely to its weight. Heavier-weight oils protect well against heat; lighter-weight oils flow better in cold. In general, if you live in a cold climate, you should use a 10W-40 or similar oil. This oil is a 10-weight oil that behaves and protects against heat like a 40-weight oil. In warmer climates, you should use a 20W-50 oil. This oil doesn't flow as well at the colder climates, but gives an extra "edge" on the hotter end.

The question of whether to use synthetic or traditional "dinosaur" oil often comes up among car buffs. *Consumer Reports* (July 1996) did an extensive test on the two types of oil, and after tearing apart engines and measuring wear, their examiners couldn't find any discernible differences. Still, some people swear by synthetic oil. In general, you should not use the synthetic oil if you have an older car with old seals in the engine. There have been many documented cases in which the addition of synthetic oil has caused an otherwise dry car to start leaking. If you own an older 911 that doesn't have fresh seals in the engine, I would stick to the nonsynthetics.

Fill your oil tank from the oil filler neck in the engine compartment. I recommend removing the oil dipstick so that you don't pour oil all over the end that you need to hold. Add about 8 quarts to the oil tank, and add an extra quart if you have a 1973 or later 911. Put the dip stick back in, and the oil cap back on.

Now, take the car out for a drive and bring it up to operating temperature. The oil level can only be accurately checked with the engine running at idle and at operating temperature. If the oil level is low, add more while the engine is running. One to 2 quarts of oil added to the tank will make the oil level on the dipstick rise from the low mark to the high mark. One rule of thumb is to fill the oil tank until the dashboard gauge reads just above its half-way point. Make sure that you double-check the dipstick when you are finished. If you add too much oil, it will eventually find its way into the breather hoses, and could make a mess of your engine compartment. Make sure that you dispose of your old oil at a respectable recycling station.

BASICS
PROJECT 3 • FAN BELT REPLACEMENT

 Time: 30 minutes

 Tools: Pulley wrench, 24-mm socket (nondeep socket)

 Talent:

 Applicable Years: All

 Tab: $15–$30

 Tinware: Pulley shims, outer pulley half, fan belt

 Tip: Use exactly six shims when installing the pulley.

PERFORMANCE GAIN: Prevention of fan failure and engine overheating

COMPLEMENTARY MODIFICATION: Replace air conditioning belt

1 The fan belt is removed by holding the pulley steady with the pulley wrench, and then loosening the 24-millimeter nut that holds the whole assembly together. Don't attempt to remove the pulley without the wrench—doing so can damage the pulley. Take a look in the tool kit that should have come with your car—each one came with a pulley wrench as standard equipment.

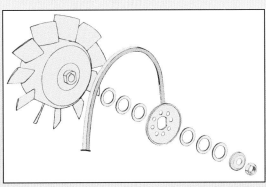

2 The proper order of assembly for the fan hub. Start with five shims on the inside, and then move them to the outside as needed to obtain the proper tightness.

One of the most important tasks in maintaining your 911 is properly replacing and tensioning the fan belt. If the belt and pulley are not properly attached, they can come loose and stop the cooling action of the fan on the motor. If you don't notice the temperature gauge or the alternator lamp illuminate, you might overheat your engine and destroy it! Needless to say, the fan belt is very important.

Ironically, it's also one of the least understood items on the car, and is often improperly tightened. The system uses a set of shims that regulate the thickness of the virtual pulley created by the pulley half and the fan. As you add more shims between the pulley half and the fan, the tension on the belt decreases, because the pulley is wider and the belt rides lower in the valley. In an opposite way, when you remove the shims from between the pulley half and the fan, it pinches the belt tighter; this makes it higher and farther toward the outside of the pulley and increases the tension on the entire belt. The system is similar to the 356's, and has worked well for many years.

The key to installing the belt is following a set procedure to guarantee the proper seating of the pulley and tensioning of the belt. Start by installing five shims on the inside of the pulley and one on the outside. It is very important to note that the pulley must always have a total of six shims on it, inside and out at all times. If you don't place the extra shims on the outside of the pulley, the nut will bottom out, and the belt won't tighten properly. If you are missing some shims, get some and put them in right away.

Make sure to tighten the pulley completely. Tighten it as much as you can, then turn the starter over a bit, then retighten. This will give the belt a chance to become unpinched from the pulley. You should feel the point at which all the shims are tight against the fan and the outer pulley half—you won't be able to tighten it any more no matter how hard you try. The final factory torque specification for this nut is 40 N-m (29.5 ft-lbs).

The belt's tension should be enough to let your finger deflect the belt about 1/4 to 1/2 an inch at the halfway point between the two pulleys. If the belt is too tight, move some shims to the inside. If it's too loose, move some to the outside. At all times, keep the total number of shims inside and out at six.

BASICS
PROJECT 3 • FAN BELT REPLACEMENT

 Time: 30 minutes

 Tools: Pulley wrench, 24-mm socket (nondeep socket)

 Talent:

 Applicable Years: All

 Tab: $15–$30

 Tinware: Pulley shims, outer pulley half, fan belt

 Tip: Use exactly six shims when installing the pulley.

 PERFORMANCE GAIN: Prevention of fan failure and engine overheating

COMPLEMENTARY MODIFICATION: Replace air conditioning belt

1 The fan belt is removed by holding the pulley steady with the pulley wrench, and then loosening the 24-millimeter nut that holds the whole assembly together. Don't attempt to remove the pulley without the wrench—doing so can damage the pulley. Take a look in the tool kit that should have come with your car—each one came with a pulley wrench as standard equipment.

2 The proper order of assembly for the fan hub. Start with five shims on the inside, and then move them to the outside as needed to obtain the proper tightness.

One of the most important tasks in maintaining your 911 is properly replacing and tensioning the fan belt. If the belt and pulley are not properly attached, they can come loose and stop the cooling action of the fan on the motor. If you don't notice the temperature gauge or the alternator lamp illuminate, you might overheat your engine and destroy it! Needless to say, the fan belt is very important.

Ironically, it's also one of the least understood items on the car, and is often improperly tightened. The system uses a set of shims that regulate the thickness of the virtual pulley created by the pulley half and the fan. As you add more shims between the pulley half and the fan, the tension on the belt decreases, because the pulley is wider and the belt rides lower in the valley. In an opposite way, when you remove the shims from between the pulley half and the fan, it pinches the belt tighter; this makes it higher and farther toward the outside of the pulley and increases the tension on the entire belt. The system is similar to the 356's, and has worked well for many years.

The key to installing the belt is following a set procedure to guarantee the proper seating of the pulley and tensioning of the belt. Start by installing five shims on the inside of the pulley and one on the outside. It is very important to note that the pulley must always have a total of six shims on it, inside and out at all times. If you don't place the extra shims on the outside of the pulley, the nut will bottom out, and the belt won't tighten properly. If you are missing some shims, get some and put them in right away.

Make sure to tighten the pulley completely. Tighten it as much as you can, then turn the starter over a bit, then retighten. This will give the belt a chance to become unpinched from the pulley. You should feel the point at which all the shims are tight against the fan and the outer pulley half—you won't be able to tighten it any more no matter how hard you try. The final factory torque specification for this nut is 40 N-m (29.5 ft-lbs).

The belt's tension should be enough to let your finger deflect the belt about 1/4 to 1/2 an inch at the halfway point between the two pulleys. If the belt is too tight, move some shims to the inside. If it's too loose, move some to the outside. At all times, keep the total number of shims inside and out at six.

BASICS
PROJECT 4 • REPLACING THE AIR FILTER

 Time: 15 minutes

 Tools:

 Talent:

 Applicable Years: 1965-1989

 Tab: $40

 Tinware: New air filter

 Tip: Replace your air filter every 10,000 miles

! PERFORMANCE GAIN: Better air flow into your fuel injection system

COMPLEMENTARY MODIFICATION: Install an aftermarket air filter, and replace your CIS air box straps

Every 10,000 miles or so, you should change the air filter in your 911. The air filter protects the fuel injection system and the air intake system from dust and debris that can be sucked in under normal operation.

On the early 911s, the circular air filter was contained in a housing that spanned the top of the carburetors or the Mechanical Fuel Injection (MFI). To replace the air filter, you simply disconnect the long "snout" on the air filter housing, and remove the old one. Make sure that you don't drop any of the attachment screws into the engine compartment—they can be very difficult to fish out. The new air filter must be aligned properly within the housing in order to replace the "snout" on the air cleaner.

With the introduction of the Continuous Injection System (CIS) on 911s starting in 1973, Porsche implemented a new type of air filter. The CIS air filter is contained within the plastic air cleaner housing and held on with flexible rubber straps. Simply detach the straps at the top of the air box, and remove the filter from the air intake housing. Check the rubber straps to make sure they aren't cracked and worn out, and replace them if they show signs of wear or age.

1 On the early cars, the air filter housing covered the mechanical fuel injection system or carburetors. The circular air filter is located inside the housing, and is accessed by removing the long "snout" of the air cleaner housing. You don't need to remove the retaining screws to replace the air filter. Simply loosen them up and rotate the "snout" until it comes off.

2 The CIS cars (1973–1983) house the air filter under a plastic air intake housing. This housing is held onto the CIS air box by two rubber straps. Access to the filter is gained by disconnecting the straps and removing the housing. Inspect the straps when you remove the filter, as these have a habit of breaking when they age.

3 The Carreras (1984–1989) and 911 Turbos housed their air filter in a box on the right side of the car (see orange stripe). This box is held together with clips (indicated by arrow). To replace the air filter, simply unsnap the metal clips and pull out the old filter.

On the 1984 and later 911 Carreras, Porsche implemented the Motronic Fuel Injection system, which uses a square air filter mounted on the right side of the engine compartment. The filter is located in the intake system, inside a box held on with clips. Simply remove the clips to replace the air filter.

For the 911 there are basically two different types of air filters—the stock paper or cloth air filters and aftermarket units. These aftermarket units utilize an oil-soaked fabric to achieve freer air flow. The bottleneck for air flow in the 911 engine is not the air filter. The primary advantage of the aftermarket units is that you usually only have to purchase one, and it will last the life of your car. The bottom line is to carefully research any aftermarket filter before you install it to your car. Make sure that it filters as well as or better than the original Porsche specifications for your year car.

BASICS

PROJECT 5 • FUEL FILTER AND ACCUMULATOR REPLACEMENT

Time: 1 hour

Tools: Wrenches

Talent:

Applicable Years: 1965-1989

Tab: $10-$80

Tinware: New filter, new accumulator

Tip: Replace the accumulator if you are having a CIS warm start problem.

PERFORMANCE GAIN: Cleaner running fuel system

COMPLEMENTARY MODIFICATION: Replace fuel pump, or fuel lines.

One of the simplest tasks to perform on the 911 is replacing the fuel filter and fuel accumulator (on CIS-equipped cars). With older cars that might have rusty tanks, keeping the filter fresh and clean is a very important part of keeping the fuel system running clean. Even microscopic particles can build up and clog the tiny holes that are a key part of the carburetors or fuel injection system. This project details the replacement of both the fuel filter and the fuel accumulator. For the early cars (1965–early 1973) and the late-style Carrera (1984–1989), you only need to be concerned about replacing the fuel filter.

The fuel accumulator is part of the Bosch K-Jetronic system, or CIS, that was used on the 911 from mid-1973 through 1983 and 911 Turbos up until 1989. The accumulator contains an internal spring-loaded diaphragm that prevents vapor lock by keeping the system pressurized after the engine has been shut off. Vapor lock occurs when the fuel pump and lines become heated up by the engine. The gasoline in the lines and the pump actually evaporates and transforms into a gaseous state. If the fuel pump is turned on when the fuel is in this state, it tries to

pump the vaporized gas, which it cannot do. The only remedy is to wait for the gas to cool down to the point where it liquefies once again and can be pressurized and pumped by the fuel pump.

Vapor lock rarely appears when the car is running. This is because the fuel in the system is constantly pressurized and recirculated back into the tank. Fuel is pumped from the tank to the fuel injection system, and then the excess is returned back to the tank through a return line. This process of recirculation keeps the fuel pressurized in the lines so that it doesn't have a chance to evaporate. The process of circulating the fuel back into the tank also helps to remove heat from the fuel system. The added pressure in the system from the action of the pump also reduces the chance of the fuel evaporating.

If you are having warm-start problems on your CIS engine, there are a couple of things that you can do. First and foremost, replace your filter and your fuel accumulator. As mentioned previously, the purpose of the accumulator is to keep the system pressurized, so if you are experiencing warm-starting problems, then chances are this unit is not performing adequately. If you think you might get stuck somewhere and need to leave quickly, carry a can of compressed air with you (often used to clean dusty computer equipment). Since it's compressed as a liquid, it has a tendency to absorb heat as it expands. Blow this compressed air over the lines in the engine compartment and the fuel pump in the front of the car, if you can reach it. This should help cool down the fuel system a bit quicker.

Another important component of the system that often fails is the one-way check valve inside the fuel pump. A faulty check valve allows the system to become depressurized when the ignition is turned off, thus defeating the purpose of the fuel accumulator. If a replacement accumulator doesn't solve your fuel-related CIS starting problem, then you might have to replace your fuel pump.

Another smart idea is to keep the fuel tank full most of the time, and not let it run down low. The CIS system recirculates the fuel back to the tank, so a full tank will act like a large cooling center for the fuel. When you shut the engine off, you might want to try leaving the fuel pump running (turn the key one notch toward the starting position) for a minute or two. This should help cool the system and reduce the chance that vapor lock will form in your lines. When the engine is turned off, temperatures have a tendency to spike, as the cooling effects from the fan are stopped.

The replacement of the fuel filter is quite easy on the 911, although access to the area where the filter

1 Shown here, to the left of the engine compartment, is the fuel filter (left) and accumulator (right). The working space is tight—you might want to remove the large black plastic blower hose that connects the blower motor to the fan. Make sure that you let the car sit for a couple of hours before you release the connections. If the fuel accumulator is working, the system will still be pressurized, and fuel might spray out. The accumulator typically holds the pressure for about half an hour, but this time varies from car to car.

Be careful when you remove the steel lines from the tops of the filter and the accumulator. If you can fit them in there, use two wrenches to disconnect the lines, which when corroded can be very difficult to remove. Place one wrench on the filter, and the other on the line. Using this method will reduce the probability of you damaging one of the lines or the accumulator.

Sometimes a faulty fuel accumulator will cause various warm-start problems on the CIS-equipped 911. Try replacing your accumulator if you have problems with vapor lock or difficulty starting when the car has been running for awhile. Remember that the fuel pump check valve works *with* the accumulator—a faulty check valve will generate the same symptoms as a faulty accumulator. A new fuel pump costs roughly five times as much as an accumulator, so most people replace the accumulator first.

is located may be a bit difficult. On cars equipped with the large black blower hose, I recommend that you remove this hose to gain easier access to the fuel filter area.

The first step is to make sure that the fuel in the system is unpressurized. As mentioned previously, the fuel accumulator is spring-loaded to keep the fuel in the system pressurized when the engine is turned off. I recommend that you only disconnect the fuel filter and the accumulator after the car has been sitting a while, preferably overnight. If the replacement must be made shortly after the car has been run, open the connection to the top of the fuel accumulator slowly and carefully. You want to make sure that you depressurize the system slowly, so that fuel doesn't fly everywhere. Make sure that you wear safety glasses, as gasoline can sting your eyes.

To remove both the fuel filter and the accumulator, simply disconnect the fuel lines from both the top and bottom of both units. Depending on how long it's been since these were replaced, it may be difficult to unscrew these lines from the units. If necessary, disconnect the line from the top of the filter and the bottom of the accumulator, and remove the

two as an assembly. This will allow you to take the two over to your workbench to disconnect the hard metal line that joins them together. These two units are simply held on with a hose clamp that can be unscrewed easily.

Make sure that you have a few paper towels handy, as there will be some fuel spillage from this process. Also make sure that you perform the replacement in a well-ventilated area, as the gasoline fumes can build up. I also recommend wearing gloves—gasoline is not the best chemical to get on your skin.

Installation of the new filter and accumulator is a snap. Simply install the new units using the original hose clamps, and attach the fuel lines. Before starting the engine, make sure that all the fuel you may have spilled has evaporated, and that your fuel lines are tight. Take the key and turn it toward the ignition position without starting the engine. I also like to disconnect the CD box as well, just to make sure that there are no sources of ignition around. When you are confident that the fuel system is pumping fuel through the new filter and accumulator without leaking, start the engine.

BASICS
PROJECT 6 • WASHING YOUR CAR

Time: 1 hour

Tools: Bucket and hose

Talent:

Applicable Years: All

Tab: $20

Tinware: Car washing soap, four or five cotton terry towels

Tip: Don't use household detergent, and don't use a chamois.

PERFORMANCE GAIN: Slicker looking 911

COMPLEMENTARY MODIFICATION: Buy a cover.

1 Truly a sight to be seen, Beverly Frohm's 1970 911E has held up over the years very well, thanks to meticulous care and attention. This car is living proof that you can place miles on a car (more than 300,000 to date), and still maintain a fabulous concours-quality shine. By following commonsense guidelines and washing the car often, the 911 can theoretically last forever.

One of the most basic maintenance tasks for your car is cleaning it. While this includes the art of washing your 911, it also includes the reconditioning and protection of both the exterior paint and chrome, and the interior.

The first step in washing your car is to determine exactly what it needs. If the car is simply dusty, and has been sitting in the garage, then you probably only need to wash it with plain water (no soap). Wet the car down and use a wash mitt to remove any dust that might have settled on the car inside the garage.

It's not recommended to use a chamois to dry your car. The chamois can trap small particles of dirt in its porous material, and can actually cause scratches in the surface of the paint when it's used to dry off the car. A really good alternative is 100-percent cotton terry towels. Make sure the towels have been washed at least once, and don't use a rinse or softener. The softener is an additive that can cause streaks, and it inhibits the towel's absorbency.

When washing the car, remember to get the valance panels and the lower rockers. As these panels are closest to the ground, they have a tendency to get the dirtiest. If your car is dirtier than simple dust accu-

mulation, then you will need to use a bit of car wash soap. Make sure that you don't use normal household soap or detergent, as this will remove the wax from the surface of the paint. As the wax is oil-based, normal detergents will attack and remove it. The car wash soaps are very mild, and shouldn't remove the layer of wax that you have on your car.

Rinse the car completely with water from a hose, taking care not to spray the water in any areas where your seals may be cracking. If you're like many Porsche owners, your 911 usually doesn't see much water, and the overall watertight seal of the interior may not be as solid as desired. If your car does leak water, then toss some towels inside the car near the windows to make sure that you catch any water before it reaches the carpet. Put a towel over the engine compartment grille. Make sure that you remember to remove the towel before you start the car!

After the car is completely rinsed, start drying it immediately. It's best to dry the car off out of the sun. Pull the car into the garage and dry it off in there. Removing the car from the sun helps to keep those ugly water spots from appearing.

The key to keeping the paint free of scratches is to make sure that the towels are clean and free of any debris. Handle the towels as if they were going to be used for surgery. Don't leave them outside, or if you drop them on the ground, don't use them again until they have been washed. Small particles of dirt trapped within the towels can cause nasty scratches in the paint. If you happen to encounter a water spot, use a section of a damp, clean terrycloth towel to gently rub it out.

When you are finished with cleaning , it's time to tuck the car away. It's recommended that you use a car cover if your car is spending most of its life in the garage. The cover will protect it from dust accumulation, and it might also help protect against items falling on the car, or cats jumping on it. For cars stored outdoors, covers usually are not a great idea. They have a tendency to trap water, and the wind can make the cloth cover wear against the paint. If your car is not perfectly clean, then dirt particles trapped between the car and the cover will have a tendency to scratch the paint.

SECTION TWO
ENGINE

The Porsche 911 engine is not one of the easiest on which to perform repairs. The tight enclosure of the engine compartment makes it pretty difficult to reach in and access many of the fuel injection components. There are indeed a few things that can be done with the engine in the car (valve adjustment, some fuel injection work, Carrera chain tensioner installation), but most major operations need better access. In these cases, the only thing to do is to remove the engine—a task that many believe to be very difficult. The reality is that removing and working on the 911 engine is not a difficult job—if you have the right tools and a bit of the right knowledge, which I hope to provide here.

ENGINE

PROJECT 7 • ENGINE REMOVAL

 Time: 10 hours

 Tools: Socket set, hex key set, floor jack, jack stands, furniture cart, blocks of wood

 Talent: 👤👤👤👤

 Applicable Years: All

 Tab: $0

 Tinware: None

 Tip: Have a friend assist you with actually lowering the engine.

 PERFORMANCE GAIN: Ability to fix and repair specific engine problems

COMPLEMENTARY MODIFICATION: Repair oil leaks, replace fuel injection hoses, install Carrera chain tensioners, replace clutch

The car referenced in this project is a 1982 911SC. Other models will vary in parts and configurations, but the procedure for dropping the engine is almost the same for all the 911s. The following checklist outlines the steps you need to take:

- Disconnect battery
- Remove fuel pump relay
- Empty oil from engine sump (Project 2)
- Empty oil from oil tank (Project 2)
- Raise rear of car on jack stands (Project 1)
- Disconnect hard oil line
- Disconnect and remove rubber oil line
- Disconnect clutch cable (Project 9), arm, and helper spring assembly
- Disconnect starter solenoid electrical connections
- Disconnect reverse backup switch and speed cable/sender wire from transmission
- Disconnect heater hoses from heat exchangers
- Disconnect and remove shift coupler
- Disconnect A/C compressor and tie to side of car

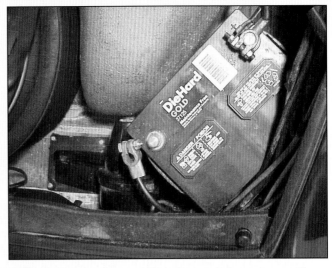

1 It is very important to remember to disconnect the battery negative cable prior to starting to remove the engine. The starter is connected to the battery at all times, and attempting to remove it when it's "live" can be hazardous to both the car and you. It's also wise to remove the red fuel pump relay from its socket as well (see photo in Project 26). If you decide to work on the electrical system of the car while the engine is out, and you turn on the ignition with the fuel pump relay in place, there is a chance that you could spill out gasoline from the disconnected lines in the engine compartment.

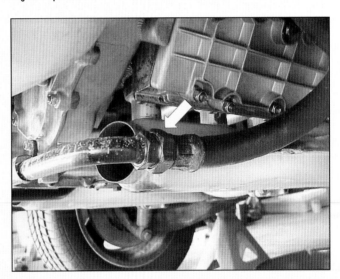

2 After the rear of the car is raised and the oil emptied, begin disconnecting the oil lines. The rear hard line connection (shown by arrow) may be difficult to loosen due to many years of rust and corrosion underneath the car. Be careful not to damage this line when you are applying force to remove it. Use two wrenches—one to turn the line, and another to hold the other end of the line steady. Do not apply force to the line itself, or you may damage it.

- Disconnect all fuel lines
- Disconnect main engine wire harness
- Disconnect breather hoses
- Disconnect accelerator linkage bar
- Disconnect cruise control cable
- Disconnect oxygen sensor
- Remove four nuts that hold the engine to the transmission
- Remove engine motor mount bolts

3 The line that connects the oil tank to the engine needs to be completely removed (shown by arrow). Two hose clamps connect the line to the bottom of the oil tank, and the bottom of the engine oil cooler. Inspect it carefully upon removal, and use a brand new one upon reinstallation if there are any cracks or if the line looks brittle. Have a drip pan ready, as excess oil in the line will spill out when you remove it.

4 The clutch cable assembly under the transmission needs to be disconnected. For 911s from 1976 to 1986, disconnect the clutch cable and remove the circlip that holds the small lever arm in place (shown by yellow arrow). Then remove the small coil spring from the lever arm (white arrow), and pry off the lever arm itself from the shaft, using a small screwdriver. The remainder of the assembly arm (red arrow) should now be able to be removed from the shaft. Be careful of the U-shaped helper spring (green arrow), as it is loaded pretty tight, and will spring back slightly when you pull the larger arm off of the shaft. See Project 10 for more information on the helper spring removal. For earlier 911s, the process is a bit simpler, as the clutch cable is connected directly to the throwout arm

- Lower engine
- Pull engine away from transmission
- Lower down onto cart and remove

If you follow the procedure carefully, and check/double-check to make sure that everything is disconnected, the actual process of lowering the engine is not difficult. Different years will vary in what you need to disconnect, but in general, the procedure outlined above and in the photo series should give a clear indication of the steps. The general rule is to carefully inspect all the areas and components (lines, vacuum hoses, electrical connections) that connect the engine with the rest of the car. Cars equipped with Sportomatic transmissions have quite a few extra lines and hoses.

With this particular engine drop procedure, the transmission is left in the car. It is good practice to support the transmission with a jack stand after the engine is removed from the car, to decrease the load on the transmission mounts. If you want to remove the transmission with the engine, then a few extra steps are required. You need to disconnect the CV joints from the transmission mounting flanges; disconnect the transmission ground strap; unbolt the

transmission mounts; disconnect the speedometer cable; and remove the rear sway bar, if it gets in the way. Once this is done, the entire engine and transmission assembly can be lowered out of the car and disconnected later.

When lowering the engine, it is very wise to have an assistant on hand. Not only can this person provide emergency assistance in case something goes wrong, but it's also important to have an extra set of eyes that can watch for anything that was overlooked during the entire process. The process of pulling the engine away from the transmission can be a little tricky. Make sure that your assistant is watching the surface where the engine and the transmission meet to keep tabs on the progress. When the studs on the engine case finally exit the transmission housing, the engine will become slightly unstable on the jack, so make sure that you have a hand free to steady it.

Keep in mind that you may need to jack up the car higher than you expected in order to remove the engine from underneath the car. It is quite common to lower the engine all the way down to the ground, only to find that you need to raise the car much higher to pull it out from underneath. Use a

5 Disconnect the starter electrical connections. Double check once again that your battery is indeed disconnected, as you can seriously injure yourself if your socket wrench touches the chassis while loosening the positive lead. Make a note of which terminal each wire is connected to, as it is easy to mix them up when reconnecting them.

6 The reverse back-up light switch is hidden at the rear of the transmission, located right above the transmission mount bar (shown by arrow). Be careful when pulling out these wire leads, as the small brittle connectors can easily pull off of the wires. If your 911 is equipped with a mechanical speedometer, and you are removing the transmission, then disconnect this cable and pull it out of the way.

7 Disconnect the heater hoses from the heat exchangers. They should be attached to the top of the heat exchangers by hose clamps. Once the engine is out of the car, these should be checked. If they are original equipment, they probably need replacing. Newer high-temp aerospace hoses are now available as more durable replacements. See Project 43 for more information.

jack pad inserted into the car's side jack hole and raise one side slowly at a time, gradually increasing the height of the jack stands placed under the torsion bar covers. It also may be useful to remove the rear valance panel, or even the rear bumper, to gain additional clearance to pull the engine out from underneath your car.

Once you have the engine out of the car, it's really handy to have a furniture cart to place it on. Make sure that you don't crush any of the oil lines or fixtures when you place it on the cart, and try not to let the engine rest on the heat exchangers. Use blocks of wood to make sure the engine case actually rests on the cart.

You might want to consider doing a few things to the engine while it's out of the car. It's a very wise idea to spend a little money now, and do maintenance tasks that can only be performed when the engine is removed. Some of these include:

Replace the oil pressure switch. These often leak with age, and are pretty much impossible to get to on the CIS (Continuous Injection System) or the 3.2L Motronic Injection engines. See Project 21.

8 Behind the front seats in the center of the car is a small trap door that allows access to the shift coupler. Remove this panel and disconnect the shift coupler by removing the small hex screw that attaches it to the transmission selector rod. Do not disconnect it by loosening the 13-millimeter clamp bolt, as you will have to readjust the shift linkage later on if you do. Disconnecting this coupler is a very important step, especially when dropping only the engine. As the engine is lowered, the transmission selector rod will rise up in the air. If the coupler is still attached to the selector rod, you may bend the selector rod and damage your transmission. When reinstalling the coupler, be careful not to strip out the delicate aluminum threads that hold the screw. If the coupler bushings are worn or missing, they should be replaced. See Project 37 for more details.

9 In the engine compartment, disconnect the A/C compressor from its mounting bracket, and place it over the side of the car. Do not disconnect any of the A/C hoses, as this will allow Freon to escape from your system and render it useless. Tie the compressor down with a flex-cord, and make sure that you place a thick towel beneath it to protect your car's paint.

10 All the fuel lines that are connected to the engine need to be disconnected. On the 911SC, there are three separate connections. The fuel lines should be disconnected at the fuel filter and fuel accumulator, if possible (white arrows). Be aware that some fuel will spill out of the lines when you disconnect them, so keep any source of potential flame (shop light, etc.) away from the area. Prior to disconnecting the fuel lines, you may want to remove a few of the engine compartment heater hoses. The large plastic one that connects the blower motor to the fan shroud usually gets in the way of almost all tasks in the engine compartment.

11 Disconnect all the main engine wire harnesses. On some models, there may be connectors that you cannot easily see without sticking your head inside the engine compartment. Feel around the sides and back of the engine to make sure that you have disconnected everything. For the 911SC, there is one wire set that connects to the chassis near the engine compartment fuse box, and one that connects to the front of the engine compartment. The back-up lamp and starter connections need to be disconnected and pulled aside as well.

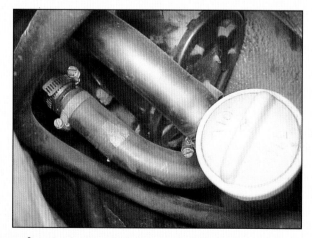

12 The oil tank breather hoses need to be disconnected. These are usually attached with hose clamps that are easily removed. There may be two or more, depending upon the type of fuel injection used on the engine.

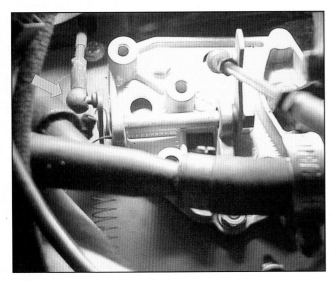

13 Begin the removal of the accelerator linkage bar by disconnecting it from the bell crank located on the transmission. The other end of the rod should simply snap out of the fitting on the top of the engine, inside the engine compartment (shown in photo), indicated by the yellow arrow. Access is usually tight in this area, and may require some effort to obtain the necessary leverage to remove the accelerator bar.

14 If your car has cruise control, disconnect the control cable from the throttle bracket. The cable is held on with two small screws (shown by arrow). Be careful not to drop these as you remove them—they can be difficult to retrieve. You also need to disconnect the two vacuum hoses from the control unit.

16 Four nuts hold the engine to the transmission. The white arrow is pointing to the lower right one on the transmission. Removing these nuts will not make the engine less stable because there are four studs that exit the engine case and are inserted into holes in the transmission case. One or two of these nuts may be difficult to reach using standard tools. You might need to obtain some extensions and universal joint socket wrenches to obtain the right angle.

15 The oxygen sensor connector needs to be disconnected. Don't tug too much on the wire, as it might become separated, and new oxygen sensors tend to be expensive. If you wish to remove the sensor from the exhaust instead, make sure that you soak it in some WD-40 overnight, to make sure that the threads loosen up a bit. See Project 34 for more details.

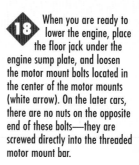

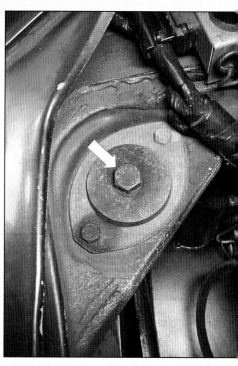

18 When you are ready to lower the engine, place the floor jack under the engine sump plate, and loosen the motor mount bolts located in the center of the motor mounts (white arrow). On the later cars, there are no nuts on the opposite end of these bolts—they are screwed directly into the threaded motor mount bar.

17 The fourth nut that keeps the transmission and the engine together is also one of the nuts that holds on the starter. The nut is a 10-millimeter barrel nut, and requires a 10-millimeter hex key or hex socket to remove it. This nut is not visible from any angle, so removal is especially difficult, and must be done "by feel." The lower barrel nut that holds on the starter is similar to the one on top and does not have to be removed in order to remove the engine. If you drop down the engine slightly before removing this nut, you may be able to reach it from inside the engine compartment.

19 After the fan clears the rear bumper, pull the motor out and away from the transmission. Do not lower the motor all the way to the ground unless it has been disconnected from the transmission, or you may damage your transmission mounts. When disconnected, lower the engine to the ground, and pull it out from underneath the car. If you need more room, you can jack the car up higher, remove the rear bumper or valance, or remove some of the fuel injection components to make the engine fit under the rear of the car.

Replace the oil thermostat O-ring. This seal often wears out, causing large amounts of oil to flow from the top of your engine. See Project 21.

Replace the oil breather hoses. These wear out with age, and sometimes leak oil. Replace them while you have the chance to access them. See Project 21.

Replace the clutch and flywheel seal. I recommend that you inspect and replace the clutch disc when you have the engine out of the car. The flywheel seal, which can often leak, should be replaced as well. See Project 8.

Replace the CIS intake manifold hoses. The CIS fuel injection system used from 1973 to 1983 relies on a strong vacuum seal. The intake manifold hoses should be replaced while you have access to the engine. See Project 31.

Replace the oil cooler seals. Although you can replace these with the engine still in the car, I recommend that you tackle this job when access is much easier. See Project 21.

Install the Carrera chain tensioners and adjust the valves. These two tasks can be performed with the engine in the car, but they are significantly easier to perform with it removed. See Project 16 and Project 18.

Replace the pulley seal. Under the crankshaft pulley, the pulley seal can sometimes fail. If you have access to it with the engine out, it's wise to replace it. See Project 21.

When you are ready to reinstall the engine, the procedure is somewhat the reverse of the removal process, with one exception. With 1977–1986 cars, when mating the engine and transmission back together, you must be sure that the clutch release fork mates properly in the groove of the throwout bearing. Peek through the small hole in the top of the transmission case when you are mating it with the engine to make sure that the throwout arm is properly set inside the groove of the bearing.

ENGINE
PROJECT 8 • CLUTCH REPLACEMENT

 Time: 20 hours

 Tools: Flywheel bolt removal tool, clutch alignment tool, hex key socket set, flywheel lock

 Talent: ▮▮▮▮

 Applicable Years: 1965-1986

 Tab: $450

 Tinware: Flywheel, pressure plate, clutch disc. throwout bearing, flywheel, seal, pilot bearing, clutch fork, pilot bearing guide clips and bushings, helper spring, clutch cable

 Tip: Replace the flywheel seal, even if it still looks good.

 PERFORMANCE GAIN: Reduced slippage of the clutch, and better acceleration

COMPLEMENTARY MODIFICATION: Replace clutch cable and flywheel seal

1 The 911 complete clutch package should include everything that you need. This particular package is for the 915 transmission from 1972–1986. Shown here are:1-Pressure plate, 2-Flywheel (resurfaced and cleaned), 3-Spring-centered clutch disc, 4-Clutch alignment tool, 5-Throwout bearing and clips, 6-Clutch throwout arm, 7-Helper spring, 8-Flywheel seal, 9-Flywheel bolts (quantity nine), 10-Pilot bearing.

One of the most common repair procedures for the 911 is the replacement of the clutch assembly. Unfortunately, it is a rather big process that involves removing the engine. The good news is that it's really not a very difficult job if you have some information, and a few hints and tips.

The first step is to make sure that you gather all the required parts for the job before you begin. It is very frustrating to get halfway through a replacement job, only to find out that you need a part or a tool that you don't have. Here is a list of what you will need to replace the clutch on your 1965-1986 911:

- Pressure plate
- Clutch disc (I recommend that you use the spring-center type instead of the rubber-centered type)
- Throwout bearing
- Replacement throwout fork (1972–1986 only)
- Pilot bearing (for flywheel)
- Resurfaced flywheel (good core usually required)

- New flywheel bolts (six for the 1965–1977 911s, and nine for the 1978–1989 911s)
- New clutch cable
- New flywheel seal
- Clutch helper spring (1977–1986 only)
- Transmission fluid
- Throwout bearing guide clips (1965–1969 911/912 only)
- Throwout arm retainer clip (1965–1969 911/912 only)
- Throwout fork arm bushings/seals (one bushing for the 1965–1969 911s, and two seals for the 1972–1986 911s)

In addition, you will need the following special tools:

- Clutch alignment tool
- Heavy-duty torque wrench
- 911 flywheel bolt removal tool
- Flywheel lock tool

As mentioned previously, the first step in replacing the clutch is to remove the engine from the car. Project 7 details the steps required for the removal process in preparation for performing the clutch job. The early 911s (1965–1969) were equipped with the 901 transmission, and had a 215-millimeter push-type clutch system, in which the pressure plate was pushed inward to disengage the clutch. While still using the same transmission design from the earlier years, in 1970 Porsche moved to a 225-millimeter pull-type design, in which the pressure plate is pulled away from the flywheel to release pressure on the disc. In

33

2 The procedure for removing the flywheel seal is a bit tricky. The goal is to remove the seal without damaging any of the important mating surfaces that surround the seal. Using two screwdrivers, place one across the end of the crankshaft to use as a brace to pry the seal out with the other one. Don't worry about damaging the seal—you will be replacing it anyway.

3 This photo shows the new flywheel seal and pilot bearing installed on the 915 flywheel. Make sure that the new seal is mated flush with the case by tapping it with the blunt end of a hammer or socket ratchet. Don't forget to place a little lithium grease on the pilot bearing before you attach the clutch disc and pressure plate to the flywheel.

4 Tightening the flywheel bolts requires a flywheel lock, and a heavy-duty torque wrench. You can make your own lock using a thin strip of metal with two holes drilled through it. Bolt one end to the flywheel, and place the other around one of the studs in the engine case. When tightening down flywheel bolts, start with one bolt and move across the center, tightening them to about 50 percent of their final torque value. Repeat the procedure several times, increasing the torque value about 20 percent or so until you have reached the final torque. Check and recheck the bolts to make sure they are torqued to the correct specifications.

1972, Porsche unveiled the 915 transmission, and still kept the push-type flywheel. In 1987 Porsche released the G50 transmission, complete with a hydraulically operated clutch mechanism. For the purpose of this project, we'll focus primarily on the early transmissions, from 1965 to 1986.

The first thing that you need to do after you remove the engine is to remove the pressure plate from the flywheel. The pressure plate is attached using hex-cap key screws and should come off quite easily when they are removed. You may have to use the flywheel lock to keep the crankshaft of the engine from turning while removing the bolts. Remove the starter ring (1970–1986) and place it on top of the engine. It is very important not to forget the reinstallation of the starter ring—it is a mistake that most professional shops have made at least once.

The clutch disc should fall out after you remove the pressure plate. On the early cars, only one type of clutch disc was used. This clutch disc used a spring-center system that cushioned the shock of clutch engagement. The springs help to make the ride a bit smoother when the clutch is reengaged. Sport-type performance and racing clutch discs often have a stiffer center-spring setup, or no springs at all to give a much quicker response when engaging the clutch.

Starting in 1978, Porsche used a rubber-center clutch disc design that didn't seem to hold up as well as the spring discs. Very often with age, the rubber eroded and disintegrated, rendering the clutch useless. With the use of the spring discs, the driver of the car can clearly feel a lack of performance from the clutch, prior to it failing. Unfortunately, with the rubber-centered discs, clutch failure can be sudden and rather abrupt, leaving you stranded.

With this in mind, I recommend that you install the spring-center clutch disc replacement instead of the rubber-centered type that was installed as original equipment. The performance is very similar, but the reliability and durability of the older, spring-type design has been proven superior.

Now, the flywheel needs to be removed. Install the flywheel lock, and use the flywheel bolt tool to remove the flywheel bolts. Be careful that you don't strip out the bolts. The heads of the bolts are very shallow, and the tool has a tendency to slip if you don't hold it perfectly vertical. If one of the bolts strips out, the only recourse is to grind the head of the bolt off with an angle grinder, which will most likely cause some damage to your flywheel.

After the bolts are removed, the flywheel should simply pop off. Take the flywheel to your local machine shop and have the machinists clean, check, and resurface it for you. If the flywheel is too worn to resurface, then you will need to replace it with a new one.

The flywheel seal is a troublesome spot for leaks, and it is recommended that you replace it while you have access to it. To remove the old seal, carefully take a screwdriver and pry it out. Be careful not to touch or mar any of the metal sealing surfaces around the seal. It's OK to destroy the seal as you get it out—it's going right into the garbage after it comes out. The new seal installation process is simple—just tap it in straight with a dull hammer.

Installation of the new flywheel is almost always easier than the removal process. For 1965–1979 911s, install the flywheel pilot bearing inside the center of the flywheel by carefully tapping it in with a dull hammer. If you pound on it too much, you will destroy the bearing and have problems later on. Tap it in straight until it is flush with the top surface. The 915 pilot bearing (for 911s from late 1979–1986) bolts onto the flywheel itself. On both types of pilot bearings, make sure that you put a little bit of lithium grease on the bearing before you install it.

Tightening the flywheel bolts is a chore. Start with one bolt, and then move across the center to one on the opposite side. Set your torque wrench at about 20 N-m (15 ft-lbs) to start, and torque down all the bolts. Then repeat the process after increasing the wrench torque value by about 20 N-m (15 ft-lbs). Don't tighten the bolts in a circle, but crisscross your pattern. Final torque value for the 1965–1977 911 is 150 N-m (110 ft-lbs); for the 1978–1986 911 it is 90 N-m (66 ft-lbs).

Once the flywheel is installed and torqued down, place the clutch disc against the surface of the flywheel, and support it there with the clutch alignment tool. The purpose of the tool is to keep the disc centered while you bolt down the pressure plate. If the disc is not centered, you will have great difficulty remounting the engine to the transmission.

If you have a 1972–1986 911, you will need to install and attach the throwout bearing to the pressure plate. Assemble the bearing according to how the old one was put together, and be careful to place all the rings and spacers in their correct orientation. If you have a 1965–1969 911, you can just install the pressure plate on the flywheel—the throwout bearing is installed on the transmission. Install the pressure plate and bolt it down, pressing the clutch disc in place. Make sure you reinstall the starter ring on 1970–1986 911s. When you are finished, you should be able to easily remove the alignment tool, and the clutch disc should not move at all.

Now that you have completed all the tasks related to the engine, it's time to move to the transmission. On the 1977–1986 911s, it is a wise idea to replace the shift throwout fork (cost is on the order of $65) because they sometimes bend and break over the years. Tap out the small pin that holds the fork to its shaft, and it should slide right off. There are two small seals that fit on each end of the arm as it rides on the shaft. Make sure that you replace these seals if yours are deteriorated or missing.

On the early 911s, the throwout fork is prohibitively expensive to replace, so most people don't bother. Three important items to replace, though, are the throwout bearing guide clips, the plastic bushing

5 Place the new clutch disc against the flywheel, and set its center alignment using the clutch alignment tool. If you don't use the tool throughout this procedure, you will have great difficulty mating the engine back up with the transmission. The tool sets the location of the clutch disc so that the input shaft from the transmission can easily mate with the clutch disc when the transmission and engine are rejoined.

6 Install the pressure plate with the alignment tool in place. Make sure that you attach the throwout bearing and check its operation before you mount the pressure plate to the flywheel. The alignment tool should easily slide in and out of the clutch disc in this configuration.

7 The 915 transmission throwout arm is often a source of clutch problems. Over many years of use, it has a tendency to develop cracks and break. It is a wise idea to replace this arm while you have the engine out. New ones are relatively cheap insurance against having to remove the engine again. Make sure that you replace the thin upper and lower seals (shown by arrows) that flank both the top and bottom of the arm.

on the inside of the arm, and the throwout arm retaining clip. Using a hex key, remove the bolt that holds the retaining clip to the throwout arm. On the back side of the arm you will see the small ball cup bushing. Pick the old one out and tap in the new one, adding some lithium grease as well. Reattach the arm using a new retainer clip. When you install the new throwout bearing, make sure that you use new guide clips and grease the guide bearing shaft. If the shaft is significantly worn, replace it with a new one.

The final step is reinstalling the engine and transmission, adjusting the clutch (see Project 11), and taking the car for a spin!

ENGINE
PROJECT 9 • CLUTCH CABLE REPLACEMENT

 Time: 2 hours

 Tools: Hex key set

 Talent:

 Applicable Years: 1965-1986

 Tab: $20-55

 Tinware: Clutch cable, cable retaining pin

 Tip: Replace your clutch cable and eliminate it as a cause of problems before you do any expensive clutch work. Carry a spare cable in your front trunk.

 PERFORMANCE GAIN: Smoother clutch motion and shifting

COMPLEMENTARY MODIFICATION: Rebuild your pedal cluster, replace your clutch helper spring, adjust the clutch.

1 The clutch clevis is screwed onto the end of the clutch cable, and attached to the lever arm with a snap retainer pin. Removal of the pin is not always easy, but it can be accomplished with a little bit of patience. Be careful not to drop the snap retainer, as it may be difficult to fish out of the area directly below.

Prior to replacing your entire clutch mechanism, it is recommended that you replace the clutch cable, and eliminate it as a possible source of clutch problems. It is common for a failing cable to exhibit the same symptoms as a bad or worn out clutch. A very stiff clutch pedal, or difficulty releasing the clutch, may be caused by the cable binding or separating. Replacing the clutch cable and the helper spring on late 915 models (Project 10) may solve more clutch problems that you would imagine. While you have access to the area, it may be a wise idea to rebuild your pedal cluster as well and replace the old plastic bushings with durable bronze ones (Project 40).

Replacement of the cable is not a difficult task. Begin by removing the driver side carpet and floormat, and unbolting the wooden foot pedal cover from the car. Underneath you will see the pedal cluster and the accelerator pedal. The clutch cable is attached to the right side of the pedal cluster, using a U-shaped clevis (sometimes called a trunnion pin or retaining fork) and a snap-on retainer. The retainer has a small pin that attaches the cable to the arm on the pedal cluster. Using a small screwdriver, remove this retaining pin from the U-shaped clevis. If the cable hasn't been replaced in a long time, it may require some WD-40 or a significant amount of force to remove the pin. Don't be concerned about destroying the retainer pin, as they are inexpensive and easily replaced.

After you get the retaining pin removed, you should be able to unscrew the U-shaped clevis from the end of the clutch cable. If it is frozen onto the end of the cable, try spraying a little bit of lubricant in the area. Don't be afraid to cut it off either, as you will be throwing out the old cable anyway.

Now, move under the car. You will have to elevate the car on jack stands for this procedure (see Project 1). Under the car, you should see the point where the clutch cable exits out through the firewall, and where it attaches to the throwout arm on the transmission. The early 911s had a single throwout arm that was a very simple design. Starting in 1977, 911s with the 915 transmission used a more complicated system that incorporated an omega-shaped (Ω) spring.

Underneath the car, the cable should be attached to the transmission throwout arm. On the early 911s, the clutch cable was inserted into a hole in a flange on the transmission, and then attached to the throwout arm. To remove the cable, simply unscrew the two nuts on the end of the cable, and pull it through the transmission flange. On the 1977–1986 911s, the cable is hooked onto a large arm connected to the helper spring, and clamped onto a flange on the transmission. If you loosen the nuts that clamp the cable to the transmission, it should come loose and slide right off of the hook.

Installing the new cable is straightforward. You don't need to lubricate the cable before you install it, but a little bit of white lithium grease can't hurt. Slide the new cable into the hole in the firewall, pushing it all the way back until its end is flush against the small tube on the firewall. Make sure that the cable is firmly seated on this tube—otherwise it might slip off later and affect your clutch adjustment.

Attach the new cable under the car the way you removed it. Clutch adjustment is performed by altering the position of the mounting nuts, but we'll cover that in Project 11. Make a best guess at where the nuts should be and hand-tighten them. Make sure that you don't forget the second tightening nut on the early 911s—this prevents the clutch adjustment from coming loose later on.

Moving back inside the car, reaffix the clutch cable to the pedal cluster, using the clevis and the retaining pin. The clevis should be screwed onto the cable along with its locknut, and the distance from the outer face of the locknut to the end of the cable should be about 20 millimeters or 0.8 inch.

After you have the new cable installed, it's time to adjust the clutch. Project 11 covers this in detail.

2 Shown here is the underside of the 1977–1986 915 transmission. The clutch cable is attached to a long lever arm that is assisted in its travel by a horseshoe-shaped helper spring. This spring gives the clutch some of its "snap-in" feel when it's engaged. The long lever acts on a smaller lever that is connected directly to the throwout arm and the throwout bearing. Backlash on the smaller arm is removed by the small coil spring that removes slack from the system.

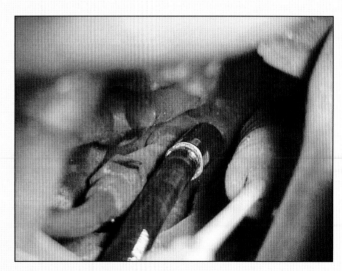

3 When installing the new clutch cable, make sure that the cable is mounted securely within its fitting against the firewall. If the cable is not mated properly, the clutch will fall out of adjustment the first time you press on the pedal.

ENGINE
PROJECT 10 • REPLACING YOUR CLUTCH HELPER SPRING

 Time: 1 hour

 Tools: Snap ring pliers, Dremel rotary tool

 Talent:

 Applicable Years: 1977-1986

 Tab: $70

 Tinware: Helper spring, associated small parts as needed

 Tip: Cut out the clutch helper spring if you have trouble removing it.

 PERFORMANCE GAIN: Smoother clutch motion and shifting

COMPLEMENTARY MODIFICATION: Replace your clutch cable, adjust clutch

In 1977, Porsche changed the design of its clutch release lever to incorporate what is commonly known as a helper spring. This spring aids in the engagement and release of the clutch by giving the pedal a "snap-in" feel. As the clutch gets used more and more, the helper spring has a tendency to wear out, leaving the car with a clutch that feels as if it is about to give way. It is recommended that you replace both the clutch cable (see Project 9) and the helper spring before you do a full-blown clutch job.

The first step in replacing the helper spring is to remove the clutch cable. The cable is mounted to a flange on the underside of the transmission, and hooked into a large throwout arm that actuates a smaller arm connected to the throwout bearing. Loosen up the two nuts that hold the cable, and remove the hooked end of the cable from this arm.

Now, remove the circlip that holds the large arm to the transmission. Try not to destroy the circlip, but if you do, replacements are easily available. After the circlip is removed, you should be able to use a large screwdriver to remove the arm from the transmission. Be careful of the helper spring as you pull the arm off,

1 After the new helper spring is installed onto the large throwout arm, mount it back onto the transmission. Make sure that you orient the helper spring properly, as it is easy to install it backward. With the arm in the position shown in the photo, pull back using a screwdriver or crowbar on the lever, and the helper spring should snap the arm into place. The final resting location of the spring should be extremely close to the heat exchangers (see Photo 2 of Project 9). Wear eye protection, and watch your fingers when snapping the spring into place.

as the spring is under tension, and will spring back when it slips off its pin. Wear eye protection and keep your hands away from the spring as you pull it off. You don't have to worry about it flying off, though, because it is firmly attached to the long arm.

Once you have the arm assembly removed from the transmission, take it over to a workbench to begin the disassembly. Remove the small circlip that attaches and secures the helper spring. Once this circlip is off, try to remove the helper spring, using a screwdriver or a pry bar. Chances are the spring will not come off. If this is the case, then it will be necessary to cut the spring off using a Dremel rotary tool. Start with the outer layers of the spring, and cut inward. When you get to the last layer of the spring, cut about halfway in, and then take a screwdriver and try to break the remainder of the spring off.

Once the old spring is off, check the shaft and the bearings in the arm to see if they turn freely. If not, press them out and replace them with new ones. Once you've confirmed that your bearings are in good condition, take the new helper spring and tap it on to the shaft with a small hammer. Make sure that you place the spring on the shaft in the proper orientation—it is possible to place it on backward. Replace the small circlip, or use a new one if you destroyed the old one getting it off.

Now, move back under the car and replace the arm on its shaft, on the underside of the transmission. To properly install the helper spring, you will need to set it against its pin and then use a big screwdriver or crowbar to pry it into place. Make sure that you keep your hands away from the area when you are doing this and wear safety glasses. When the helper spring is snapped back into position, its curved side should be right up against the heat exchangers.

Reconnect the clutch cable and adjust your clutch (Project 11). Test the clutch to see if there is an improvement, and you may find that all of your worries about having to replace your clutch were needless.

ENGINE
PROJECT 11 • CLUTCH ADJUSTMENT

 Time: 1 hour

 Tools: Feeler gauges, wrenches

 Talent:

 Applicable Years: 1965-1986

 Tab: $0

 Tinware: None

 Tip: Don't tighten up the locknut on the clutch cable until you are sure that it's completely adjusted.

! PERFORMANCE GAIN: Better, smoother shifting

COMPLEMENTARY MODIFICATION: Clutch cable replacement

Whether you have just installed a new clutch cable, or simply need to adjust it a bit from regular driving, the procedure is simple and straightforward. There are a few different types of clutch cable assemblies used on the 911, and the adjustment processes vary slightly for each of them.

911 (1965–1976)

The early 911s had a relatively simple clutch adjustment mechanism. Despite the fact that there were four different clutch adjustment mechanisms during this period, the procedure is very similar for all of them. To adjust the clutch, release the adjuster nut near the underside of the transmission until the clutch pedal free play at the pedal is about 1 inch. The free play is measured by pulling back on the clutch pedal from inside the car. The pedal should travel about 1 inch when you pull it toward you.

Now, tighten up the locknut underneath the transmission. Start the car and with it at idle, press in the clutch and wait about 10 seconds. Then select reverse with the shifter. If the transmission grinds going into reverse, you will need to readjust the cable

1 Before 1977, the 911s have a single arm that the clutch cable is attached to. Adjustment of the cable is performed by rotating the small nut (shown by the arrow) until the proper throw is obtained. Although there were four different variations on this design, the principles for adjustment are the same. Adjust the nut until you obtain about 1 inch of free play in the clutch pedal. Then check your results by starting and driving your car. Keep in mind that if your cable is too loose, the car will be impossible to shift into gear without grinding or stalling. If the cable is too tight, the clutch will never engage, and the car won't move.

2 In 1977, Porsche installed a helper spring mechanism (see Project 10) to give a better feel to the clutch pedal. This mechanism is a bit more complicated to adjust, but involves less guesswork. With the clutch cable disconnected, adjust the small screw on the small actuating lever so that the clearance is 1.2 millimeters (shown by the arrow). After the clearance on the small actuating lever is set to 1.2 millimeters, hook up the clutch cable and adjust the nuts on the clutch cable until the clearance gap decreases to 1.0 millimeter. At this point, tighten up all the nuts on the cable and drive the car to test the clutch setting.

at the release fork end, under the transmission. The grinding indicates that the clutch is not disengaging all the way when you press in the clutch pedal. You use reverse to check the gears grinding because the reverse mechanism doesn't have any synchros that will disguise poor adjustment in your clutch.

When the clutch pedal is pressed completely to the floor, the travel on the throwout release fork should be about 0.6 inch (15 millimeters). Of course, this distance is highly dependent upon the condition of your clutch components. Worn clutches may require more movement, as new clutches may require less. If the release fork doesn't move enough to disengage the clutch, you will need to adjust the cable again, or check the other end of the cable, which is attached to the pedal cluster. If you need to tighten the cable more than the amount that you can at the transmission, you will have to adjust the clevis and pin on the clutch cable that attaches to the pedal cluster. See Project 9 for more details on gaining access to the clevis end.

Depending upon the wear in your clutch disc and pressure plate, you may have to play with these adjustments quite a bit until you get the right feel. Unfortunately, there is no exact science for adjusting the clutch on these early cars. The rule of thumb is that you tighten the cable under the car if the transmission grinds into gear, and loosen the cable if you cannot engage the clutch to the drivetrain (the clutch slips). Adjust the nut only three to four turns at a time. The clutch is quite sensitive to changes in the cable length, and once you get into the ballpark, only minute changes in the cable are necessary to dial in the clutch to your preferences.

911 (1977–1986)

For 911s with the late-model 915 transmission, there is a specific factory adjustment procedure that works quite well. With the cable completely disconnected, adjust the small stop bolt attached to the large release lever arm, until you have a clearance of 1.2 millimeters between the stop bolt and the smaller actuating lever arm (see photo). Use a feeler gauge to measure this gap. Once you achieve this distance, tighten the locknut to keep the screw from turning. Now, attach the clutch cable end to the small hook on the lever arm. Using the nuts captured on the clutch cable, tighten up the cable until the previgap decreases to 1.0 millimeters. Tighten both nuts on the clutch cable, step on the clutch pedal, and recheck the measurement. Readjust if the clearance has changed from the 1.0-millimeter baseline.

If you have trouble meeting this distance, within the range of the adjustment nuts, you might

3 The total throw of the clutch cable should be 25 ±0.5 millimeters as measured at the transmission. If this distance is not within the specified range, adjust the rubber stop that is attached to the wooden floorboard behind the clutch pedal arm in the passenger compartment.

need to readjust the clevis at the pedal cluster end of the cable. See Project 9 for more details on this procedure.

Once you have the primary adjustment set, you need to measure and check the amount of cable travel at the release lever (see photo). You will need an assistant for this task. Measure the distance that the release lever travels when the clutch pedal is depressed. The total travel of the clutch cable should be 25±0.5 millimeters. If the travel is not in this range, adjust the rubber stop under the clutch pedal accordingly. Refer to the photos accompanying this project for the exact locations of the clutch adjustment points.

911 (1987–)

The clutch on the 911 from 1987 to present isn't adjustable. The clutch master/slave system that is implemented with the new G50 transmission is pretty much maintenance free, and self-adjusts for wear on the clutch components. You can, however, set the total clutch pedal travel using the adjustable stop on the wooden floorboard behind the pedal. The total horizontal travel for the pedal should be 150±10 millimeters.

ENGINE

PROJECT 12 • 911 ENGINE TEARDOWN

 Time: 16 hours

 Tools: Cam shaft removal tool, cam shaft holder, snap ring pliers, heat exchanger removal tool, heat stud removal tool

 Talent: ⚒ ⚒ ⚒

 Applicable Years: All

 Tab: $0

 Tinware: None

 Tip: Take pictures while you work in case you forget where something goes during reassembly.

 PERFORMANCE GAIN: Knowledge of how the engine works

COMPLEMENTARY MODIFICATION: Engine rebuild

One of the best ways to learn about how an engine works is to tear one apart. In most cases, doing so is educational, and you usually don't have to worry about breaking anything since the motor will be rebuilt anyway.

The first step is to remove the engine from the car. For complete details on this procedure, see Project 7. After the engine is out of the car, it's probably a wise idea to place it on an engine stand. Not only is the engine up in the air and more accessible, but you can actually flip it upside down and rotate it around as you work on it.

The first items to be removed from the engine are the fuel injection components. If you are planning on using the injection system again, I recommend that you take meticulous notes and pictures of the whole setup before, and during, disassembly. Draw vacuum hose routing diagrams, and make sure that you clearly label all the connections. Take your time doing this, and also make sure that you create clear labels that will last a long time—it might take you longer than you think to rebuild your motor. Be careful of any left-over fuel in the injection system and carburetors—this can be an unforeseen danger if there are any open

1 Here is the starting point, now that the engine is out of the car. It is recommended that you use an engine stand to perform your disassembly work. This engine was disassembled on blocks of wood because all the engine stands were being used to rebuild other motors at the time. The first recommended step is to remove the fuel injection from the top of the motor. In most cases, it can be removed as a single unit, after unbolting it from the intake manifolds on the top of the cylinder heads. This 1982 911SC motor is being torn down for a rebuild. Plug the intakes to the heads with paper towels to keep out debris. Tackle the chain end of the motor first, removing the motor mount, chain covers, and the chain tensioners.

2 Removal of the cams requires the use of two special tools: a Porsche cam holder tool and a 46-millimeter crowfoot wrench. Both tools are absolutely necessary to remove the cams—don't try to get around using them. So much force will be needed to remove the large 46-millimeter nut that you will probably need an assistant, and even then it will be difficult. In the early 1980s, Porsche updated the hardware used to attach the camshaft to the engine. The newer-style hardware requires the Porsche tool 9191 rather than the original P202. Porsche documentation contradicts itself on when this change took place. The 1982 911SC shown here has the old-style retaining nut installed. Check your car's camshafts before spending your money on the tool.

flame sources or even hot halogen lamps in the near vicinity. You can also opt to remove the entire fuel injection system, fan, and fiberglass shroud as one complete assembly. Doing so helps to keep the hoses and fuel injection components hooked up properly.

After you get the fuel injection components removed and labeled, it's time to remove the fan, engine shroud, sheet metal, and fan housing. For detailed information on removing the fan housing, see Project 20, Replacing Your Alternator. The fan shroud is screwed onto the top of the motor with a few sheet metal screws. As you remove screws and other components, it's good to label them in plastic bags for future reference. Nothing is worse than reassembling your motor, and not being sure where everything goes.

With the fan and sheet metal removed, remove the clutch assembly and the flywheel. Refer to Project 8 for more details.

3 Once the cam nut has been removed, the head studs (shown by the arrow) can be loosened and the cam towers removed. Removing the head stud nuts requires an extra long 10-millimeter Allen head tool that can reach down into the recesses of the heads. Sometimes these nuts are heavily rusted and are very difficult to remove. Spray some WD-40 on the difficult nuts and let them soak overnight before trying to remove them from the studs.

4 Once the head stud nuts are removed, you can pull off the cam towers and the heads as a single unit. In this photo, the cam tower is upside down, with the exhaust ports on the top. Visible on the first head is extensive oil residue in the blow-by area, caused by the broken head studs.

5 The rocker arms can be removed by loosening up their attachment bolts in the cam towers. The rocker shafts are secured with a cap that expands when tightened, so be careful to loosen them up fully before removing them from their mounts. The heads can now be simply unbolted from the cam towers. The rocker arms and shafts need to be removed to reach all of the nuts that secure the heads to the cam towers.

6 Looking at the bank of pistons and cylinders, it is obvious why this motor is coming apart. The arrows point to broken head studs. Sludge left over from oil leaking out of the heads surrounds the head studs. Theoretically, there shouldn't be any oil in this area, but this motor had other problems as well. The Dilavar studs used in 1982 seemed like a good idea at the time, but the seven broken studs on this motor (five on the opposite side) tell a different story. If you are shopping for a 911SC or a 3.0-liter engine, insist that your mechanic remove the valve covers during the prepurchase inspection to check for broken head studs.

Once you have the fuel injection and fan assembly removed, it's time to tackle the long block. Start with the timing chain at the rear of the motor. Unbolt the motor mount, A/C compressor brackets, and smog pump/bracket (if so equipped) to gain access to the chain housings. Remove the rear chain housing covers, their associated oil lines, and unbolt the two tensioners. You won't be able to remove the chain until you split the case, but you can lift it off the camshafts and move it out of the way.

Removing the camshaft nuts is a task that requires two specific Porsche tools, and it cannot be easily done without them. First, a 46-millimeter crowfoot wrench is required to turn the nut, and special Porsche tool P202 is required to hold the camshaft steady while you loosen it (for pre-1982 cars; see Photo 2). The torque specification for this nut is 150 N-m (110 ft-lb), so it will probably require the skills of two relatively strong people to remove it. Again, I cannot stress how difficult this would be to do without the special Porsche tools.

The next step is to remove the rocker arms from the cam towers. Carefully place each rocker arm and associated screws in a marked plastic bag indicating the cylinder number and whether it was part of an intake or exhaust valve assembly. Many expert mechanics believe that replacing the rockers and shafts in the same positions that they were removed from will reduce the likelihood that they will leak.

Once the rockers are removed, you can pull out the camshafts. After you remove the camshafts, you can then detach the chain housings. The next step is to remove the heads and the cam towers. Remove all the 10-millimeter head stud nuts, and simply pull the cam towers and heads off of the cylinders. With the rockers removed, you should have clear access to the

nuts that hold the heads to the cam towers. Unbolt the heads and separate them from the cam towers.

Now, turn your attention to the engine case. Carefully remove the cylinders from the pistons and label them. It is important to keep all the cylinders matched with their respective pistons when you are reusing them. Each piston can be removed from its rod by removing the small circlip that holds in the wrist pin. Once the circlip is removed, use the handle end of a long screwdriver to tap out the wrist pin. Make sure that the piston doesn't fall from the engine case. Now, remove the oil cooler and the oil breather console on top of the motor.

With the pistons removed, you can now move to separate the case. There is a cover for the front of the intermediate shaft that needs to be removed prior to the case coming apart. Also make sure that you remove the engine sump plate from the bottom of the case. Be sure that you remove all fasteners from the case before attempting to open it. Work slowly and carefully—there are a lot of fasteners, including two hidden deep inside the timing chain area.

To separate the case, tap it with a rubber hammer. Don't use any sharp tools to pry the case apart—you might damage the parting line mating surface, which will cause leaks later on. The case should come apart pretty easily. If not, double-check to make sure that you have indeed removed all the fasteners. You should be able to lift the left side of the case off of the right side without any major components falling out. Once the case is open, you can remove the crank and rods, the oil pump, timing chains, and the intermediate shaft.

Tearing apart your motor is a fun process, even if you are not planning to rebuild it yourself. If you keep careful inventory of your parts, you can now easily take them to your mechanic or engine machine shop in reparation for rebuilding.

7 Slide the cylinders off of the pistons. Be gentle in the process, as these are very expensive to replace. It is the hope of most people that their pistons and cylinders are still in good enough condition to be reused, since new sets cost anywhere from $1,500 to $3,000.

8 Remove the snap rings that hold on the pistons (shown by the arrow). Reach in with a small screwdriver, and pry the rings out of the pistons. If you are not planning to split the case, make sure that you don't drop the circlips down into the recesses of the engine. Cover the openings to the case with some plastic, because the snap rings have a tendency to fly out when they are removed.

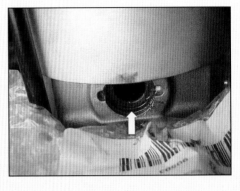

9 Quite possibly the hardest step is removing the head studs. Installed by the factory using Loctite, these can really be difficult to remove. Using a propane torch to heat up the case always helps, as does the use of a special collet head stud removal tool. If the stud breaks off, then you may be forced to use other means to remove it from the case (see Project 95: Removing Broken Studs). Only remove the studs if you are planning to replace them.

10 The final step is to separate the case. An engine stand is especially useful in this stage. After removing all of the case fasteners, the two halves should separate with a few light taps with a rubber mallet. Don't use any tools to pry the case halves apart, as you might damage the fragile mating surfaces in the center. Make sure to double-check that you have removed all the fasteners before you start hitting the case with the mallet. The left side should be lifted off of the right side of the case.

ENGINE
PROJECT 13 • MACHINE SHOP 101

 Time: As long as it takes

 Tools: A good quality machine shop

 Talent: –

 Applicable Years: All

 Tab: $50–$1,500

 Tinware: Valve guides, valve seats, new valves—if needed

 Tip: Find a machinist who has time to answer your questions.

 PERFORMANCE GAIN: Tightly machined parts for a better running engine

COMPLEMENTARY MODIFICATION: Blueprint your engine

If you are planning to have your motor rebuilt, or having a top-end rebuild performed, you will probably need to take some of your parts to your local machine shop. Some tasks require special, precise tools and knowledge that only a machine shop possesses. This section aims to take some of the mystery out of what happens to your parts when you drop them off.

One of the most useful services of any machine shop is its ability to clean and bead-blast sheet metal, flywheels, heads, body parts—just about anything you want. If for some reason you can not use a blasting procedure (on engine cases or oil coolers for example), most machine shops have advanced cleaning tanks that are similar to industrial-sized dishwashers for greasy, oil-soaked parts.

One of the most common procedures to be performed at the machine shop is reconditioning cylinder heads. The first thing that needs to be done is to separate the valves and springs from the heads. The heads are placed on a specialized spring compressor, which compresses the valve and allows the removal of the retaining clip that secures the valve and spring together. The valves can then be removed from the

1 It all begins here with the bead blaster. A bit better than sand blasting, the bead blaster is kinder to the surface of the metal when it is used. Paint, oil, dirt, and grime are no match for the bead blaster.

2 You can often assess the condition of the valve guides, simply by placing a good valve in each of them and seeing how much it wobbles. If it doesn't move around too much, further measuring of the valve guide wear will be required. In most cases, the valve will wobble, indicating that the guides are worn and should be replaced.

3 The old and new valve guides are placed side by side here for comparison. In many cases, the valve guide design and materials used over the years has improved. In particular, the valve guides from the 2.7-liter motors used from 1974 through 1977 were often known to wear out after about 60,000 miles. Newer materials can increase that limit up to 250,000 miles or more.

assembly. Then the heads are either cleaned or blasted until they look new.

The heads are then inspected to see if they need new valve guides. In most cases, the guides will be worn beyond the recommended Porsche specifications, and need to be replaced. One quick test to see if the valve guide is worn is to insert the valve into the guide and look to see if it can wobble back and forth. If the guide doesn't wobble, then a more precise small-bore gauge will be needed to accurately measure the guide. If the guide is worn, it needs to be removed. One of the most common methods of removing valve guides is to tap threads into the guide and screw in a cap screw. This screw now gives the valve guide puller a grip for removing the valve from the head.

Advances in valve guide technology have resulted in newer types of materials with higher wear strengths. Newer guides may look different from the older ones, and should last considerably longer. After the guides are pressed into the heads, they are reamed to make sure the inner bore is within the proper specifications.

The heads contain valve seats, which are steel inserts that are pressed within the aluminum casting. In most cases, it is not necessary to replace the seat in the head. The seat is machined in precise alignment with the new valve guide. A machine that aligns itself with the new guide cuts the seat at a specific angle so that the valve will seat and seal properly.

The valves themselves are machined as well to match the angles of the valve guides and the valve seats. For a valve to be reused, it must still have a significant amount of material on both the outer edge, and on the valve stem itself. In general, a valve can be used for one or two rebuilds before it needs to be replaced. Exhaust valves should only be used once, unless they are the more expensive sodium-filled ones. The sodium-filled valves dissipate heat better than standard stainless-steel valves, and thus are less affected by thermal shock than steel valves. The valves are set into a valve grinding tool, and precisely ground to the angle that matches the angle on the valve seats.

Machining the valve, guide, and the seat are all precision processes that need to be aligned together. If a machine shop is sloppy, or its equipment is out of alignment, you might be in for trouble later on. In some cases, the cheapest machine shop might not do the best-quality job. Unfortunately, it's very difficult to check the tolerances on the valves after you get them back from the shop.

Another common procedure at the machine shop is honing used cylinders. The honing process places a crisscross pattern on the inside of the cylinders that allows the rings to seat properly when the engine is being broken in. The honing process also helps to ensure that the cylinders are round when the new rings are installed. Two types of cylinders were primarily used on the later 911s, Nikasil and Alusil. The Nikasil cylinders, manufactured by Mahle, can be easily honed on a standard machine, while the Alusil cylinders cannot. The Alusil cylinders, manufactured by Kolbenschmitt, have a coating on the inside of the cylinders made from a special material that doesn't respond well to the honing process.

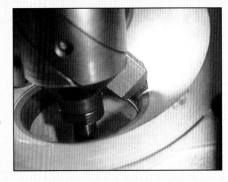

4 The heads are machined on a special jig that is aligned to cut the valve seats to match the valves exactly. A special cutting tool cuts the angle of the seats, while the machine holds the heads aligned to the inner bore of the valve guide.

5 The tool used for grinding the valve seats is made of special tool steel, and is ground to reflect the desired profile and angle of the seats.

6 Valves can usually be reused if there is enough material on the edge for a regrind. The valve on the left is a brand-new one; the one on the right doesn't have enough material left on its edge for another regrind. Intake valves can usually be used again with no problems, but the exhaust valves should only be used once, unless they are the more expensive sodium-filled ones. These exhaust valves dissipate heat much better than plain stainless-steel ones, and thus have a longer life. Sodium-filled exhaust valves typically have a small divet in the center of the valve head.

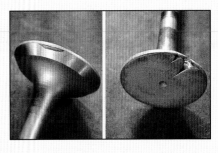

7 Here are two valves that have seen better days. The valve on the left has been ground so thin that its edge has cracked off. The valve on the right came from an engine that exhibited signs of the valve getting too hot. If the seat and the valve don't meet and mount perfectly, hot spots will build up in the valve, causing cracks like the ones in this valve.

8 If there is enough clearance left on the valve, it can be reground to match the valve seats. The process is performed on a special valve grinder that can be set to match the angle of the valve to the angle of the valve seat.

9 The honing machine places a crisscross pattern on the inside of the cylinders, helps the rings seat, and helps keep the compression high.

10 Your best asset in rebuilding your engine is your machinist. Look for one who doesn't mind answering your questions. Beware of those who insist that they know what's best without explaining why. Sometimes the cheapest machine shop isn't the best bet. Try to find one with machinists who take pride in their work. Ask around, as stories of bad shops tend to spread quite easily from the mouths of disgruntled customers.

The crankshaft should also be taken to the machine shop before using it in a rebuild. The crank is put through a process called magnafluxing, which can isolate and identify microscopic cracks that may lead to later failure. In general, the 911 cranks are very strong, and aren't normally susceptible to cracking. But it's better to be safe than sorry.

If a bearing spun in your 911 motor, your machine shop might recommend that you regrind the crankshaft. I recommend that you find a good used standard crank that doesn't need to be reground. The grinding process removes the hardened surface on the crank and makes it wear out faster.

It's also a wise idea to get the crank polished. The bearing surfaces require a smooth surface to properly create a thin oil film to ride upon. If the surface is a bit rough, it disrupts the flow of oil around the bearing. Polishing the crank keeps the oil flowing smoothly around the bearing surfaces, and increases engine bearing life.

The connecting rods are important parts that need to be reconditioned at the machine shop as well. New wrist pin bushings should be placed at each rod's end. There is also a procedure called resizing that makes sure the size of the rod bearing that fits around the crankshaft is the correct size. Over the life of the motor, rods sometimes stretch, causing the rod bearing surface to become slightly out-of-round. To correct this, the smaller half of the rod is removed and a small amount of material is removed from the mating surface. The rod is then remated with its other half, and the bearing surface is machined to the original factory specifications. Removing the small amount of material from the smaller rod half is common, and doesn't affect the strength or reliability of the rod.

It may also be necessary to regrind your camshaft. In general, the 911 motors do not exhibit large amounts of wear on the camshafts, but a regrind and polish close to original specifications may be necessary. If the camshaft is pitted, then it may be necessary to weld the pits, regrind the shaft, and retreat the metal to reharden the surface on the lobes of the cam.

The most valuable tool in the machine shop is your machinist. Make sure that you choose one who takes pride in his work, is more than willing to answer your questions, and offers to show you around the shop. Remember that all the attention to detail that you may take rebuilding your motor could be useless if your parts are not machined correctly.

Make sure that your machine shop understands this, and can identify the two different types prior to honing your cylinders.

You should also take your engine case into the machine shop to be cleaned and checked. Make sure that the case is not sandblasted, as the sand may get caught in the tiny oil passages that feed various parts of the engine. The shop will check the engine case to make sure that all the bearing surfaces are round and aligned with each other. If they are not, then a procedure called align boring is performed. In many cases, machine shops will outsource this particular job, because the machines required for the job can be large and expensive. The process of align boring increases the outer diameter of the bearings to a specific size, while aligning all the bearing surfaces within the case. After the case is bored out, you must use oversized bearing sets instead of the standard sets.

ENGINE
PROJECT 14 • REBUILDING YOUR ENGINE

 Time: 50 hours

 Tools: Cam shaft removal tool, cam shaft holder, snap ring pliers, heat exchanger removal tool, valve adjustment tool, torque wrenches, ring compressor

 Talent: 🔧🔧🔧🔧🔧

 Applicable Years: All

 Tab: $2,500–$6,000

 Tinware: Engine gasket set, O-rings, valve covers, piston rings, sealant, pistons and cylinders (if required), rod bearings, main bearings, intermediate shaft bearings, rod bushings, timing chains, head studs

 Tip: Buy your favorite mechanic a six-pack of beer right before you start, so you can flood him with questions later on.

 PERFORMANCE GAIN: More horsepower, longer lasting engine

COMPLEMENTARY MODIFICATION: Turbo valve covers, Carrera chain tensioners, larger pistons, Carrera oil pump upgrade

1 It all begins with your checked and/or line-bored case. The aluminum 2.0-liter, 3.0-liter, and 3.2-liter cases make excellent rebuild candidates. If you have a 2.2-liter, 2.4-liter, or 2.7-liter case, there are a few modifications that you will want to do to make it stronger. Most important is the addition of Heli-Coil inserts in the cylinder head stud mounting holes. This will decrease the likelihood that the studs will pull out of the soft magnesium. You also want to ensure that all three mounting surfaces for the cylinders are level. The magnesium cases have a tendency to warp over time, and rebuilding the motor without machining the case will likely result in an oil leak. It's also wise to reinforce one of the center engine case studs, which has a tendency to pull out from the case.

2 Assemble the rods and crank away from the case. It's a good idea to mount the crank to the flywheel and use it as a stable base for tightening up the rods. Use plenty of assembly lube here, and red Loctite on the rod nuts. The rod nuts and bolts should always be used only once. They are designed to stretch, and deform when torqued up to their final specifications. Make sure that the two rod halves match each other—the numbers stamped on both sides should always be kept together.

One of the most talked-about and most revered jobs on a Porsche 911 is a complete engine rebuild. Many mechanics will chatter all day about the mysteries of the design of the 911 motor that make it a very difficult beast to rebuild. In all honesty, it's just another engine, slightly different in design from most of the other ones out there. To rebuild a 911 motor takes plenty of time, patience, and a little bit of know-how. This project is not designed to be a tutorial on the process of rebuilding your motor, but is organized to give you a broad overview of the tasks involved, and the steps required. At the very least, this section will provide you with enough information to ask your engine rebuilder questions about what he is doing to rebuild your engine.

The rebuilding process starts with the engine case. Depending upon what size and year engine you have, you may want to make some modifications to the case to make it more durable. The earlier cases, as well as the magnesium cases, will require the greatest

amount of modifications. The earlier cases can be modified to later specifications by adding piston squirters for better lubrication, boat-tailing the main bearing ribs for better oil circulation, and align boring the intermediate shaft to accept the later bearing shells. As the 911 engine grew and additional smog restrictions were imposed, the magnesium cases became taxed beyond their ability. This weakness often resulted in the case yielding and becoming warped under the pressures of operation. These shortcomings in the case construction were especially profound in the 1974–1977 2.7-liter models, when the added stresses of increased displacement and stricter smog restrictions caused the cases to weaken considerably. There are quite a few modifications that should

3 The crankshaft, intermediate shaft, and oil pump are all shown installed in this photo. Use a new bend-up lock tab when installing the oil pump. Make sure that you properly install the timing chains before you go too far in the process. Even if you forget to install the chains, you can always install a master link chain later on. The master link chain allows you to disconnect the chain and remove it from the intermediate shaft without reopening the case. Everything that is a moving bearing surface should be coated with assembly lube—no need to be shy about spreading it on there. However—make sure that you don't get the assembly lube on the case mating surfaces. Don't forget the two thick O-rings on the oil pump and the one that seals the lower oil passages within the case (not shown).

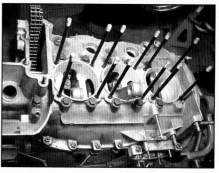

4 The two case halves are together, and the new head studs are installed in this photo. The consensus of the Porsche experts is that the Dilavar studs are to be avoided, and original-style steel head studs should be used instead. Make sure that all the studs are at identical heights (133–134 millimeters), and use some red Loctite when installing them. Remember when installing the through bolts on the case to insert the small O-rings that stop oil leaks. I recommend that you use silicone sealant under the washers as an added precaution.

5 Perhaps the "most dangerous" part of rebuilding the engine is installing and compressing the new piston rings. Make sure that you stagger the gaps on the rings, and also be very careful that you don't break one. If you do, the entire top end of the engine will need to be removed and the engine will need to be reringed. If you are in doubt, pull the cylinder out and check.

6 A tricky process is the actual installation of the piston/cylinder assembly onto the rods. Some builders prefer to install the pistons and then place the cylinders over the pistons while the engine is on the stand. While this is easier, it's also much easier to break a ring this way. The cylinders must be installed in a particular order, or you will not be able to slide in the wrist pin for the last one. Make extra sure that you don't drop any of the small wrist pin snap rings down into the engine while you are installing the pistons.

be performed to the magnesium cases in order to strengthen them, but a detailed explanation of these modifications is beyond the scope of this article.

The case should be taken to your local machine shop and checked for straightness. If a bearing has previously spun inside the case, or some other destructive event has occurred in there, the bearing surfaces may need to be align bored. This is the process of aligning all the bearing bores together as well as squaring them relative to the case. As a result, you may then need to use an oversized bearing set. This is a common procedure, and the oversized bearing sets are readily available. Have your shop thoroughly clean the case as well. Do not have the case sandblasted, as you do not want to get any particles of sand lodged in the fine oil passages within the case.

The case should be mounted on an engine stand that is designed for the 911 engine. There are general-purpose engine stands that will work, although they will not be able to give you the support that you need when the engine gets significantly heavier. If you are rebuilding your own motor, make sure that you borrow a 911-specific engine stand, or invest in one for yourself.

If you are installing new head studs, make sure that you install them before you put the case together. It's a bit too easy later on to drop small items and/or shavings into the case if you need to redress some threads on the holes. I recommend that you use the older-style steel studs instead of the Dilavar or late-style 993 head studs. Many years of research combined with polling mechanics around the world has led me to this conclusion.

7 The cylinders are all installed, and the air guide sheet metal is ready to be installed. Make sure that the long fins on the pistons are installed on the exhaust side, or your pistons will overheat and seize. Also make sure that you install the sheet metal in the proper orientation. A seemingly minor mistake on the sheet metal can translate into serious heat problems for the motor later on.

8 Bolt the heads to the cam tower before attaching them to the engine block. This avoids any alignment problems that may be caused by the case not being completely flat on the piston mounting surfaces. Liberally coat the mating surfaces of the cam tower with the Loctite 571 case sealer while using an acid brush. Use new seals and

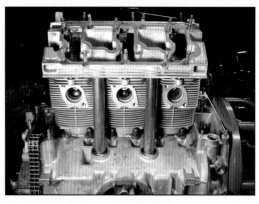

oil return tubes. Make sure that you wet the seals with a little bit of motor oil before you install them. Immediately after bolting the heads to the cam tower, bolt the cam tower and heads assembly to the motor, tightening down the head stud nuts to the proper torque. You want to make sure that you have the entire assembly torqued down before the sealant cures. This photo shows a dry-run test fit of the heads and cam towers that was made prior to the installation of the air guide sheet metal. It's a wise idea to make sure that you have all your fasteners, washers, and sealants lined up before you assemble the cam towers and the heads.

The crank and rods should be assembled on a workbench. Bolt the crank to the flywheel to make a handy stand for assembly. Make sure that you test fit all the rods, and don't ever recycle the rod nuts or bolts. Use red Loctite on the rod nuts, and apply plenty of assembly lube to the bearing surfaces. The assembly lube allows the parts of the engine to be turned and rotated during assembly, and also provides lubrication during the first few moments when the engine is started and no oil pressure is available. Apply it in an even pattern covering the entire surface, but don't lay it on too thick.

Each rod consists of two parts that are numbered and matched together. Make sure when you take your rods to the machine shop that they machine them to be round again (see Project 13). Also make sure that you have the wrist pin bushings replaced.

When placing the crank and rods in the case, make sure that you fully lubricate the main bearings with assembly lube. Also make sure that the oil pump and intermediate shaft are properly installed and that you have also installed the two timing chains. The backlash alignment between the aluminum gear on the intermediate shaft and the drive gear on the crankshaft should be checked as well. It's also a wise idea to pour a little bit of motor oil into the oil pump prior to installing it.

Closing up the case is an important step, of course. Use an appropriate case sealer (the orange

Loctite 571 case sealer is preferred) and apply it evenly with an acid brush. The Loctite sealer doesn't cure with contact with air—it cures with metal-to-metal contact, so don't be concerned if the excess that drips out when the case is sealed never hardens. The long through bolts that hold the case together need to have small O-rings placed on each end. This is because oil flows through these passages, and will leak out if not properly sealed. It's also wise to put some high-temp silicone around the O-rings as an added measure. Make sure that you torque all the fasteners to the required torque, and don't forget the one or two hidden fasteners in the recesses of the case.

Once the case is together, you will be feeling a bit proud of yourself, as it will look like it's coming together. The next step is to assemble the pistons and cylinders. This is perhaps the trickiest part of the process. It is very easy to break a piston ring here. Work slowly and carefully, and assemble the pistons and cylinders on a workbench. Some people recommend putting the cylinders on after the pistons are attached to the rods. However, it's easier to break a ring during this process because you don't have a really good angle on the pistons, and you also don't have any surplus working room.

The installation of the pistons/cylinders to the rods is a bit tricky. In order to get the snap ring that holds the wrist pins in place, you will need to plan out your assembly procedure. Don't forget the copper

9 When attaching the valve train, don't overtighten the rocker arm shafts, as they tend to leak if stretched a bit too much. On the older 911 engines, the rocker arms sometimes have a tendency to leak, despite the design of this compression fit. The solution is to install a small seal in the groove of the rocker arm prior to installing it into the cam tower. See Project 21 for more details.

10 A very important step in the rebuild process is the setting of the cam timing. This is measured by using a dial indicator gauge that is mounted to the top of the valve. When the valve lift reaches a certain height, the engine must be at top dead center. The procedure calls for adjustment of the cams until the valve lift reaches its required specification. See Project 15 for more details. With the timing set, the cam nuts can be tightened. Installing the chain tensioners is a snap when you have clear access to the front of the motor. This photo shows the newer-style Carrera chain tensioners installed. For more information on this upgrade, see Project 16, Installing Carrera Chain Tensioners.

sealing gasket (wet it on both sides with some case sealer). Also don't forget to install the cylinders with the large cooling fins facing down, and the pistons with the dimple facing up (if equipped with CIS pistons). These are important details that will wreck your engine rebuild if not closely watched.

Once the pistons and cylinders are installed, assemble the heads to the cam towers. Using the same Loctite case sealer and an acid brush, liberally coat the mating surface of the cam tower. When finished, bolt the heads to the cam tower. Now, mount the cam towers and heads to the engine. Don't forget to install the cooling sheet metal in its proper orientation. Make sure that you also remember the cylinder head gasket that sits on the top of the cylinders. Also don't forget the large washers that go under each of the head stud nuts.

With the cam towers in, you can install the cam into the cam towers. The chain housing and chain tensioner equipment is next. The assembly here is pretty straightforward—see Project 16 for more details on installing the chain tensioners and associated oil lines. Now, install the rocker arms and set the adjustment screw for the intake valves on cylinders one and four. The rocker arms have a compression-type fit that prevents oil from seeping past the interface, but it doesn't always work. There is a secret fix for this problem—a little seal that goes in the groove of the rocker arm and prevents nasty oil leaks (see Photo 6 of Project 21). For some reason, these only seem to leak on the exhaust side of the engine. Make sure when you are tightening down the rocker arms that you don't overtighten them, as you can create friction that will cause the rocker arm to not turn smoothly. Check each of the rocker arms after you tighten them down to make sure they move freely.

The cam timing should be performed with only the two intake rockers installed on cylinders one and four. Without going into extensive detail, the cams are set by measuring the amount of valve lift with respect to the orientation of the crankshaft. Small adjustments are required in the camshaft sprocket in order to achieve the desired results. It is in this step that you can choose to advance your timing to a setting that is

11 The completed long block, looking shiny and new! Most of the work is done, but to do the job right, there is still a lot of work to be performed on the fuel injection system. Hoses, clamps, and seals should be replaced where necessary, and all parts should be cleaned as well as possible.

12 Sandblasting or beadblasting your intake manifolds really adds the finishing touches to the fuel injection. It's also a wise idea to use new screws and washers for attaching the engine shroud to the block. Carefully reassemble the fuel injection system according to the notes and pictures that you took when you removed it.

a bit more aggressive than the stock factory setting. See Project 15 for more details. When the timing is complete, install the remainder of the rockers. Leaving most of the rockers uninstalled while adjusting the cam timing reduces the chances that your valves may accidentally hit the tops of your pistons when setting the cam timing.

Once the timing is set, the cam nuts are tightened and the remaining rockers are installed, you can adjust the valves. With the engine out of the car, this typical four-hour job takes only about a half-hour. After you seal up the valve covers and the timing covers, your long block is completed!

The final steps, of course, are the reinstallation of the fuel injection components, the addition of the exhaust system, and the reinstallation of the motor back into the car. Break-in procedures are very important and should be followed very carefully. Use non-detergent oil if possible, as this will help the rings will seat properly. When first starting the car, make sure that you disconnect the CD box and let the engine turn over until the oil pressure light in the dashboard

goes out. This should take about a minute or less. When you finally start the engine, let it run at about 2,000 rpm for 20 minutes. Take a stopwatch with you, 10 minutes can easily seem like half an hour. Check under the car for major oil leaks, and shut it off if you see oil pouring out from underneath. Before driving the car any significant distance, take it to your mechanic and have him check the mixture. If the car is set to run rich, it might prevent the rings from seating properly. Expect lots of smoke and a bit of a sulfur smell as the rings go through the seating process. The best thing that you can do for the car to break it in is to just drive it. In general, do not take the motor past 4,000 rpm during the first 500 miles. It's also a wise idea to change your oil every few hundred miles until you reach about 1,000 miles on your new engine.

Hopefully, when you are done, you will have a strong-running motor. The rebuilding process is not difficult if you have the right tools and the right instructions. For more information on rebuilding your 911 engine, see my upcoming book, *Rebuilding Your 911 Engine*, when it is released in 2002.

ENGINE
PROJECT 15 • SETTING AND ADJUSTING THE CAM TIMING

Time: 2 hours (with engine removed)

Tools: Cam bar tool, 46-millimeter crowfoot wrench, dial indicator gauge, cam pin extraction tool

Talent: 🔧🔧🔧

Applicable Years: All

Tab: $10

Tinware: Chain housing cover gaskets

Tip: Double-check your settings when you are done — it's easy to make a costly mistake

PERFORMANCE GAIN: Advancing the timing can give you increased power and better low-end response on the 911SC.

COMPLEMENTARY MODIFICATION: Rebuild your engine.

Other than the very expensive factory manuals, there really isn't a very good source of documentation on the process for setting the cam timing on the 911 motor. This is not meant to be a weekend-type project, but more of a knowledge base, so that you can be up to date when your mechanic talks about setting the cam timing on your newly rebuilt 911 motor.

Obviously, the best time to set the cams is when the motor is being rebuilt. However, the cam timing can be changed and altered with the engine in the car. Quite a few things need to be removed or placed out of the way—engine mounts, A/C compressor, spark plugs, valve covers, some heater hoses, fuel injection components—but it is indeed possible. For the sake of simplicity, we will assume that you are putting the motor together on a bench, but the same procedures apply to the motor when it's in the car.

The first step is to make sure that the valves are adjusted properly. This is a very important step, and if the valve clearances are slightly off, then it will affect the timing setting that you will dial in for the cams. The

clearance on both intake and exhaust valves should be 0.10 millimeter (0.004 inch). Take a look at Project 18, Adjusting Your Valves, for more information.

Once you are assured that the valves are set at their proper clearance, you need to attach a dial indicator gauge to the cylinder Number One intake valve in order to read the amount of physical valve lift. Make sure you properly convert all the numbers if you don't use a metric dial gauge. The gauge should be mounted to one of the studs located on the cam towers. Make sure that the gauge tip is perfectly parallel to the valve, and positioned exactly on the edge of the spring retaining collar. Adjust the dial gauge so that the indicator arm is pressed in at least 10 millimeters (about 0.4 inch). This will provide enough clearance for the dial indicator arm to travel as the valve moves up and down.

Now, rotate the engine so that the Z1 mark on the crankshaft pulley lines up with the case half underneath the fan. If you are adjusting the timing with the distributor installed, make sure that the distributor is pointing at the small notch in its housing, indicating Top Dead Center (TDC) for cylinder Number One.

Using the special cam holder tool (Porsche tool P202, or 9191 on post-1982 cars), rotate the camshafts so that the small punch marks on the cams are pointing upward. If you are performing this step on an engine that has already been assembled, you need to remove the large cam holding nut that constrains the camshafts.

It is very important to note that when the cam nut is removed, and the cam is disconnected from the timing chain, it is possible to have the valves hit the top of the pistons when you are turning either the camshafts or the crankshaft. Turn the crankshaft and the camshafts very slowly, and if the slightest resistance is felt, make sure that you rotate the camshafts slightly to relieve the pressure. Moving quickly at this stage in the game can cause great harm to your engine.

If you are assembling the motor from the ground up, then you will need to place the aligning dowel pin into the cam sprocket. In this position, one of the alignment holes of the camshaft will line up with one of the holes in the sprocket. They are slightly offset to give a significant degree of adjustment. Using Porsche tool P212 (or the screw tip on an old spark plug), place the pin in the only hole that is lined up with the sprocket. You can look through the camshaft sprocket, and it will be obvious which hole the pin needs to go into. Simply place the pin in there and unscrew the tool—the pin will not fall out.

With the engine at TDC for cylinder Number One, and the small punch mark on the cams pointing upward, the engine now can be timed for firing on cylinder Number One. Start with the left side of the motor, and use Vise-Grips to clamp the end of the wheel sprocket lever arm to the edge of the chain housing. This is done to increase the tension on the chain and to get a more accurate reading. On the right side, it's a bit more difficult. Make sure that you keep a lot of tension on the chain throughout the timing process. If you have a mechanical chain tensioner, you can use it on the right side of the motor during the timing process and swap it out before you seal up the chain housings. The mechanical chain tensioner was used originally on Porsche race cars, and is not spring loaded. You can purchase these tensioners from most parts houses and use the tensioner as a tool for keeping the chain's tension tight during the timing process.

Reset the dial gauge to zero and rotate the crankshaft 360 degrees, until the Z1 mark appears again. If you sense any resistance at all while turning, rotate the other camshaft to relieve any conflict with the pistons. At this point, the dial indicator gauge should read a few millimeters less than the point that you zeroed. It is this distance, or valve lift for cylinder Number One, that needs to be set to a specific amount when the camshaft is at TDC for cylinder Number Four (where it should be now). On the 911SC type 930/10 motor, this value of intake valve stroke in overlapping TDC with 0.1-millimeter valve clearance must be set between 0.9 and 1.1 millimeters. To determine this value for your particular motor and cams, check the Porsche factory specifications book for your year car.

In order to change the value at which the camshaft is currently set, simply remove the small alignment pin and rotate the camshaft until the dial gauge reads the specified amount. Replace the alignment pin, attach the large spring washer, and tighten down the large cam nut, but not to the final torque specification. Turn the crankshaft 720 degrees, and check the measurement. It should be the same value that you just set. If it's not, remove the alignment pin and repeat the procedure.

At this point, the crankshaft should be at TDC for cylinder Number Four. This is 360 degrees off the point where you originally set the dial gauge to read zero. At this point, remove the dial gauge, and place it on cylinder Number Four, and repeat the entire timing process for cylinder Number Four. The gauge should be set to zero before you make any additional turns of the crankshaft (it should be 360 degrees off from TDC on cylinder Number One).

It's a wise idea to double-check the measurements prior to tightening the cam nut to its final

1 The dial indicator gauge can be installed using the special Porsche tool holder (sometimes called a Z-block), or if you have a flexible holder, you might get away with clamping it to one of the studs on the cam tower. Make sure that the gauge is parallel to the valve, and not cocked at an angle. Setting up the gauge at an angle will affect your final timing setting.

2 Set the dial indicator tip to sit on top of the valve spring retaining collar. The indicator needs to measure exact valve lift, so make sure that it doesn't slip, and is firmly mounted. Also make sure that it has enough play to measure the entire lift of the valve.

3 When placing the small alignment pin into the camshaft sprocket, it will line up with only one hole of the sprocket mounting flange. The two flanges are angularly offset to allow a slight degree of adjustment when setting the timing. Place the alignment pin in the hole and then unscrew the tool—the pin shouldn't fall out.

4 When all the timing is set, and you are convinced that it's correct, tighten the nut to its final torque using a torque wrench, the 46-millimeter crowfoot wrench, and Porsche tool P202 or P9191. Porsche tool P9191 are required for most cars after 1980. The crowfoot wrench and tool P202 are used for most cars before 1980. However, the 911SC used in this book has the early-style cams installed. Check your cams before you purchase the tool. This is a task that cannot be done without the use of these two tools, as the final torque for the cam nut is extremely high (150 N-m for the early 911SCs).

torque. Also make sure that your dial gauge is a metric gauge, and if it isn't, don't forget to convert your units over before you're finished.

ENGINE

PROJECT 16 • UPGRADING TO THE LATE-STYLE 911 CARRERA CHAIN TENSIONERS

 Time: 5 hours

 Tools: Socket set, flared wrenches, hex key set

 Talent:

 Applicable Years: 1965-1983

 Tab: $450

 Tinware: Carrera chain tensioner kit, spacers, an oil line adapter for 1969-1973 cars, muffler gaskets

 Tip: Have an oil pan ready to catch extra oil runoff after you remove the chain housing covers.

 PERFORMANCE GAIN: Protection against chain tensioner failure, quieter engine

COMPLEMENTARY MODIFICATION: Replace or upgrade chain ramps, install tensioner guards, install improved idler arms

The design of the 911 engine incorporates a dual-cam system that is driven by timing chains connected to the main crankshaft. One of the weak points of the early 911 motors (through 1983) is the mechanical spring-loaded tensioners that maintain the tightness and accuracy of the chains. After many years of faithful service, these tensioners have a tendency to fail. If a chain tensioner fails, there is the distinct likelihood that the chain will slip off of one of its sprockets. The result can be catastrophic failure, as the pistons will most likely hit the valves, resulting in a complete engine rebuild and a $6,000–$10,000 repair bill.

In 1984, Porsche developed a better tensioner. With the introduction of the new chain tensioners, Porsche also developed a bolt-on kit that could easily be retrofitted to all of the early cars from 1969 to 1983. Engines from 1965 and 1966 cannot use the bolt-in upgrade because the cam tower lines attach differently. If you rebuild your early 1965–1966 911 engine and use a late-style chain housing and cover, you can then use the newer chain tensioners. Engines from the 1967 year can also use this method to install the upgrade. Smog pumps from the 1968 engines will not fit unless the left cover is slightly machined.

The kit comes complete with everything that you need to perform the job on 1974–1983 cars with CIS. Pre-1974 cars need an oil line adapter, because the location of the oil pressure sending unit changed in 1974. The 1973 911Ts with CIS fuel injection are a special case. They need a different, special adapter, because their oil pressure senders are mounted at the rear, like 1974 and later cars, but they use a smaller thread size than the later cars.

Early cars also need a set of spacers for the chain sprocket idler arms, if you reuse the old idler arms. When you install pressure-fed tensioners, I advise you to replace the chain sprocket idler arms with the 1980 and later design (Part Number 930.105.509.00 left and 930.105.510.00 right). These arms have a wider base and two bushings where they mount. The new design prevents binding of the idler arm, which can cause premature chain tensioner failure.

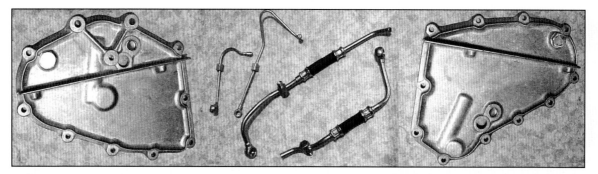

 The Carrera chain tensioner kit comes complete with just about everything that you need to perform the upgrade. Shown here are the new chain housing covers, two flexible oil lines, and two small hard oil lines that together replace your standard cam tower oil lines. The new chain housing covers are universal and should fit all 911s from 1969 through 1983. The kit comes complete with all the mounting hardware that you need (not shown here).

2 The old-style sealed spring-loaded chain tensioners were prone to failure. An inexpensive alternative to installing the pressure-fed Carrera chain tensioners the addition of a safety collar around the shaft of the ten-ner. While not as good as a pure replacement, the safety llar can provide some emergency help when tensioners fail. potential pitfall is that it is not easy to detect tensioner fail-e, and the repeated pounding of the collar may cause it to ar and begin to lodge metal bits inside your engine. The lar is only for use on the early sealed tensioners, and not e pressure-fed ones.

3 The new pressure-fed chain tensioners are both hydraulic and spring loaded. The spring tension exerted on the chain is supplied by a mechanical spring and an oil-pressurized tensioning system that is fed by the engine's oil pump. This redundant tensioning system decreases the likelihood of chain tensioner failure. The pres-sure-fed tensioner is fed the oil by tapping into the pressur-ized oil line that supplies the cam towers. When installing the upgraded idler arms, reuse the old sprocket and mounting hardware. Ensure that the sprocket retainer shaft has its small scoop pointed upward—this is to catch oil and lubricate the bearing.

4 The newer-style chain ramps are manufactured out of tough plastic, and are known to stand up better than the ones used on the early cars. It is recommend-ed that you replace the ramps if they show pitting, which may be caused by the chain flapping up and down. Two odd-shaped bolts that pass through the case create the mounts for the chain ramps. Make sure that you don't install the ramps backward—the four inboard chain ramps closest to the crankshaft point with their longer end toward the shaft; the two outboard ones point their longer ends out toward the wheels. The chain ramps pull off of their mounting posts, and the new ones simply snap on.

The procedure for installation is quite straight-forward. The first step is to drain the oil from the car (see Project 2). Now, place the engine at Top Dead Center (TDC) by putting a wrench on the pulley nut and rotating until you line up the Z1 mark on the crankshaft pulley with the seam of the case. Remove the distributor cap, and make sure that the rotor is pointing to the small notch on the distributor hous-ing. If it's not, rotate the motor another 360 degrees until it does.

Removal of the muffler is required to gain access to the rear of the motor. Remove the muffler by loos-ening the bolts that attach it to the heat exchangers. Then loosen the two muffler clamps. Once the muffler is off of the car, remove the rear engine shelf. Attachment of this piece varies from year to year, and may require the removal of a heater hose or two. On air conditioned cars, you need to temporarily dis-mount the compressor and move it out of the way. Remove the bolts that hold the compressor onto the bracket and pull it out to the side of the car. See Project 7 for more details. Once the compressor is out of the way, remove the compressor bracket that is located right in front of the chain housing cover.

The distributor needs to be removed as well in order to gain access to the left cam oil line. Make sure that you have a timing light handy, as you will need to

reset the ignition timing on the engine when you replace the distributor.

Once you have access to the rear of the engine, remove the left and right chain housing covers. If your chain ramps are looking worn, this is a good time to replace them. Make sure that the chain is kept tight around the cam either by wedging some wood in between the chain and the case, or by tying the chain together near the outboard chain ramps. A good pair of Vise-Grips makes an excellent clamp as well. The goal is to assure that the cam doesn't move and that the chain doesn't skip on the cam gears. If the chain does come off of the cam gears, then you will have to retime the cams as detailed in Project 15.

Removal of the chain tensioner is straightforward. Starting on the left side, simply remove the 13-mil-limeter hex nut that secures the tensioner, and slide it out. Again, make sure that you keep tension on the chain. Once the chain tensioner is out, you can also remove the idler pulley if you are planning to upgrade to the later style pulley arms.

If you are using your original idler arms and have an early car, insert the aluminum spacer on the shaft. Now, install the new chain tensioner. Do not remove the small retaining pin until the tensioner is installed and secured in place. Make sure that you remember to install the small orange O-ring on the

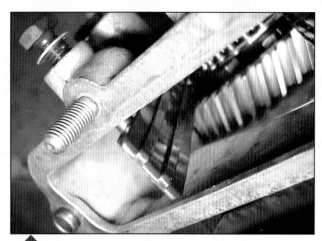

6 **Above and Below** — Make sure that you properly attach the hard oil line brackets and mounting hardware. Failure to do so will result in the lines vibrating too much, and will lead to their premature failure.

5 Chain ramps should be replaced one at a time to ensure tension is kept in the chain. This photo shows an engine during assembly, and affords a unique view of how the inboard chain ramps are mounted. When removing the bolts that hold the ramps, make sure that you don't lose the ramps inside the engine, or you may have difficulty fishing them out. Some of the bolts for the inboard chain ramps may require removing the engine mount for access. If this is necessary, support the engine with a floor jack or jack stands before disconnecting the engine mount. There are also two different types of chain ramps—use the black ones everywhere except for the slightly different brown ramp, which is installed on the lower right.

tensioner where it feeds through the chain housing. Wet the O-ring slightly with a bit of clean motor oil before you install it. Retighten the 13-millimeter hex nut, pull the retaining pin, and then attach the new chain housing cover, using the new gasket that was included with the kit. The housing cover will offer a bit of resistance as it fits down over the O-ring.

The right side replacement is similar, but a little bit trickier, because it is easier for the chain to lose its tension. Be extra careful securing the chain when performing the replacement on the right side.

Make sure that you don't forget to pull the retaining pins out of the chain tensioners. If you do forget, there will be no tension on your chain. When you go to start your engine, the chain will slip off, causing catastrophic damage.

After you have reattached the two chain cover housings, you need to install the new cam tower oil lines. Lay them out on your workbench and make sure that you have all the fittings, gaskets, and washers that you need. The lines have both banjo fittings and straight line fittings with an aluminum sealing ring that fits under a hex cap cover. Attachment of the outboard banjo fittings is straightforward, but the inboard ones are a bit trickier. Make sure that you have the inboard straight oil lines placed exactly

square into the inboard fittings, and the tapered sealing rings have their small edge pointing downward. Do not use too much force on any of the fittings—they will usually seal perfectly if installed properly. You may need to remove some hoses or other additional equipment in order to obtain the necessary room that you need to tighten all the fittings. Once the lines are tightened, install the small support brackets in place. Engines from 1967 through 1972 require removal of the two upper studs on the left chain housing cover, and replacement with the two longer studs (M8 x 60) that should be included with the kit.

Once you have replaced and reinstalled your muffler (use new exhaust gaskets), hoses, distributor, and sheet metal, refill the car with oil, start it up, and check for oil leaks. Small leaks around the lines can usually be eliminated with a half turn or so on the fittings. Don't forget to reset the ignition timing—when reinstalling the distributor, make sure that the rotor points to the notch in the distributor housing. See Project 23 for more details.

Although you won't get an extra 25 horsepower from this upgrade, you will get peace of mind. The old style tensioners are almost guaranteed to fail at one time or another, and the upgrade to your car is cheap insurance against engine failure.

ENGINE

PROJECT 17 • UPGRADING TO TURBO VALVE COVERS

 Time: 1/2 hour

 Tools: 13-millimeter socket

 Talent:

 Applicable Years: 1968-1989

 Tab: $185

 Tinware: Turbo valve covers, valve cover gaskets and hardware

 Tip: Drain the engine oil prior to removing the lower valve covers.

PERFORMANCE GAIN: Prevents a very common oil leak

COMPLEMENTARY MODIFICATION: Adjust your valves at the same time

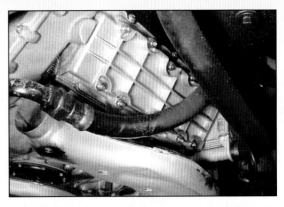

1 Stiffening ribs on the Turbo valve covers strengthen the lower valve covers and reduce the chance of warping. The additional heat from the engine's exhaust system necessitates this additional stiffness. For a photo of the magnesium valve covers, see Photo 1 of Project 21.

One of the most popular upgrades to the 911 engine is the installation of the 911 Turbo valve covers. The valve covers originally installed on almost all 911s from 1968 through 1977 were manufactured out of magnesium. The magnesium was originally used to cut down on the overall weight of the engine. Unfortunately, the magnesium covers were a poor match for the 911 engine and its stressful environment. It is very common for the magnesium valve covers to warp after many years of temperature cycling during the normal operation of the engine.

As the valve covers leak, the oil will spill onto the tops of the heat exchangers, causing the car to smoke a bit when driving. You may also notice the smell of burning oil as the heat from the exhaust burns away the oil on top of the exchangers. If oil is dripping from the cam towers, chances are your valve covers are indeed leaking. If not, then you might have an oil leak coming from somewhere else. See Project 21 for more information on fixing these other oil leaks.

As original equipment, magnesium valve covers were bolted to the aluminum cam towers of the engine. No one can quite agree on what causes the

warping; however, this inevitably leads to valve cover leakage. While replacing the valve cover gaskets with better silicone beaded ones may help the problem, the best solution is to replace the covers entirely with what has come to be known as the 911 Turbo valve covers.

First used on the 911 Turbo (930), these covers are made entirely of aluminum. The aluminum covers are stronger and less likely to corrode than their magnesium counterparts. Additionally, the late-model lower Turbo valve covers are reinforced with aluminum ribs that stiffen and support the structure of the cover, further decreasing the likelihood of warping.

If your 1968 and later 911 is equipped with the original magnesium covers, then you should definitely upgrade both the upper and lower covers to the later-style Turbo aluminum covers. For cars manufactured after 1978 and later, I recommend that you replace your lower valve covers with the reinforced Turbo ones. The upper valve covers on these 911s were already cast out of aluminum.

To check to see if your original magnesium covers (darker in color than the aluminum ones) are warped, place them on a flat surface (glass table) and see if they rock back and forth. If they do, then you should most certainly replace them with the improved aluminum Turbo valve covers.

Installing the covers is a bolt-on process, and no modifications are required. Simply remove the old valve covers and replace them with the new ones. Make sure to use new valve covers gaskets, and torque the nuts down on the valve covers to about 8 N-m (5.9 ft-lbs).

If your car still leaks even with the installation of the Turbo valve covers, you might want to take them to your local machine shop and have them milled flat. Sometimes the casting process used in manufacturing the covers can leave them slightly deformed. Milling the mating surface assures that they will be completely flat when bolted to the car. This can also work to resurrect the early 1966-1967 valve covers as well.

ENGINE

PROJECT 18 • VALVE ADJUSTMENT

 Time: 3 hours

 Tools: 24-millimeter socket, 13-millimeter wrench, valve adjust tool, adjustable mirror, spark plug socket

 Talent:

 Applicable Years: All

 Tab: $20

 Tinware: Valve cover gaskets and hardware

 Tip: Use a shop light, and disconnect hoses that get in your way.

PERFORMANCE GAIN: Greater horsepower, and quieter valve train

COMPLEMENTARY MODIFICATION: Change oil, upgrade to turbo valve covers

One of the most common and expensive maintenance tasks on the 911 is adjusting the valves. This should be done about every 10,000 miles on the later-model 911s (1978 on), and about every 6,000 miles for pre-1978 cars. If the valve clearances are too tight, the valves might not close all the way, hampering performance. If the clearances are too loose, the valves won't open all the way, and they'll be noisy.

Adjust the valves with the engine stone cold, or the settings won't be accurate when the engine warms up. Don't start the engine for four hours before adjusting the valves; letting it sit overnight is better. Before you start, disconnect the spark plug wires and remove the distributor cap and wires as an assembly. You should also remove the spark plugs and replace them with new ones when you're finished. You may need a deep spark plug socket to reach all the plugs. See Project 22 for more details.

Drain the engine oil (if you don't, it'll run out the bottom valve covers), and remove the valve covers from both the top and the bottom of the engine. It's

1 A 24-millimeter socket and wrench is the best way to rotate the motor. Make sure that you only rotate it clockwise, as rotating it significantly in the other direction can result in damage to the chain tensioning system. Make sure that your pulley and fan belt are tight prior to turning the motor, or the belt will slip on the pulleys. Removing the spark plugs and placing the transmission in neutral decreases the amount of force required to rotate the engine.

a tight fit, and you may need some extensions to get to all of the nuts.

Next, set the Number One piston at top dead center (TDC); the Z1 mark on the crankshaft engine pulley should line up with the split in the case, and the rotor on the distributor will point at the little notch in its housing. You can rotate the engine clockwise by using a 24-millimeter socket on the fan pulley nut. Don't turn the engine counterclockwise; it can damage the chain tensioner parts. If the engine doesn't turn because the belt slips, replace or tighten your fan belt (Project 3). Removing the spark plugs and placing the tranny in neutral will make turning the engine easier.

When the Number One piston is at TDC, it's time to adjust the valves for that cylinder. The intake and the exhaust valves can be adjusted at the same time. The intake valves are on top of the engine inside the engine compartment; the exhaust valves are located underneath the engine. For each valve, loosen the 13-millimeter retaining nut around the adjustment screw, and turn the screw counterclockwise. Place the feeler gauge between the valve stem and the swivel foot screw, and tighten down the screw. A coat of engine oil on the feeler gauge blade helps you feel when the adjustment is correct. When you have tightened down on the feeler gauge, tighten the retaining nut

2 The crankshaft pulley has a mark of Z1 (shown by the arrow), referring to top dead center for either cylinder Number One or Number Four. When the crankshaft is lined up with this mark and the distributor is lined up with the notch in its housing, the motor is at top dead center (TDC). In the combustion cycle, the spark plug has just fired, and both the intake and exhaust valves are closed.

3 The distributor must be pointing to the small notch in the distributor housing (shown by the arrow) in order to make sure that the engine is at top dead center (TDC) for cylinder Number One. At this point, both valves are closed, and the rocker arm feet should have a physical gap between them and the top of the valve.

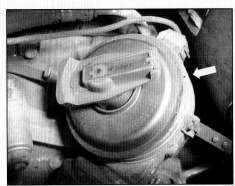

4 The special feeler gauge is an important tool in the adjustment process. Normal feeler gauges will not fit well down into the recess of the cam tower. Make sure that you adjust the valve so that you can still easily remove the feeler gauge from between the foot and the valve. Also make sure that you have a few extra feeler gauge blades handy, as they are very easy to break when you are reaching around into the recesses of the engine.

5 Use a 13-millimeter wrench and a screwdriver to tighten up the adjustment screw-foot. Make sure that you double-check the clearance after you finish by removing and reinserting the feeler gauge.

while holding the adjustment screw in place with a screwdriver. Recheck the clearance after tightening the nut, as the clearances often change in the process.

Now, rotate the engine crankshaft 120 degrees using the fan pulley. A mark on the crankshaft engine pulley will indicate the 120-degree position. Repeat the adjustment procedure for cylinder Number Six. When finished, rotate the engine another 120 degrees, and adjust the valves for cylinder Number Two. Repeat the rotation and adjustment procedures for the remaining valves following the engine firing order 1-6-2-4-3-5 (see diagram).

When you are finished, rotate the engine back to TDC for cylinder Number One; the distributor rotor should be pointing at the notch in the housing. Now, go back through the rotation procedure and check all valve clearances with the feeler gauge. If any feel too tight or too loose, readjust that valve.

When the process is complete, replace the valve covers and tighten them to about 8 N-m (5.9 ft-lbs),

and always use new valve cover gaskets and mounting hardware. After adjusting the valves, you might feel a significant increase in power, and a significant decrease in the valve train noise.

6 The firing order for the 911 engine is 1-6-2-4-3-5. Adjust the intake and exhaust valves together in this sequence, then check all the clearances again. Sometimes the rocker arms sit slightly differently the second time around.

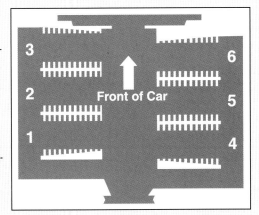

ENGINE
PROJECT 19 • OIL LEVEL SENDER REPLACEMENT

 Time: 1 hour

 Tools: Socket set

 Talent: ☆

 Applicable Years: All

 Tab: $60

 Tinware: New oil level sending unit, gasket

 Tip: Never depend on this gauge for accurate readings—always check the dipstick at idle when the car is warm

 PERFORMANCE GAIN: Semiaccurate oil level readings

COMPLEMENTARY MODIFICATION: Oil change

1 The brand new oil level float is a bizarre looking part. It's shaped so that it can barely fit inside the hole in the side of the tank. Installation requires a bit of maneuvering to place the sender inside. *Tom Sharpes*

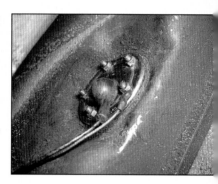

2 The sender is accessible from the outside of the tank, looking in from the rear wheel fenderwell. The primary signal wire is connected to the center of the unit, and a ground is connected to one of the mounting bolts on the unit. Make sure that you don't drop any dirt or debris in the tank when you install the new unit. *Tom Sharpes*

3 If, after you've installed the new unit, your gauge still isn't working, it's likely a problem with your actual dashboard gauge. You can only replace the gauge as a unit. The old ones simply pop out of the dash and can be replaced with a brand-new one after reconnecting all the wires in the rear. *Tom Sharpes*

If the oil level readings in your dashboard gauge are a little off, it might be time to replace your oil level sender. Quite possibly the most dangerous part in the car, the oil tank level gauge is indeed mostly useless. Its measurements are only accurate when the car is warm and at idle. At all other times, the gauge will read artificially low or high values. Sometimes the sender or the gauge will stick, leading to more false readings. In general, the safe rule is to only check the oil using the dipstick located in the filler neck of the engine compartment. The oil should only be checked when the car is fully warmed up, and at idle.

If your oil tank level gauge is pegged at full, then you probably have a problem with the sender. Replacement units are relatively inexpensive, at around $60, and the process of installing the new unit is quite simple.

The oil tank level sender is located on the outside of the tank, which is in the rear right fender of the 911 behind the wheel. All 911s had their oil tanks in this location except for the 1972 911, which had it in the front. The sender unit is held on with five small nuts that need to be removed. It's a wise idea to clean the area of any dirt or debris that may have been flung up

into this area from the tires. When you remove the sender, you don't want any dirt falling into the tank.

The sender unit is an unusual shape, and some wiggling may be required to remove it from the tank. The new one should be installed in the same orientation as the old one. The sender can only mount on the holes one way, so you can't really mess up the rotation. Make sure that you use a new gasket, and tighten the nuts snug.

If your gauge still reads irregularly after installing the new unit, you may need to replace it. Unfortunately, the oil level gauge is not available as a separate unit—you have to purchase the entire gauge. The old gauges simply pop out of the dashboard, and the new ones can be pushed back in after all of the electrical connections are reattached. See Project 88 for more information on removing the gauges.

ENGINE

PROJECT 20 • ALTERNATOR TROUBLESHOOTING AND REPLACEMENT

 Time: 4 hours

 Tools: Hex key set, wrenches, 911 pulley tool

 Talent:

 Applicable Years: All

 Tab: $65–$300

 Tinware: New alternator brushes or a rebuilt alternator, new alternator belt

 Tip: Replace the brushes and check the electrical grounds before you replace the alternator.

PERFORMANCE GAIN: Higher charging output

COMPLEMENTARY MODIFICATION: Clean and paint the fan, upgrade the fan to 11-blade type

One of the nice things about the configuration of the 911 engine is the relative ease with which you can replace the alternator. The alternator is located directly in front of the fan—a great location because of the amount of cooling air it receives. The replacement and repair process is straightforward, and should take you about an afternoon to complete.

The first thing that you need to do is to make sure that your alternator is indeed the cause of the problems with your charging system. Sometimes bizarre electrical problems can be caused by a number of faults other than the alternator. It's important to troubleshoot the system prior to replacing your alternator.

The first thing to check is the fan belt. Is it tight and amply turning the fan? If not, then retighten it, according to the procedures outlined in Project 3. Modern fan belts rarely break, but they get brittle and glazed with age, and can slip on their pulleys. Replace it with a new one.

The next item to check is the voltage at the battery. This should read a little more than 12 volts with the

engine off. When the car is running, the voltage should read at in the range of 13.5 to 14.5 volts with the engine at 2,000 rpm. If your battery appears to be leaking, then your voltage regulator has probably failed. The battery will usually only leak acid if it has been overcharged at a much higher voltage. If the voltage measured at the battery is more than 16 or 17 volts, then the regulator is probably bad. If your battery has boiled over and has acid overflowing out the top, make sure that you clean up any spilled acid immediately. Dousing the area with a water and baking soda solution should help considerably to neutralize the acid, and prevent it from eating away at the metal.

1 The alternator is attached to the fan and the fan housing. The housing is strapped to the engine case using a long metal strip that needs to be loosened and disconnected before the housing can be removed. Remove the coil and the few select screws that attach the fiberglass engine shroud to the fan assembly. The long metal strap does not need to be completely disconnected from the case—leave it attached to the case at the bottom. *Tom Sharpes*

2 Once the housing is disconnected from the engine, remove the rear cream-colored plastic air guide that surrounds the rear of the alternator. This piece is held on with nuts that are attached to studs located on the alternator. Be careful not to crack this piece when you are reinstalling it. Using too much torque on the nuts can easily damage the air guide upon reinstallation. *Tom Sharpes*

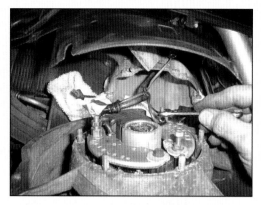

3 Carefully label and disconnect the connections to the alternator. Remove the large, thick ground strap as well. Be aware that the wires are quite old, are subject to heat from the engine, and may be more brittle than you would think. Try to avoid moving them around or bending them too much. Inspect the connectors carefully, and replace any that look damaged or rusted. Double-check the wires upon reinstallation. It's very important not to confuse and mix up the terminals to which the wires are connected. *Tom Sharpes*

4 The alternator should slide out of the housing. It may need some gentle coaxing, but be careful not to damage the studs that mount it to the housing. Some light taps with a soft hammer should force it loose from the housing. Try to tap evenly around all of the studs—it's easy for the alternator to get jammed inside the fan housing. *Tom Sharpes*

The following guidelines are useful for troubleshooting your alternator:

Alternator indicator lamp is on with the ignition key off.
- Alternator has failed, and diodes have shorted out. Replace alternator, and in the meantime, disconnect battery to prevent it from becoming completely drained.

Alternator indicator lamp does not light when ignition key is turned on.
- Alternator bulb has burned out
- Regulator has failed
- DF wire is disconnected or broken from alternator
- Alternator has failed, and internal windings are open

Indicator lamp remains on after engine is started and running above 2,000 rpm.
- Regulator has failed
- Battery lead to alternator has been disconnected
- Alternator is not firmly grounded
- Alternator internal bushings are dirty or worn
- Alternator is bad

Indicator lamp is dim after starting, and gets brighter as engine rpm increases.
- Battery lead to alternator loose or bad
- Ground connections are bad
- Battery is bad
- Alternator is bad due to open diode failure

Indicator lamp is dim after start-up, but gets dimmer and goes out when engine rpm increase.
- Low-charged battery
- Poor connections to battery

Indicator lamp is dim after start-up, and gets dimmer as rpm increases, but never goes out.
- Regulator has failed
- Alternator is failing

An important item to check on your car is the transmission ground strap. The engine is electrically isolated from the chassis by rubber motor mounts. If the transmission ground strap is missing or disconnected, then you might have a whole bunch of problems, including electrical system malfunctions and difficulty turning over the starter. See Project 87 for the exact location of the transmission ground strap.

All 911s up to 1981 had external regulators, and from 1982 on, the alternators had built-in ones. If you've determined the regulator to be working properly, then you should probably remove the alternator for testing and inspection. Before starting any work, make sure that you disconnect the battery. The positive battery terminal is directly connected to the alternator, and it can be dangerous to work on if it's live.

The first step is to remove the fan belt. Refer to Project 3 for detailed instructions on fan belt removal. Removing the fan housing itself is a very easy process. The entire assembly is affixed to the

5 The fan is pressed onto the alternator shaft, and requires some effort to remove. Don't use too much force in prying it off, or you may damage the bearings inside the alternator. If you have any doubts, take the fan to your local

machine shop and have them remove it with a press. This is a good time to upgrade to the 11-blade fan if your 911 doesn't have one already installed. *Tom Sharpes*

6 Some of the 911 alternators have brushes in the rear that can be easily removed and replaced. Remove the brushes and inspect them carefully if your alternator is not working well. If the contacts are as short in length as they are in the photo (shown by the arrow), they are worn and need to be replaced. If they are long, then you probably have some other

internal problem with the alternator that is causing it to malfunction.

engine case by a metal band that is tightened around the fan. Loosen this band by removing the one or two large cap screws that secure it. There should also be two nuts that secure the coil, and a few fiberglass shroud screws that need to be removed. Once the assembly is loose, the fan can be pulled away from the engine far enough to access the nuts and electrical connections in the rear. Be careful not to pull too hard, because the wires that are connected to the alternator are not very long.

Once you have access to the rear of the fan, remove the plastic air flow guide that surrounds the alternator. You should now have enough access to disconnect and remove the wires from the rear of the alternator. Make sure that you mark them, or take a picture of the entire assembly so that you know where each wire goes when it's time to reconnect them. You can destroy your alternator, and portions of your car's electrical system, if you hook the connections up improperly. Also make sure that the alternator was properly grounded to the engine, as this can cause it to malfunction. The ground strap is a thick copper cable that connects the housing of the alternator to the engine case. Disconnect this ground strap before attempting to remove the alternator.

After the alternator is disconnected electrically, you should be able to remove it, along with the fan assembly, from the car. The fan is pressed onto the alternator (ultimately held on with the pulley nut) and the alternator is bolted into the fan housing. If you are planning to replace just the brushes on the alternator, then you can remove them now without removing the alternator from the housing. On a side note, almost every Porsche parts diagram has the

brushes mislabeled as a "support." There must have been something lost in the translation from German!

Remove the brushes by unscrewing the small assembly from the back of the alternator, and inspect them to see if they are significantly worn. If so, then replace them. (They typically cost about $50.) If you think you need to replace your entire alternator, then gently tap it out of the housing with a soft hammer. The fan is pressed onto the shaft of the alternator, and needs to be gently removed. Don't bang on the alternator shaft too heavily, as this may damage the bearings inside.

The installation of the new alternator is simply the reverse of the removal process. Make sure that you reconnect all of the wires to their proper terminals when you are done.

In the mid-1970s, Porsche implemented a 5-blade fan instead of the normal 11-blade one on the 911 engine. The purpose of this fan was to provide less cooling to the engine, forcing it to run hotter. This was accomplished solely for the task of meeting emissions requirements. The hotter the engine, the better the gases burned, and fewer emissions were produced. However, this didn't help the longevity of the engine. These engines overheated easier, and generally lasted a significantly shorter time than their predecessors. One upgrade that should be performed on every 2.7-liter motor is the replacement of the original 5-blade fan with an 11-blade one. The two fans are interchangeable, and can be switched when replacing or removing the alternator. The only other part that may need to be replaced is the pulley half—it must be matched specifically to the size of the fan. Also, different-sized fans and pulleys used different-length belts—make sure that you get the one that's appropriate for your setup.

ENGINE
PROJECT 21 • FIXING COMMON OIL LEAKS

 Time: 12 hours

 Tools: Need full set

 Talent:

 Applicable Years: All

 Tab: $40–$200

 Tinware: New gaskets, O-rings, valve covers

 Tip: Replace all the seals that might leak while you have the engine out of the car

 PERFORMANCE GAIN: No more oil leaks!

COMPLEMENTARY MODIFICATION: Installation of Turbo valve covers, installing collapsable oil return tubes

1 Valve covers are notorious for leaking, especially on the 911s equipped with magnesium valve covers. If yours are leaking, replace the gaskets first. Silicone beaded gaskets are more pliable and supposedly stop oil leaks much better than the standard gaskets. If your oil leaks persist, consider upgrading to Turbo valve covers (see Project 17).

One of the most frustrating aspects of owning an older Porsche is the inevitable existence of oil leaks. The 911 engine in particular has a lot of different seals and connections that can often deteriorate with age, resulting in a large number of oil leaks. Unfortunately, some of these leaks cannot be fixed without the engine removed from the car, or the fuel injection components removed from the top of the engine. It's a wise idea to start with the leaks that are easiest to fix, and then move onto battling the harder ones later.

Perhaps the easiest oil leak to fix is the one involving the valve covers. Early covers manufactured out of magnesium had a tendency to warp and leak past the valve covers seals. The easiest solution to this problem is to replace your valve covers with 911 Turbo valve covers. These covers are manufactured out of aluminum and are reinforced to reduce the warping that is often associated with the magnesium covers. For more information on installing the Turbo valve covers, see Project 17.

Some of the most common oil leaks cannot be fixed, unfortunately, without removing either the engine or the fuel injection components. Some of the components and areas most susceptible to leaking are located in the front of the engine near the flywheel and are completely blocked by the fuel injection components. One such spot is the location where the crankcase breather hose is connected. Tightened around its fixture with a hose clamp, this hose can sometimes come loose or split, spilling oil all over the top of the engine. The solution is to replace the hose and retighten it with a new clamp. The crankcase breather cover where the hose mounts is also a problematic area for oil leaks. This small cover for the top of the engine has a gasket that seals it from leaking. Replacement is simple—remove the cover and install the new gasket with a slight bit of gasket sealer.

Right near the crankcase breather hose is the oil pressure warning lamp switch. This component often leaks not only out of its housing, but at the connection to the case. The solution is to replace the entire sender (about $10). Make sure that the new one is tightened properly in the case, and also use a new metal crush washer gasket. Be careful not to overtighten the switch (20 N-m/14.6 ft-lbs max), as this may ultimately cause its housing to separate and leak oil. This can sometimes be blindly repaired without removing the engine or fuel injection—even though you can't actually see what you're doing. On early cars, the oil pressure sending unit, which also often leaks, was installed in this location.

Directly adjacent to the oil pressure switch is the thermostat, which controls the flow of oil to the oil

2 The crankcase breather hose mounts to the top of the engine and is sealed to the case by the gasket shown here. Replacement of this gasket requires removal of the engine or fuel injection system, and should be replaced every time that you have access enough to reach it.

3 The crankcase breather hose could be another source of oil leaks. It sometimes has a habit of coming loose and slipping off of its mount. Make sure that you have a clamp on the hose to secure it to its mount (shown by the arrow).

4 The oil cooler thermostat O-ring is another source of troublesome oil leaks. Replacement is almost impossible without removing the engine or the fuel injection system . Install the O-ring wet by placing a little bit of oil on the O-ring seal before you install it.

cooler. The thermostat has an internal O-ring, which seals itself against its housing and prevents oil from leaking out across the top of the engine. The thermostat can see somewhat high oil pressures, so it is especially prone to oil leaks around this seal. To repair the problem, simply remove the two 10-millimeter nuts that hold the thermostat to the case. Gently pry up the edges of the thermostat with a screwdriver, replace the O-ring, and then reinsert into the case. It should be noted that all O-rings when installed should be liberally coated with fresh, clean motor oil.

Located in the same general area is the oil cooler. The three seals that mate the oil cooler to the engine case also have a tendency to become brittle and leak. Replacement requires the removal of the oil cooler—a task that can be accomplished with the engine in the car. You need to disconnect the oil line that mates to the oil tank and loosen the surrounding sheet metal to gain access to the three nuts that mount the cooler. Wet the seals with a bit of fresh oil when you remount the cooler. If you suspect that the oil cooler itself might be leaking, then it may be a wise idea to have the oil cooler pressure tested for leaks at your local machine shop.

Connected to the oil cooler is an S-shaped hose that attaches to the oil tank. This rubber hose can develop cracks and leak over the years. It's best to replace this hose if there are signs of weakness in the rubber. The hose is simply connected with two hose clamps, and is easily removed. Make sure that you empty the oil from the engine and the tank prior to

disconnecting this hose, or you will have a mess on your hands. The other oil lines that run under the engine and mate to the tank have a tendency to leak as well. Carefully inspect all lines for oil leaks, cracks, and breaks when you are looking under the engine.

The oil tank level sender has been known to cause a leak from its seal with the tank. For more information on replacing the sender and this seal, see Project 19.

Under the valve covers lie the rockers, which have been known to occasionally leak. The factory originally didn't supply a seal for these rockers, using instead a compression fit to seal the oil inside the internal cambers. The Porsche factory workshop manual summarizes the design quite well:

The rocker shafts are designed so that tightening of the Allen screw compresses the two cone-shaped pieces (nut and bush) against the coned ends of the rocker shaft and spreads the ends. As the rocker shaft ends spread, the rocker shaft is tightened in its bore in the camshaft housing and thus prevented from turning or axial movement.

However, this design doesn't always work too well. If the shafts or the cone-shaped pieces don't mesh properly, then there might be room for oil to seep out. A secret fix is a small rubber seal that fits into the small groove of the rocker shaft, and helps to seal the internal chamber. This part was a race-motor part that was not originally used on the production

5 The oil pressure switch, located all the way behind the fuel injection, is one of those annoying $3 parts that have a tendency to fail. It is recommended that you swap this part out with a new one every time that you have access to it, usually when the engine or fuel injection system is removed.

6 The rocker arm seal is one of the best-kept secrets. Not an original production engine part, this little seal fits in the small groove of the rocker arm (shown in the photo), and helps to seal the shaft and prevent leaking. Normally, the expansion of the end of the shaft in the cam towers is supposed to seal the rockers, but this sometimes fails, especially on rebuilt engines.

7 When the engine is out, access to the oil cooler is easier. The oil cooler seals are well known for their ability to spring leaks. Replacing of these three seals (two identical-sized ones on top, one on the bottom) is easy once the oil cooler has been removed.

8 The flexible oil cam lines deteriorate over time, and spring leaks at the points where the rubber meets the hard lines (shown by the arrow). These lines are generally pretty accessible from the rear of the car. The only component that might get in the way would be the distributor, which is easily removed.

engines, but works pretty well to stop these oil leaks when installed. The part number for this rocker arm shaft seal is 911.099.103.52, and you need 2 of them for each rocker, for a total of 12.

Another common oil leak comes from the oil return tubes. The seals at the end of the tubes expand and contract many times over the years, and develop small oil leaks. For more information on the replacement of these seals, please see Project 25, Replacing Oil Return Tubes.

At the lower rear of the engine are the cam housing covers. These are sealed with thin paper gaskets that can develop leaks if not installed properly. Replacement of these gaskets is a bit of a pain, requir-

9 This photo shows the distributor O-ring that seals it to the engine case. Although not a high oil pressure area, this seal does sometime fail. Make sure that you place the engine at top dead center before you remove the distributor. That way, you can make sure that you replace the distributor into its proper position again.

10 The oil pressure sender can leak from its base or directly from the main unit. Replacement is easy, as the unit is located near the rear of the car (on the later cars). Wrap a bit of Teflon pipe sealing tape around the connection to ensure that it won't leak.

11 The main shaft seal is located under the crankshaft pulley. Replacement requires removing the motor mount, the pulley, and a few other parts to reach the seal. It can be removed and pressed in, in a procedure similar to replacing the flywheel seal (Project 8). This photo shows the seal as installed inside of the Number Eight bearing, prior to the crankshaft being installed into the engine case.

ing removal of the muffler, and the rear engine shelf sheet metal. For more information on replacing these gaskets, please see Project 16, Upgrading to Carrera Chain Tensioners.

On the top rear of the engine are the camshaft oil feed lines. These lines supply the cam towers with oil to lubricate the cams and the rocker arms. These lines have a tendency to vibrate and develop leaks over the life of the motor. Replacement is an easy process, although you might have to remove the distributor to reach one of the fittings. Make sure that you use new sealing rings when you remount the lines. Project 16 details the installation of these lines in further detail.

Adjacent to the right cam oil line on the later cars is the oil pressure sending unit. This unit has a tendency to leak where it is attached to the case, and also from its own housing. Carefully inspect the sender, and replace it if you think that it might be leaking. Since access to the sending unit is fairly straightforward, it is not necessary to be cautious—don't replace it unless it is leaking. On the early cars, this unit is located toward the front of the engine compartment.

The flywheel seal is another one of those common and mysterious leaks on the 911. Unfortunately, the flywheel seal cannot be replaced without removing the engine and the clutch. For more information on the replacement of this seal, please see Project 8, 911 Clutch Replacement.

On the very rear of the engine is the pulley seal. In order to replace this seal, you need to remove the muffler, rear engine shelf, the motor mount bar, and the rear pulley. Removal and replacement of the seal is similar in nature to the replacement of the flywheel seal. Be careful not to scratch the outer surface of the crankshaft when you replace the seal.

ENGINE
PROJECT 22 • IGNITION TUNE-UP

 Time: 1 hour

 Tools: Torque wrench, spark plug wrench, screwdriver

 Talent:

 Applicable Years: All

 Tab: $20–$200

 Tinware: New spark plugs, cap, rotor, points and plug wires

 Tip: Replace your cap and rotor every 15,000 miles.

 PERFORMANCE GAIN: Smoother running engine

COMPLEMENTARY MODIFICATION: Upgrade your old Marelli distributor to the Bosch model.

One of the most common systems on the 911 to require maintenance is the ignition system. Without a doubt, the cap, rotor, and ignition points should be periodically replaced as they tend to wear out over time. In addition, the spark plug wires have a tendency to get old and less effective as they age. Last, but not least, new spark plugs are extremely important to a good tune-up as well.

I recommend changing the plugs, rotor, cap, and points every 15,000 miles or so for 911s after 1977. For the earlier cars, it's wise to replace them a bit sooner, around 10,000 miles. With important moving mechanical/electrical parts such as these, it's very important to keep them in top condition. I have seen many cars refusing to run properly because the owners hadn't replaced the cap, rotor, or points in many, many miles.

The first thing to be replaced should be the spark plugs. Make sure that the car is stone cold before attempting to remove the plugs. If you try to pull them out of the aluminum heads when they are hot, there is a high likelihood that the steel plugs could damage the threads in the aluminum heads.

With the car cold, carefully pull on each rubber end of the ignition wires and remove them from each spark plug. Make sure that you don't pull on the wire itself, as this can damage it. Repeat this for all six spark plugs, and leave them hanging in the engine compartment.

Once the wires are removed, insert the spark plug remover into the access hole where the plug wires were connected. You will probably need an extension on your socket wrench to reach inside. Especially for the 911, I recommend the use of a swivel-foot spark plug socket that can bend and twist into the tight spaces required. Make sure that the tool has a firm grip on the spark plugs, and remove them from the engine.

Spark plugs are good indicators of how your car is running. Check your spark plugs carefully, as signs of problems with the engine or fuel injection can sometimes be indicated by clues from the spark plugs. However, modern gasoline formulations sometimes can make the spark plugs black or sooty, even when the car is running properly. For an excellent description of various spark plug problems commonly found in 911s, check the ignition system chapter of the *Haynes Porsche 911 Automotive Repair Manual*, by Peter G. Strasman and Peter Ward. Although brief in many sections, this manual should be in the collection of every 911 owner. It's probably the second-best value in books for your 911, the first being the book that you are reading right now.

Installation of the new plugs is straightforward. Make sure that the small round tips on the end of the plug are firmly attached. It's a wise idea to double-check the spark plug gap to make sure that the gap is properly set. Refer to the Technical Specification book available from Porsche or your car owner's manual for the proper gap for your year 911 and engine.

Carefully install the plugs into the engine, making sure to stop if you encounter any significant resistance during the installation. If you use a heavy hand during the install, you might cross-thread the spark plug holes, which means that your engine will have to be taken apart for repair! Torque the spark plugs to 25–30 N-m (18–22 ft-lb) with a torque wrench. Do not use any antiseize compound on the spark plugs.

The ignition wires should probably be replaced every 60,000–90,000 miles. Although the 911 wires are known for being very rugged, the constant heating and cooling of the wires in the engine compartment can lead to hardening of the metal inside, which then degrades performance. I recommend replacing the plug wires every 60,000 miles, or sooner if you are having problems with your ignition system. This figures out to be about once every five years, if you drive the car every day, and about once every 10 years for occasional driving.

The replacement process for the wires is easy. Simply pull off the old wires and strap down and plug in the new ones. I recommended that you label the distributor cap before you remove the old wires, as it can get confusing when you remove them all at once. Some of the older wires may really be attached to the cap tightly, so you may have to wiggle them slightly to negotiate their release.

I recommend that you use the stock 911 shielded plug wires on the CIS cars. These are of very high quality, and aftermarket products really only serve to change the color or appearance of the wires in your engine compartment. The stainless-steel sheath on the outside of the stock wires helps to insulate and isolate the ignition signal that is running through the wire. Make sure that you attach the ground straps from the ignition wires to an appropriate plate on the engine (usually attached to one of the bolts that mounts the coil).

The cap, rotor, and points are perhaps the most common items to replace on the ignition system. I recommend that you inspect and replace them every 10,000 miles or so. To replace the cap, simply undo the small straps that attach it to the distributor, and unplug

the ignition wires from the top. If you unplug all the wires from the cap at once, label the wires, so you don't mix them up.

The rotor simply pulls off of the top of the distributor (under the cap). The new rotor can only be installed one way—there is a notch in the rotor that will make it line up with the distributor shaft. Make sure that you push the new rotor down all the way on the shaft. New rotors are also available with a built-in rpm limiter. These rotors will not let you overrev your engine. They are available with rev-limit cut-offs at 5,800, 6,500, 7,000, or 7,300 rpm. It is important to note, however, that an rpm limiter will not protect your engine from overrevs that may be caused by a missed shift during driving. Starting in 1978, an electronic rev limiter was built into the the ignition CD box.

The replacement of the points is a bit trickier, and applicable only to the 1965–1976 cars. The capacitive discharge system used on the 911 should prevent the points from pitting, although they can wear out after many cycles of opening and closing. The points are located under the rotor, and are screwed into the top plate of the distributor. The distributor contact breaker points together make a switch that tells the ignition system when to fire a spark. The gap should be set to an initial value, and then reset when you can check the dwell angle of the car with a meter (see Project 23). For the proper points gap value, check your owner's

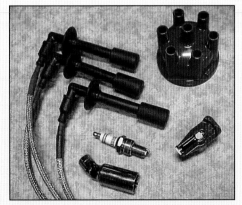

1 This photo shows the basic components of an ignition tune-up needed for a 911SC. The plug wires are the stainless-steel variety, which were installed as stock equipment. The cap and rotor are original Bosch, as well as the standard Bosch platinum plug. On the earlier cars, you will need to replace your ignition points as well. A very handy device is the swivel spark plug socket made by the Sears Craftsman line. Sold for about $10, it's very useful for reaching into the rear recesses of the 911 engine compartment.

2 After pulling out the spark plug wires, use the spark plug socket to remove the plug. Make sure that your socket has the rubber insert inside of it that prevents the plug from falling out. Spark plugs can be a pain to fish out of the inside of the 911 engine.

manual, or the *Porsche Technical Specifications Book* for your year car.

To properly set the points gap, the distributor needs to be rotated until the points are open to their maximum distance. Rotate the crankshaft of the engine (see Project 18) so that the lobes of the cam inside the distributor push the points open to their maximum amount. Use a feeler gauge to set this amount, and then tighten down the screw that holds the points in place. Setting this gap is only a temporary measure—you will have to set the dwell angle later on after the engine is started. After you set the points gap, make sure that you set the ignition timing for the car (Project 23).

On some of the early cars, Porsche installed a distributor manufactured by Marelli. These distributors are no longer available, and at the time of writing this book, all of the supply of original caps, rotors, and points has been exhausted. There is an aftermarket company making replacement points that fit Marelli distributors. The part number is 911.602.960.00 and is manufactured by IKAR, which makes a lot of Mercedes parts. Regardless of that, the caps and rotors are nowhere to be found. Many people have called hundreds of Porsche dealers and shops around the world looking for them, to no avail. The only real practical solution is to upgrade to the Bosch distributor that was also used as an adjunct to the Marelli one. This Bosch distributor is still available, and so are the basic tune-up parts. The cost of the distributor is around $700 for a new one; used ones are very difficult to find because everyone is looking for them to replace their old Marelli distributor. If you have an older 911 with one of these older distributors, you will eventually have to upgrade it to the Bosch one. The good news is that the Bosch distributor is a drop-in replacement for the Marelli and requires no modifications to the engine.

3 Installing the new cap and rotor is very straightforward. About the only thing that you can mess up is the location of the ignition wires on the top of the cap. Unplug and replace each wire individually, as it is very easy to get confused and plug a wire into the wrong socket.

4 If you happen to own an early car equipped with an original Marelli distributor, you will probably want to upgrade to the Bosch distributor. The maintenance parts for the Marelli distributor (cap, rotor) are no longer manufactured, and they are impossible to locate. The new Bosch distributor is a drop-in replacement, and replacement parts are common.

PROJECT 23 • SETTING THE TIMING, DWELL, AND IDLE SPEED

 Time: 1/2 hour

 Tools: Timing light, tachometer, dwell meter

 Talent:

 Applicable Years: 1965-1983

 Tab: $0

 Tinware: –

 Tip: Be careful not to accidently place anything near the fan when you are setting the timing.

! PERFORMANCE GAIN: Smoother running engine

COMPLEMENTARY MODIFICATION: Ignition tune-up

One of the most important and basic tasks to perform on your 911 is setting the ignition timing. The timing setting is what determines when the spark is going to be fired for each particular spark plug. If the timing is a bit off (retarded or advanced), your car may not perform at its maximum efficiency and power. It's very important to check the timing periodically to make sure that it's within the correct range for your car.

Two basic adjustments need to be made to set the timing on early 911s (1965–1977). The distributor rotation needs to be determined, and the gap between the points needs to be set. On the later cars (1978–1983), Porsche used an electronic breakerless ignition system that eliminated the need for the points. On the earlier cars, a cam, located on the main shaft of the distributor, controls the breaker points. As the distributor rotates, the cam pushes the points open. At this point the coil releases its stored energy and sends a charge to the spark plug determined by the position of the rotor inside the distributor cap. In 1984, the factory employed the use of the Bosch Motronic engine management sys-

tem, which integrates control of the fuel injection and ignition systems. The timing and dwell of the Motronic system is controlled by its central computer, and cannot be adjusted.

By far, the most important adjustment is setting the position of the distributor for adjustment of the timing. Make sure that your points gap is properly set (see below) prior to adjusting the timing of the distributor. This measurement is performed using a timing light with the engine running and warmed up. The timing light is attached to the spark plug wire for cylinder Number One, and gets its power from the terminals in the fuse box panel on the left side of the engine compartment. Connect the ground connection of the timing light to the fan housing, or the braided shielding of the ignition wires. The timing light uses induction to sense the voltage running through the spark plug wires. Make sure that you attach the sensor around the wire where it is not protected with the stainless-steel sheath, otherwise you might have difficulty obtaining an accurate reading.

Strap the sensor around the spark plug wire for cylinder Number One, which is located on the left side of the car, toward the rear of the car. Make sure that the car is warmed up before you take the timing measurement. Also make sure that your idle speed is set to the correct range. For details on setting the idle speed for your 911, make sure that you look at Projects 29–31, which are specific to each different

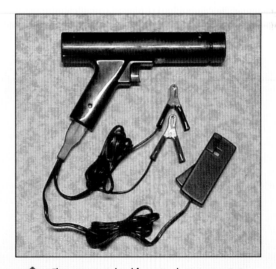

1 The most essential tool for setting the timing is a timing light. This device attaches to one of your ignition wires, and then flashes a light whenever the engine fires the spark plug that the sensor is attached to. Using this strobe effect, the timing can be set on the engine.

This photo of the engine compartment shows how to hook up the timing light. Attach the positive clip to one of the fuses on the left side of the engine (yellow arrow). The black ground for the light can be attached to any metal point on the chassis, but the most convenient spot is usually the ground for the spark plug wires (green arrow). The white arrow shows where the inductive sensor is placed around the spark plug wire. Make sure that you don't attach it around the shielded section of the wires, as this will result in a weak signal to the lamp.

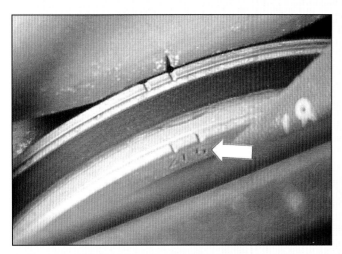

At the specified rpm, aim the light at the bottom crankshaft pulley. With this engine, a 911SC 3.0-liter, the timing should be set so that the second mark appears lined up with the notch in the bottom of the fan housing when the timing light flashes. This mark, labeled with the number 5 and shown by the arrow, indicates five degrees before Top Dead Center (TDC).

type of fuel injection system. To properly set the timing, you may have to remove the vacuum hoses from the distributor. Check the *Porsche Technical Specifications Book* for the exact details on what you need to do to properly set the timing. Sometimes this information is written on stickers attached to either the engine shelf, or the inside of the rear deck lid.

With the car running and the idle speed set, aim the timing light at the crankshaft pulley located directly underneath the fan. If all is working properly, the timing light should strobe on and off, and you should be able to see the timing mark on the pulley. Different-year 911s had different timing points, but it should be marked with a number 5 or similar marking. This mark indicates the timing mark for five degrees before top dead center, or after top dead center, depending upon the year and engine. If you have a more advanced adjustable timing light, you can set the light to time the car to just about any setting simply by dialing in the value on the light.

The timing setting is changed by rotating the distributor slightly. Take a 13-millimeter wrench, and loosen up the nut that holds the distributor secure to the engine case. While the engine is running and the timing light is shining on the pulley, gently rotate the distributor until the timing mark on the pulley lines up with the notch in the fan housing. It may take a few tries to get it right, and keep in mind that small movements in the rotation of the distributor are all that are needed. Once you have the correct setting, tighten down the nut on the distributor. Be very careful not to place any tools or fingers near the fan when the engine is running, and watch the cord of the timing light as well.

On the pre-1977 911s, you must set the dwell angle for the points as well as the timing position of the distributor. The dwell angle is the number of degrees of rotation that the points will stay closed when the distributor is rotating. The angle is adjusted by moving and rotating the position of the points with respect to the to the cam. The farther the points are moved away from the cam, the smaller the dwell angle.

The difficult part of this equation is that changing the dwell angle changes the timing of the motor.

Therefore, it's wise to set the distributor to the correct location, then adjust the dwell angle, and then go back and adjust the distributor again. You measure the dwell angle using a dwell meter that is hooked up to the points and to ground. The meter will accurately tell you the angle of dwell based on the frequency and length of the points opening and closing. The dwell angle is changed by moving the points closer to or away from the distributor cam. They are attached to the distributor using a small screw that must be loosened in order to move them. With the engine off, unclip the distributor cap, loosen the screw, and move the points away from the cam to decrease the angle, or move it closer to the cam to increase the angle. Since there are so many different years and engines used with the 911, check the technical specifications book available from Porsche for the exact dwell angle, and the exact setting for the ignition timing. In general, the 1965–1968 911s should be set with an initial gap of 0.016 inch and the 1969–1977 911s should have an initial gap of 0.012 inch.

You can measure the dwell angle on 1965–1968 911s by hooking your meter up to the positive and negative terminals of the coil. On 1969–1977 911s, you will need to use a different technique, since the capacitive discharge system won't give you an accurate signal. Don't hook up the dwell meter to the coil, or you may damage your capacitive discharge system and your meter. Instead, hook the signal wire of the dwell meter directly to the points wire that is coming off of the distributor. In some cases, it may be easiest to hook the dwell meter to a long screwdriver and place the tip of the screwdriver on the contacts where the wire is plugged into the distributor. You should be able to get an accurate reading from the distributor using this method.

Keep swapping between setting the dwell and the timing until you have the two measurements correct. Keep in mind that if you removed vacuum advance or retard hoses from the distributor, then you might have to reset the idle for your car once you reconnect them.

It's also important to follow the proper vacuum hose settings when timing the car. On some models with vacuum advance or retard, you may need to dis-

The inside view of the Bosch distributor shows the points and the gap that needs to be set prior to setting the timing. The arrow points to the gap that should be initially set using a feeler gauge. This is the same Bosch distributor that is the upgrade for the Marelli distributor for the 1969–1971 911s.

connect or plug the hoses to get an accurate reading. Again, check the technical specifications book for the exact timing procedure.

It's also important to check the total timing advance that occurs at 6,000 rpm. Check it with the engine warm. Refer again to the Porsche technical specifications book for your year car as to which vacuum hoses you need to disconnect from the distributor. Checking the total advance at 6,000 rpm may seem scary and very loud, but it's necessary to make sure that the ignition system is advancing properly. You want to make sure that your total advance at 6,000 rpm does not exceed the value specified in the technical specifications book. If it does, then you may have detonation or pinging at higher rpm. If the total advance is beyond the specification, rotate the distributor until it comes back into spec. As a result, your idle timing will change. If you find that you cannot adjust both the idle and total advance values to the proper specifications at the same time, then you might have some internal components of your distributor that are worn, or some vacuum hoses that are clogged or improperly installed.

Time: 4 hours

Tools: Wire clippers, wire strippers

Talent:

Applicable Years: All

Tab: $350

Tinware: MSD electronic ignition system, tachometer adapter, Bosch hi-spark blue coil

Tip: The MSD is an excellent replacement for a failed or fickle Bosch CD box.

PERFORMANCE GAIN: 10 or more horsepower increase on lower-end and non-CD 911s (1965-1968)

COMPLEMENTARY MODIFICATION: Perform ignition system tune-up, addition of MSD rpm module selector

One of the best upgrades that you can perform on your 911 is the installation of the Multiple Spark Discharge, or MSD, ignition control system. This unit replaces the capacitive discharge unit, or CD box, in the 911 ignition system with better and updated technology. The CD box is the small metal box on the left side of the engine compartment that makes a high-pitched whine when the ignition is turned on. If you need to replace the CD box, I recommend that you replace it with one of the better and cheaper MSD units.

Similar to the original Bosch CD box, the MSD system uses a capacitive discharge ignition design. Other Porsches such as the 356, 912, and 914 use a standard inductive ignition system that cannot match the performance of the capacitive discharge design. On these older inductive systems, the coil must step up the voltage and store the electrical charge at maximum strength in between each firing. When the rpm of the engine increases, the coil doesn't have enough time in between firing to ramp up to its maximum voltage. This results in a weaker spark and a loss of power at higher rpm.

With such capacitive discharge systems as the OEM Bosch CD box and the MSD unit, the ignition system contains a capacitor that can be charged much quicker (less than one millisecond) than the inductive coil. With a capacitive discharge system, the voltage sent to the coil is always at full strength, even when the engine is running at a high rpm.

In addition to the benefits of the capacitive discharge system, the MSD unit fires more than one spark per cycle. During the course of an ignition stroke, the MSD unit rapidly fires full-power sparks over 20 degrees of crankshaft rotation. This multiple spark firing aids in the combustion process and helps the fuel burn more completely, resulting in more power, and less emissions. The amount of multiple sparks fired decreases as the engine rpm increases, and above 3,000 rpm, the MSD system only has enough time in the ignition cycle to fire a single high-powered spark. Within the range above 3,000 rpm, the performance of the MSD system is comparable to the stock Bosch CD system. The MSD system also incorporates a rev limiter within the ignition system that limits the maximum revolutions of the engine. Some of the early cars can use a rev-limiting rotor, which performs a similar purpose; the later 911s had a rev-limiting function built into the CD box or the tachometer itself. The MSD system allows you to adjust this rpm level by plugging in modules into the unit.

The main MSD unit recommended for the 911 is the 6AL, part number 6420. This kit contains all the wires, connectors, mounts, and crimping hardware that you will need to install the unit in your 911. The kit is very well manufactured (made in the United States), and the unit is known for its high reliability. Racers under harsh conditions typically use the MSD systems in their cars.

In addition to the MSD main unit, you may also need to purchase the tachometer adapter. For early 911s with points, this tachometer adapter is required to convert the MSD signal back into one that the tachometer can recognize. Without this adapter, the tachometer might be confused by the multiple spark signal, and give a false reading. The technical gurus at MSD couldn't give me a definitive answer when asked which models needed the tachometer adapter. Apparently, changes and differences in individual cars result in unpredictability in determining whether or not the system will require the adapter. Some cars may require it, and other, seemingly identical cars, may not. According to MSD, it may be related to manufacturing tolerances inside the VDO tachometers used on the 911. Either way, the tachometer adapter should make the system work for any 911 tachometer. I recommend that you purchase and install it to avoid any potential tachometer problems. Use tach adapter 8910 if your 911 uses points (1965-77) or adapter 8920 if your 911 has a magnetic pickup (1978-83).

Another option for the MSD system is the rpm selector. This allows you to manually dial in the rev-limited amount that you would like to use for the unit. The unit itself allows you to use small plug-in modules to select the rev-limiting rpm, but this selector allows you more flexibility. The stock unit contains a rev-limiting plug-in for 6,000 rpm, so if you want to use a value other than this, you will have to purchase another set of relatively inexpensive plug-in modules.

The final item you will have to acquire is a new coil. The MSD system will not work with the standard CD coil that is stock on the 911. The standard Bosch blue coil (0.221.119.027) is the recommended coil to use with the system, and is relatively inexpensive (about $30).

Installation is relatively straightforward, and can easily be completed in about four hours. The installation instructions that come with the unit are clear and concise, so the remainder of this project will focus on information specific to the 911 installation that is not covered in the MSD installation documentation.

The physical mounting of the unit is important. The natural place for mounting the unit is in the same place as the old CD box—try to mount it there if possible. The MSD unit replaces the CD box, so you don't need it any more. There is a market for good, used Bosch CD boxes, so you might want to resell your old one and recoup some of the costs of purchasing the MSD system. The Bosch CD unit is mounted on an aluminum metal plate that is mounted to the left side of the car, under a plastic cover. Unplug the electrical connections from this plate and remove it so that you can drill holes in it for mounting the MSD unit. Use the supplied rubber mounts in the kit to elevate the unit off of the plate.

The thick red wire that exits the unit should be connected directly to the battery. Since this is hardly possible with the 911 battery being in the front trunk, you should connect it to the large electrical connection on the starter. This wire is connected to the battery (check it with a voltmeter) and should be live all the time. Make sure that you disconnect the battery before unscrewing this connection. The large black wire is a ground wire, and should be connected to one of the bolts that mount the aluminum plate to the left side of the car.

There are two wires (black and orange) that exit out of the unit and are covered with a black sheath.

1 The MSD Unit and tachometer adapter are shown here. The kit contains all the small parts you need for installation (not shown here). The tachometer adapter is recommended for all 911s. The MSD box is slightly bigger than the stock Bosch CD box, but will still fit in the prescribed mounting area.

These are to be connected to the new Bosch blue coil that should be installed in place of the older black one. The orange wire is connected to the positive (+) terminal of the coil, and the black wire is connected to the negative (-) terminal.

The thinner red wire needs to be connected to a switched voltage source. The best place to do this is to tap into the electrical connector that used to go to the CD box. Peel back the rubber insulation, and underneath you should find a red wire. Tap the thin red wire from the MSD unit into the red wire that comes into the CD box connector. It's a wise idea to use some male spade connectors and plug right into the CD box connector, so that you don't destroy the wiring or the connector.

The white MSD wire is connected to the points if your car has them (1965-77). Cars with magnetic pickups use the magnetic pickup wire in the MSD unit.

The tachometer wire inside the CD box connector is black with a purple stripe down the side. This wire needs to be connected to the tachometer output on the side of the MSD unit. In addition, the tachometer adapter from MSD needs to be installed inside the engine compartment. Simply wire the tachometer adapter into the system as described in the MSD installation documentation.

When you are finished installing your MSD system, it's advisable to install a new cap, rotor, and spark plugs. MSD recommends that you set the gap on your plugs to a much wider distance, in the range of 1.27 to 1.49 millimeters, which is much larger than the factory specification of 0.7 ±0.1 millimeters. MSD also recommends that you play around and adjust the spark plug gaps until you obtain the performance that you are looking for. The recommended values are simply good starting points.

When you're all done, you should have a system that gives you more lower-end power and torque, and also burns the fuel better for cleaner emissions. It's very common to simply upgrade to the MSD system if there is a problem with the standard Bosch CD box. The cost of the MSD system, although expensive, is usually less than a new or rebuilt Bosch CD box.

ENGINE

PROJECT 25 • REPLACING OIL RETURN TUBES

 Time: 1–2 hours per side

 Tools: Channel locks, hose clamps

 Talent:

 Applicable Years: All

 Tab: $25 per tube

 Tinware: Expandable oil return tubes

 Tip: Attach a hose clamp to the tube so that you can get a better grip on it.

 PERFORMANCE GAIN: No more leaks onto your heat exchangers

COMPLEMENTARY MODIFICATION: Replace or repair your heat exchangers

Among the more frustrating parts that leak oil on the 911 are the oil return tubes. Years of heating and cooling and expansion and contraction can leave the rubber seals brittle and worn out. It is very common for them to leak oil right onto the heat exchangers, which results in the car smoking when it's started, and also can result in smoke entering the passenger compartment through the heater system. The good news is that the tubes can easily be replaced with expandable replacements that don't require the removal of the engine.

How can you tell if your oil return tubes are leaking? Contrary to popular belief, the dry-sump oil system of the 911 actually contains a large amount of oil in the sump when the engine is off. This oil can easily leak out of the bottom of the engine overnight, depositing a large amount of oil on the floor of your garage. In order to determine exactly where your oil

leak is coming from, wash off the bottom of the motor, and then let it run for a while as you check where the oil leak is coming from. If the oil appears to be coming from the bottom of the oil return tubes on either the engine side or the outer cam tower side, chances are that the seal has failed and needs to be replaced.

The process of replacing the oil return tubes is not very difficult, but it is a task that requires a significant amount of patience. It's also highly recommended that you have a spare oil return tube or two handy, as these are very easy to accidentally destroy during the installation process. If you are removing the heat exchangers, I recommend that you replace the oil return tubes in pairs, both left or both right. They will eventually leak, and it's a wise idea to replace them now while you have access.

The first step is to remove your heat exchangers from the car. Check to make sure that this is necessary, as on some 911 models there exists enough room to perform this replacement without their removal. Removal of the heat exchangers in itself can be a very difficult step, especially if the bolts are frozen and stuck. Refer to Project 44 for more details on the safe removal of the heat exchangers. After the heat exchangers have been removed, it's a wise idea to empty the oil out of the car. This is not an absolutely vital step, but I recommend it just to make the whole process a bit cleaner.

Removal of the old tube is a somewhat easy, yet destructive process. Simply take a large pair of Vise-Grips and crush the old return tube in the middle. The ends should begin to pull out of the engine case and the cam towers. Compress and wiggle the old tube until you can get one end out free and clear. The other end of the tube should simply pull out. Make sure that you have a drip pan nearby, as there is a likelihood that at least some oil will spill out.

Now, move to your workbench, and assemble the parts of the new expandable tube. First take the circlip and slide it onto the longer tube. Slide it up past the grooves as shown the first photo of this project. Then place the two smaller seals on the two inner grooves of the larger oil return tube. Finally, place the two larger seals on the end of each tube. Prior to installing each of the four seals onto the tube, make sure that you wet them first with a little bit of clean motor oil, moly lube, or dielectric

1 The expandable oil return tube kit is designed specifically to replace old, worn-out tubes and seals that were installed the last time the motor was assembled. The kit contains the two rubber seals that fit on each end of the tube, an additional two seals that mate the tubes together, a large circlip, and the two tube halves. The tube is shown with the proper seals installed and the proper location of the circlip, prior to assembly.

2 The trick to getting the collapsible return tubes installed is getting each end compressed into its respective location, whether it be the engine case or the cam towers. The best method of achieving this is to use Channel Locks or a set of adjustable Vise-Grips, and tap the tube into the hole. Be gentle, however, as too much force can dent and damage the tubes. The tube shown in this photo is manufactured by a different company from the one in the previous photo, but the installation process is very similar. While the tube is shown installed here, one of the installation problems is the difficulty involved with getting past exhaust pipes and other components. Sometimes it helps to remove the exhaust before replacing the tube.

grease. This will help the seals seat properly, and should help prevent leaks. A few different types of tubes are available. Installation instructions may vary slightly, based on the particular type of tube that you choose to use.

When all the seals and the circlip have been installed properly, take the two tubes and slide them into each other. Crawl under the car and insert the end of the longer tube into the cam towers. The shorter tube should be placed into the engine case. The reasoning behind this is underscored by the fact that if the oil is going to leak, it's probably going to leak when the engine is warm, and the oil is thin. Because the oil returns from the cam towers back to the engine case, the tubes should be oriented in order to minimize the amount of contact that it will have with the two inner seals when the oil is warm.

The tube should now be ready to be expanded into place. The toughest part is getting a good grip on the oil return tubes. One idea is to use Vise-Grips or Channel Locks, but these sometimes have a habit of destroying the tubes. Another idea is to use a hose clamp. Simply tighten the clamp around the tube, and it should provide enough leverage for you to push the tube into its socket. Either way, be careful when installing the tubes, as it is very easy to damage them.

After you get the first side installed, and the tube is firmly mounted in its hole, push on the opposite tube until you can slide the circlip into its groove. When the circlip can fit entirely into the groove, then you know that the tube is completely expanded.

Refill the oil if you emptied it, and take the car out for a spin to check for oil leaks. If everything was done correctly, there shouldn't be any leaks coming from the tubes. After installing the new tube, you may actually find that your leak was caused by something else. Take a look at Project 21 if this is the case.

ENGINE

PROJECT 26
• INSTALLING/UPGRADING THE 911 FRONT-MOUNTED OIL COOLER

 Time: 6–15 hours

 Tools: Oil line wrenches

 Talent: 𝕏𝕏𝕏𝕏

 Applicable Years: 1965–86

 Tab: $500–$2000

 Tinware: Oil cooler, oil cooler foam seal, fan, oil lines, relay and socket, horn bracket and fender strut, cooler hoses, mounting kit

 Tip: Get all the parts together before you begin.

 PERFORMANCE GAIN: Better engine cooling

COMPLEMENTARY MODIFICATION: Change your oil (this project is enough by itself)

One of the most popular upgrades for the 911 is the addition or upgrade of the external oil cooler. The external oil cooler takes oil directly from the engine, and funnels it up the side of the car to an oil cooler located in the front right fender of the car.

In 1969 on the 911S, a front-mounted radiator-style cooler was mounted as standard equipment in the front right fender well. In 1973, the newer trombone, serpentine, loop, or cooling pipe cooler, as it was called, replaced the radiator-style cooler. This style of oil cooler was used through 1983. The cooler was standard equipment on the 1973 911S, as well as the 1974–1975 Carreras, but was optional on all other models up to 1977. In 1980, Porsche began using a 28-tube all-brass oil cooler in place of the trombone cooler on all European 911SCs and Turbos. This cooler was claimed to have reduced the operating temperatures over the trombone cooler by 30 degrees Fahrenheit.

The early trombone oil cooler wasn't designed to act as a traditional cooler. The oil cooler itself is just a few loops of piping that radiate heat. Some radiation of heat occurs in the trombone cooler, but a large part of the cooling process occurs in the lines running up the side of the car. A thermostat mounted near the engine controls the amount of oil redirected to the front oil cooler.

Realizing that this arrangement wasn't satisfactory for cooling the engine, Porsche developed the all-brass cooler. This brass cooler was used on all U.S. and European 911 Carreras in 1984. Then, Porsche released an even better oil cooler. Returning to the finned, radiator-style cooler, the Carrera oil cooler was mounted in the same spot as the previous ones, but had a large seal and stone guard to protect it from rocks and debris thrown up by the tire.

In 1987, Porsche added one more option to the fray. An electric fan attached to the front of the oil cooler. Controlled by a thermostat on the top of the cooler, it added additional cooling for the motor. The Carrera oil cooler with the fan attached is the desired upgrade for just about any 911 lacking one (all 911s made before 1987). This setup allows you to maintain the stock look of your car, and obtain better cooling with a minimum of modifications to the chassis.

So what's required to implement this cooler setup? It depends upon what you have on your car right now. Here is a list of all the parts and widgets you'll need if your 911 does not have an external cooler installed right now:

- Carrera finned radiator-tyle cooler (about $450 used, 930.207.053.00)
- Cooler to fender seal (about $70 new, 930.207.353.00)
- Rock guard and air guide for cooler (should come with cooler, but $45 used, 930.207.319.02)
- Rubber mounts (3 required, 930.207.239.00)
- Supply and return oil lines that run down the side of the car (if your car doesn't already have a front-mounted oil cooler) ($200 used)
- Thermostat in right rear fenderwell (about $100 used)
- Flexible adapter lines to connect the cooler to the oil lines
- Fan for oil cooler
- Seal between the rock guard and the cooler (930.207.361.00)
- Thermoswitch for oil cooler (930.606.118.00)
- Relay and relay socket for oil cooler (911.615.109.01 and 901.612.333.00)

1 The Carrera oil cooler, mounting kit, and flexible oil lines are shown here. Not shown in this picture is the horn bracket, the fender strut, or the large spongy seal that mates the cooler to the inside fender. When purchasing a used oil cooler, make sure that you obtain it from a reliable source that will guarantee its condition. As these coolers age and get beaten around, they sometimes have a tendency to leak. Make sure that any cooler you purchase has been completely inspected and pressure tested for leaks.

2 The relocation of the horns is the trickiest part of this project. A new hole must be drilled in a very tight space for the fender strut to be mounted to the inside of the car. This hole, indicated by the white arrow, can be drilled in the sheet metal support that is welded to the inside of the fender well. It is possible to reach behind this area to place a nut on a mounting bolt. The green arrow shows the nut that is welded to the fender strut. The bolt that threads into this nut is located at the bottom of the headlamp bucket. The yellow arrow points to the spacer used for the fender strut, since the newer-style struts do not align exactly with the older-style valance panels.

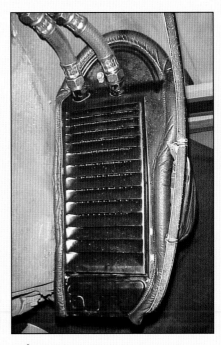

3 The Carrera oil cooler is shown installed here in the front fender well. The lower bracket must be welded to the inner fenderwell in order to firmly mount the cooler. Note how the large seal that surrounds the cooler mates with the inside walls of the fender. The rock guard for the cooler is clipped onto the side of the cooler, and prevents rocks and debris from hitting the finned portions of the cooler.

4 Installation of the oil lines from the rear of the car is not too difficult a process if you have all the correct parts. Shown here are the lines and the thermostat, which is located in the rear right fenderwell, just in front of the wheel. The two lines that bend downward go to the rocker panels and run to the front-mounted oil cooler. The two lines that exit out of the thermostat go to the engine and the oil tank.

- Enough wiring to hook up oil cooler fan and relay
- New horn mounting bracket and fender support (911.635.107.00 and 911.504.080.00)
- Upper bracket for mounting oil cooler (930.207.927.00)
- Lower bracket for mounting oil cooler

The first step of installation is gathering all these required parts. Some can be sourced from reliable used parts suppliers. Make sure that any oil cooler that you purchase comes with a warranty and has been properly cleaned and pressure tested. Oil coolers are expensive; you would hate to get stuck with one that leaks.

When you are ready to install the new cooler, the first step is to remove the old one. Jack up the car and remove the front right wheel. This will give you plenty of access to the oil cooler and the lines. Now, take two wrenches, and disconnect the long metal

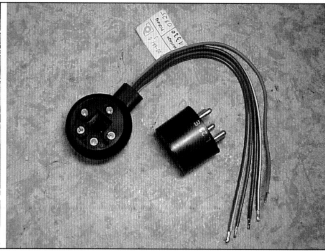

5 The wiring of the cooler fan should be routed through a relay that can easily be placed in one of the free spots in the 911 relay/fuse box. Shown on the right is a standard black relay and socket that can be easily used to power the fan. The fuse box on the left offers a handy placement for the relay, right next to the other ones that control the major systems of the car.

lines from the cooler. Be very careful when disconnecting the hard metal oil lines from the small flexible oil cooler lines. A set of thin Porsche tool wrenches were designed to be used in this process.

When removing the lines, make sure that you hold both ends steady with another wrench. The lines themselves are not strong enough to support the twisting motion on the ends, and you can actually twist and damage the metal lines as you remove them. Work slowly and carefully, and don't forget to support the lines when trying to disconnect them. The lines themselves might be slightly rusted and corroded. In this case, it may be wise to soak the area in WD-40 the night before. Another trick is to heat the entire connection with a small propane torch. This loosens up the joint, and makes it easier to disconnect. Be careful not to accidentally burn your paint when you are using the torch.

A very important note to make here is that you should be aware that the lines will leak oil when they are disconnected. Make sure that the right-side strut and brake assembly is out of the way when you disconnect the line, otherwise you will soak it in oil. If this happens, you will probably have to take it apart piece by piece to clean your brake rotor and pads.

Once you have the lines disconnected, you should be able to easily remove the cooler from its bracket. Be careful when removing it, because it will most likely be full of oil. Now, set up the new Carrera oil cooler to be installed. Install the top bracket into the flange at the top of the wheel well. This bracket

is angled, and has a small stud sticking out of it. Attach one of the rubber mounts to the bracket, and then bolt the bracket to the car. The rubber mount that mates to the oil cooler should be pointing toward the rear of the car.

Affix the two rubber mounts to the bottom of the cooler. Make sure that you place the small rock shield that covers the bottom in the correct orientation. It should be attached to the rubber mounts, fitting flush up against the right angle bracket. Install the right-angle bracket to the bottom of the oil cooler, capturing the air guide.

Now, make sure that the rock guard is firmly attached to the oil cooler. A set of clips, similar to the headliner clips, should keep the shield firmly planted onto the cooler. There is also a seal that goes around the two oil inlets, between the cooler and the shield. Make sure that seal is in place prior to clipping the rock guard together with the cooler.

Now, press on the large spongy seal that goes around the edge of the cooler. This seal is quite flexible, and should be pressed onto the cooler until it snaps and locks onto the edge. Make sure that this seal follows the edge of the cooler around every curve and turn that the shield makes.

The thermostat should be installed and wired at this point. The original factory thermostat clicked on the fan at about 240 degrees Fahrenheit—way too hot for some people's tastes. An alternative thermostat switch, actually a semi-compatible BMW part (61-31-1-364-273), will start the fan running at a much-cooler 210 degrees Fahrenheit. Install this thermostat switch, using a new aluminum sealing ring to make sure that it won't leak. Run the two wires from the switch to the fan, and couple them with the fan's own two wires. These wires need to be routed into the front trunk. I recommend threading them through one or more of the holes that exist for the wiring of the front headlamps and side marker lamps. You can create your own wiring or use the factory oil cooler wiring harness.

Another problem you will probably experience is a conflict with the horns. The large fan on the front of the car will most certainly interfere with the horns. The solution on the later Carreras was to install a different fender strut and horn support bracket. The old one can be removed by loosening the three bolts, including the one that is located inside the headlamp bucket. You will need to remove the headlamp to do this (see Project 71).

With the fender strut removed, you will need to attach the new one. Unfortunately, the new fender strut has slightly different mounting holes, so you will need to drill a hole into one of the support pieces on the inside of the fender. Attach the fender strut to the fender, and then use the hole in the fender strut to align your hand drill to the proper spot to place the hole. Refer to the photo in this project for more clarity. On the outside of the fender, you will probably need a small spacer, as the new fender strut does not match up perfectly with the older valance.

Once you have relocated the horns, it's time to install the oil cooler. Lift the cooler up into the fender well, and let it hang on the upper bracket. Fasten down the bracket with a nut to make sure that the cooler doesn't fall off, but leave it slightly loose at this time. The lower bracket eventually needs to be welded. We will assume here that the welding of the bracket is going to be done by someone else. The best bet in this case is to install the cooler, mark the location of the bracket, and then drive the car to the welder so that the bracket can be attached. The cooler does not need to be removed in order to weld the bracket in place—it can be pushed and manipulated out of the way. You can drive the car a short distance with the cooler hanging from the one top bracket. Just make sure that this bracket is installed very tightly when you leave your garage.

Once the cooler is mounted, you can now attach the oil lines. Loosely attach them to the hard oil lines that come from the engine. Then try to mate them with the openings on the oil cooler. This may require some tugging and bending of the oil lines, as they are a tight fit. If necessary, remove the oil cooler, and

bring it closer to the metal oil lines. Have an assistant hold the cooler for you while you get the threads on the lines started. Once the nuts have been started on the threads, remount the oil cooler to the top bracket. Finally, tighten up the lines after the cooler has been placed back into position. Make sure that you use two wrenches to prevent the lines and the oil cooler connections from twisting.

With the oil cooler installed, and the lines attached, the only thing remaining is the welding of the lower bracket, and the wiring of the fan. Bob Tindel, technical advisor for Pelican Parts, offers us a good procedure for integrating the fan wiring into the car:

- Grab your relay and relay socket. Examine the relay and socket to determine which relay pin sockets connect to which terminal on the relay.
- Wire terminal 30 of the relay socket to the bottom of fuse 13 (counting from the front of the car, in this case an SC. This fuse is a 25-amp, for the sunroof, rear wiper, and mirrors). Use heavier-gauge wire, such as 10 gauge.
- Wire terminal 87 to the fan motor positive terminal, using 10-gauge wire.
- Wire terminal 86 to the bottom of fuse 14, using 16-gauge wire (16-amp fuse, wiper/washer and cigarette lighter).
- Wire terminal 85 to the thermoswitch, using 16-gauge wire (if you want to include a manual switch, also run a 16-gauge wire from terminal 85 to one terminal of a switch, and connect the other switch terminal to ground. A rear wiper switch works well for this, and can be located in the stock position. On many cars, the hole is already cut in the metal dash. You can locate it by pressing on the dash along the left of the steering wheel below the instruments. Cut out the vinyl with a razor knife, and the switch snaps into place).
- Wire the fan motor ground terminal to ground.
- Before buttoning everything back up, confirm that the fan works properly and that it blows in the desired direction. It should activate when the ignition is on and the manual switch is closed, or the thermostat should turn it on at about 210 degrees Fahrenheit.

Now take the car to your welding shop to have the lower L-bracket welded to the side of the car. Needless to say, if you have your own welding equipment, you can install the cooler, take the measurement, and install the bracket yourself.

6 A brand-new product, this oil cooler scoop replaces the side marker light on the right side of the car. Molded and formed out of fiberglass, the matte surface matches the rubber of the 1974–1989 911s perfectly, and looks very much like a standard factory accessory. The scoop channels air from the front of the car into the fenderwell where the front-mounted oil cooler is located. This area is sealed off most of the time, and actually receives very little fresh air. At the time of this printing, the scoop is available only from Pelican Parts (1-888-280-7799).

7 On the late-model Carreras, Porsche notched the bumper to allow more airflow into the region where the fender-mounted oil cooler is located. This particular car is a 911SC, with the bumper removed and notched by a local machine shop. Notching the bumper and adding the oil cooler scoop are probably the two best methods for increasing the air flow to your oil cooler.

If your car doesn't have the oil cooler lines that run up to the front of the car, you must install them and the thermostat yourself. You will need new lines that extend from the oil tank to the thermostat and from the thermostat to the engine. The process is not very difficult.

First, remove the rocker panel from the right side of the car. This will provide access to run the lines down the side of the car. It is wise to examine a car with the lines already installed, to get an idea of where they should be mounted. The mounting tabs and brackets are held into the side of the car with sheet metal screws. Simply drill a small hole and then screw in the small rubber/metal brackets that hold the lines. The early cars use a different rear oil line setup from the later cars (1975 and up), so make sure that you get the appropriate lines. Specifically, the rear-mounted oil line will not fit onto cars with the later-style heat exchangers.

There are many options besides the factory Carrera oil cooler for installation into your 911. Mocal carries one that will fit into the fender well and costs much less than the stock factory oil cooler.

What about air circulation in the fenderwell? The later-style Carrera bumpers have a small cut made in them to allow more air to reach the inside of the fender, where the oil cooler is mounted. If you don't have this bumper, your oil cooler will be isolated in the fenderwell, and insulated with the spongy seal. Fortunately, there is a new product that solves this problem. It is a bolt-on air scoop that replaces the 911 side marker lamp, and provides additional cooling to the inside of the fenderwell. For the cars without the cutout bumper, this scoop provides the necessary air and cooling that is needed to take full advantage of the oil cooler.

For more information on this installation, see the following resources:
- http://www.pelicanparts.com for the installation procedure for both the Mocal oil cooler and the oil cooler scoop
- *Up-Fixen der Porsche* Series from Porsche Club of America. Volume IX contains a detailed article on this procedure
- Porsche Cars North America has a Technical Bulletin, dated December 17, 1984, regarding the upgrade of the brass tube oil cooler to the new Carrera radiator style cooler. Part Identifier 1741, Number 8406

ENGINE

PROJECT 27 • REPLACING MOTOR & TRANSMISSION MOUNTS

 Time: 2 hours

 Tools: –

 Talent: 👤👤

 Applicable Years: All

 Tab: $80–$200

 Tinware: Motor mounts, transmission mounts

 Tip: Replace one side at a time.

 PERFORMANCE GAIN: Stiffer shifting, less vibration from the drivetrain

COMPLEMENTARY MODIFICATION: Upgrade to solid mounts (recommended for racing).

1 The transmission mounts can easily be seen from underneath the car. Shown here are the mounts on a later-style 911, which are replaceable. On the early cars, these mounts are embedded into the steel transmission mount bar and cannot be replaced. Used transmission mount bars with good rubber mounts can still be found, but they are becoming increasingly difficult to locate.

Old, worn-out motor and transmission mounts can cause shifting problems, because the drivetrain is no longer firmly held in its position. A visible sign that the motor mounts need replacing is the appearance of cracks in the rubber of the mounts. The rubber will deteriorate over the years and will need to be replaced, even if the car has relatively few miles on it.

The first step in replacing the motor mounts is to place a jack under the engine and support it. Make sure that you use a block of wood to protect the bottom of your engine case from damage. See Project 1 for more details. Once the engine is supported, you can begin removing one of the bolts that fasten and hold the motor mount bar to the mounts. The mounts themselves are located in the engine compartment, along the back shelf (see the photo in Project 7, Engine Removal). Remove the long bolt from the center of one of the motor mounts. On the later cars, these bolts are threaded into the motor mount bar itself—there is no nut on the other end. These bolts are often rusted in place and should be lubricated generously with WD-40 from the bottom. A stuck bolt can actually bend the mounting cross-bar when you are trying to remove it.

It is advisable to replace each motor mount, one at a time. Otherwise, the weight of the engine may cause it to shift, and it may become misaligned. Also, the motor may drop down slightly from its normal position. Replace the mount on one side and then replace the one on the opposite side.

Once the center motor mount bolt is removed, then you can simply remove the entire motor mount by removing the two smaller bolts that attach it to the chassis. These bolts have corresponding nuts that must be kept from turning when they are being removed. Access to these nuts is gained by reaching underneath the rear engine shelf. Once you have the motor mount removed, simply install the new one in the same place. Tighten up all the nuts, and perform the same procedure for the opposite side.

The transmission mounts are very similar to the motor mounts, except for the early cars. Unfortunately, the early cars have a one-piece mount and support bar design that is no longer available. The rubber transmission mounts are embedded into the 2-foot-wide support bar that mounts the entire transmission to the chassis. Sometimes, good used mounts can be found, but they are getting scarcer every day. To replace this one-piece mount, support the transmission with the jack, and unbolt the mount from the chassis and the transmission. Depending upon the configuration of your car, you may have to remove the rear sway bar in order to remove the transmission mount.

The later-style 911s (1972–on) were equipped with a transmission mount bar that incorporated replaceable mounts. These mounts are very similar to the engine mounts, and should be replaced in a similar manner. Make sure that the transmission is well supported with a jack before you remove either of the transmission mounts. As with the engine mounts, work on one side, and complete the installation prior to removing the mount on the other side.

SECTION THREE
FUEL
SYSTEMS

Without a doubt, the fuel injection system on your 911 can be one of the most finicky to diagnose and troubleshoot. While one can write volumes about fuel injection systems alone, this section not only introduces the various 911 fuel delivery systems, but focuses on identifying common problems and potential pitfalls. Reading through it will help you to identify problems with your own system, and gain familiarity with those installed in other 911s.

FUEL SYSTEMS
PROJECT 28 • CARBURETOR REBUILD

 Time: 12 hours

 Tools: Socket set, compressed air, parts cleaner, cotton swabs, aerosol carb cleaner

 Talent:

 Applicable Years: All with Weber carburetors

 Tab: $50

 Tinware: Carburetor rebuild kit

 Tip: Rebuild each side at a time, in case you forget where something goes.

 PERFORMANCE GAIN: Cleaner running engine, better throttle response

COMPLEMENTARY MODIFICATION: Install jets optimized for your car

The Weber triple-barrel carburetors are the most popular for installation on a late-model 911. This project will cover the rebuilding of the Weber carburetors in detail. The procedure is similar for the Solex and Zenith carburetors and differs mostly in the method that the float levels are set.

The key to maintaining well-functioning carburetors is keeping them clean. There are many very small passages within the carburetor that can become clogged from dirt or old fuel, and prevent the car from running properly. Typical carburetor problems include backfiring, flat spots, missing, lack of power, and general uneven performance. You can usually figure out that your carburetors need rebuilding when they become insensitive to adjustments that are made when attempting to tune and balance them (see Project 29).

The first step is to remove the two carburetors from your 911. They should be mounted to each intake manifold by six studs on each side. Be careful when removing the fuel lines that are attached, as there will most likely be fuel in the lines. Likewise, when you remove the carburetors from the car keep

1 Disassembly begins with the removal of the intake funnels (sometimes called velocity stacks), and the upper mounting plate for the air filter. Removing the small locking hex nuts will now allow the top cover assembly to be removed from the carburetor body.

2 Remove the air correction screw in order to gain access to the channels and passages within the carburetor body. Make sure that you spray plenty of carb cleaner and compressed air down all the passages to clean them out. The cleanliness of these passages and chambers is directly related to the ability to tune and balance the carburetor.

3 It's not wise to disassemble the bottom part of the carburetor that contains the throttle valves. If the bushings are heavily worn, additional and more expensive rebuilding will be required. You can tell that the bushings are worn if the throttle valves stick in the throttle bodies. Very often when the shaft bushings wear, the throttle valves will actually dig a groove into the body of the carburetor. If this is the case, the carburetor body is worn beyond repair and should be scrapped.

4 The venturis are held in by a set screw that secures them within the inner housing. They can be gently coaxed out of the main carburetor body after removing this screw, and then cleaned. Make sure that you are careful to keep track of all the small parts you remove from the carburetor. Many of these parts are very difficult to find these days, and can only be swiped out of older, junked carburetors.

5 Place the main carburetor body into a parts cleaner, and force cleaning solution into all the passages in the carburetor body. It's also wise to let the housing sit for a while in the cleaning solution. Years of dirty fuel and deposits need to be dissolved and swept out of the internal passages.

6 A cotton swab dipped in carb cleaner makes an excellent tool for cleaning hard-to-reach places. Make sure that you rinse all parts under fresh carb cleaner before letting them dry. It is important not to get cotton fibers stuck in the small passageways of the carburetor.

7 The complete carb kit contains all the gaskets, sealing rings, and floats that you need to completely rebuild one carburetor. In many cases, the carburetor kits are universal across different sizes of carburetors, so don't be worried if you have a few extra gaskets left over when you're finished. When installing the paper gaskets, make sure that you match up the proper-sized ones for your size carburetor.

8 An important step to perform is the adjustment of the float height. Wedge a paper towel between the float and the housing to elevate it off the bottom of the housing. Using a straight edge, measure the height of the float tab to the carburetor upper face, and adjust it until the measurement is 18 millimeters. If you happen to have a specialty float gauge, you can also use it to measure the float height.

9 With the float tab exactly 18 millimeters from the carburetor upper face, the height of the float should be between 12.5 and 13 millimeters from the upper face. Do not measure the height from the weld seam of the float; use the top surface of the float. If this measurement is incorrect, bend the float tab slightly until you obtain the required measurements. Additionally, check the height of the needle valve. When installed with its sealing washer, the needle valve should hang down exactly 18 millimeters from the top of the carburetor housing.

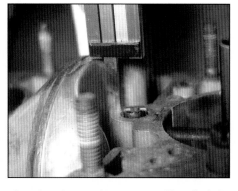

10 The accelerator pump assembly can be a little tricky because the parts are spring loaded and compressed. Make sure that you don't damage the new rubber diaphragm when you install it. Also make sure that you install all the parts correctly and in the right orientation. It's quite easy to get confused here.

11 The completed and rebuilt carburetor. Place a little lithium grease on the linkage assembly to reduce the wear in this area, and make sure that you use a new air cleaner when you rein-stall the carbs in the car. Make sure that you install a new fuel filter in your car as well. You do not want dirty fuel to get inside your newly rebuilt carburetors.

in mind that the fuel bowls might still be full of gasoline, which can easily spill out.

When you get the carbs on your bench, you should carefully inspect them to make sure that they are not worn beyond repair. Very often the throttle valve bushings become worn, and the valves themselves begin to wear a groove in the throttle body. If the throttle shaft is loose in its bearings, then you should probably take the housing to a professional rebuilder. They will need to drill out and remove the old bushings, then install and ream new ones in their place. The alignment and tolerances of this procedure are critical, and should probably be left to a professional. If the shafts are loose and you don't replace the bushings, then the throttle valves will most likely permanently damage the throttle body in the very near future, and your carburetor will be junk.

The task of rebuilding is straightforward. The entire process is simply a teardown and reassembly with new gaskets. I recommend that you rebuild each side one at a time, so you have a reference point in case you forget where a particular part is installed. (The left and right carburetors are identical.)

Carefully remove all the parts and pieces of the carburetor, and clean them in parts cleaner. It is not necessary to remove the throttle valves and the linkage from the bottom of the carburetor housing. These parts can be cleaned in place. Make sure that you flow carb cleaner through every passage and area of the carburetor. When finished, blow compressed air through all the passages. If you don't have an air compressor, use one of those compressed cans of air that are designed to blow out dust from computer equipment. It's also important to note that you should always use eye and hand protection when working with any solvents or cleaners.

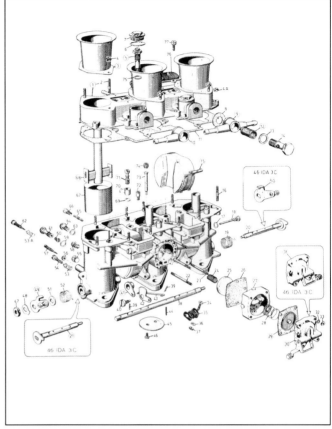

12 This exploded view of the 911 carburetor shows you where and how every little piece goes when reassembling the unit. Work slowly, and double-check to make sure that you don't forget to reinstall any parts. Legend: 1. Cover 2. Stud 3. Air horn 4/4A Nut 5. Needle valve 6. Washer 7. Plug 8. Washer 9. Union 10. Union 11. Gasket 12. Fuel filter 13. Washer 14. Bolt 15. Float 16. Stud 17. Washer 18. Fulcrum pin 19. Throttle spindle 20. Throttle spindle 21. Throttle spindle 22/23. Stud 24. Spring 25. Plate 26. Diaphragm 27. Accelerator pump housing 28. Spring 29. Diaphragm 30. Cover 31. Cover 32. Spring washer 33. Nut 34. Screw 35. Linkage 36. Washer 37. Nut 38. Throttle spindle 39. Clip 40. Pivot 41. Arm 42. Cam 43. Linkage 44. Roll pin 45. Throttle valve 46. Screw 47. Nut 48. Tab washer 49. Lever 50. Lever 51. Spacer 52. Spring 53/53A. Spring 54. Idling adjustment screw 55. Progression hole inspection plug 56. Locknut 57. Air compensating adjustment screw 58. Choke retaining screw 59. Washer 60. Main jet 61. Holder 62. Mixture adjustment screw 63. Washer 64. Drain plug 65. Idling jet 66. Holder 67. Choke 68. Auxiliary venturi 69. Washer 70. Pump jet 71. Delivery valve 72. Inlet and discharge valve 73. Emulsion tube 74. Air corrector jet 75. Washer 76. Filter gauze 77. Screw

Some of the fittings are made out of brass, and extra care should be taken when removing them. Brass is a soft metal, and the fittings may easily strip out. If any of them seem very difficult to remove, try soaking them overnight in WD-40.

FUEL SYSTEMS

PROJECT 29 • CARBURETOR ADJUSTMENT, BALANCE, AND TUNING

 Time: 1 hour

 Tools: Carb sync tool

 Talent: ♦♦

 Applicable Years: All

 Tab: $25

 Tinware: –

 Tip: Adjust the carbs, and then drive the car around for a while and recheck all your adjustments, and have plenty of patience.

 PERFORMANCE GAIN: Better engine performance

COMPLEMENTARY MODIFICATION: Check the engine timing

Well-adjusted carburetors are key to good engine performance. If your carbs are unbalanced, different cylinders in your engine will receive different amounts of fuel and air, and the all-important air/fuel mixture ratio will be off. This will result in less horsepower, a poor idle, and higher emissions. It's a wise idea to check the balance of the carburetors each time you perform a major tune-up on your engine. The most popular system for use on the 911 is the Weber triple-throat carburetors. This project will discuss the procedure used for balancing Weber carburetors.

If your carburetors are poorly balanced, you will have a multitude of problems with your engine. The engine will have a tendency to spit and backfire through the exhaust. Unbalanced carbs may also give the engine an uneven idle, or make the car very difficult to keep at idle without stalling. It's important to make sure that your engine is in good overall health (good compression), and that your idle jets are clean as well. Dirt in the idle jets, poorly adjusted valves, or a burnt exhaust valve can also result in

the same symptoms that are associated with unbalanced carburetors.

The first step in adjusting your carburetors is to make sure that the rest of your car is tuned and performing properly. Make sure that your valves are properly adjusted (Project 18), and the timing and dwell are set properly (Project 23). Make sure that your spark plug wires are in good condition, your plugs are new, the carburetor floats are properly adjusted (Project 28), and the idle jets are clean. Let the car warm up to its normal operating temperature before starting to adjust the carburetors. Once the car is warm, begin by adjusting the idle to about 1,000 to 1,100 rpm. You want to set the idle to be a little bit higher so that the car will not die out when you are making adjustments. Adjust the engine to this value by carefully turning the idle adjustment screws located on the ends of the carburetors.

Now, remove the air cleaner from the top of the carburetors. Now, disconnect one of the two small drop links on the throttle linkages, so there is no connection between either of the two carburetors.

Once you are sure the timing is set correctly, and the idle speed is set to your working range of 1,000–1,100 rpm, it's time to synchronize each of the carburetor throats. A special synchronization tool (sometimes called a Unisyn or synchrometer) is used to measure the airflow being sucked into the manifold by each carburetor throat. The goal of the synchronization task is to make sure that the amount of airflow into each throat is the same for all six cylinders.

Start with cylinder Number One, located on the rear left side of the engine. Place the synchronizer over the top of the carburetor stack and adjust the tall glass stack to a vertical position. Turn the adjusting disc on the synchronizer until the small indicator bubble inside the glass rises about halfway up the height of the synchronizer. This basically calibrates the synchronizer tool for Number One.

Now, place the Unisyn on one of the throats of the right bank of cylinders. Adjust the idle adjustment screw located at the end of the carburetor until the ball in the Unisyn is at about the same height as it was on Cylinder One. The idle speed should either rise or drop off a bit from the level that you had it set at.

Starting with cylinder Number One, adjust the mixture adjustment screw at the base of the carburetor. On each Weber carburetor, there are three mixture adjustment screws that have a spring wrapped around the inside to prevent them from turning. Turn this screw in until the idle begins to drop. Then back off the screw about 1/8th of a turn or until the idle comes back to its previous level. The goal is to turn in all the mixture adjustment screws right to the point where they begin to affect the idle. Repeat this procedure for each cylinder on each side of the car. If your mixture adjustment screws are turned in too far, then you will be starving your engine of air. This will result in a popping-type backfire out of the exhaust. When all the mixture adjustment screws have been set, then readjust the idle adjustment screws located on each end of the carburetor until the idle is adjusted back to 1,000–1,100 rpm. Use the Unisyn to make sure that both banks of carburetors are drawing the same amount of air while the car is at 1,000–1,100 rpm.

Next, take the Unisyn and measure the level of airflow that each cylinder is drawing through the carburetor. Make a note of the level of the highest cylinder—you will adjust all the other carburetors to the level of this cylinder. There are three air correction screws that are located at the base of the carburetors and, they have a small nut that locks them down to prevent them from rotating. Adjust the air correction screws so that the level of each cylinder as shown by the Unisyn is equal to the reading on the highest-level cylinder. Adjusting the carburetors in this fashion will give the car a strong idle and make it run very evenly. If, for some reason, you cannot adjust all the cylinders to the reading on the highest cylinder, adjust that one down slightly to the point where all the cylinders can be synchronized together. After adjusting all the air correction screws, reset the idle back to the 1,000–1,100-rpm range, using the Unisyn to verify that both sides are evenly balanced.

Once all the cylinders are set and synchronized, it's time to adjust your linkage. The accelerator linkage must open each carburetor by the same amount at the same time. In other words, both the left and right carburetor linkage must be synchronized with each other as the throttle is depressed.

All of the links and ball joints should be tight and have almost no slop or backlash. If there is significant wear on these joints, they should be replaced, as you will find it very difficult to adjust the linkage and balance the carburetors. To adjust the linkage, you will need to change the length of the linkage arms by rotating the ball joints at the ends of the arms. The linkage has two drop links, whose length controls when the throttle bodies are opened and closed. If one carburetor opens earlier than the other, you need to decrease the length of the throttle linkage drop link until they both open at the same time. The drop links are threaded with both a left- and right-handed thread (similar to the tie rods), so you can get a very fine adjustment simply by rotating the drop link in either direction. Tighten up the retaining nuts

1 The Unisyn synchronizer is a very useful tool for balancing your carburetors. Make sure that it completely covers the top of your carburetor or velocity stack when taking measurements. Once you have the synchronizer set for a particular cylinder, don't change the diaphragm setting until you are finished checking all the other cylinders. Also, avoid looking directly down the stacks of the carburetors while the car is running. If a backfire occurs it can come up the stack and hit you in the face.

2 It's also very important to make sure that your linkage is properly adjusted. The small drop links (shown by the yellow arrow) that are connected to the throttle and control the butterfly valves need to be appropriately adjusted. Make sure that they are opening the valves at the same time. The white arrow shows the idle adjustment screws that are located on the end of each carburetor.

on each end of the drop link when you have finished adjusting the linkage.

In addition to checking both the idle mixture and the linkage, you should also check the adjustment of the accelerator pumps. These pumps are designed to inject extra fuel into the carburetor throats under acceleration. There are two of them, and they are located in the center of each carburetor. They directly affect the performance of the 911 up to about 30 miles per hour. This pump jet squirts out a stream of fuel when the throttle is opened from being completely closed. It may be easier to perform this test if you remove the velocity stacks on top of the carburetors.

To check the adjustment of the accelerator pumps, place a small vial under the pump jet located inside the carburetor throat. You will have to fashion a small wire to hold the vial, as space is pretty tight inside the carburetor throat. Pump the throttle completely from closed to open twice, and measure the amount of fuel in the vial. For cold weather, the factory recommends 0.55–0.65 cc of fuel. For warmer weather, it's recommended to have 0.40–0.50 cc of fuel. Adjust the length of the small linkage attached to

3 This photo clearly indicates the adjustment points for the Weber carburetor. The white arrows indicate the idle adjustment screws. The green arrows point to the idle mixture adjustment screws. The yellow arrows indicate the air correction screws, and the red arrow points to the accelerator pump adjustment rod. The location of the idle jets, which must be kept clean, are indicated by the blue arrows.

the accelerator pump on the carb to increase or decrease this amount.

Early Weber carburetors don't have adjustable accelerator pumps. A poorly adjusted accelerator pump will tend to make the car hesitate under acceleration. This symptom is also experienced when the diaphragm on the carburetor is cracked or leaking. It's very common on 911s that have been sitting for many years for the rubber diaphragm to break. Replacing the diaphragm during a routine carburetor rebuild will solve this problem (see Project 28).

When finished, go drive the car and check the performance of the engine. Often several attempts will be required to properly tune and balance the carbs. When you have completed the entire procedure, it's a wise idea to go back and check all the measurements one more time. If you find that you are having difficulty balancing or tuning the carburetors, it may be that they need to be rebuilt. Vacuum leaks around seals and worn throttle bodies will make the carburetors almost impossible to properly tune. If a carburetor throat doesn't seem to respond to any changes in the idle mixture screw, then this is a clear indication that the idle jets may be clogged, or your carburetor may need rebuilding. See Project 28 for more information on rebuilding Weber carburetors.

Another problem common to carburetors is the clogging of the idle jets. These clogged jets will cause the engine to run rough. The solution is to simply pull them out of the top of the carburetors and clean them out with a little bit of carburetor cleaner and compressed air. You should make sure that your jets are clean before attempting to tune and balance the carburetors. Refer to Project 28 for more details. Dirt in the idle jets will make the car run sluggish, as if you have lost power in a cylinder.

Another common problem with Weber carburetors is that they sometimes spit out the top of the velocity stacks. This is usually caused by a design defect in the early specifications of carburetors used on early 911s. The spitting is caused by the idle jets

being too small. The cure for this problem is to install larger idle jets. In the old days, you could check the jetting of your carburetors by taking a close look at the spark plugs. Unfortunately, you can't read spark plugs as well with today's unleaded gas formulations. With today's unleaded fuel combined with lots of additives, the plugs will often look black and sooty, even if the engine is running well.

Clean fuel is especially vital to good-working carburetors. It's a smart idea to add an extra fuel filter right before each carburetor just to remove any excess dirt that may clog the idle jets. Unlike high-pressure fuel injection systems, carburetors don't get cleaned by the pressurized fuel flowing in and out of the small passages. It's also very important to make sure that the air filter is clean when you reinstall it.

It's important to note that Weber carburetors have no choke or starting circuits. You must use your foot on the accelerator pedal to pump the accelerator pumps in the carburetors when first warming up the engine. When starting the car warm, take the pedal and floor it, then turn the key. Don't pump the accelerator pedal when the car is warm, as you will probably flood the engine. Weber carburetors have a tendency to boil the fuel over when the car is warm, and dump it into the combustion chamber, flooding the engine. Holding down the pedal is the correct procedure because chances are that there is already a lot of fuel in the combustion chamber. When the car kicks over, simply release your foot from the pedal and bring the car down to idle.

If after going through the entire adjustment procedure, the engine still doesn't perform properly, you may have some problems that are caused by other factors. If your engine is not in good health and has a compression leak, then you may get backfiring through the carburetors. If the small passages within the carburetors are clogged, then they might need to be rebuilt. If turning either the idle mixture screws or the air correction screws doesn't affect the idle of the engine, then you may have to rebuild the carburetors.

PROJECT 30 • MECHANICAL FUEL INJECTION TROUBLESHOOTING AND ADJUSTMENT

Time: –

Tools: MFI tune-up tools

Talent:

Applicable Years: 1969-1973

Tab: –

Tinware: –

Tip: Make sure that all your systems are propery checked.

PERFORMANCE GAIN: Lots of extra horsepower from a well-tuned MFI system

COMPLEMENTARY MODIFICATION: –

One of the most complicated fuel delivery systems ever created was the Bosch mechanical fuel injection system, or MFI. The system was a precursor to the more modern electronic controlled fuel injection systems, and is actually a marvel of mechanical engineering. The system functions in a similar manner to the electronic systems that followed it, yet all the controls were almost completely mechanical. As a result, there is lots of tuning and adjustment required for the complicated system.

Unfortunately, there isn't a whole lot of information available on the subject. This project will give an overview of the MFI system, and also some pointers on tuning and adjusting it. For more information, I recommend that you consult the factory workshop manuals, or if you can find it, the Porsche technical bulletin "4532.20 Check, Measure, Adjust" for the mechanical fuel injection system.

The MFI system consists of two main parts, the injection/distribution pump, and the throttle bodies.

The electric fuel pump located in the front of the car supplies pressurized fuel to the injection/distribution pump. The injection pump is the heart of the system, and is responsible for metering and providing the fuel to each cylinder. The pump itself consists of two main parts, the fuel pump assembly, and the compensating unit. The fuel pump assembly is responsible for the actual delivery of fuel to each of the cylinders, while the compensating unit is responsible for adjusting the fuel delivery according to the levels set by both the accelerator and the speed of the engine. Precise coordination of all the elements of the engine is required for the system to function properly.

The MFI system was mostly used on diesel cars, on which a timed injection system is absolutely necessary (diesel cars don't have ignition systems). In 1966 Porsche first used an MFI system on the 225-horsepower Carrera 906 with a 2.0-liter engine. This engine was later installed in the venerable 911R. The advantage of an MFI system is that the fuel delivery is metered to the rpm of the engine. In general, the system supplies fuel to the cylinders in a more precise and aggressive manner than carburetors can deliver. Because the system was designed with a closed, nonvented fuel supply, the emissions were also much better than carburetors. Even compared to the electronic fuel injection systems of today, the MFI system has a very high injection pressure. Fuel is squirted out of the injectors at a remarkably high 220–250 psi. This high pressure aids in the atomization of the fuel, which in turn increases the surface area of the mixture. This results in a more efficient and complete burn of the fuel.

The entire goal of any fuel injection system is to provide the proper mixture of air and fuel to the engine. The MFI system uses the injection pump to coordinate the amount and delivery of the fuel. The velocity stacks and throttle bodies mounted to the top of the heads regulate the airflow into the cylinders. In order to achieve the ideal air/fuel ratio, these two systems must be carefully coordinated. A lot can go wrong with the MFI system, but when it works it performs very well.

The fuel pump half of the injection pump works similarly to the valve train in the engine. A small camshaft inside the pump rotates around, and pushes on small cylinders. These cylinders act as plungers that push fuel through the lines to each cylinder. As the engine rotates, the camshaft pushes the small fuel pistons up and down as each cylinder is fired. Close coordination with the timing of the engine is required to get the process just right. In a similar manner to the method in which the ignition system fires sparks, the

1 The three primary components of the Mechanical Fuel Injection system are the injection/distribution pump (upper left), the velocity stacks (upper right), and the throttle bodies (lower right). This is a recently rebuilt pump for a 2.4S motor. The large gold can on the top is the barometric compensator, which should never be used to pick up the pump. The large silver cylinder hanging off of the rear of the pump is the shut-off solenoid. The large black cylinder on the back of the pump is the thermostat that is connected to the hose, which provides hot air from the heat exchangers. The velocity stacks are made of plastic and have bearings pressed into them for the throttle body linkage. The throttle body shown here has new butterfly valves, and newly adjusted linkage arms.

fuel pump side of the injection pump pushes fuel through the lines to each cylinder in a timed and controlled manner. When the fuel reaches the cylinder, it exits through an injector embedded inside the cylinder heads. This side of the fuel pump is lubricated with oil fed from the engine. Two oil lines that connect to the top of the engine provide an oil supply and return for the internal mechanicals of the pump.

In addition to providing spurts of fuel that pulse with the speed of the engine, the injection pump regulates the amount of fuel pushed during each spurt. In order to accomplish this, the plungers themselves are designed with a corkscrewlike groove cut into their side. The plungers are allowed to rotate in their bores, amounting to only half a turn. As the plunger turns, the corkscrew effect basically allows more fuel to enter each plunger. The rotation of these plungers is tied into the throttle position. The greater the throttle position is, the more the pistons will turn, and more fuel will be delivered.

To recap, the up-and-down motion of the fuel pistons occurs in time with the rpm of the engine. The rotation of the fuel pistons is connected to the position of the throttle or accelerator. While this relationship is fine for many operating conditions, to obtain the required air/fuel mixture ratio, the engine must be supplied with different quantities of fuel under varying engine speeds and loads. Internal to the injection pump, a centrifugal governor works in conjunction with the throttle position lever to meter the fuel fed into the system. In addition, a barometric compensator is used to adjust to changes in altitude that might affect the air/fuel ratio. A warm-up thermostat linked to the heat exchangers senses when the car needs a richer mixture upon cold start-up. Finally, a shut-off solenoid reduces fuel delivery to the injection system when the throttle is closed, and the engine is coasting in gear.

Because the internal mechanisms of the MFI pumps are coordinated precisely with the timing of

the engine, each pump is specifically designed to work with a specific engine. Swapping pumps from engine to engine is not a wise idea, and the car will probably never run correctly. The pump, distributor, and camshafts of the engines must be matched together for the MFI system to operate properly.

In many ways, the MFI system combines elements of the modern fuel injection systems and the older-style carbureted systems. Like carburetors, the MFI system uses a set of throttle bodies to meter and control the airflow intake into the system. Since the entire goal of the fuel injection system is to maintain the proper air/fuel mixture, the throttle bodies must be properly synchronized with the fuel injection pump. All of the linkage rods in the entire system must be properly aligned and synchronized. If one or more are off, then the car will not run properly. Of paramount importance is the length of the connecting rod that runs between the pump regulator lever and the cross shaft. The length of this rod must be set at exactly 114±0.2 millimeters from ball center to ball center, in order for the fuel injection system to function properly.

There are a whole set of Porsche protractor tools that are used to adjust these rods. The tools are attached to the rods on the throttle bodies, and also on the injector pump. Changes in the angles of the throttle body butterfly valves have to correspond with angular changes on the pump lever. It's very difficult to accurately check and measure these settings without these tools.

Also very important is the adjustment of the air bypass screws. These are used to balance the amount of air entering each cylinder when the car is idling. To check these values, use a synchrometer similar to the one used to adjust carburetors (Project 29). Close the air correction valves, and then open them up five half-turns for 2.0 and 2.2 engines, or three half-turns for 2.4 engines. Start the car and let it warm up. Using the hand throttle, set the car to idle at 3,000 rpm.

Measure the airflow over each of the velocity stacks, and then write down the average of all the measurements. Now, using the air correction screws on the throttle bodies, adjust each cylinder until the average number is reached. If the screws open up more than four full turns, then there is probably carbon buildup on the inside of the passageways, and the throttle bodies need to be cleaned.

The adjustment of the idling speed is not performed at the injection pump, but rather with the air correction screws. To change the idle speed, evenly turn each of the six air-correction screws. Be careful to turn each one the same amount. Adjust the screws until the idle reaches 900 ±50 rpm.

There are two different mixture adjustments on the MFI system. One adjusts for idle and low rpm, and the other for higher rpm when the engine is under load. You should not adjust these unless you have a carbon monoxide meter handy and hooked up to the car. Make sure that the car is warm when performing the adjustments, and also make sure that the engine is off when you turn any of the adjustment screws, or you can damage the pump.

To adjust the idle mixture of the MFI system, you will need to turn the small adjustment screw that is located on the back of the pump. You must use a special long tool to reach through the blades of the cooling fan to turn the adjustment screw. The adjustment screw is spring-loaded and must be pushed in toward the pump in order to engage the mechanism that controls the mixture. The adjustment screw is indexed, and you should feel it click as you turn it. To richen up the mixture, turn it clockwise. To lean it out, turn it counterclockwise. Turn it only about one or two clicks at a time, and only when the engine is off. Make sure that you monitor your readings with a carbon monoxide meter after you change the mixture, and only take measurements when the engine is warm. On the 2.0-liter engines, you may have to use a flexible shaft to reach inside and access the mixture adjustment screw.

To adjust the higher rpm, or part-load mixture, you need to remove a small hex socket-head bolt from the rear of the pump. Inside the pump, there will be another socket-head receptacle that you can turn to adjust the mixture. Turn the screw clockwise to lean out the mixture, and counterclockwise to richen it up. Note that this is in the opposite direction from the other mixture adjustment. For the 2.0-liter engines, you may have to loosen up the starter solenoid lever on the pump in order to gain access to the screw.

In general, when you are adjusting the mixture, make sure you take detailed notes of where you

2 Shown installed on the 911, the throttle bodies and velocity stacks are placed directly on top of the cylinder heads. The complexity of the throttle linkage is shown here. Each of these rods must be carefully measured and adjusted or the mixture for one or more of the cylinders will be off. Also shown here is the microswitch that indicates the throttle is completely released (shown by the arrow). This switch activates the shut-off solenoid, which prevents the pump from dumping raw fuel into the cylinders when there is no air to mix it with. The injectors for the MFI system are screwed directly into the cylinder heads, making these heads somewhat unique.

started, so that you can restore the car back to its original condition. Failure to do this may seriously disturb the balance of the MFI system, and make your car run poorly.

When installing the pump back onto the engine, there are a few things to be concerned about. First, the pump should always be carried by the bottom. The gold tin can that looks like a good handle on the top of the pump is actually the barometric compensator, and can be seriously damaged if you pick the pump up by it.

Once the pump is mounted on the engine, the toothed drive belt must be properly set in order to synchronize the pump with the main crankshaft. There is a mark located on the pulley hub of the MFI pump. Make sure that this mark is aligned with the small notch on the case of the pump. Then place the engine at TDC for cylinder Number One. Refer to Project 18 for more details on this procedure. Then rotate the engine 360 degrees. The engine should now be at TDC for cylinder Number Four. Then rotate the engine until the FE mark on the crankshaft pulley aligns with the mark at the bottom of the fan housing. At this point, install the toothed belt. The pump should now be synchronized with the engine.

So what can go wrong with the MFI system? Apparently a few potential problems have been isolated over the past 30 years. The MFI systems are often known for running too rich. One of the causes of this problem is that the heater hose that connects to the thermostat on the back of the pump is not properly installed. This hose is connected to the heat exchangers, and heats the element inside the pump

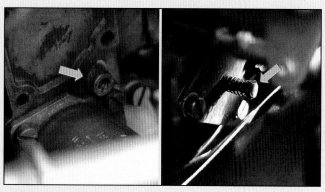

3 These photos show the locations of the two mixture adjustment screws. The one on the left is the part-load mixture adjustment, or higher-rpm adjustment. The hex socket-head screw shown here needs to be removed before the adjustment socket inside can be accessed. The photo on the right shows the low-rpm or idle mixture adjustment screw, which needs to be pushed in and turned in order to change the mixture. You should feel distinct clicks when you turn the screw in either direction. Only make adjustments when the engine is off, lest you damage the pump.

to lean out the mixture. When the car is cold, the mixture is rich to aid in starting and warm up. If the hose is disconnected or damaged, then the element does not get heated, and the pump is set to run rich all the time. Make sure that the hose on your car is firmly connected, and installed properly. There is also another hose that is connected to the heat exchangers that is attached to the air cleaner on 1972–73 911s. This hose is part of the emissions control, and doesn't affect the performance of the engine.

The shut-off solenoid is used to stop fuel delivery when the engine's rpm is high, yet the accelerator pedal is not pressed. This occurs when coasting along in gear, either down a hill or along the highway. The shut-off solenoid significantly reduces the delivery of fuel to the engine during this moment. Without the shut-off solenoid in operation, raw fuel would be dumped into the cylinders with the throttle bodies closed. In this condition, stepping on the accelerator can generate a huge backfire in all cylinders. The shut-off solenoid is controlled by a small microswitch linked to the main throttle rod. Make sure that this switch is properly adjusted to be electrically closed when the throttle is completely closed (foot off gas pedal).

Another source of problems with the MFI systems is the throttle bodies wearing out, similar to carburetors. The bearings on the butterfly valves in the throttle bodies can become worn out after about 100,000 miles. Sometimes the valves are so loose that they can be heard flapping when the engine is running. If the bearings on the butterfly valves in the throttle bodies

become too loose they can cut a groove in the sides of the chambers. If a groove is scored, the throttle bodies need to be scrapped. It's wise to have the throttle bodies rebuilt and new bearings installed before significant damage occurs.

Sometimes the oil seals in the pump fail, causing gasoline to leak out of the pump and into the crankcase of the engine. If you are checking the oil on an MFI car, and the oil level appears to be rising, it is most certain that your pump is leaking gas into the oil. The oil will also smell a bit like gasoline. Empty and change the oil at once—as the gasoline will eat up the bearings inside of the engine and force you to perform a rebuild—then have the pump rebuilt.

The timing of the engine is crucial for the proper operation of the MFI systems. Since the fuel is delivered at a very high pressure within a specific moment of time, the ignition spark must be correctly coordinated with the injection system, or the car will perform poorly. Double- and triple-check the timing on MFI cars to make sure that it is set correctly.

The factory technical publication has a pretty good checklist to follow when you are looking for problems with your MFI system:

• Check the air cleaner for blockages and clogs
• Check the engine to ensure that you have appropriate, even compression in all the cylinders
• Examine the spark plugs for deposits and also inspect the ignition wires (see Project 22)
• Check the dwell angle of the points (see Project 23)
• Check and set the ignition timing (See Project 23)
• Check the fuel pressure and flow to the injectors
• Inspect the injectors for dirt and buildup
• Check the injection timing and synchronization with the engine crankshaft
• Measure and adjust the MFI system linkage arms for their proper correlation to the MFI pump
• Perform an emissions test to check carbon monoxide levels at idle and under load

With a little bit of know-how and the right tools, the MFI system can be made to perform quite well. The 911S in 1969 was one of the first production Porsches to use the MFI system and was rated at 170 horsepower—quite a feat for a 2.0-liter motor. If you are planning on performing your own tune-up and maintenance work on your MFI system, I suggest that you obtain a set of the measurement tools, a set of factory manuals, and the MFI technical bulletin (4532.20).

FUEL SYSTEMS

PROJECT 31 • TUNING AND ADJUSTING CIS FUEL INJECTION

 Time: –

 Tools: Mixture adjustment tool

 Talent:

 Applicable Years: 1973-1983

 Tab: –

 Tinware: Fuel injection manifold hoses

 Tip: Spray carb cleaner around the injectors and hoses to check for vacuum leaks.

PERFORMANCE GAIN: Better running engine

COMPLEMENTARY MODIFICATION: Replace air filter

1 The CIS idle speed is set in a similar manner to the setting of the speed on carburetors and the MFI system. A throttle bypass system regulates the amount of air that passes into the fuel injection system when the throttle is at rest. This screw is indicated by the white arrow. You should adjust the idle until it reaches about 950 rpm. If you have problems achieving this setting, then you might want to double-check the mixture adjustment.

For more than 10 years, Porsche used the Bosch K-Jetronic Continuous Injection System (CIS) on all production 911s. The system in general is very reliable, and was only bested in 1984 by the introduction of the Motronic engine management system, which controls both ignition and fuel injection together.

The CIS meters the amount of fuel provided to the cylinders as a function of the air drawn into the engine. The CIS airflow sensor plate measures the amount of air that is being drawn into the system. This sensor plate is attached to a fuel distributor that evenly meters the amount of pressurized fuel sent to each injector. The system doesn't differentiate among the six injectors—it sends the same amount of fuel to them at all times. Unlike pulsed-injection systems, like the Motronic system, or even the earlier Mechanical Fuel Injection system, the CIS injectors distribute fuel to the cylinders at all times. The opening and closing of the intake valves controls the influx of fuel to the combustion chamber.

Through 1979, CIS was a semi-open-looped system, which means that it didn't monitor the out-put gases from the engine to see if the air/fuel mixture was set at the appropriate levels. In 1980, emissions requirements forced the introduction of an oxygen sensor into the system, which helped the engine to better run at the appropriate mixture level through the regulation of fuel pressure inside the fuel distributor.

Maintenance and Adjustment

The two primary adjustments for the CIS are the idle speed and the mixture adjustment. The mixture can be adjusted by turning a small hex screw that is located between the fuel distributor and the sensor plate. Use a long hex key or the special mixture adjustment tool to turn the screw.

The screw is indexed so that it should click when you rotate it. Turn it clockwise to richen up the mixture, or counterclockwise to lean it out. The mixture should only be adjusted when the car is hooked up to a carbon monoxide meter. Make sure that you rev the engine for a few seconds before you take a reading from the meter, and that you don't leave the tool in the adjustment screw—the screw itself must be free to move up and down without any weight on it.

The idle speed is adjusted by allowing more air to by-pass the closed throttle. Using a large flathead screwdriver, simply rotate the screw clockwise to reduce the idle, and counter clockwise to increase it. The idle should be set to be about 950 rpm.

3 The intake mani-
fold hoses
(shown by the
arrow) are common
sources for vacuum leaks.
If the carb cleaner spray
test indicates that there is
indeed a vacuum leak
near the hoses, then they
should be replaced.
Unfortunately, this
requires the removal of
the fuel injection system
from the top of the
motor—a task that is not
easy, considering the tight
clearances in the engine
compartment. Also a
source of vacuum leaks
are the injector seals and
the plastic inserts that fit
into the base of the intake manifolds. Check and replace these if you find evi-
dence of vacuum leaks near the base of the manifolds.

2 The mixture is adjusted by placing the adjustment tool between
the fuel distributor and the large rubber boot (shown by the
arrow). The screw is indexed so that you can feel distinct "clicks"
as you rotate it. Turn it clockwise to richen up the mixture, and counterclockwise to lean it out. Make sure that you have the exhaust gases
checked while you are performing the adjustment so that you can verify
that you are in the proper operating range.

Troubleshooting

So what can go wrong on with the CIS? Plenty. Although the CIS has a reputation for reliability, it is also known for having a few characteristic problems. Warm- and cold-start problems are common, as well as back-firing and poor performance at start-up. On the early 911s, the CIS didn't even operate properly until the car was warmed up. A hand throttle was a standard part of the car to facilitate easier starting and warm-up. On the later-model CIS cars, the addition of the auxiliary air valve eliminated the need for the hand throttle.

One of the most common problems for the older CIS cars is the existence of vacuum leaks. The entire system works almost entirely on vacuum. Any vacuum leaks will cause problems in regulating the mixture, and may also result in an uneven idle. To check for vacuum leaks, spray some carb cleaner or starting fluid around the hoses and injectors of the fuel injection system. If the engine idle increases, then you probably have a vacuum leak that needs to be tracked down. Make sure that you have a fire extinguisher handy—if there is arcing in the spark plug wires, you may ignite the carburetor cleaner.

Another common problem is the warm-up regulator (WUR), or control pressure regulator. Contrary to popular belief, the WUR regulates the system's fuel pressure at all times. Cars that have difficulty adjusting the mixture may be suffering from a defective WUR. This failure may also contribute to starting problems.

Since the CIS depends upon correct fuel pressure for proper operation, the fuel pump and fuel accumulator must be in working order. Using a CIS fuel pressure tester, verify the proper operation of the fuel pump by measuring the pressure when the ignition is turned on. The pressure measurements need to be taken at specific times, and at varying engine temperatures. For more details on these specifications, see the *Porsche Technical Specification Book* for your year 911. Also make sure that your fuel accumulator (Project 5) and the pressure check valve in the fuel pump are operating properly.

Sometimes the idle on the CIS cars will oscillate up and down. An incorrectly set mixture will often cause this to occur. Recheck the mixture with an exhaust gas analyzer to make sure you are in the proper operating range.

Hot-start problems are common with CIS systems and may be caused by a faulty fuel accumulator (see Project 5) or a faulty fuel pressure check valve in the fuel pump (see Project 33). Cold-start problems can often be attributed to the thermo-time switch or the warm-up regulator.

For more information than you will probably ever need on the CIS, take a look at the book *Bosch Fuel Injection & Engine Management* by Charles O. Probst. It provides an excellent guide for understanding the physics behind the CIS, and also includes an invaluable troubleshooting section.

FUEL SYSTEMS

PROJECT 32 • POP-OFF VALVE INSTALLATION

 Time: 4 hours

 Tools: 2-inch hole saw, vacuum cleaner, electric drill

 Talent:

 Applicable Years: 1973-1983

 Tab: $40

 Tinware: none

 Tip: Use the template supplied with your kit to guide your placement of the pop-off valve..

PERFORMANCE GAIN: Protection of your air box from explosive backfires

COMPLEMENTARY MODIFICATION: Air filter replacement

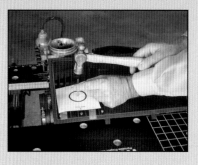

1 Position the template on the air box and punch a guiding hole with a nail and hammer. Be careful not to tap too hard, as you don't want to crack your air box. The pictures that are shown in this project are of an air box that was removed from the engine for clarity in the photos. It is not necessary, nor is it recommended, to remove the air box for this procedure.

2 Drill a pilot hole using a small drill, then switch to the hole saw. Make sure that you hold the drill absolutely vertical when you are drilling the hole. Access may be a little tight if you are drilling from inside the engine compartment. A right angle drill is useful for this procedure.

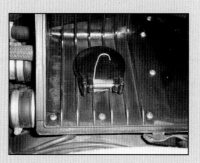

3 Test fit the pop-off valve prior to mixing up the epoxy. Make sure that you place epoxy around the entire circumference of the pop-off valve—you don't want any air leaking through the hole.

During 1973, Porsche introduced a new type of fuel injection for the 911T. The Continuous Injection System (CIS) is vacuum-controlled and depends on tight seals to accurately meter and distribute fuel to the cylinders. If the CIS has a vacuum leak, problems with steady idling and other general performance issues will result. Check out Project 31 for more information on troubleshooting CIS systems.

One problem with having a tightly sealed vacuum system like CIS is that excess air pushed back into it from a backfire has almost nowhere to escape. CIS cars often backfire, especially the early ones when started cold. A large backfire can send enough compressed air through the intake manifold to explode the black plastic CIS air box, located in the engine compartment. Replacement air boxes from Porsche are hundreds of dollars, and good used ones can be hard to find. Even if the force doesn't destroy the air box, the occasional backfire can blow apart or weaken seals and increases the likelihood of a vacuum leak.

The pop-off valve installation procedure is simple—just drill a hole in the bottom of the air box and epoxy the valve in place. First, remove the air filter housing to provide access to the inside of the air box.

Using the template that comes with the pop-off valve kit, map where you want to drill the hole. I would drill a small pilot hole before using the hole saw. The hole must be drilled at exactly a right angle to the floor of the air box; the pilot hole is a big help in achieving the proper alignment. The ridges on the air box floor may cause difficulty when drilling. Going slowly, work your way down with the drill until the hole is complete. If the clearance is too tight, a right-angled drill will help.

After drilling the hole, vacuum out any plastic chips left in the air box (it's okay to miss a few). Fit the pop-off valve in the hole, filing the edges if necessary, so that it fits flush with the ribs in the box's bottom.

Before you epoxy the valve in place, clean both edges of the hole and the valve with some alcohol to remove any oil or gas residue. Apply the mixed epoxy liberally to the valve and lightly around the edges of the hole. Install the valve in the box, rotating it slightly to ensure that the epoxy is spread on all surfaces. It's important to create an airtight connection here. Install the valve with the hinge parallel and closest to the rear of the car. Let the epoxy dry at least 24 hours before starting the engine. Now your CIS should be well-protected from backfires.

PROJECT 33 • FUEL PUMP REPLACEMENT

Time: 3 hours

Tools: Socket set

Talent:

Applicable Years: All

Tab: $250

Tinware: Fuel pump and new fuel lines

Tip: Try to empty as much of the tank out as possible before you begin

PERFORMANCE GAIN: Better running fuel injection, quieter pump, fewer starting problems

COMPLEMENTARY MODIFICATION: Replace fuel lines

Some common fuel injection problems can be traced back to a faulty or nonoperational fuel pump. If your pump is noisy and loud, or the fuel pressure in the engine compartment is below what is needed for proper fuel injection operation, it's probably time to replace it.

The 911 fuel pump is a not as simple a device as one might think. The fuel actually runs through the pump and acts as a coolant and lubricant for the entire assembly. Therefore, if you let your car run out of gas, make sure that you turn off the pump immediately, or you might damage the internal components of the pump. Not much is worse than a broken or faulty pump leaving you stranded on the side of the road.

Typical fuel pump problems can sometimes be headed off in advance. If the pump is noisy, and making loud clicking noises, chances are that the bearings inside are worn and should be replaced. If the pump continues to make noise even after the

ignition is shut off, internal check-valves in the pump may be showing signs of failure. The pump could seize up, or the pressure to the fuel injection system could drop. Either way, the car will not be performing at its peak. Another symptom of failure is the pump getting stuck, and then finally kicking in after turning the ignition on and off a couple of times. This could be a clear sign that you are living on borrowed time, and that you should replace the pump immediately. Check the electrical connections to the pump before you replace it to make sure that it's not an electrical problem.

Before removing and replacing the fuel pump, try to get as much fuel out of the tank as possible. Be careful to turn the ignition off immediately if you let the car run dry, as this can burn out your fuel pump. Of course, if you are replacing it anyway, it doesn't really matter. Drive the car around until the fuel light goes on. The lower the fuel in the tank, the lower the pressure will be on the hoses, and you will have a greater chance of blocking the fuel intake hose before you disconnect it. Make sure that you also perform the replacement procedure in a well-ventilated area that is free from any sources of ignition (gas/water heater, electrical cord, or lamp). If you need additional light, use a cool fluorescent lamp and keep it far away from the pump. Fuel will spill out when you replace the pump and you don't want it getting anywhere near the lamp. Also make sure that you wear gloves, as gasoline and its components are known carcinogens that can easily be absorbed through the skin. Before you start working on the pump, disconnect the battery ground. You would hate to have the pump accidentally turn on when you are working on it. It's also a wise idea to have a fire extinguisher handy.

Another method of draining the tank is to attach a hose to the fuel line in the engine compartment. To do this, however, you need a special fitting that attaches to either the fuel pump or fuel accumulator. Attach the fitting to the bottom of the fuel pump or the bottom of the fuel accumulator and run the line into the gas tank of another car. Then turn the ignition on, and the fuel should be pumped directly into the other car's tank.

The belly pan located underneath the car covers and protects the fuel pump. Jack up the front of the car (see Project 1), remove this pan (see Project 59), and you should clearly see the pump. On some

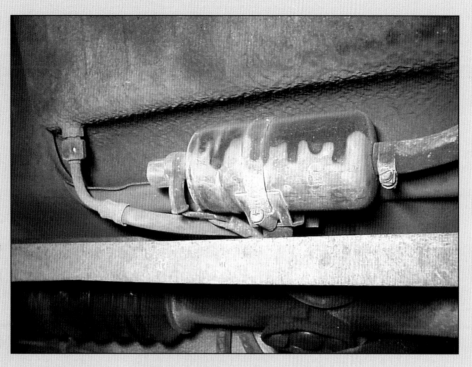

1 The fuel pump is located under the front belly pan. Access to the pump and its lines are obtained by removing this pan. Make sure that you work on the pump only in a well-ventilated area, and that you have as much of the fuel removed from the tank as possible. Keep all sources of ignition away from the pump while you are working on it. Be sure to wear gloves and safety glasses while you work with the fuel pump. Gasoline is notoriously unpredicatble, and you might find that it leaks out more than you expect. Think ahead, imagine the worst thing that could happen, and plan for it. Always have a fire extinguisher handy.

of the very early 911s, a mechanical pump similar to the one on the 356 and the 912 was used instead of the electric pump. This pump was located in the engine compartment and ran off of an attachment that connected it to the valve train. We won't cover this fuel pump in this project since not very many 911s used them.

Once you have access to the fuel pump, you'll need to clamp the lines. There are a few methods of doing this, but the easiest way seems to be by placing a pair of Vise-Grips on the line and clamping down. Tom Woodford of Factory Tour suggests that you cover the tips of the Vise-Grips as well with some duct tape so that the ridges of the tool don't damage the line. Also, make sure that you take a close look at the line itself to see if there is any damage or cracking in it. If there is, you should drain the tank fully, and replace the line. It's also a wise idea to clamp more than one Vise-Grips tool on the line to make sure that it is blocked as much as possible. Again, draining the tank to the lowest possible level will reduce the amount of fuel pressure in the line, and will make the Vise-Grips approach of clamping the line most effective.

Once you are confident that the lines are appropriately blocked, loosen and disconnect the hoses from each end of the pump. They should only be clamped on with small hose clamps. Again, inspect the fuel lines for cracks or other deterioration. Now, disconnect the electrical connections from the pump. Finally, loosen and remove the large clamp that holds the pump to the chassis. The pump should be easy to remove from the car at this point.

The installation of the new pump is straightforward, and basically the reverse of the removal procedure. Make sure that the rubber insulators completely cover the electrical connections to the pump. If they are cracked or worn, they should be replaced. When you have finished replacing the pump and reattached and clamped the hoses, slowly release the Vise-Grips and check the lines for leaks. Inspect the area where the Vise-Grips were clamped to make sure that no damage occurred to the lines.

Take the car out for a drive before you reinstall the belly pan. Fill the tank up with gas, and check again for leaks under the tank. When you are confident that the hoses are tight, then reinstall the belly pan, and you're done.

FUEL SYSTEMS

PROJECT 34 • OXYGEN SENSOR TROUBLESHOOTING AND REPLACEMENT

 Time: 1/2 hour

 Tools: Wrench

 Talent: 🔧

 Applicable Years: 1980-

 Tab: $50-$350

 Tinware: New oxygen sensor

 Tip: The grommet that goes in the engine sheet metal comes attached to new OEM sensors

! PERFORMANCE GAIN: Better air/fuel mixture and better engine performance

COMPLEMENTARY MODIFICATION: Catalytic converter replacement

1 The oxygen sensor (O_2 Sensor) is attached to the top of the catalytic converter. The sensor measures the amount of oxygen in the exhaust prior to the catalytic converter acting on the exhaust. The sensor is one of the key elements in a "closed-loop" feedback system that regulates the amount of fuel injected into the engine. The test port, located directly below, allows the measurement of exhaust gases to be made before they enter the converter. The catalytic converter pictured is an aftermarket unit, and not an original Porsche catalytic converter.

The oxygen sensor is one of the most important elements of the modern fuel injection systems. A finely tuned fuel injection system with an oxygen sensor can maintain an air/fuel ratio within a close tolerance of .02 percent. Keeping the engine at the stoichiometric level (14.6:1 air/fuel ratio) helps the engine generate the most power with the least amount of emissions.

The oxygen sensor is located in the exhaust system of the engine, and senses the oxygen content of the exhaust gases. The amount of oxygen in the exhaust varies according to the air/fuel ratio of the fuel injection system. The oxygen sensor produces a small voltage signal that is interpreted by the electronic control unit (ECU) of the fuel injection system. The ECU makes constant adjustments in fuel delivery according to the signal generated by the oxygen sensor in order to maintain the optimum air/fuel ratio.

There are a few signs that your oxygen sensor may be failing. In general, it is difficult to diagnose problems with the sensor, unless all of the other compo-

nents in the fuel injection system have been checked and determined to be operating correctly. Some of the symptoms of a failed oxygen sensor system are:

- Irregular idle during warm-up
- Irregular idle with warm engine
- Engine will not accelerate and backfires
- Poor engine performance
- Fuel consumption is high
- Driving performance is weak
- CO concentration at idle is too high or too low

In general, if the oxygen sensor is not working, the car will be running very poorly, and will also be outputting a lot of harmful emissions. If you disconnect the oxygen sensor and ground it to the chassis, the ECU will think that the car is running really lean, and will try to richen the mixture. At the other extreme, if you disconnect the oxygen sensor, and replace it with a small AA battery that supplies 1.5 volts, the ECU will think that the car is running really rich and attempt to adjust the mixture to be leaner.

Needless to say, troubleshooting the complete fuel injection system is beyond this project's scope. If you think that the oxygen sensor may be causing some of your fuel injection problems, it should be replaced. In general, I recommend that you do this every 30,000 miles. The oxygen sensor is located on the left side of the car, right before the catalytic converter. Removing the rear left wheel will make access much easier. The sensor is simply unscrewed from the converter. If there is a lot of rust in this area, it may be advisable to spray the area with some lubricant and let it sit overnight prior to attempting to remove the sensor. When you install the new oxygen sensor, it is a wise idea to place some antiseize compound on the threads so that they will not rust and seize up. It's also important to note that the rubber grommet that is attached to the wire on the oxygen sensor usually comes preinstalled with each new original equipment sensor.

100

FUEL SYSTEMS

PROJECT 35 • TUNING THE MOTRONIC ENGINE MANAGEMENT SYSTEM

 Time: –

 Tools: –

 Talent: –

 Applicable Years: 1984-89

 Tab: –

 Tinware: –

 Tip: The Motronic system should be mostly maintenance free.

 PERFORMANCE GAIN: Better-running engine

COMPLEMENTARY MODIFICATION: Add a performance chip

In 1984, Porsche replaced the 10-year-old Continuous Injection System, or CIS, with a new type of computer-controlled fuel injection from Bosch AG. This new type of injection system, called Motronic, is technologically leaps and bounds above the CIS system in terms of performance and emissions control.

The CIS system sprays fuel into all the manifolds at the same time, relying on the opening and closing of the cylinder valves to regulate the amount of fuel that enters the combustion cylinder. While very effective at delivering fuel, the CIS system is not the most efficient. When the valve to the cylinder head is closed, it still injects fuel onto the closed valve. This extra fuel has a tendency to cause multiple backfires, especially when the engine is cold. Even properly tuned CIS systems are infamous for their backfires that can cause damage to the plastic CIS airbox (see Project 32).

Overview

The Motronic system that was implemented on the 1984 911 Carrera is what is commonly called a pulsed injection system. The fuel injection system only sprays fuel into the intake manifold when it is required in the combustion cycle. In this manner, the system can more accurately control the fuel levels and fuel delivery, and help to better maintain the ideal stoichiometric air/fuel ratio of 14.6.

The Motronic system takes fuel injection one step further, and incorporates an engine management system that also controls the ignition system. The marriage of ignition and fuel injection is a natural fit, because they are completely reliant on each other for proper engine operation. The Motronic system not only times and meters the fuel, but it also decides when to fire the spark to make combustion happen.

The central Motronic computer controls the ignition and fuel injection system. The computer takes input from a variety of sensors placed about the engine. An engine rpm sensor indicates how fast the engine is running. An airflow sensor measures the amount of air that is being drawn into the engine, and thus the amount of load on the engine. An oxygen sensor measures the exhaust gases exiting the engine in order to correctly meter the mixture. Timing sensors and cylinder head sensors also provide additional information for the computer.

The computer itself is able to take all the input from the sensors, and calculate the best ignition timing and fuel delivery to create the most horsepower with the least amount of emissions. The computer has a Read-Only-Memory (ROM) computer chip inside that contains what is known as a data map based on engine dynamometer and emissions tests performed at the factory. At any split second, the computer can read in all the input from the engine, compare it to the map in the ROM chip, and decide how much fuel to deliver and when to fire the ignition.

The advantages of such a system are numerous. Gone are the mechanically complex methods of advancing the timing with counterweights and vacuum advance units. Points inside the distributor are a thing of the past as well. Instead, the engine relies on the computer to control all fuel- and ignition-related decisions. In milliseconds, the computer can gather input data, access the ROM chip, and interpolate the best settings for the engine.

Storing all the computer data on a ROM chip also allows for the chip to be swapped out for different applications. Certain aftermarket manufacturers sell chips for the 911 Motronic system that are not as conservative as the factory chips. They promise gains of about 10–15 percent more horsepower at various rpm. While some of these chips may not be legal in all 50 states, they do seem to work. Check with your local auto repair shop to see which chips are legal in your area.

Tuning and Adjustment

Because the Motronic system is so integrated within its computer, it doesn't need many adjustments. It should basically run by itself. The only major adjustments it might need are the CO level and the idle adjustment. The CO level should only be adjusted by a qualified mechanic equipped with a CO meter. The CO adjustment is made by turning a small screw located in the bottom rear left-hand corner of the airflow meter. This screw is normally covered by a plug that you'll need to remove.

The other common adjustment is of the idle speed. While the computer should regulate the system on its own, you might need to adjust the speed manually. On the left side of the engine compartment, between the coil and the rear regulator plate, there is a small test port with three small sockets. To adjust the idle, first disable the idle volumetric control. Bridge a wire from terminals B and C. Then, using a small nut driver, adjust the bypass screw on the throttle housing until the car reaches the desired idle speed.

Troubleshooting

In general, the Motronic system is very reliable. Problems arise when the sensors to the system are not functioning properly. In general, the debugging of the Motronic system is not for the home mechanic, as the system requires a handful of specialty tools and knowledge that are not easily acquired. Most problems associated with the Motronic system are electrical in nature, and involve complex testing of these electrical devices, or the less complex method of simply replacing parts until the problem is fixed.

Sometimes the relay for the system fails. This relay is actually two relays in one: one for the Digital Motor Electronics (DME) system, and the other for the fuel pump. If you find that the system is acting erratically, or the fuel pump is not getting power, try replacing this relay. The relay is located next to the engine control module (ECM) underneath the driver's seat.

For a more complete understanding of the Motronic system, take a look at the book *Bosch Fuel Injection & Engine Management* by Charles O. Probst. It provides an excellent overview into the theory, practice and implementation of the Motronic system.

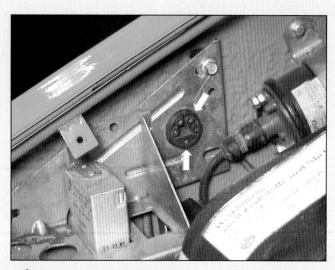

1 To properly adjust the idle on the Motronic system, you need to disable the idle volumetric control. The two white arrows in the photo show the two jumper plugs that must be connected to disable the control system prior to adjustment. This plug is located on the left side of the engine compartment.

2 In this photo, the yellow arrow indicates the airflow bypass screw, which regulates the idle for the engine. The green arrow points to the location of the mixture adjustment screw, which is located under a protective cap. This cap must first be removed prior to adjusting the mixture. Make sure that you have a CO meter on hand to properly adjust the mixture.

SECTION FOUR
TRANSAXLE

The transmission, drive axles, and pedals and shifter have been combined into one section because they are interrelated. The drivetrain system of the 911 is unique in that it is mounted toward the rear of the car, and is a transaxle that incorporates the differential within the transmission. While the rear-engine design of the car allows for the use of the transaxle design to save space and weight, it can impede ease of shifting. The projects in this section explain and guide you through the pitfalls and problems associated with the 911 rear transaxle design.

TRANSAXLE

PROJECT 36 • REPLACING TRANSMISSION FLUID

Time: 1/2 hour

Tools: 17-millimeter Hex Key (901,915), 19-millimeter socket (G50)

Talent:

Applicable Years: All

Tab: $15-$50

Tinware: Transmission fluid

Tip: Make sure that you have a drip pan and plenty of paper towels.

PERFORMANCE GAIN: Longer life for your transmission

COMPLEMENTARY MODIFICATION: Use Swepco transmission fluid for better shifting

The 911 differential and the transmission both share the same lubricating fluid. It's very important to make sure that the fluid in your transmission is at the proper level, or your transmission will experience significant wear. The synchro rings and sliders (see Project 38) all depend on a slick surface in order to match speeds when shifting. If your transmission is low on oil, the wear on these components will accelerate significantly. In addition, shifting the car will be more difficult. One of the first things that you should check on a 911 that is having problems shifting is the level of the transmission oil. Keeping the differential and all the associated gears well lubricated should also help increase your fuel mileage.

The transmission oil also helps to keep temperatures down inside your transmission. The engine is one of the primary sources of heat for the transmission, as it conducts and radiates through and around the points where the engine and transmission are mounted. The transmission also creates heat itself as the gears and synchros turn within its case. Keeping the transmission fluid at its proper level helps to miti-

gate heat problems. Having a large reservoir of oil to spread the heat throughout the transmission helps to keep temperatures down. On some of the higher-performance Porsche transmissions, there is even an external transmission cooler that operates similarly to the engine cooler.

The transmission fluid should be changed every 30,000 miles or about once every two years. Check your owner's manual for more details on the scheduled requirement for your year 911. This number is a rough estimate, and may vary depending upon your use of your 911 (track vs. street). There are many moving parts in the transmission, and they have a tendency to drop small microscopic metal particles into the oil. Specifically, the synchro rings wear down slowly over time, each time you shift. While the transmission bearings are not as sensitive as the engine bearings, they can still exhibit wear from these particles in the oil.

The 901 transmission has two plugs for filling and emptying the transmission oil, located on the side of the case. The 901 transmission was used on 911s from 1965 through 1971. The 901 transmission requires a 17-millimeter hex key to remove the M25x1.5 plug. On the 915 transmission, used on 911s from 1972 through 1986, the plug is the same, but located on the bottom of the transmission instead of the side. With the G50 transmission, used on 911s from 1987 on, the locations of the plugs were similar to those on the 915, but the plug changed to a 10-millimeter hex-key plug.

If you are simply checking the level of oil in your transmission, start by removing the top filler plug on the side of the transmission. This is the plug you remove to add fluid. When you have the plug removed, take your finger, and stick it inside the hole, point it toward the ground, and see if you can feel any fluid in there. Make sure you do this when the car is cold, and parked on level ground. If you can feel the fluid level with your finger, your fluid level is about right, or perhaps will need only a little topping off.

If you cannot feel the fluid level, you will need to add transmission oil to the case. If you are planning to change the oil, remove the small plug on the bottom of the transmission case (on the side for the 901 transmissions). It's a wise idea to try to empty the transmission oil when the car is warm, as this will make the oil flow out easier. Make sure that you have a drain pan capable of handling at least five quarts of transmission oil. Check the fluid in the pan for any unusual metal pieces or grit in the oil.

While the fluid is emptying out, you can use this time to clean out the drain plugs. The bottom drain

1 Shown here are the filler and drain plug for the 915 transmission used on the 911 from 1972 through 1986. The drain plugs on the other transmission models are similar as well. You need a 17-millimeter hex key to remove the plug from the transmission. The bottom plug is magnetic, while the top plug was originally not. A worthy upgrade is to replace your top plug with one of the lower magnetic ones.

plug should have an integrated magnet in it that traps metal debris. Using a cotton swab or a paper towel, carefully clean out all of the black debris and particles that may have found their way in there.

While the plug on the bottom is magnetic, the top plug that shipped originally from the factory isn't. A simple upgrade is to install one of the bottom magnetic plugs into the top filler plug location. The added magnet can't hurt the transmission, and may help to remove some additional particles.

Replace the bottom plug on the transmission, but don't overtighten it (24 N-m or 17.6 fl-lb maximum). These plugs do not have a tendency to leak (transmission oil is thicker than engine oil). If it does leak later on, you can always tighten it a little more. Now, add transmission oil to the case. The best method of doing this is with a hand-operated oil pump. These are available from most auto parts stores and attach to the top of the plastic transmission oil bottle. They work very similar to the liquid soap dispensers you find in most bathrooms. Pump the transmission case full of fluid until it just starts to run out the filler hole. Replace the filler plug and clean up the few drips that might have run out of the hole. Tighten down the filler plug in a similar manner to the drain plug.

In many cases, generic transmission gear oil will suffice perfectly. However, for those 911 owners wishing to have the best of everything for their car, there is Swepco 201 Multi-Purpose Gear Lube. This gear oil is excellent for transmissions, and many Porsche owners swear by it. The current rumor is that

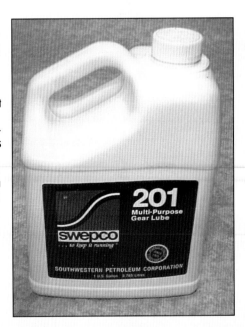

2 The gold standard for transmission oil is Swepco 201. Used by racers and Porsche owners worldwide, many would swear that it gives new life to an old, worn-out transmission. Customers' stories from the parts supply world seem to indicate that using Swepco on a transmission with worn synchro rings can prolong its life and fend off that costly transmission rebuild.

adding Swepco 201 will prolong the life of many transmissions and also help to postpone a costly rebuild. While this can hardly be proven, a lot of owners will agree that using Swepco 201 creates a difference that you can feel while shifting. For the G50 transmission (1987 and later), I recommend using a synthetic blend that is more suited to its Borg-Warner synchro design.

TRANSAXLE

PROJECT 37 • SHIFTING IMPROVEMENTS

 Time: 3 hours

 Tools: Socket set, Hex Keys

 Talent:

 Applicable Years: All

 Tab: $35-$85

 Tinware: Shift coupler or coupler bushings, shift rod bushing, shifter bushing

 Tip: Install all the bushings using a little lithium grease.

⚠ PERFORMANCE GAIN: Better, more precise shifting

COMPLEMENTARY MODIFICATION: Install the factory short shift kit

Porsches have never really been known for their supreme shifting abilities. Very often on the older 911s, the shifting ability deteriorates as the years go by. While many people blame their transmissions and prepare for a full rebuild, their worries may be needless. In many cases, the shift bushings have simply worn out and need to be replaced. Worn bushings can result in sloppy shifting, misplaced shifts, and grinding when engaging gears. Most people are amazed at the improvement that occurs when they replace their bushings. A mere $45 spent on new bushings is a heck of a lot cheaper than a $1,500 transmission rebuild.

The first step in replacing the bushings is to gain access to the shifter. On the later 911s, the center console surrounds the shifter, and needs to be removed. Three screws secure the console to the chassis floor. The front access panel of the console hides the two screws located in the front of the car. The rear screw is usually hidden under the carpet, and requires some fishing around to locate.

Once you have the center console removed, you should be able to pull away the carpet and gain access to the shifter. Be careful not to tear your carpet when

1 You can gain access to the shifter by removing the center console. The console is held in place by three screws that mount it to the floor of the chassis. In order to access the two screws in the front, remove the front-most part of the console. The third screw may be difficult to locate, as the carpeting usually covers it.

2 Pull the carpeting back to reveal the shifter, which is mounted to the chassis floor. Unbolt the shifter and remove it from the floor. The bottom of the shifter contains the shifter bushing, which wraps around the shifter rod. Remove and replace this bushing, using a little lithium grease spread inside the bushing. Make sure that the bushing is on tight; air tends to get trapped inside the ball cup, and can unexpectedly pop the bushing off of the end of the shifter.

3 Removing the access panel behind the front seats reveals the shift rod coupler. The two bushings in the coupler often wear with use, as sometimes does the small cone screw that holds the coupler in place.

pulling it back. The original carpet was glued to the floor, and it has a tendency to weaken with age.

The shifter is bolted down to the floor with hex socket cap screws. Simply place the car into first gear, unbolt the shifter from the floor, and remove it from the chassis. Placing the transmission in gear prior to removing the shifter helps to keep the transmission selector rod from moving when disconnecting the shift rod coupler later on. The shifter bushing is a ball cup bushing, and is located at the base of the shifter handle. Remove the old one and pop on the new one. Make sure that you put some lithium grease in the new bushing before you install it.

Now, move behind the front seats and remove the small access panel that is located on the center tunnel. Underneath, you will find the shift coupler that connects the shift rod to the transmission selector rod. Using a permanent marker, mark the location of the coupler with respect to the shift rod—you will need to line it up again later. Make sure that you mark the rotational position of the coupler, as well as its location along the length of the shift rod. Remove the coupler by loosening up the hex key cone screw, and the clamp on the shift rod.

The two bushings that are located within the shift coupler often wear with age. The center pin of the coupler needs to be pressed out and removed in order to fit the new bushings. Installation of the new bushings is not an easy job, and is perhaps best left to a machine shop with a heavy-duty press. It's quite easy to damage the aluminum coupler if you don't have the proper tools. An alternative to replacing the bushings is the replacement of the entire coupler. For only a few dollars more, you can replace the coupler with a brand-new one, and forget about the hassle of pressing out the center pin.

With the shift coupler disconnected, the shift rod bushing can be removed. This bushing is located behind the shifter in the center tunnel. It's held in place by a bracket that mounts to the top of the center tunnel. To remove this bracket, unbolt it from the top of the tunnel. Then disconnect the ball cup bushing adapter that is mounted to the end of the shift rod. It may require some maneuvering in order to get the adapter off and the bracket out. Install the new bushing into the mounting bracket, and then replace it in the center tunnel.

On the 1973 and earlier cars, the shifter has a concave ring-shaped bushing that tends to wear out over the years. In addition, the lockout springs within the shifter assembly tend to become weak with age. When you have the shifter out of the car, it's a wise idea to disassemble it and replace these parts. For all year cars, it's a wise idea to clean and grease the shifter while you have access to it. If you want to install a short shift kit (Project 39), this would be an excellent time to do it.

When reinstalling the entire shifting system, make sure that you line up the coupler in the same place that you marked previously. If you weren't happy with the alignment of the previous shifter and you often "nicked" gears when shifting, you might want to readjust your shifter.

The procedure for adjusting the shifter is simple. Reattach the shift coupler to the transmission, but keep the clamped end of the shifter rod very loose. With the transmission in first gear, place the shifter into the upper left-hand corner of the shift pattern. Now, clamp down on the shift coupler. The shift assembly should be properly adjusted in this position, and the shifter should cleanly lock into all gears,

4 New bushings installed in the coupler make a world of difference when shifting your 911. These bushings cost about $20 for a pair, and a new coupler itself is only about $50. Be careful when reinstalling the coupler. If the screw hole in the coupler is not perfectly lined up with the hole in the shift rod, you can cross-thread the coupler when tightening the cone screw. If this happens, the coupler is destroyed, and needs to be replaced.

5 The shift rod bushing supports the shift rod in the tunnel. To replace this bushing, remove the bracket that holds it in place. It is held on by two screws that fit through the top of the center tunnel.

6 The new bushing snaps into place inside the bracket. Be sure to spread some lithium grease on the shift rod before you place it through the bushing.

including reverse. However, depending upon transmissions, chassis, and linkages, this doesn't always work on the first try. It may be necessary to loosen up the coupler clamp again, and play with the final adjustment of the shifter.

When you have all the bushings replaced, and the shifter adjusted, the car should show a remarkable improvement. If you are still having problems with shifting and grinding, you might want to check your clutch adjustment (Project 11), or your motor and transmission mounts (Project 27), or the fluid level in your transmission (Project 36). Another upgrade that is a good complement to this project is the addition of the Porsche factory short shift kit for the 915 transmission (see Project 39).

TRANSAXLE

PROJECT 38 • REBUILDING FIRST GEAR ON THE 901 TRANSMISSION

 Time: 5 hours

 Tools: Impact wrench, 30-millimeter deep socket, synchro removal tool, snap-ring pliers

 Talent:

 Applicable Years: 1965-1971

 Tab: $50-$300

 Tinware: Synchro ring, first gear dogteeth, first/reverse slider (if worn), transmission end-cover gasket

 Tip: Having the right tools is a requirement for this job.

 PERFORMANCE GAIN: No more grinding into first gear

COMPLEMENTARY MODIFICATION: Add Swepco fluid to the transmission, and replace the shift bushings.

One of the most frustrating elements of owning a classic Porsche is the existence of a worn-out transmission. Porsche transmissions in particular have not been known for their excellence in shifting ability. Combine this with the fact that there really isn't too much information available on repairing them, and you have a recipe for poorly maintained transmissions. Adding to the problem is the fact that internal transmission parts and repair tools can be some of the most expensive parts to purchase.

Well, a little bit of relief is available. For early 911/912 owners (1965–1971), there is a relatively easy fix to repair first gear on the five-speed 901 transmission. The 901 is unique, in that the gears for first and reverse are located at the rear of the transmission (the part that faces the front of the car) and are easily accessed without tearing apart the transmission. That's the good news. The bad news is that you need to remove the engine from the car in order to get the transmission out. But

1 This is what is visible when the rear cover is removed. The first-gear shift fork (manufactured out of brass) is wrapped around the first/reverse slider. Before you play around with the shifter (it's good to familiarize yourself with how it works), make sure that you place a nut and spacer on one of the end cover studs (shown by the arrow). This will prevent the intermediate plate from separating from the transmission housing.

2 After removing the shift fork and slider, you will need an impact wrench to get the center stretch bolt off of the assembly. Removing the bolt without the help of an impact wrench is nearly impossible, since the shaft turns freely.

3 Removing of the snap ring reveals the thrust block, the anchor block, and the brake band. It is important to remember that first gear uses only one brake band, while all the others use two. Surrounding the whole assembly is the synchro ring (shown by the green arrow). It is important to reassemble the unit exactly as shown here. The thrust block (yellow arrow), brake band (tan arrow), and anchor block (red arrow) must be assembled in their proper order and positions in order for first gear to function properly.

once you have access to it, repairing that nasty grind into first gear is relatively simple.

Before you decide that your first gear is trashed, you should check a few other factors that might be contributing to grinding. Make sure that your motor and transmission mounts are firm and not cracked (Project 27). Also make sure that your clutch is adjusted properly (Project 11). Check that your transmission shift linkage bushings are in good condition, and that your shift linkage is properly adjusted (Project 37). If all of these check out in good condition, then it's probably wise to take a closer look at the transmission itself.

4 The all-important synchro hub removal tool is shown here. I don't recommend attempting this job without access to this tool. Buy it or rent it—the amount of time you will save will be tremendous. Without it, you will have to cut off the dog teeth synchro hub, a tedious job that could damage your first gear. The tool wraps itself around a groove in the synchro hub (dog teeth), which then allows you to knock out the gear from the tool using the large center punch. A couple of good smacks with a hammer will affirm that this really can't be done without the use of this tool. If you have a press available, the procedure is made a little bit easier.

5 Old and new synchro hubs side by side offer up a good reason why first gear on this transmission didn't work too well. The normally pointy gear teeth are completely worn down and rounded off at the edges. Not only does this cause additional grinding, but it also makes it more difficult to shift into first gear when the teeth finally synchronize. Having a transmission that is difficult to place into first is likely to have worn dog teeth like these on the synchro hub.

The first step, obviously, is to remove the engine and transmission from the car. For more information on this particular task, see Project 7. Once you have the engine and transmission separated, it's a wise idea to place the transmission on an engine stand. It's easier to keep it steady, and you won't find yourself bending over too much.

An important step to take before you start working on the transmission is to drain all the transmission fluid out of it. If you forget this all-important step, you will be reminded of it when you start to take it apart, and transmission fluid empties out all over your garage floor.

Removing the rear cover is as simple as unbolting the nuts holding it on. Be careful when you remove the rear cover, because the reverse gear and bearings are attached to a shaft that is pressed into the cover, and they might fall out. After the rear cover is off, take one of the nuts, and reattach it to one of the studs with a spacer between the nut and the intermediate plate. This will prevent the intermediate plate (the approximately 1.5-inch-thick plate that is wedged in between the case and the end cover) from separating from the case. When you are playing with the gears on the transmission, this plate will try to separate from the case.

Once you have the rear exposed, remove the brass shift fork and the first/reverse slider. This fork is simply bolted onto the shift rod for first/reverse gear. Now exposed, the first gear synchro hub assembly requires the use of an impact wrench for removal. There really is no other way to remove the expansion bolt, because there is no practical means of keeping the transmission pinion shaft from turning. Use a 30-millimeter deep socket to remove the bolt using the impact wrench.

The disassembly of the synchro hub starts with the removal of the large snap ring that holds on the synchro ring. Use a pair of snap-ring pliers to remove the ring from the assembly. It's a wise idea to wear safety glasses during this step. Carefully remove the synchro ring, the anchor block, the thrust block, and the brake band, keeping in mind their original positions so that you can reassemble them easily later on.

The dog teeth, or synchro-hub, should be inspected at this point. If the teeth are badly worn, the hub needs to be replaced. Chances are if the transmission was grinding, then the synchro hub is probably worn beyond recognition. When the synchro ring wears out, it allows the internal teeth inside the transmission to contact each other when they are not turning at the same speed. This results in that awful grinding noise when changing gears. The grinding of the gears is not really what you hear, but it is the grinding of the synchro hub and the slider that create this horrible noise.

6 The other half of the equation is the slider. This is what the dog teeth (synchro hub) mate to when they are engaged in gear. While usually showing less wear than the synchro hub, the slider has a tendency to wear out more quickly when the synchros have been worn beyond their useful life. Shown here is a slider with semirounded

points similar to the worn dog teeth. Also shown is a worn groove in the middle (indicated by the arrow) that occurs from the synchro ring wearing on the slider. New sliders have a slight groove that locks in the synchro ring when the transmission is in gear.

7 The final piece of the puzzle is the synchro ring. After this begins to wear, everything else goes downhill as well. The old and the new rings side by side show how significantly the synchro ring can wear. The arrow points to the subtle, yet important contoured surface on the new ring that is completely worn away on the old one. This surface

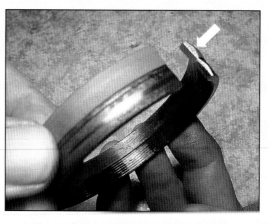

is an important factor in preventing the gears from grinding. When it wears away, the teeth on the synchro hub and slider begin to grind and gradually become destroyed. It is important to replace the synchro ring before this starts happening. The worn synchro ring also contributes to the transmission popping out of gear when driving. When operating normally, the synchro ring snaps into the slider and holds the transmission into gear.

To remove the synchro hub from first gear, you will need a synchro hub removal tool. I don't recommend attempting the removal of the synchro hub without this tool, as it will almost certainly have to be cut off of the gear with a small rotary tool. First gear can be very expensive to replace if you accidentally damage it while cutting off the synchro hub. Buy or rent the tool—it's a good investment.

Installation of the new synchro hub is straightforward—simply tap it on with a soft hammer. Reassemble the unit with the brake band, thrust block, anchor block, and the new synchro ring constrained by the large snap ring. Your new assembly can be installed back into the transmission using the impact wrench again. Make sure that the expansion nut is zapped on tightly as you don't want this assembly to come loose in your transmission. The factory torque specification for this bolt is about 114 N-m (84 ft-lb).

The slider deserves careful inspection before it's installed back into the transmission. Carefully assess the points that mate with the synchro hub for wear. If you have doubts about whether to replace the slider, have your mechanic or a transmission specialist assess its condition. If you were performing this repair on the Porsche 914, it would be less of a concern because the slider can be replaced in about a half hour on that car, without removing the transmission. On the 911, how-

ever, you will need to drop the engine again, so extra consideration is worthy here. It's not an easy decision, because new sliders cost around $325.

After you've reassembled the slider and shift fork, carefully check to make sure that the first-gear slider locks onto the synchro hub and stays in place. It's common for these parts to wear to the point where they will have a tendency to slip out of gear. Make sure the fit is tight, and that they are firmly locked together.

Now, replace the end cover on the transmission. Make sure that you properly reassemble reverse gear, and align and replace all the bearings and spacers that fit on the rear cover shaft. Also use a fresh transmission cover gasket, and make sure that you scrape off the remains of the old one with a razor blade prior to installation. Tighten the nuts up on the case to about 23 N-m (16.9 ft-lb). I also recommend that you replace the shift rod selector seal in the end cover. The old seal simply pries out and the new one can easily be pressed in.

When you finally get back into your car and start driving it, you may experience some difficulty getting the car into gear, as the break-in period makes shifting pretty tough. Don't worry—the new synchro ring needs to be worn in just a bit before you will feel a significant improvement. Adding Swepco 201 transmission fluid may help the break-in process as well.

PROJECT 39 • INSTALLING A SHORT SHIFT KIT

Time: 3 hours

Tools: Hex key set, needle-nose pliers, 22-millimeter socket for later cars

Talent: 🔧🔧🔧

Applicable Years: 1965-1986

Tab: $130

Tinware: Short shift kit, new shift bushing

Tip: Use screwdrivers to align the compression springs with the top retaining plate

PERFORMANCE GAIN: Quicker shifting between gears

COMPLEMENTARY MODIFICATION: New shift boot, new shift bushings, new shift knob

There are currently two popular types of short shift kits on the market. One of them is a Weltmeister aftermarket unit, and the other is a genuine Porsche kit. The Porsche factory kit is only applicable to 911s from 1973 through 1986 with the 915 transmission. The kit will reduce shifter travel by 20 percent on 1973–1984 911s and 10 percent on 1985–1986 models. The Porsche kit replaces just about everything in the shifter with new parts, so if your shifter is worn, the install will renew its performance.

The Weltmeister kit uses an adapter plate and a new shift arm to decrease the throw. This adapter plate raises the level of the entire shifter by about a half-inch. The Weltmeister kit fits all 911s, including the Turbo, from 1965–1986. Installation is similar to the Porsche kit, except that the kit doesn't provide replacements for the major internal pieces of the shifter. The installation process utilizes the older components. It is important to note that the installation process is not a quick job, and converting your shifter back to its original state will easily require another three hours.

The installation of the factory short shift kit is pretty straightforward. The first step is to remove the shifter from the car. This is documented in Project 37, Shifting Improvements. Once the shifter is out, place it on a workbench and begin disassembly by removing the two nuts that hold on the top carrier plate. Be careful when you remove this plate, because there are two heavily loaded springs that are compressed up against it. The carrier plate will spring off when you remove the two nuts—make sure that your hands are out of the way and your safety glasses are on.

The shift handle is held on with a pin that is constrained using two circlips. Using needle-nose pliers, remove the circlips from the pin, slide it out, and remove the shifter handle. Unscrew the large hex pivot bolt at the end of the shifter and remove the internal pivot fork that rocks back and forth. Loosen the retaining nut before you try to remove the bolt. In order to completely remove the pivot fork, the small roll-pin on the opposite side must be pushed into the housing. Use a small hammer to tap out the roll-pin so that you can remove the pivot fork.

The new pivot fork replaces the old one, and the hole for the shifter should be located on the top of the fork when installed. Tap the roll pin back into place, and reinstall the hex bolt. Make sure that you tighten down the bolt to the point where you can slightly move the pivot fork back and forth. Tighten up the retaining nut to make sure that the bolt doesn't come loose.

Now, install the new shift handle into the fork. Make sure that the tab welded on the shift handle points to the right side of the shifter. The longer end of the retaining pin should point toward the left side. Reinstall the two circlips on both ends of the pin. Now, place the guide plate back into its normal position.

The final and most difficult part of the conversion is installing the carrier plate, the buffer plate, and the two springs. Insert the springs into the buffer plate and place it in the shifter. Now, use two small screwdrivers inserted through the holes in the carrier plate to constrain the springs to the carrier plate. Using this method should allow you to compress the top carrier plate back into its proper position without having the springs fly out. It may be wise to wear gloves and safety glasses during this stage, as the springs will be tightly compressed and could be dangerous if they fly out. These springs are sometimes called the shift lock-out springs, because they keep you from accidentally putting the car into reverse. If you have found them to be weak when shifting into reverse and fifth, you should replace them with new ones at this time.

When compressing the top plate, work on one side of the shifter at a time. Press down one side until you have enough clearance on the top stud to attach one of the nuts. Don't worry about putting the small

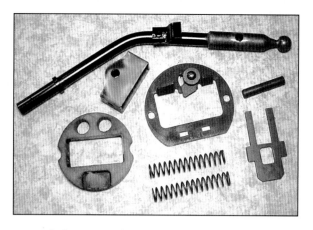

1 The factory short shift kit contains all the pieces and bits that you need to install it into your 911. The kit basically replaces all the parts in the shifter except for the housing and some fastening hardware. If your original shifter is worn, and needs to be replaced, the short shift kit should provide you with everything that you need to both replenish the shifter and shorten the shift throw.

2 This photo shows the original shifter disassembled. Be careful when removing the lock pawl carrier plate, as it is heavily spring-loaded and the springs will come flying out if you are not careful. Cover the entire assembly with a towel when you are removing the second bolt on the carrier plate. The towel will prevent the springs and the plate from flying out of control.

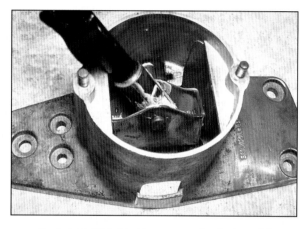

3 The short shift kit's fork is offset to accommodate the shorter shift. Make sure to install the fork with the hole facing toward the top of the shifter, and install the shift handle's lock tab on the shifter's right sider. The rear of the shifter has the single large mounting hole in its base.

4 When installing the new carrier plate, use two small screwdrivers to hold the springs in while you position the nuts for tightening. This may require a few attempts to get it right. Remember to wear safety glasses when working with the springs under pressure.

washer back on—you can do that later. Place one nut on the stud and tighten it down slightly. Then move over to the other side and compress the carrier plate all the way down, and attach the other nut. Tighten both nuts up tight when you are finished. Then, remove one of the nuts, and place the washer underneath. The other nut (if still on tight) should be strong enough to hold the top carrier plate in position. Retighten the nut with the washer underneath, and then repeat for the opposite side.

At this point, your shifter should be completely reassembled, and ready to be placed back into the car. It's a wise idea to replace your shifter bushings for clearer, crisper shifting (see Project 37), if you haven't already done so. It's also a good time to replace your shift boot and knob, if they are looking worn.

On a side note, many people install short shift kits in their cars thinking that it will fix problems that they are having with their transmission. This will not solve any problems, and will in most cases make a poorly shifting car shift even worse. The reason for this is that with the short shift kit, the torque arm on the shift lever is much shorter, giving you much less "resolution" on your shifter. It's similar to having a gas pedal that only travels 1 inch over its range instead of 2–3 inches. You have less precision in how much throttle you want to give the car. In a similar manner, with the short shift kit you will have less precision on where the shift rod is placed. It's a wise idea to tackle the core problems with your transmission (synchros, shift bushings) before installing the short shift kit.

TRANSAXLE
PROJECT 40 • REBUILDING YOUR PEDAL CLUSTER

 Time: 4 hours

 Tools: Bench vise, hammer, hand drill

 Talent:

 Applicable Years: All

 Tab: $25

 Tinware: Bronze bushing kit, new pedal rubber, black paint, white lithium grease

 Tip: If you can't easily get out the press pin, take it to your local machine shop

⚠ PERFORMANCE GAIN: No more squeaky or binding pedals

COMPLEMENTARY MODIFICATION: Replace your clutch cable, check/replace your master cylinder

O n the older 911s, the pedal cluster will often stick and bind. This is usually caused by rainwater leaks starting to rust out the assembly or a master cylinder that has leaked corrosive brake fluid over the bushings. The original pedal clusters were installed with plastic bushings that tend to wear away over the years. Rebuilding the entire assembly with new bronze bushings is easy and straightforward, and can possibly solve some of your shifting and clutch problems as well.

These bushings will perform better than the stock plastic ones, and should last a lot longer. Replacing the plastic bushings will also ensure that your pedals will not squeak anymore, or worse, get stuck in the down position. Besides the bronze bushing kit, you will need new rubber pedal pads, black paint, and white lithium grease for lubricating the entire assembly.

Removing the pedal cluster is not difficult, but can be tricky if it's your first time. The first step is to remove the carpet and the wooden floorboard, and disconnect the clutch cable. See Project 9 for more information on this procedure. Now, unbolt the

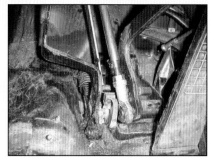

1 With the floorboards removed, you can see the pedal cluster. The plastic bushings that were originally used as OEM equipment have probably worn out a long time ago. Before you remove and disassemble the cluster, make sure that the bushings have not already been replaced with the bronze ones by a previous owner.

2 This photo shows the pedal cluster completely disassembled. The bronze bushing kit contains seven new bushings that need to be installed into the cluster. These bushings, shown by the arrows in the picture, should easily slide into the pedal cluster, and don't need to be tapped in with a large amount of force.

3 Starting in 1977, the clutch return spring was moved to the outside of the pedal cluster. This heavy-duty spring is very difficult to install, and usually requires the work of two very strong people to wrestle it into place. One person must pull and stretch the spring, while the other person guides it onto its hook.

assembly from the car. The pedal cluster and the master cylinder are bolted together on the early cars, so you need to disconnect the master cylinder in order to remove the pedal cluster. Do this by removing the two nuts that attach the master cylinder to the pedal cluster. The nuts can be reached from underneath the car, after removing the belly pan covering the steering rack. To actually remove the cluster from the car, you may need to unbolt and disconnect the accelerator pedal as well. I suggest vacuum cleaning the area near the cluster before removing it. The job will be far more pleasant, and you won't track dirt across the car's interior when you remove the cluster. Make sure to unhitch the clutch cable and accelerator cable as well. See Project 9 for more details.

Once you have the pedal cluster removed from your car, take it over to your workbench and begin

4 It's a wise idea to closely examine your pedal cluster prior to disassembly so that you're familiar with how it is supposed to be reassembled. The location and orientation of the pedal springs looks obvious when the assembly is together, but once it's in pieces, it can be difficult to determine which part goes where. Refer to these photos when reassembling the pedal cluster, or take some photos of your own during the process.

the disassembly. A roll pin pressed into the end of the clutch pedal holds the majority of the cluster together. The first step to try when removing the roll pin is to place a bolt on one end and tap it carefully with a hammer. Make sure that the base of the clutch pedal is firmly mounted in a vise so that you don't dent, damage, or bend any of the parts on the cluster. Tapping the pin with a hammer might make it move slightly, but in most cases probably won't be enough to remove it.

Another removal method involves drilling the inside of the pin out before trying to remove it. The pin has a hollow center, so it should be relatively easy to get the drill bit started in the pin. Drill out the pin by increasing the size of the drill bit that you use, until the inside of the pin is significantly larger in diameter. Now, the pin should be easier to press out. Try to tap it out with a hammer, or you can place it in a vise with a screw behind the roll pin and compress the vise until the pin is pressed out. If all else fails, you can probably take it to your local machine shop, where they have the proper tools to press out the pin in about one minute.

Once you have the roll pin out, the rest of the cluster should come apart quite easily. Remove the nut that holds on the inner cylinder of the cluster and pull it out. At this point it should be easy to completely disassemble the entire cluster. Take a screwdriver and remove all of the older plastic bushings. At this time, you might want to take your pedal cluster parts to your local machine shop to have them sandblasted and painted. This gives it a very nice appearance, and will also protect it from rust in the future.

Once the parts are cleaned up, insert the new bushings into the cluster. Refer to the photos in this section for the exact location of where each bushing is to be installed. Make sure that you place a light coat of white lithium grease on all the bushings in the cluster. The bushings themselves should not require too much force to be pressed into their mating surfaces.

Once you have the bushings installed, reassemble the cluster and carefully install the brake pedal and clutch pedal spring. Make sure that you inspect the two springs to ensure that they haven't been damaged or corroded to the point where they might fail. It's a wise idea to renew both these springs while you have the pedal cluster apart.

While you have the cluster out and apart, it's also a good idea to test and adjust your brake pedal switch. On the earlier 911s, this switch is activated by the brake pedal and triggers the rear brake lights. Check to make sure that the switch is operational, and adjust it if the actuation point is not where you think it should be.

It's also a good time to replace the pedal pad rubber on your cluster. The old ones simply slide off the back of the pedals, and the new rubber is pressed and fit onto the pedal with a little effort.

Reassembly into the car is similar to the removal procedure. Make sure that you properly reattach your clutch cable, throttle cable, and remount the master cylinder. Make sure that you don't wrap the throttle cable around the clutch cable. If this happens, when you push in the clutch, the engine will speed up.

Before you reinstall the cluster, inspect the front floor of the car. If the area under the cluster is rusty, then you might want to consider some preventative maintenance through the use of some sandpaper and rust-prevention paint.

TRANSAXLE
PROJECT 41 • REPLACING CV JOINTS

 Time: 4 hours

 Tools: CV bolt removal tool, circlip pliers

 Talent:

 Applicable Years: All

 Tab: $160

 Tinware: CV Joints, or complete axles, CV joint grease, gaskets, CV boots

 Tip: If you are planning on replacing all four CV joints, it's cheaper to purchase a complete axle.

 PERFORMANCE GAIN: Smoother drivetrain

COMPLEMENTARY MODIFICATION: Replace your rear wheel bearings

One of the most common suspension items to replace or service on the 911 is the constant velocity, or CV, joints that connect the wheels to the transmission. These bearings, packed in grease, get a tremendous amount of mileage through the years, and thus have a tendency to wear out after about 100,000 miles or so. One of the clear signs that the joints need replacing is the distinct sound of a clunk, clunk, clunk coming from the rear axle when the car is in motion.

In some cases, the boots that cover and protect the CV joints will be torn and need replacing. The procedure for replacing the boots is very similar to the procedure for replacing the entire joint. New boots should be installed each time a new CV joint is installed.

If you are planning on replacing both the inner and outer joints, then you should probably purchase a brand-new axle. The new Lobro axle

contains both the inner and outer CV joints, as well as the boots that cover and protect them. In addition, the complete axle is usually about the same cost as if you purchased just the CV joints and the boots. Plus, the entire assembly ships with everything installed. All you need to do is to bolt it up to the car.

The complete axle is also a good option for replacing the CV joints on the late-model 911 1984–1989 Carreras. The inner CV joints are an integrated part of the stub axle, and are not available separately. The Carrera axle ships with the two CV joints and the stub axle as a simple replacement unit.

The first step is to jack up and raise the car (see Project 1 for details). You don't need to remove the road wheels, although it is recommended that you do so in order to gain yourself some additional working room. The next step is to start removing the bolts from the CV joints. Start by making sure that you have the correct tool. On some early 911s, the bolts need a six-point or 12-point star-pattern removal tool to loosen them up. On some others, the bolts used only a standard Allen hex pattern. Either way, you must have the correct tool for the removal task, or you might strip out the CV bolts. If you do strip out the bolts, the only way to remove the bolts is to grind them off, which is not a fun task. Sometimes on the early cars, the bolts have been replaced with bolts that are easier to remove. For instance, it's common to find that the bolts on the early cars have been replaced with bolts similar to the simpler hex pattern. Either way, it's recommended that you use a socket tool to remove the bolts and reinstall the bolts, since you will have to torque them with a torque wrench when you are finished.

In order to gain access to the CV bolts, rotate the wheel of the car until you can clearly get your socket

1 Shown here is a complete axle for a late-model 911 Carrera (1985–1989), a CV joint for the 911SC, and a CV boot for an early 911. On these later cars, the outer CV joint is not available separately, but must be purchased as a complete axle. This is because the joint is integrated into the stub axle and cannot be separated. If the boots are damaged and leaking, then you should replace them, because dirt and debris can find their way inside.

REPLACING CV JOINTS

2 The four CV joints are located in the rear of the car, attached to both the transmission flanges and the stub axles on the trailing arms. It's recommended to replace the joints in pairs—either both of the inside ones or both of the outside ones. Chances are if one of the joints is showing signs of wear and deterioration, then the other three will not be far behind.

wrench on the bolts. Then, pull the emergency brake and place the transmission into first gear. This will allow you to loosen the bolts without having the axle spin. When you have removed all the bolts that you can from this angle, release the brake, take the car out of gear, and rotate the wheel until you can reach the next set of bolts. If you are planning to remove the whole axle by removing both the inner and outer joints, then work on the bolts on both the inner and outer joints at the same time.

Once you have the CV bolts disconnected, it's now time to separate them from the transmission or the stub axle. On the early cars, there are roll pins that help align the CV joints with the flange. Using a small screwdriver, poke into the CV joint seal that is located between the CV joint and the transmission. With the emergency brake released and the car out of gear, rotate the wheel around

as you gently pry the two apart. On the later cars, there is no pin holding the joint and the flange together, so they should simply come apart. Make sure that you wear safety glasses when working underneath the car. You would hate to have an axle fall on your face.

If you are replacing the entire axle, or the boots on both sides, simply remove the axle and take it over to your workbench. If you are only replacing one boot or one CV joint, you will have to continue to work underneath the car. The CV joints are held onto the axles using a large circlip. Remove this circlip, and the joints should come right off. In general, it's a really bad sign if large balls from the bearing start falling out. That's a clear indicator that you need to replace the joints. If you are reusing the joints again, make sure that you carefully place them in a plastic bag, and avoid getting any dirt or grime in them. Even a crystal of sand or two accidentally placed in the joints can help them wear out prematurely.

Once you have removed the joints, replacing the boots should be easy. Simply disconnect the small clips that hold the boot to the shaft and slide it off. The new ones are installed in a reverse manner.

When installing the new CV joints, make sure that you pack them with plenty of CV joint grease before installing them on the car. Also make sure that you place plenty of grease in and around the boot. Move the joint in and out as you insert the grease to make sure that you get it well lubricated. When ready, place the new boot on the axle and then place the CV joint on the axle. Reattach the circlip so that the joint is attached to the axle.

Now, insert the CV joint back into either the stub axle flange or the transmission flange, making sure that you don't forget to install the new CV joint gasket. Pack a little more grease into the recesses of the flange before you remate the joints together. Finally insert the bolts, and tighten them up. Using a torque wrench, tighten up the bolts to 83 N-m (61 ft-lb) for cars with four M10 bolts on the flanges, (and 47 N-m (34 ft-lb) for cars with six M8 bolts on the flanges.) For 1965-68 911s, tighten them up to 47 N-m if you have the Nadella axles (M10 bolts), or 43 N-m if you have the early Loebro CV joints (M8 bolts)." You may need to drop the car down onto the ground to tighten to this spec without turning the wheels.

Once you have the entire assembly back together, take the car out for a drive, and check the rear for noises. All should be smooth and quiet, and the boots should no longer leak.

SECTION FIVE
EXHAUST

As with most air-cooled cars, the 911's climate control and exhaust systems are very closely related. The heater and defroster system on the 911 gets its heat by circulating air next to the hot exhaust pipes. Unfortunately, this is not the most efficient design for heating the passenger compartment, but the only one available on air-cooled cars. Although the design of the system leaves much to be desired, a lot can be done to make sure it's operating as well as possible. These projects will help you get the most out of your heating and air conditioning systems.

EXHAUST

PROJECT 42 • REPLACING YOUR CATALYTIC CONVERTER

 Time: 2 hours

 Tools: –

 Talent:

 Applicable Years: 1980–

 Tab: $350

 Tinware: Catalytic converter, CAT by-pass pipe, new gaskets

 Tip: Installing a new CAT can improve your performance and help the environment

PERFORMANCE GAIN: Increased power from better flow

COMPLEMENTARY MODIFICATION: Check and replace the O2 sensor, install new muffler

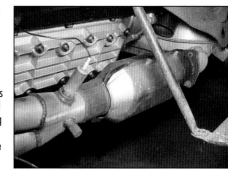

1 Installed on your car, the new catalytic converter should instantly improve performance. Years of use can clog old converters, causing restrictions that prevent the engine from running properly. If your O_2 sensor has recently failed, there is a chance that your CAT has become clogged. Under these conditions, the car has a tendency to run rich, which can seriously damage the converter. Also check for cracks that can create exhaust leaks.

One of the most important emissions devices ever invented is the catalytic converter. The converter works by altering harmful exhaust gases into more environmentally friendly byproducts. The first converters used a platinum-coated ceramic honeycomb or aluminum-oxide pellets coated with platinum to convert HC and CO into water vapor (H_2O) and carbon dioxide (CO_2).

Troubleshooting converter or "CAT" problems can be a bit frustrating. Some clues that the car may have a CAT problem include loss of power at higher rpm and speed, even though the car idles perfectly fine. Many mechanics troubleshoot the fuel injection system first (indeed a smart place to start), but never really think that the problem might be a clogged CAT. If you remove the CAT, you should be able to clearly see through it. Chances are if you shine a bright light on one end, and you can't see any light through the other end, then it's clogged. The 911 CAT has a right angle built in, so you can't really see directly through, but some reflected light should be able to shine through.

Of course, to inspect the CAT, you need to remove it. The process of removal simply involves the unbolting of the CAT from the exhaust system. You don't need to remove the muffler or the heat exchangers. I would recommend that you remove the left rear wheel, as it will gain you a lot of access room for the job.

It is very common for the nuts and bolts on older cars to rust, and make exhaust components very difficult to remove. This very well may be the case with your CAT. If so, then you might need to grind off the nuts and/or heads of the bolts to get the CAT off of the car. It's not an easy job, and it is complicated by the lack of room underneath the car. If you have extreme difficulty, then take the car to your local mechanic.

Original Porsche converters can easily cost more than $1,000, although good aftermarket ones are available for about $350. If your car is having problems passing an emissions test, it may be a sign that your CAT is worn out and needs to be replaced. You may also be surprised at the additional horsepower that you might gain. Any clogs in the CAT will directly affect the efficiency and power of the engine.

Another alternative is to bypass the converter completely. While this will generate less restriction than a CAT, the tailpipe emissions will basically go through the roof. Using a CAT bypass pipe in most states is legal only for off-road use, and should only be used for racing purposes. Removing the catalytic converter from your car will make it put out significantly more emissions than today's new cars. Doing so is not really worth the few extra horsepower that you will gain from polluting the air.

EXHAUST

PROJECT 43 • HEATER SYSTEM REPAIR

 Time: 2-10 hours

 Tools: –

 Talent:

 Applicable Years: 1965-1989

 Tab: $10–$500

 Tinware: New flapper boxes, gaskets, hoses, new heat exchangers, blower motor

 Tip: Fix any oil leaks prior to fixing your heating system.

 PERFORMANCE GAIN: Warmer car, better defroster

COMPLEMENTARY MODIFICATION: Install stainless steel heat exchangers

New flapper boxes are painted to avoid rusting. When installing these new flapper boxes, make sure that you inspect the flapper box cable and the high-temp heater hoses that connect the flappers to the heat exchangers. Only use hose that has been approved for high-temp use. If you use normal hose available from a hardware store, it might melt and create noxious fumes.

The heating and defrosting system on the 911 is one of the most confusing and complex systems on the car. It's also one of the most common systems to fail. Nonetheless, there is plenty that you can do to restore your heating system back to its original, somewhat lackluster performance. The heating and defrosting system for the 911 relies on hot air that is channeled from the motor to the exhaust pipes, through the sides of the chassis, and into the area behind the dashboard. Needless to say, all this traveling causes the air to lose some of its heat and velocity by the time it reaches the passenger compartment.

The source of all this hot air starts in the engine compartment. Depending upon which model and year you have, the orientation of the hoses and blower motors may vary. On most cars, there is an adapter plate on one or both sides of the engine fan that funnels air down into the heat exchangers. The heat exchangers are nothing more than an exhaust header system with sheet metal wrapped around the pipes. The air from the fan is funneled through these heat exchangers, and is heated by flowing past the hot exhaust pipes.

It's important to remember that your fresh air is circulating past the exhaust system. If there is a problem with rust in the exhaust system, you might have leakage from the pipes, resulting in a dangerous situation. Make sure that you inspect your heat exchangers carefully and replace or repair them if they look like they might be developing leaks from rust holes. For the early heat exchangers, there are separate replacement parts available that can be welded in for repair.

Another important consideration is that the heat exchangers are located right below the engine. This means that any oil leaks from the engine will have a likelihood of dropping oil onto the top of the heat exchangers, mixing with the air that is channeled into the cockpit. When the car warms up, this oil will start to burn and smoke, and you can actually have smoke coming out of your dashboard vents. With this in mind, it's a wise idea to repair all of the oil leaks that might drip on the heat exchangers before you activate your heating system. It's not a wise idea to use your heating system if you can smell burnt oil in the air.

The hoses in the engine compartment are manufactured out of aluminum and paper, and have a tendency to crack and break over the years. Inspect and replace these hoses with new ones if you find any damage to them. Ensuring that these hoses are intact is the first step to improving your heating system. Underneath the engine, there should be additional hoses that connect the heat exchangers to the hoses in the engine compartment. Inspect these too, and replace them if necessary. In particular, the A/C bracket has a tendency to poke a hole in the paper hose that runs right next to it, between the fan and the bracket.

On the 911s made after 1978, Porsche installed a separate blower motor in the engine compartment to

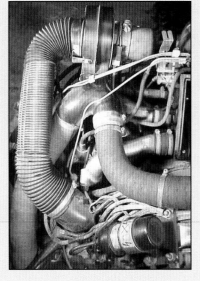

2 In the engine compartment, several hoses warrant inspection or replacement. The large plastic blower motor hose that acts as an intake from the fan often cracks and leaks air out the sides. This can actually have a detrimental effect on the cooling of your car, as this air now becomes "wasted." In order for your engine to get all the cooling that it needs, this plastic hose needs to be intact and installed. The long paper and aluminum hoses that connect the blower motor to the heat exchangers also often need replacement after many years of use. Finally, if the blower motor is not functioning properly, it too may need to be replaced. Check the connections to the blower motor to see if there is any power getting to it before you replace it (see Project 94).

3 The hidden catch for the heater pull cable is under the heater knobs. These pull handles serve a dual purpose. They act as a physical switch, pulling open the flapper boxes, and there is an electrical switch underneath the pull handles that actuates the blower motor. If you wish to improve the look of your interior, the red plastic tips on the pull handles simply pop off for replacement. *Tom Sharpes*

give an extra push to the air channeled to the cockpit. This blower motor is connected to the air intake of the fan through a plastic hose that often develops cracks over the years. It's a wise idea to replace this hose if it's cracked, as a lot of extra air can slip out of it.

Exiting the front end of the heat exchangers, the warm air enters what is known as the flapper boxes. These two boxes, located on opposite sides of the car, control the flow of hot air into the cockpit. They have flaps inside that are either open or closed. These flaps are connected via a cable to the two levers that are located between the passenger's and driver's seat. These levers also have a built-in electrical switch that operates the engine compartment blower motor

on the later 911s. It is important to inspect these boxes, as they are often susceptible to rust and deterioration. Also inspect the hoses that lead from the heat exchangers to the flapper boxes.

If you decide that you need to replace the flapper boxes, exercise care when removing them from the car. They are attached to the chassis via small studs that were welded into the car when it was assembled in Germany. If you accidentally break off one or more of these studs, you might have a difficult time reattaching the flapper boxes later on. When installing a new flapper box, make sure that you use a new seal between the flapper box and the chassis.

If the heater hoses that connect the flapper boxes and the heat exchangers are broken or ripped, then you should replace them with new ones. Be sure that you only use high-temp heater hose, as most other ordinary hoses from hardware stores will melt when exposed to the high heat from the heat exchangers. There are very good aftermarket hoses available—originally designed for the aerospace industry—that will work well in your Porsche.

The flapper box cable is another source of problems for the heater system. This cable has a tendency to break on the older cars. To replace it, you need to remove the small handle assembly located in the cockpit, between the two seats. Lift up the edges of the carpet, and find the small screws that hold the lever assembly to the chassis. When you lift up the assembly, you should be able to see the catch for the cable underneath. The new cable needs to be threaded through the two holes in the chassis firewall from inside the cockpit (not always an easy process), after first being threaded through the lever assembly. Make sure that you don't damage the cable during this process. You may find it easier to work if you pull out and remove the passenger's seat from the car.

After you have fixed all the components that make up your heater system, you should test it. The hot air from the heat exchangers is funneled behind the dash. The red lever on the climate control module determines whether the heated air will be directed at the windshield (for defrosting) or through the dash and lower vents for heating. In addition, there is a fresh air blower that mixes air from the outside with the heated air from the heat exchangers. By adjusting the volume of fresh air mixed with the heated air, you can change the temperature of the air exiting the vents. You can also change the amount of hot air released into the system by adjusting the heater lever arms between the two front seats. Pulling up the handles only part of the way will limit the amount of air that passes through the flapper boxes.

EXHAUST
PROJECT 44 • REPLACING HEAT EXCHANGERS

 Time: 2 hours

 Tools: Heat exchanger removal tool

 Talent:

 Applicable Years: all

 Tab: $100-1,000

 Tinware: New heat exchangers, new exhaust gaskets

 Tip: Be very careful when removing the old heat exchangers.

PERFORMANCE GAIN: Better heating

COMPLEMENTARY MODIFICATION: Adjust your valves, upgrade to SSI heat exchangers, install early exhaust system

1 Truly a sight to be seen, here is a picture of a brand-new 1965–1974 stainless-steel heat exchanger. These exchangers bolt up to a dual-inlet muffler, and are the type of exhaust that many people place on their 1974-and-older 911s. Stainless steel heat exchangers for the 1978–1989 911SC and Carrera are available as well. Stainless-steel heat exchangers keep their value and are a worthy investment. A used set of stainless-steel heat exchangers can simply be cleaned and bead blasted, and they will look and perform as good as new. They are basically indestructible.

One of the most important elements of your 911's exhaust system is the heat exchangers. Not only do they funnel the exhaust out from the engine, but they also provide heat for the interior of the car. However, the heat exchangers take quite a lot of abuse, and they have a tendency to be one of the first components on the car to rust. Salt, water, and other debris can easily get washed up onto the bottom of the heat exchangers, causing them to rust.

In addition, oil leaks from the engine can drip down on top of the heat exchangers, causing them to smoke when the car is running. Oil that seeps down onto the exchangers can also cause dirt and grime to buildup on the inside. When the car is warm, and the heat exchangers are hot, this grime and oil heats up and smokes. This smoke is often channeled right into the cockpit of the car. This smell of burning oil is very reminiscent of older cars of this type, and is sometimes called "that air-cooled car smell."

The only way to rid yourself of the air-cooled problems is to fix all the oil leaks on your engine (covered in Project 21) and replace your heat exchangers with brand new or good quality used ones.

Brand new heat exchangers from the factory can be quite expensive. New exchangers for a 911SC list for more than $1,000 each. The older-style heat exchangers can actually be had for less, but they are still very pricey indeed. A good compromise is a set of used exchangers that have come from a relatively rust-free environment like California. In some cases, it may be difficult to find a really good set, but if you keep scouring the classified ads from Porsche sources around the world, you should be able to find some.

Another alternative is brand-new stainless-steel heat exchangers from a company called SSI. These exchangers will most likely outlast the life of your car. Made from 100 percent stainless steel, these are guaranteed to never rust and never corrode. Occasionally you can find a set of used SSI heat exchangers, but it's not very common. These exchangers are built so tough that they are usually snatched up really quickly by people looking for them. A typical used set sells for about $500, which is about half the cost of a new set.

Removing your heat exchangers can sometimes be a very risky task. The rust, combined with the high heat of the cylinder heads, can temper the studs on the heads to the point that they have a tendency to break off when you try to remove the heat exchanger nuts. It's very important to use plenty of WD-40 and let the nuts soak for a few days before

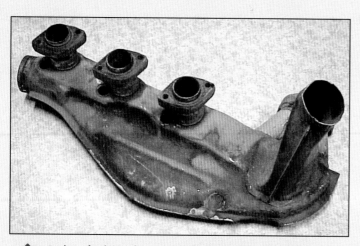

2 Good, rust-free heat exchangers can be difficult to find. This one is for a 911SC, and is one of the best examples around. The 911SC and Carrera heat exchangers, surprisingly enough, are identical for both left or right. Finding a really good used pair can be difficult, but well worth it when you consider the cost of new heat exchangers, or the cost of stainless-steel ones.

3 The heat exchangers are attached and secured to the car by their connection to the heads. The top arrow points to one of the nuts that bolt the heat exchangers to the heads. The bottom arrow points to the access hole in the heat exchangers that must be used to remove the small barrel nuts that are difficult to remove with a regular tool. Be careful when removing these nuts. The heat from the heads, combined with rust, can lead to a situation in which the stud breaks off when you try to remove the nut. If this happens, you will have a very difficult time removing the broken stud from the head.

you try to remove them from the studs. Tom Woodford of Factory Tour recommends the use of a torch to heat the nuts prior to the removal attempt. The heat from the torch will expand the nuts and reduce the chance that the studs will break off. If the studs break, then you will have a very difficult time removing them from the heads. You may have to resort to EDM methods such as the one described in Project 95. It's a wise idea to be very careful when removing the nuts from the studs.

To access the heat exchanger barrel nuts, you will need to have an angled 13-millimeter wrench and a special heat exchanger barrel nut removal tool. The removal tool is basically a very long 8-millimeter Allen hex key with a socket end on it. You can remove the barrel nuts by placing the removal tool through the access holes located in the heat exchangers. Don't worry about not being able to get the nuts out. The

nuts are a small, special type of barrel nut that will fit through the holes in the heat exchangers.

When installing new exchangers, make sure that you use new exhaust gaskets at the heads and at the exhaust pipe end. It's wise to coat the nuts with a little bit of antiseize compound to prevent them from rusting and sticking together.

While you have the heat exchangers off, take a look inside the heads to check if you can see anything that doesn't quite look right. Lots of black carbon built up on the outside of the valves and the combustion chamber is an indication that the mixture might be set a little too rich. One cylinder looking different from the others is also a sign that there is something wrong. In general, all the cylinders and their exhaust ports should look similar. If you have any doubts, you might want to take the car into your mechanic for an expert opinion.

PROJECT 45
AIR CONDITIONING ON THE 911

Time: –

Tools: Air conditioning pressure gauge

Talent: 👤👤

Applicable Years: All

Tab: $0-$750

Tinware: Freon, or R134 Upgrade kit

Tip: Replace your system with R134 if you have to spend a lot of money on a new or rebuilt compressor.

PERFORMANCE GAIN: Better cooling during the summer months

COMPLEMENTARY MODIFICATION: Replace your blower motors

The Porsche 911 has never been renowned for its air conditioning systems. At best, most of the systems on the 911 can be described as marginally cool. Part of the problem stems from the fact that the air conditioning systems on the early cars were a dealer-installed option, and never fully adopted by the factory. As it happened, the A/C systems were basically patched into the car, and weren't really well integrated into the 911.

On any car, the A/C system is a complicated beast. This project is not intended to be a repair manual for your A/C system, but to serve more as a guide to how the system works, and the maintenance involved with its upkeep.

Almost all air conditioning systems work on the theories of thermodynamics, whereby heat flows from a warmer surface to a colder one. Heat from inside the car is transferred to the cold metal fins of the evaporator. The refrigerant in the system picks up the heat from the evaporator and takes it to the compressor. The gas is then pressurized, which concentrates the heat by raising the temperature of the refrigerant gas. The gas is then sent to the con-

densers, which are located in the front and rear of the 911. These condensers cool the refrigerant and turn it back into a liquid from a gas. The liquid is then sent to the receiver-dryer, where any water vapor that may have formed in the system is removed. The receiver-dryer also acts as a storage container for unused fluid. From the receiver-dryer, the liquid flows into the expansion valve, which meters it into the evaporator located inside the car. Here the liquid absorbs heat, and becomes a cold low-pressure gas. This evaporation, or boiling of the refrigerant, absorbs heat just the way a boiling pot of water absorbs heat from the stove. As heat is absorbed, the evaporator is cooled. A fan blows air through the evaporator and into the cockpit of the car, providing the cooling effect.

The compressor pumps the refrigerant through the entire system. An electromagnetic clutch on the compressor turns the A/C system on and off. In addition to cooling the car, the system also removes water vapor from the ambient air via the cooling process. It is not uncommon to find a small puddle of water underneath your car from the condensation of the air conditioning system. A thermostat control on the evaporator keeps the condensation in the evaporator from freezing.

The late-model factory A/C systems from 1978 used a dual condenser system to try to remove more heat from the system. It is important to check that the blower motor in the front of the front trunk is working in order to achieve the maximum cooling from the system.

So what can be done to maintain and protect the system from deterioration? First and foremost, the air conditioning system should be operated at least once a week, if the outside temperature is above 50 degrees Fahrenheit. This will circulate the refrigerant in the system, and help to keep all the seals in the system from drying out. Most failures are caused by refrigerant leaking out of the system and can be prevented by making sure that the system is run frequently.

A belt that runs off of the main crankshaft operates the A/C compressor. Make sure that you don't overtighten this belt, or you may place undue pressure on the bearings inside the compressor. If you think that you might be having problems with your compressor, then check the belt first. Turn on the system, and check to make sure that the electromagnetic clutch is engaging. If not, then you may need to replace it. Check the power connection to make sure it is live before replacing. Sometimes the A/C system will not turn on the compressor if the system is not charged with refrigerant.

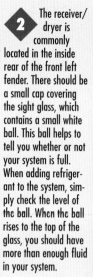

1 The workhorse of the system is the compressor. The white arrow points to the high port side of the compressor. This line comes out of the compressor and goes to the condenser, which is located on the inside of the engine grille. The low part of the system is located directly beneath. The valve for testing the pressure in the system is covered with a small black cap that needs to be removed.

2 The receiver/ dryer is commonly located in the inside rear of the front left fender. There should be a small cap covering the sight glass, which contains a small white ball. This ball helps to tell you whether or not your system is full. When adding refrigerant to the system, simply check the level of the ball. When the ball rises to the top of the glass, you should have more than enough fluid in your system.

Finally, if the rest of the A/C system appears to be functioning correctly, and you are still not getting cold air output, then you might have to replace the compressor. The compressor contains a piston with seals that may deteriorate if the system is not run for a while. Also make sure that when you are running the A/C system you keep the engine lid closed. You can open it to perform pressure tests on the valves, but at all other times keep the lid closed.

On the receiver-dryer, there is what is commonly called a sight-glass. The sight-glass is an excellent indicator of the condition of the A/C system. Find the sight glass and clean it. After running the system at maximum for about five minutes, increase the rpm to 2,000, make sure the engine lid is closed, and check the sight glass. If the glass is completely clear, the system is either fully charged or completely empty. Have an assistant turn the system on and off while you watch the glass. If the system emits cool air, or if bubbles appear when the system is off, it is fully charged.

A few bubbles in the sight glass when the system is running means that it needs a charge, or the compressor is not functioning properly. Make sure that the clutch is on, and check the sight again. If the bubbles remain, then the system needs to be charged.

If the sight glass is foamy, or if oil streaks appear, then the system is very low on refrigerant and needs to be recharged. If the sight glass is cloudy, this is an indication that the desiccant in the receiver-dryer is breaking down, and the unit needs to be replaced.

For environmental reasons, it is illegal in some states to perform your own A/C refrigerant recharging with the older R12 refrigerant, but you can check the overall charge (amount of refrigerant) of the entire system. The system's pressure can be checked using a pressure valve that is located on one of the hoses that is attached to the compressor. Before checking any of the valves in the system, make sure that you put on a pair of thick gloves and wear eye protection. If freon is released from the system, it will rapidly expand, and could cause frostbite if it gets on your hands. On a similar note, the system is pressurized, and the freon could discharge into your eyes if you are not careful.

There are two test valves on the compressor. These Schrader valves are very similar to the valves that are used to inflate your tire, and the pressure of the system should be checked with an air conditioning pressure gauge. Make sure that you check the pressure of the system while the engine is on, and the compressor and A/C system is running. Make sure that the clutch is engaged when taking the readings, and the system is set to maximum cooling.

The compressor will have two markings on its housing where the two hoses connect to it. One is marked "S" for suction, and the other "D" for discharge. The valve on the suction side should read about 10–30 psi when the system is running. The discharge side should be about 140 psi if the compressor is functioning correctly. Be careful again that you wear hand and eye protection, as the refrigerant can easily give you frostbite.

Take another set of readings when the system is off. If the system gives readings that are equal, and the gauge indicates a temperature/pressure value equal to the outside air, then the system may need a recharging.

If your A/C system needs a major overhaul, this can be a difficult and time-consuming process. For you to work on it, the entire system must be evacuated of any freon. The process of recharging the system from empty is not an easy task, either. In order to prevent water vapor and other impurities from entering the system, it needs to have a vacuum drawn on it for about a half an hour. Needless to say, the repair and replacement of most A/C components is beyond the average weekend mechanic.

The original freon that was used in the older-style air conditioned cars is no longer being manu-

3 The A/C blower motor located in the front trunk is an important part of the system that occasionally fails. The blower motor helps the front condenser cool the refrigerant in the system by blowing air over it. Check the proper operation of the motor when the system is running, and replace it if necessary.

factured. Around 1995, auto manufacturers started phasing out freon-based A/C systems, and started implementing the newer R134 systems. The cost of the replacement freon is skyrocketing as the current supplies disappear. This freon, which was once sold to the public in do-it-yourself kits, can now only be purchased by dealers who are trained in recharging these systems. If your A/C system needs a major overhaul, it's a wise idea to upgrade to the newer R134 kits available for the 911. Particularly if your compressor is broken, it doesn't make much sense to replace it with a rebuilt original one. Although the R134 system is not as efficient and doesn't cool as well as the original system, the refrigerant can be purchased inexpensively at your local auto parts stores. The typical non-factory-installed 911 A/C system uses about 28 ounces of R12 freon. The factory A/C systems with both a front and rear condenser uses about 39–41 ounces of freon.

SECTION SIX
BRAKES

Your brakes are probably the most important system on your 911. No matter how fast you go, you will always need to stop, and sometimes rather quickly. It's of paramount importance to keep your brakes in top condition. The stock 911 braking system is a really strong setup if properly maintained. The projects in this section detail the troubleshooting, restoration, and maintenance of your all-important brake system.

BRAKES
PROJECT 46 • REPLACING BRAKE PADS

Time: 2 hours

Tools: Screwdriver, isopropyl alcohol, wooden block

Talent:

Applicable Years: All

Tab: $85

Tinware: Brake pads, retaining kit

Tip: Check your brake discs when replacing your pads in case they have worn too thin.

PERFORMANCE GAIN: Better braking

COMPLEMENTARY MODIFICATION: Caliper rebuild, brake disc replacement, install stainless steel brake lines.

Replacing your brake pads is one of the easiest jobs to perform. Generally, you should check them every 5,000 miles, and replace them if their material linings reach 2 millimeters (0.08 inches) or less. In reality, most people don't inspect them very often, and wait for the scraping sound of metal on metal to tell them they're worn out. New pads have about 15 millimeters (0.6 inches) of material on them.

If you *do* get to the point of metal-on-metal contact, replace the pads immediately. Not only will you be unable to brake adequately, but you will begin to wear grooves in your brake discs. Once the discs are grooved, there is almost no way to repair them. Resurfacing will sometimes work, but often the groove cut will be deeper than is allowed by Porsche specifications. On some of the later 911s, there are brake pad sensors that indicate to you when the pads are getting low.

Brake pads should only be replaced in pairs—replace both sets of front pads or both sets of rear pads at a time. The same rule applies to the brake discs, which should be checked each time you replace your brake pads.

There are slight configuration differences between front and rear brakes, but the procedure for replacement is similar. First, jack up the car and remove the road wheel. This will expose the brake caliper that presses the pads against the disc. Make sure the parking brake is off when you start working.

The pads are held within the caliper by two retaining pins. There are also small retaining clips that hold the pins in the caliper. First remove the clips, and then tap out the pins with a small screwdriver and a hammer. When the retaining pins are removed, the cross spring that holds the pads in place will fall out.

Now the pads can be pried out with a screwdriver. Use the small holes on the pads that normally surround the retaining pin as a leverage point for removing them. This might take some wiggling, as it is sometimes a tight fit. Keep in mind that the caliper piston is also probably pressing against the pads slightly, and will add to the challenge of removal.

Once the pads are out, inspect the inside of the caliper. You should clean this area with some compressed air and isopropyl alcohol. Make sure that the dust boots and the clamping rings inside the caliper are not ripped or damaged. If they are, the caliper may need to be rebuilt.

At this point, you should inspect the brake discs carefully. Using a micrometer, take a measurement of the disc thickness. If the disc is worn beyond its specifications, then it's time to replace it along with the one on the other side. See Project 47 for more information.

Installing the new brake pads is quite easy. You will need to take a small piece of wood or plastic and push the caliper piston back into the caliper. This is because the new pads are going to be a lot thicker than the old ones, and the piston is set for the old pads. Pry back the piston with the wood, and don't use too much force. Using a screwdriver can accidentally damage the dust boots and seals inside the caliper, and is not recommended. Make sure to push both pistons (inside and outside) back in the caliper.

Be aware that as you push back the pistons in the calipers, you will cause the brake reservoir level to rise. Make sure not to have too much fluid in your reservoir. If the level is high, you can siphon out a bit to prevent it from overflowing. Make sure to have the cap securely fastened to the reservoir's top, or else brake fluid might get on your paint.

When the piston is pushed all the way back, you should then be able to insert the pad into the caliper. If you encounter resistance, double-check to make sure that the inside of the caliper is clean. You can use

REPLACING BRAKE PADS

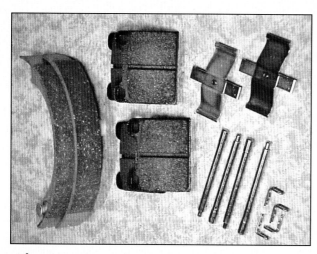

1 Shown here are some of the parts that you need to replace and refurbish your rear brakes. At the top is a pair of emergency brake shoes. These usually don't need replacing unless someone has been driving great distances with the emergency brake engaged. You need to remove the brake rotor in order to replace these shoes (see Project 51). The brake pads featured here are a complete set of rear pads shown with their accompanying retainer kit. The kit includes two new retainer springs and four pins that are used to hold the pads into the caliper.

2 To remove the old pads, pull out the small pin retainers, and tap out the retaining pins with a screwdriver and a small hammer. They should slide out pretty easily, as there is usually no load on them. If there is much difficulty encountered during the removal process, then tap on the pads slightly to remove pressure from the pins.

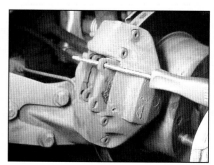

3 Pulling out the pads usually involves the use of a screwdriver for leverage. The pads are loose in the caliper, but it's a pretty tight fit, and there is usually lots of dust and debris in the caliper. Wiggle the pads back and forth in order to pry them free.

a small hammer to tap it in, but don't use too much force. When the pads are in place, insert the retaining pins and spring clip back into place. It's wise to use a new set of pins and clips when replacing your pads. Make sure that you replace the pin retaining clips inside the small holes in the retaining pins.

Tom Woodford of Factory Tour recommends replacing the brake pads one at a time. When the piston on one side is pushed back into the caliper, it will try to push out the piston on the opposite side of the caliper. Leaving the brake pad installed on one side keeps the piston from being pushed out too far.

You also may want to spray the back of the brake pads with some antisqueal glue. This glue basically keeps the pads and the pistons glued together, and prevents noisy vibration. Antisqueal pads can also be purchased as sheets that are peeled off and placed on the rear of the pads.

When finished with both sides, press on the brake pedal repeatedly to make sure that the pads and the pistons seat properly. Also make sure that you top off the master cylinder brake fluid reservoir if necessary. Brake pads typically take between 100 and 200 miles to completely break in. It's typical for braking performance to suffer slightly, as the pads begin their wear-in period. Make sure that you avoid any heavy braking during this period.

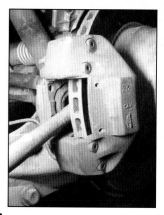

4 When you are ready to install the pads back into the caliper, use a wooden or plastic handle to push back the caliper pistons. Don't use a screwdriver, as you might damage some of the piston seals. Keep your eye on the fluid level in the master cylinder reservoir—it can overflow when you push back on the pistons.

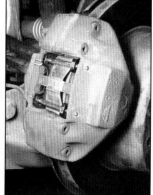

5 Don't forget to reinstall the small retaining clips for the pad retaining pins. The completed assembly should be carefully tested before you do any performance driving. Brake pads can also take several hundred miles to completely break themselves in. Exercise care when driving with brand-new brake pads.

PROJECT 47 • REPLACING BRAKE DISCS

Time: 3 hours

Tools: Impact screwdriver (if necessary), micrometer

Talent:

Applicable Years: All

Tab: $180

Tinware: Brake discs, new pads, brake pad retainer pins, new emergency brake shoes (if required)

Tip: Adjust your emergency brake while you have access.

PERFORMANCE GAIN: Better, safer braking

COMPLEMENTARY MODIFICATION: Replace brake pads, emergency brake shoes, install stainless steel brake lines, install new wheel bearings.

Brake discs (or rotors, as they are often called) are a very important part of the braking system. The brake pads rub against the discs to create a friction force that is responsible for slowing the car down. If the rotors become too thin, or develop grooves in their surface, their ability to stop the car decreases.

When replacing your brake pads, always measure the thickness of your brake discs. If they fall below the specified value for your car, they need to be replaced with new ones. Check for grooves in the rotor, making sure to take measurements of the disc in several different places. This will guarantee an accurate reading. If the brake disc has a groove in it, then it should most certainly be removed and resurfaced by a machine shop. Discs with grooves brake less efficiently, become hotter, and reduce your overall braking ability.

The measurements that you take with your micrometer should be made from the center of the disc. Use the table below to determine if your rotors need to be replaced.

If you do find that you need to replace your rotors, the process is a relatively simple one. The procedure for the front or the rear rotors is very similar, but for the sake of this project, we'll look at replacing the rears, which is slightly more complicated, due to the addition of the rear parking/emergency brake.

Step one is to jack up the car and remove the road wheel. If you haven't already, remove the brake pads from the caliper. Refer to Project 46, Replacing Brake Pads, for more details. The flexible rubber brake hose is attached to the trailing arm of the car with a large clip, which retains both the flexible line and the hard line that connects to the rear caliper. Remove this clip so that you can remove the caliper without bending the hard metal brake line.

Now, unbolt the caliper from the trailing arm where it is mounted. There should be two 19-millimeter bolts that hold it in place. After removing these, you should be able to move the caliper out of the disc's way. Exercise caution when moving the caliper around. The hard steel line that attaches it to the rest of the brake system can be flexed a little, but too much movement can cause the line to break. Bob Tindel of Pelican Parts recommends using a coat hanger to hang the caliper out of the way. This way, you will reduce the amount of stress placed on the brake line. Make sure that you do not let the caliper hang from

Type and Year	New Thickness	Replacement Thickness
Front Rotor, 911 (1965–1968) Front Rotor, 911 (1969–1977), 911 Turbo (1976–1977)	12.7 millimeters 20.0 millimeters	11.0 millimeters 18.0 millimeters
Front Rotor, 911 (1978–1983)	20.0 millimeters	18.5 millimeters
Front Rotor, 911 Carrera (1984–1989)	24.0 millimeters	22.0 millimeters
Rear Rotor, 911T/912 (1965-1969)	10.5 millimeters	9.0 millimeters
Rear Rotor, 911 (1970–1977), 911 Turbo (1976–1977)	20.0 millimeters	18.0 millimeters
Rear Rotor, 911 (1978–1983)	20.0 millimeters	18.0 millimeters
Rear Rotor, 911 Carrera (1984–1989)	24.0 millimeters	22.0 millimeters

1 The rear brake discs have a slightly different shape from the front discs. This is due to the need for an inner "drum" area that acts as the surface for the emergency brake to press against. While the 911 has disc brakes at all wheels, the rear parking brake mechanism is most similar to a drum brake system.

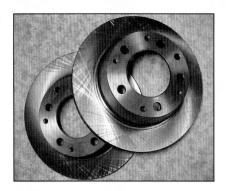

2 Before you remove your brake discs, it is important to first measure them to see if they need to be replaced. Use a micrometer to perform the measurement. If you use a dial caliper, then you might get a false reading because the disc wears on the area where the pads make contact, not on the edges of the disc. Make sure that you take several measurements to compensate for potential low or high spots on the disc.

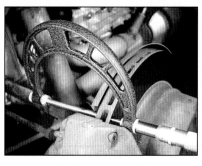

3 Removing the caliper is accomplished by unbolting the two 19-millimeter bolts that mount it to the arm. The caliper can be pushed out of the away, and doesn't need to be physically disconnected from the brake lines. Be careful not to bend the solid brake lines. Instead, remove the clip that holds both the solid line and the flexible rubber line to the trailing arm, and use the flexibility of the rubber line to allow you to pull the caliper out of the way.

4 The brake disc slides off the hub after the caliper and the two small screws that affix it in place are removed. Keep in mind that the lug nuts that hold on the wheel apply the majority of the force that constrains the disc to the hub. Note that the caliper is pushed slightly off to the side. The two parking brake shoes act on both the inside top and bottom of the rotor.

5 The new disc can be tapped on with a rubber mallet. Make sure that you have your parking brake shoes adjusted away from the inside drum, or they might interfere with the installation of the disc. New discs may not be perfectly flat, and may take a few hundred miles of break-in to achieve their maximum braking efficiency.

the rubber brake line, as this will most certainly damage the line.

Once you have the caliper out of the way, remove the two small retaining screws that hold on the brake disc. You will need a large flat-head screwdriver for this task. If these screws are really on tight, you may need an impact screwdriver for the task. At this point, make sure that the parking brake is off. You should now be able to pull the disc off of the hub. If there is any resistance, use a rubber mallet to tap the brake disc off.

If you are having a difficult time getting the disc off, it's probably because the parking brake shoes are stuck on the back of the disc. You need to adjust the parking brake so that it's not gripping the disc. For more information on this process, see Project 50, Replacing and Adjusting Parking Brake Shoes.

Installation of the new brake disc is a snap—simply push it onto the hub. Before you install the new disc, take a close look at your parking brake shoes and see if they warrant replacing. If you can see metal on the shoes, or if the previous owner had a hard time remembering to remove the emergency brake, then it might be a good time to replace these. After you

install the new discs on both sides, you should test your parking brake and adjust it if necessary. Again, refer to Project 50 for more details.

After the new disc is installed and the two retaining screws are replaced, simply reattach the caliper, and install new brake pads. Your new rotors should last a long time, and you should see an improvement in your braking after the wear-in period for your new brake pads.

BRAKES

PROJECT 48 • BRAKE LINE REPLACEMENT

 Time: 4 hours

 Tools: 11-millimeter crescent flare-nut wrench

 Talent:

 Applicable Years: All

 Tab: $65

 Tinware: New brake lines, or stainless steel brake lines

 Tip: Make sure that corroded rubber from old lines didn't end up in your caliper.

 PERFORMANCE GAIN: Better braking performence

COMPLEMENTARY MODIFICATION: Rebuild calipers, replace brake pad, flush brake system, replace master cylinder

1 Old rubber brake lines are often responsible for poor brake performance. As the car ages, the rubber begins to break down and can clog the lines, leading to very little pressure getting to the calipers. The brake lines should be renewed if they are old or if you are having problems with your brakes. The arrow points to the flexible brake line on the rear of the car that needs to be replaced.

One of the most popular projects for the 911 is replacing the flexible brake lines that connect from the main chassis of the car to the A-arms and the trailer arms. These lines are made out of rubber, and have a tendency to break down and corrode over many years. The rubber lines should be carefully inspected every 10,000 miles or so. They can exhibit strange characteristics, such as bubbling and expanding prior to actually bursting. Needless to say, failure of these lines is a very bad thing, as you will instantly lose pressure in one half of your brake system.

Faulty brake lines in the front of your 911 can cause all sorts of steering problems when braking. It is common for bad hoses to cause a car to dart from side to side to when braking. Bad hoses allow pressure to build up in the caliper, but sometimes do not release this pressure properly when the pedal is depressed.

The first step in replacing your lines is to elevate the car. Remove the wheels from each side of the car, as this will make it much easier to access the brake lines. You might want to bleed the entire system of brake fluid before you start disconnecting the lines. Refer to Project 49, Bleeding Porsche Brakes, for

more information. If you're not planning to flush your entire system, Bob Tindel of Pelican Parts recommends pushing the brake pedal down just to the point of engagement, and blocking it there. If you do this, you will lose less brake fluid, and also less air will enter into the system.

Once the brake system is dry, it's time to disconnect the brake lines. Make sure that you have some paper towels handy, as some brake fluid will leak out of the lines. Brake fluid is perhaps the most dangerous fluid to your car, as any amount spilled on the paint will permanently mar it. If you do get some on the paint, make sure that you blot it, and don't wipe it off. Be aware that your hands may contain some brake fluid, so don't even touch anything near the paint on the car with your hands.

The brake lines themselves can be very difficult to remove. The goal of this job is to remove the lines without damaging anything else. In this case, the easiest thing to damage (besides your paint) is the hard steel brake lines that connect to the flexible rubber lines. These lines have relatively soft fittings on each end, and often become deformed and stripped when removed. The key to success is to use a flared-nut wrench. This wrench is basically designed for jobs like this one where the fittings are soft and might be heavily corroded. The flared end of the wrench hugs the fitting, and prevents it from stripping. It is very important to only use this type of wrench, as it is easy to damage the fittings using a regular crescent wrench.

The other disastrous thing that can happen is that the fitting can get stuck to the rest of the hard line.

2 A required tool is the flare-nut wrench that fully wraps around the brake line. If you use a standard wrench, there is a high chance of rounding off the corners, and permanently damaging the hard brake lines. These fittings are not very strong, and will

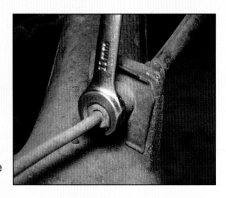

become stripped if you don't use one of these wrenches. Once the fitting becomes stripped, the line needs to be replaced (usually a special order part from Germany). Also make sure that the fitting is turning—not the line. It is very easy to twist off the ends of the hard lines when the fitting binds.

3 New stainless-steel lines are identical in size and length to the original ones that shipped with the car. The advantage to the stainless-steel lines is that they have a protective coating on the outside that prevents the ele-

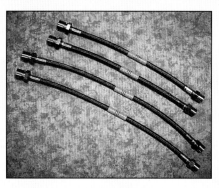

ments from attacking them as easily. There is a downside, though. The stainless-steel sheath doesn't allow you to inspect the rubber inside to see if there is any significant deterioration. Some of the aftermarket lines are made of Teflon or have Teflon components to help increase their durability.

The fitting is supposed to turn and rotate on the end of the line, but sometimes it becomes too corroded to break free. When this happens, the fitting and the steel line will usually twist together, and it will break the line. Be careful when you are removing this fitting to make sure that you are not twisting the line.

If you do damage the hard line or strip the fitting, then the replacement line is probably going to be a special order part that will have to be shipped in from Germany. You can usually find the correct length line at your local auto parts store, but then you will have to bend it into shape, and most of the time, this is a very difficult process that requires a few special tools. The moral of this story, and this entire book, is that you should use the right tool for the job (the flare-nut wrench).

After you have disconnected the hard metal line, you can now remove the flexible lines from the car. At both ends, the lines are attached using spring clips. Sometimes, depending upon the angle, these clips can be quite difficult to remove. With a good pair of Vise-Grips though, they can usually be pulled off the car.

Installation of the new lines is straightforward, and is the easy part of the job. Before you start attaching the lines, make sure that you have the correct type for your car. There are a few different types, and a few different lengths, so make sure that the ones that you are putting on are the same length and have the same fittings as the ones that you are removing.

When it comes to replacing brake lines, many people install stainless-steel braided lines on their car.

The rumor has it that the stainless-steel sheath keeps the rubber line from expanding under pressure, and actually delivers better performance than the standard lines. While this reasoning sounds good at first, it's mostly hype. The stainless-steel braided lines are usually made of the same rubber underneath, and are simply protected by the outside sheath. Even if the sheath were tight enough and strong enough to prevent the lines from expanding, it really wouldn't make a difference in braking. Even if the lines expand a little, the resulting pressure that is exerted at the caliper will be almost the same.

Regardless of the rumor mill, I will recommend that you place the stainless-steel lines on your car because the outside sheath protects the lines from dirt, grime, rocks, small animals, and other things you might run over with your car.

The other thing that might warrant your consideration is the label of DOT (Department of Transportation) certification. The original rubber lines were required to be certified under a certain set of specifications dictated by the DOT for use on U.S. highways. Often, the stainless-steel lines are aftermarket components that are not DOT certified, and are subsequently listed for "off road use only." In reality, these lines are more than adequate for use on your car, and any concern over the use of them is not really necessary. For those who want to be absolutely sure and certified, there are manufacturers who will make DOT-certified stainless-steel lines, but they are usually more expensive than the non-certified lines.

BRAKES
PROJECT 49 • BLEEDING BRAKES

Time: 2 hours

Tools: Vacuum brake bleeder, pressure brake bleeder, friendly assistant with a good right leg

Talent:

Applicable Years: All

Tab: $20

Tinware: Brake fluid

Tip: Bleed your brakes with different colored fluid so that you know when all of your older fluid has been flushed through the system.

PERFORMANCE GAIN: Stiffer and safer braking

COMPLEMENTARY MODIFICATION: Replace master cylinder, replace brake lines

Bleeding brakes is not one of my personal favorite jobs. There seems to be a bit of black magic involved with the bleeding process. Sometimes it will work perfectly, and then other times it seems that you end up with a lot of air in your system. The best strategy to follow when bleeding your brakes is to repeat the procedure several times in order to make sure that you have removed all the trapped air from the system.

The right tools are a necessary part of the job too. A few days before this book was to be sent off to my editor, I had a chance to evaluate a new type of pressure brake bleeder kit from Motive Products. Retailing for about $45, this kit attaches to the top of the master cylinder reservoir and applies pressurized air to the system. Brake fluid is forced out of the master cylinder reservoir and into the system. The pressurized kit is probably the best one around because it is the least likely to create air bubbles in the system. There was a time when no one was manufacturing pressurized bleeders, but thankfully, Motive Products now supplies this excellent-quality kit at a reasonable cost.

The pressurized system works very well because it pushes the brake fluid out of the reservoir and into the system. In this manner, it is very unlikely to create air bubbles in the system. When small air bubbles form in the brake lines, the entire system suffers as the brake pedal becomes soft. This is because air is much more compressible than the brake fluid. When you push on the pedal, the air trapped in the lines acts like a spring inside of the system. The air becomes compressed, absorbing energy from the system, instead of directing the energy toward pushing the caliper piston against the brake disc.

A second alternative is the vacuum bleeding kit. This kit works in the opposite manner of the pressure bleeder, applying a vacuum to the brake system in order to draw brake fluid out of the car. The system works well, but can sometimes cause air bubbles to form in the lines. Particularly on cars with rear brake proportioning valves, like the Porsche 914, the vacuum system can leave air trapped in these valves, giving a spongy pedal as a result. When using the vacuum bleeding system, the best approach is to bleed each corner of the car several times, to ensure that all the air is out of the system. Simply fill up your brake reservoir, attach the pump system, pump up some vacuum, and then open the bleed nipple. Brake fluid should be pulled out of the system when the vacuum is applied. If not—you may have a problem with your brake lines.

The third and most labor-intensive method of bleeding your brakes involves actually having an assistant press on the pedal while you go around to each wheel and bleed the system. Without a doubt, this is the most effective method of bleeding, and should probably be used as a final procedure when performing any brake system bleeding. This method actually pushes fluid through the system (similar to the pressure-fed system) at a high rate of velocity. Sometimes, air bubbles that are in the system can become dislodged and be cleared out by the quick rush of brake fluid when you press on the brake pedal.

The procedure for bleeding the brakes using the brake pedal is pretty straightforward. Attach a small rubber hose to the brake caliper nipple and let the other end hang inside an empty container. Ask your assistant to firmly and quickly press on the pedal three times, and hold it down the third time. Then, open up the bleed nipple by unscrewing it slightly. Brake fluid should come rushing out and the pedal should sink to the floor.

Left: One of the most popular vacuum brake bleeding kits is the MityVac kit. This kit contains a hand-operated vacuum pump and a variety of attachments to allow it to fit just about any car. The pump draws brake fluid using vacuum pressure created by the hand pump. This photograph shows the process of emptying the system of brake fluid, prior to removing a brake caliper.

Below left: This is the pressure bleeder kit from Motive Products. Brand-new, this product is a step above its now-defunct precursor, the EZ-Bleed system. It has a hand pump for pressurizing the brake fluid to just about any pressure. A small gauge indicates the pressure of the brake fluid inside the reservoir, which can hold about two quarts of brake fluid—more than enough for most brake flushing and bleeding jobs. Retailing for about $45, the bleeder kit is a useful and cost-effective tool to have in your collection.

Make sure that your assistant doesn't remove his or her foot from the pedal, because that will suck air back into the system. With the pedal still completely depressed, tighten up the bleed nipple. When this nipple is closed, have your assistant remove his or her foot from the pedal.

I recommend that you use this procedure as a final step, even if you are vacuum- or pressure-bleeding. The high force associated with the pressure from the brake pedal can help free air and debris in the lines. If the brake fluid doesn't exit the nipple quickly, then you might have a clog in your lines. Brake fluid that simply oozes out of the lines slowly is a clear indication that your rubber lines might be clogged and constricted. Don't ignore these warning signs—check out the brake lines while you are working in this area.

Another important thing to remember is that brake fluid kills—paint jobs, that is. Brake fluid spilled on paint will permanently mar the surface, so be very careful not to touch the car if you have it on your hands and clothing. This, of course, is easier said than done. Just be aware of this fact. Rubber gloves help to prevent you from getting it on your hands and your paint. If you do get a spot on your paint, make sure that you blot it with a paper towel—don't wipe or smear it. It's also important not to try to clean it off with any chemical or other cleaning solutions.

During the bleeding process, it's very easy to forget to check your master cylinder reservoir. As you are removing fluid from the calipers, it will be emptying the master cylinder reservoir. If the reservoir goes empty, you will most certainly add some air bubbles to the system, and you will have to start all over. Keep an eye on the fluid level and don't forget to refill it. Make sure that you always put the cap back on the reservoir. If the cap is off, brake fluid may splash out and damage your paint when the brake pedal is released. If you are using a pressure bleeder system, make sure that you check the level of brake fluid in the bleeder reservoir often so that you don't accidentally run dry.

If you are installing a new master cylinder, it's probably a wise idea to perform what is called a dry-bleed on the workbench. This is simply the process of getting the master cylinder full of brake fluid and "wet." Simply add some brake fluid to both chambers of the master cylinder, and pump it a few times. This will save you a few moments when bleeding the brakes.

When bleeding the system, start with the wheel farthest from the master cylinder, and work your way back toward the front left wheel. In other words, bleed the system in this order: right-rear, left-rear, right-front, left-front. This minimizes the air that getting into the system. Always bleed each caliper more than once, because bleeding the other calipers can dislodge air into the system. Surprisingly, after five times around the car a little air can still be in the system. A good rule of thumb is the more you bleed, the better your brakes.

There are few little tricks that you can use when changing your brake fluid. The company ATE makes brake fluid that comes in two different colors. It's a smart idea to fill your reservoir with a different-colored fluid, and then bleed the brakes. When the new-colored fluid exits out of the caliper, you will know that you have fresh fluid in your system. Make sure that you use DOT 3 or DOT 4 brake fluid in your car. Some of the later-model 911s with antilock braking systems required the use of DOT 4. The use of silicone DOT 5 fluid is not recommended for street use.

You should also routinely flush and replace your brake fluid every two years. Deposits and debris can build up in the lines over time and decrease the efficiency of your brakes. Regular bleeding of your system can also help you spot brake problems that you wouldn't necessarily notice simply by driving the car.

There is also a new product out called Speed Bleeders. These small caps replace the standard bleeder valves located on your calipers. The Speed Bleeders have a built-in check valve that eliminates the need for a second person when pedal bleeding the brakes. Simply open the bleeder valve for a particular caliper and step on the brake pedal. The Speed Bleeder will allow brake fluid to cleanly bleed out of the system, without sucking air back in. When used in conjunction with a pressure bleeder system, you can achieve a pretty firm pedal bleeding the brakes by yourself. I still recommend using the two-person pedal-stepping method as a final procedure, simply because the high pressure from this method can help to unclog trapped air bubbles.

BRAKES
PROJECT 50 • PARKING BRAKE ADJUSTMENT

 Time: 1 hour

 Tools: Long screwdriver, flashlight

 Talent: 👤

 Applicable Years: All

 Tab: –

 Tinware: –

 Tip: Properly adjusting your parking brake can reduce the amount of drag on your road wheels.

 PERFORMANCE GAIN: Better parking brake performance

COMPLEMENTARY MODIFICATION: Adjust clutch cable, replace brake pads

1 Removing the rotor reveals the mechanism for the parking brake adjustment. As the cog is turned, the parking brake shoes are pushed outward toward the inside of the disc. The shoes are properly adjusted when they are just about to touch the inside of the disc. Use this photo to identify the location of the sprocket when you are trying to look through the access hole in the brake disc.

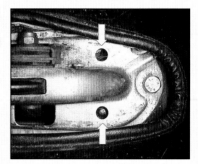

2 Pulling up the carpet reveals the cable equalizer check holes (shown by the arrows). It is important that the equalizer be level (as shown here), or your parking brake will not work properly. If not, then adjust the parking brake cables where they attach to the rear of the brake assembly.

The first step is to raise the rear of the car and remove the two road wheels. This will allow you access to the rear calipers. Make sure that the parking brake lever is released. Using a screwdriver, push back slightly on the brake pads until the brake disc is allowed to turn freely on its spindle. Remember to check the fluid level in the master cylinder reservoir, as pushing the pads back may cause it to overflow.

Once the brake disc can be moved easily, loosen the two nuts that attach the handbrake cable to the inside of the brake mechanism. If there is any tension on these cables, it will be difficult to adjust the handbrake. The adjustment of the parking brake shoes is accomplished by turning a small gear or sprocket with a screwdriver. This sprocket can only be reached through a small access hole in the brake disc.

Looking at your brake discs carefully, you will see a large hole in the disc. Rotate the brake disc until you can see the small adjusting sprocket through the hole. You may need a flashlight for this procedure. Rotate the cog until the parking brake shoe is tight and the rotor can no longer be rotated. If you are turning the sprocket a lot, and the brake disc isn't tightening up, then you

are probably turning it the in the wrong direction. Repeat this procedure for the opposite side of the car.

After you have the sprockets adjusted so that the brake shoes have just pressed up against the inside of the disc, tighten up the ends of the parking brake cables. Now, move to the cockpit of the car, and pick up the carpet that covers the rear of the handbrake/heater lever assembly. In the assembly housing, you will find two access holes, through which you will see a small lever that attaches to both parking brake cables. As you pull the lever, you should see this equalizer lever move. When the parking brake handle is up, the equalizer must be parallel with the axle of the car, or one side of the parking brake will work better than the other. If the equalizer is skewed, then adjust the parking brake cables at the point where they screw into the rear of the brake assembly. Adjust the lengths of the two cables using the two adjusting nuts until the equalizer is parallel with the axles of the car.

After you have determined that the equalizer lever is properly set, tighten up the two nuts against each other on the cables located near the rear brake assemblies. Then, back off the parking brake adjusting sprocket (using a screwdriver, poking through the brake disc) about four to five teeth. Finally, check the proper operation of the handbrake. The brake discs should be free to rotate with the handle in the down position, but fully locked by the time that the handbrake is pulled up at least four clicks. Recheck the master cylinder reservoir, and also step on the brake pedal a few times to make sure that the pistons have repositioned themselves properly against the brake pads.

BRAKES
PROJECT 51 • PARKING BRAKE SHOE REPLACEMENT

 Time: 3 hour

 Tools: 19-millimeter socket, rubber mallet

 Talent: 🔧🔧

 Applicable Years: All

 Tab: $125

 Tinware: New parking brake shoes

 Tip: Wear safety glasses when working around the spring-loaded mechanisms.

 PERFORMANCE GAIN: Better parking brake performance

COMPLEMENTARY MODIFICATION: Replace the brake pads, brake discs.

If your parking brake is not functioning properly, then perhaps it's time that you replaced your parking brake shoes. The first step in the process is to make sure that your parking brake cables and handles are adjusted properly (Project 50).

The parking brake shoes can only be inspected after the removal of the rear brake discs (Project 47). Visually inspect the shoes for wear. The shoes should have some brake lining along the top, and should not have any heavy grooves cut into them. Compare your brake shoes to the new shoes shown in Project 46 to determine if you need to replace yours.

After the brake disc has been removed from the brake assembly, remove the small parking brake adjuster by prying it out from between the upper and lower parking brake shoe. Make sure that the parking brake handle is all the way down for this procedure. Be careful while you are performing this removal, as the adjuster is spring-loaded and the springs may fly out when you are prying the adjuster out.

When you have removed the adjuster, take a needle-nose pliers and remove the long spring that that holds the upper and lower shoes together

1 Remove the small adjusting cog assembly by using a large screwdriver to push it out from between the two parking brake shoes. With some effort, the cog assembly should pop out, leaving a little bit of slack between the two parking brake shoes.

2 Using a pair of pliers, grab and unhook the parking brake spring from the brake shoes. Be careful of the spring, as it is under a lot of tension at this point. Also undo the small spring retainer (indicated by the arrow) that secures the brake shoes to the rear trailing arm. Use a pair of Vise-Grips and a pair of needle-nose pliers to twist the spring and unlatch it from the assembly. Be very careful when installing the new shoe, as the retaining springs have a tendency to snap out of place and fly out.

near where the adjuster was mounted. Again, be careful of the spring, as it may fly off unexpectedly. Make sure that you wear safety glasses during this entire procedure.

Now, remove the washer and conical spring retaining mechanism at the top of the assembly. Press in the spring, and then rotate the special spring washer so that you can slide it out of its retainer. Make sure that you don't lose the parts if they happen to fly out.

Move to the front of the brake assembly (toward the front of the car), and remove the long spring from the two brake shoes. Use the needle-nose pliers again, and be careful not to catch your fingers in the process.

After all the springs have been removed from the parking brake assembly, both the top and the bottom shoes should simply lift off of the assembly. The new shoe should be installed in an opposite manner to the removal process. Reassemble the parking brake by attaching the long spring toward the front of the car first, then the upper conical spring, and then the spring toward the rear. When you are finished, test the assembly by operating the emergency brake handle a few times. Carefully check the springs and make sure that they are properly seated in the restraining holes in the brake shoes.

Reinstall the brake disc, and make sure that you recheck and adjust the parking brake mechanism (Project 50) before you reinstall the caliper and the brake pads.

BRAKES

PROJECT 52 • MASTER CYLINDER REPLACEMENT

Time: 4 hours

Tools: Torque wrench

Talent:

Applicable Years: All

Tab: $150

Tinware: New master cyclinder, new brake fluid

Tip: Make sure that you keep all brake fluid away from your paint.

PERFORMANCE GAIN: Better braking, no more leaky master cylinders

COMPLEMENTARY MODIFICATION: Wiper reversal, install stainless steel brake lines, new brake discs, pedal cluster rebuild.

Without a doubt, your brakes are one of the most important systems on the car. The heart of the brake system is the master cylinder, which controls the hydraulic pressure of the entire system. Unfortunately, over many years, the master cylinder has a tendency to wear out and leak. The leakage can occur internally or externally, resulting in a weakened braking system. If you have any problems with your brakes, and you think that it's related to the master cylinder, you should probably replace it.

On the early cars without power brakes, the master cylinder is located underneath the car, covered by a large panel often called the belly pan. To gain access to the master cylinder, you need to remove this panel. The master cylinder is bolted to the pedal cluster, with the chassis of the car sandwiched in between. Access to the master cylinder is usually pretty good if you have the front of the car raised off of the ground. See Project 40 for more details.

The cars equipped with power brakes have the master cylinder located in the front trunk compartment. Prior to removing the master cylinder, it's a wise idea to confirm that your brake vacuum booster is working properly. While you can usually tell during normal driving, Bob Tindel of Pelican Parts suggests an alternative method of testing. Press the brake pedal a few times when the engine of the car is off. Holding down the brake pedal with a light touch, start the engine. The brake pedal will give way slightly under your foot, indicating that the vacuum booster is pulling on the pedal. If it doesn't, then you might want to consider replacing the vacuum booster, or checking the vacuum hoses that supply the booster.

In order to remove the master cylinder on the power brake cars, you need to first disconnect the actuation rod and mounting nut from inside the cockpit of the car. Remove the floorboard (see Project 40 for additional details) and remove the small pin that holds the actuating rod to the master cylinder. In addition, there is a small nut that holds the master cylinder to the chassis. Remove this nut before you move back into the front luggage compartment.

In the front trunk of the car, you now need to start removing a few things. Start with the carpet and remove the front cover to the air blower (see Project 69 for more details). It's a wise idea to hang on tight to all nuts, bolts, and tools during this entire procedure, as it is difficult to retrieve items that are dropped in the front trunk. Remove the fresh air hoses that get in your way, and also remove the silver, rectangular cruise control brain if your car is so equipped. Now disconnect the vacuum lines from the brake booster and the overflow hose from the reservoir.

Location	Tool Size	(Thread)	Torque-N-m	(Ft/lb)
Master cylinder to brake booster	13-millimeter	(M8)	25	(19)
Brake booster console to trunk floor	13-millimeter	(M8)	25	(19)
Brace strut to console	17-millimeter	(M10)	46	(35)
Brake lines to master cylinder	11-millimeter	(M10 X 1)	14	(11)
Bleeder screws in calipers (front)	9-millimeter		3	(2)
Bleeder screws in calipers (rear)	7-millimeter		3	(2)

Whether your car has power or manual brakes, removal of the brake lines is very important. As with the installation of new flexible brake lines, it is very important not to strip out the fittings on the lines. You should always use an 11-millimeter flare-nut wrench to remove the fittings from the master cylinder. See Project 48 for more details. It's also a wise idea to spray the area with some WD-40 or other lubricant if the lines seem to be heavily corroded. This will usually be the case more with the early cars, because the master cylinder is under the car, where it is more susceptible to the elements.

Before you remove the master cylinder, make sure that you siphon off as much brake fluid as you possibly can from the reservoir, using a turkey baster or other tool. Disconnect the hoses connecting the master cylinder to the reservoir. Remember to avoid spilling any brake fluid on your paint. On the manual brake cars, the master cylinder is held in using two nuts attached to the pedal cluster. On the power brake cars, the vacuum booster holds in the master cylinder, using four nuts mounted to the floor of the front trunk.

After you have the master cylinder removed, you can take it over to your workbench. Unbolt it from the vacuum booster and separate the two units. If your new master cylinder is missing any small hoses or fittings, transfer them from the old one. Reattach the new master cylinder to the brake booster, being careful not to torque the nuts past the value of 25 N-m (18.4 ft-lb). If you overtighten these bolts, you may permanently damage your brake booster, which is a very expensive part to replace. Make sure that you install the small O-ring into the master cylinder before you attach it to the brake booster.

When reassembling the master cylinder in your car, it's important to use the proper torque values. Follow the specifications in the table on page 138.

When the master cylinder is reinstalled, it's time to bleed your brake system. You may want to dry-bleed the master cylinder on the bench to prime it before you start the install. For more information on bleeding your brakes, see Project 49. Following the bleeding of the brakes, reassemble all the surrounding parts in the trunk that you have disassembled, and make sure that everything is tightened. Reinstall all the carpets and the floorboard in the cockpit.

When you are ready to drive the car, make sure that you test the brakes beforehand. Don't drive near other cars, and prepare to use the emergency brake if necessary. It's probably a wise idea to bleed the brakes again a few days after you install the new master cylinder, to make sure that you have gotten all of the air out of the brake system. If the emergency brake warning

1 On cars with power brakes, the connection to the master cylinder and the retaining nut are right above the foot pedal. Remove the actuating lever by removing the small pin that attaches it to the pedal cluster (shown by the white arrow). Also shown in this photo is the mounting bolt for the master cylinder assembly (green arrow).

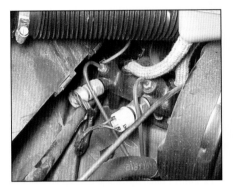

2 This photo affords us a great look at the master cylinder in power-assisted 911s. The two main brake lines are the metal ones exiting diagonally out of the master cylinder. The fluid is fed from the reservoir to the top of the master cylinder via the cloth-braided rubber hose. The two electrical switches that exit out of the side of the master cylinder are used to detect pressure drops in the system.

3 Make sure that you use the appropriate torque values when tightening the connections to the master cylinder. Overtightening the vacuum booster can damage it internally. This is also a good time to bench-bleed the master cylinder. This process basically fills the master cylinder with fluid and primes it prior to installation in the car. Bench-bleeding the master cylinder can save a little time later on, but it can also get a little messy.

lamp lights up on the dashboard, you might need to either manually reset the switch on the master cylinder (for manual brake cars) or briefly remove the battery ground strap on the power brake cars.

BRAKES
PROJECT 53 • REBUILDING YOUR BRAKE CALIPERS

Time: 6 hours

Tools: Flared-end wrench to remove brake lines

Talent:

Applicable Years: All

Tab: $60

Tinware: Brake caliper rebuild kit, brake fluid, silicone assembly lube

Tip: Soak the caliper in parts cleaner overnight if possible.

PERFORMANCE GAIN: Better braking—no more sticking calipers

COMPLEMENTARY MODIFICATION: Replace the flexible brake lines, replace brake pads and discs.

If your car is pulling to one side when braking, then there is a good chance that you might have a sticky caliper that needs rebuilding. The rebuilding process is a actually a lot simpler than most people think. It basically involves removing the caliper, taking it apart, cleaning it, and then reinstalling all of the components with new seals. Very often, the most difficult part of the task is the process of actually removing the caliper from the car.

The first step is to jack up the car and remove the caliper. Refer to Project 47 for details on removing the caliper from around the brake disc. Refer to Project 48 for more details on disconnecting the brake line from the caliper.

Once you have the caliper free and clear from the car, take it over to your workbench, and begin the disassembly process. You don't have to disassemble the two halves of the caliper if they weren't leaking. However, if you fully want to clean out the caliper, then you should take it apart. Keep in mind that sometimes it's difficult to reassemble them without having them leak, so be forewarned. Most caliper kits also do not contain the O-rings that seal the two halves to each other.

Now, you can remove the pistons from the calipers. One method of removal, suggested by Bob Tindel of Pelican Parts, is to use compressed air to blow out the pistons. Using a small screwdriver, remove the dust boots that surround the piston. You may need to remove the retaining ring in order to remove the boots from the caliper. Place a small block of wood in the center of the caliper to prevent the pistons from falling out of the caliper. Then, take a C-clamp and clamp down one of the pistons. Blow compressed air through the caliper bleeder hole to force the piston out of its chamber. Start slowly, and gradually increase pressure until the piston reaches the block of wood. Make sure that the piston doesn't come all the way out of its chamber. After the piston is far enough out that you can get a grip on it, remove the C-clamp and place it on the other side so that you are keeping the already extended piston from traveling out any further. Blow compressed air through the bleeder hole again, and the other piston should move out of the other half. Be careful when working with compressed air—it is more powerful than it appears, and can make the pistons suddenly fly out of the caliper unexpectedly.

Using a rag to protect the sides of the pistons, carefully remove them from the caliper using either your hands, or a large pair of Vise-Grips. Make sure that you don't touch the sides of the pistons with any metal tools, as you don't want to scratch this surface.

If the pistons are frozen, then more radical methods of removal may be necessary. Disassemble the calipers into their two halves. Then, using a block of wood, pound the half of the caliper on the block of wood until the inside piston begins to fall out. If the piston starts to come out and then gets stuck, push it back in all the way and try again. Eventually, the piston should come out of the caliper half.

Another method is to use the car's brake system to release the pistons. Reconnect the caliper to the car and have an assistant pump the brakes to force out the inner pistons. Make sure that one piston doesn't fall out of the caliper, or you will have difficulty removing the other one.

Once the pistons have been removed from the caliper, carefully clean both the inside and outside of the caliper using brake cleaner or another appropriate solvent. All of the passages should be blown out with compressed air, and it's a good idea to let the whole assembly sit in some parts cleaner overnight. If the piston or the inside of the caliper is badly rusted or pitted, then the caliper should be

1 Rebuilding calipers is a lot easier than you would normally think. The basic principle involves tearing apart the caliper, cleaning it, and then reinstalling the pistons with new seals and clips. Professionally rebuilt calipers, like this one, are usually sandblasted so that they return to their original gold color. Rebuilding your calipers may solve a lot of mysterious brake problems that you may have been experiencing. Because the process of rebuilding seems difficult, it's usually the last project tackled when overhauling the brakes.

2 Make sure that you replace the inner piston seal. This seal is what keeps brake fluid from leaking out past the cylinder. Make sure that you clean the entire inner cylinder for dirt, debris, and corrosion. Be careful not to scratch the inside of the caliper cylinder while you are working on it, or you may have problems with the caliper leaking when you reassemble it.

replaced. A little bit of surface rust is OK—this should be polished off using a coarse cloth or some Scotch-Brite. Make sure that you thoroughly scrub out the entire inside of the caliper and the pistons so that they are perfectly clean.

After the caliper and pistons have been cleaned and are dry, coat the caliper and piston with silicone assembly lube. If you can't find this silicone assembly lube at your local auto parts store, then make sure you coat the entire assembly with clean brake fluid. Do not get any lube or brake fluid on the dust boot.

Insert the new piston seal into the inside of the caliper piston groove. It should fit smoothly in the groove, yet stick out only slightly. Make sure that you wet the seal with a little brake fluid. Now, insert the piston into the caliper. It should slide in easily—make sure that it doesn't get cocked. On the top of the piston, there is a portion of the groove that is recessed. It is important to align this recess at a 20-degree angle to the brake pads (refer to the diagram at right). This angle is required to keep the brake pads from squealing when pressed against the brake disc.

After you make sure that the piston angle is correct, push the piston into the caliper half. Make sure that the piston angle is correct when you have the piston pushed back into the housing. If it is not correct, then you need to pull the piston out again (compressed air, etc.) and realign it.

When both pistons are installed, fit the dust boot around the pistons and attach the retaining clip. On the rear calipers, it helps if the pistons are sticking out about 1/8 of an inch from the housing in order to get the boot to fit.

Once the dust boots are installed, remount the caliper back onto the car. Install the brake pads (Project 46), bleed the brake system (Project 49), and you should be good to go. Make sure that you carefully check the brakes on the car before you do any significant driving.

3 This diagram shows the proper orientation of the caliper pistons inside the caliper. The notches on the caliper must be offset at 20° before you reattach it to the car. The pistons are designed to reduce brake squeal when installed at this orientation.

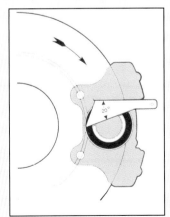

SECTION SEVEN
SUSPENSION

The setup of your 911's suspension is highly dependent on your own driving habits. Fortunately, the suspension is one of the easier items to modify and tune to your preferences on the 911. Whether you're an avid autocross racer or a regular street driver, the projects in this section will detail upgrades and maintenance required to tailor your 911 to your own driving profile.

SUSPENSION

PROJECT 54 • INSTALLING A CAMBER STRUT BRACE

 Time: 4 hours

 Tools: Socket set, 22-millimeter socket, breaker bar

 Talent: ▮ ▮ ▮

 Applicable Years: All

 Tab: $200

 Tinware: Camber strut brace kit

 Tip: Don't remove the rear outside nut on the shock towers— this will cause your car to lose its alignment.

> ⚠ **PERFORMANCE GAIN:** Better handling through sharp turns

COMPLEMENTARY MODIFICATION: Install new shocks, align the front suspension

The 911 is reknowned for its agility and superb handling, but the chassis design causes a key weakness in this area. Unlike the Porsche 914, famous for its excellent handling, the 911 has no firewall welded into its chassis front. As a result, the shock towers are isolated and unsupported. They often bend and flex under heavy cornering, to the detriment of your car's handling.

Generally, the stiffer the chassis, the better the car handles. Camber strut braces are designed to maintain the distance between the shocks under heavy cornering. A bar linking the top of the shock towers ensures that the towers do not bend when the chassis flexes.

There are a few brands of camber bars out there, and they are all similar. The Cambermeister bar by Weltmeister is an excellent kit available for easy bolt-on installation. The designers at Weltmeister have done extensive research on the 911's chassis dynamics, and designed the Cambermeister kit to lock in the proper camber value regardless of the tower deflection. The kit prevents tower expansion and contraction and helps keep your 911 cornering at its best.

Installation of the Cambermeister bar is straightforward, and can be easily completed in an afternoon. The kit comes with detailed instructions that are very clear and easy to follow. The installation of the kit requires you to remove some of the undercoat material that covers the shock towers. Be careful when doing this, as it is easy for a bit of material to fly out and hit you in the eye. Remember to wear eye protection when chipping away at the coating.

The kit bolts onto the top of the shock towers, and doesn't require you to have your car realigned. However, the addition of the Cambermeister bar will allow you to dial in a bit more negative camber to your alignment if you need it. The chassis of many 911s are built with a wide spectrum of variations and adding the Cambermeister bar will help

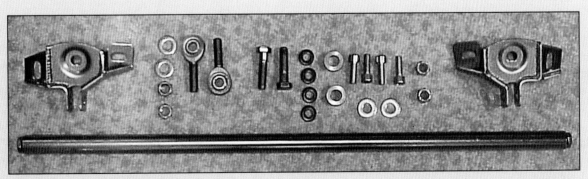

1 The camber strut brace kit should include all of the mounting hardware that you need to install it. The kit shown in this picture is manufactured by Weltmeister, and is a high-quality example of many of the kits that are available. Custom-made attachment brackets are the key to getting the bar to fit to the top of the strut towers.

3 The installed strut tower bracket integrates nicely with the existing hardware. Since all 911 chassis are slightly different, you will have to adjust the brackets to best suit your car. Make sure that there is significant clearance between the bracket and the hood before you close it. On some models, you may have to grind or file down a small section of the bracket to maintain adequate clearance with the hood.

2 After you remove the necessary screws, remove the rubber undercoating material that is applied to the top of the strut towers from the factory. Make sure that both the front and rear attachment plates are clean and free of the material. The strut tower bracket uses both these plates as a mounting surface.

you dial in more accurate alignment values. Any good alignment shop with a professional alignment rack should be able to take advantage of the additional adjustment. The camber bar will also help prevent the body sag that often occurs with older 911s.

As with any changes to the suspension of your 911, the driving feel might change significantly. The entire car's suspension system needs to be properly balanced in order to obtain the correct feel for the handling of the car. The designers at Weltmeister specifically recommend some of the following changes to take advantage of the reduced change in camber:

- Adjust the front sway bar to a stiffer position. This is accomplished by shortening the sway bar arm (if adjustable), or by installing a thicker sway bar.
- Soften out the rear sway bar. This can be accomplished by lengthening the adjustable arms, or by using a smaller-diameter bar.
- Reduce the amount of front toe-out (if your car is set that way). Since the bar will be reducing your flex, you can dial in the suspension to an amount that is closer to ideal.

The installation of the tower camber brace should improve your handling significantly. It might be a wise idea to upgrade and replace your front shocks while you are working on the shock towers. It's also good practice to get the car aligned after the installation. If you are planning to perform any other suspension upgrades to the front of your car (lowering the car, adding a Turbo tie rod kit), it is recommended that you perform them all at once, since you would normally have to get the car realigned after each install.

SUSPENSION
PROJECT 55 • LOWERING THE 911

Time: 1-4 hours

Tools: Tape measure

Talent:

Applicable Years: All

Tab: –

Tinware: –

Tip: Check the torsion bars to make sure that they don't need replacing.

PERFORMANCE GAIN: Lower center of gravity

COMPLEMENTARY MODIFICATION: Replace torsion bars, realign the suspension

The U.S. spec cars were equipped with a much higher ride height than the European cars. This was to accommodate the stricter U.S. standards for bumper height elevation. It's a popular modification to lower the 911 back to the European specs or even lower, in order to achieve a lower center of gravity for better handling. The lowered look also looks a bit sleeker.

Lowering the front end of the 911 is a snap—the suspension was designed to be easily adjusted. The 911 uses a pair of torsion bars in the same manner that many cars use coil springs to support the front suspension. There is an adjustment screw on the bottom of the front suspension that resets and alters the base position of the torsion bars. This allows the adjustment of the height of the car through a significant range.

It should be noted that lowering the front of the car has some slight drawbacks. The front of the car will be lower, and hence the front spoiler or valance panel will be increasingly prone to curb damage and breakage from speed bumps. In addition, lowering the 911 front end also changes the alignment of the front suspension. Specifically, the toe-in and camber of the car is affected. If you decide to lower the front

end, I recommend that you have the car professionally realigned when you are finished.

Another problem to consider is bump steer. Lowering the car will result in the tie rods no longer being parallel to the ground. While this shouldn't affect handling, when the car travels over a bump, the steering wheel will rotate violently in your hand. The solution for this problem is the installation of the bump steer kit (see Project 56). This kit raises the steering rack back up to be aligned with the tie rods, thus reducing the amount of bump steer. I recommend that you install this kit under your steering rack if you lower your 911. Installing the Turbo tie rods (Project 59) will also help solve bump steer problems.

The lowering procedure is simple, and all adjustments should be made with the car level on the ground. Make sure that you have a tape measure handy when you start so that you can keep both sides of the car at the same level. The factory measures the height of the front suspension as the difference between the height of the center of the road wheel, and the height of the center of the torsion bar. Therefore, as this difference increases, the car rides lower to the ground. The standard U.S. spec for the ride height for almost all 1965–1989 911s is 99 millimeters ±5 millimeters. The maximum difference between the left side and the right side should be less than 5 millimeters. The European specification is 108 millimeters ±5 millimeters. To lower the car to this height, simply loosen the adjustment bolt on the front suspension. Again, make sure that the left and right sides of the suspension are equal. If you have difficulty turning the screws with the car on the ground, lift up the front suspension a bit using a floor jack. Make all measurements only after you have pushed down on the car a few times to level it. Also make sure that your trunk is empty and your spare tire is installed in the front trunk. Keep in mind that the car will also ride lower with a full tank of gas (approximately 150 pounds of extra weight). There may also be a spacer installed on the top of your shock tower that can be removed if you are lowering your car.

Balancing the left and right height of the car should also help to improve your handling. In general, the adjustment screws for the left and right sides should be dialed in roughly equal amounts. If they are not, this might indicate that one of the torsion bars is old and worn, and needs to be replaced. Another method of checking the left-to-right balance is to measure the distance of the wheel to the top of the fender. This, however, can sometimes give inaccurate results if one of your fenders is slightly tweaked.

1 Here is the adjustment bolt for the front suspension. Make sure that you don't loosen the bolt so much that it is no longer pressed against the torsion bar end. A simple wrench can be used to lower the car in seconds. Be aware, though, that changes in the height of the front suspension will affect the toe-in alignment and camber specifications. Remember to have the car realigned after any height adjustment. Sometime this bolt gets a bit rusty—use generous amounts of WD-40 before attempting to remove it.

2 The rear radius arm on this 911SC contains an assortment of adjustment bolts. The bolt located closest to the torsion bar cover keeps the ride height secure (green arrow). The bolt second from the right is used to adjust the height of the radius arm (red arrow). There is some degree of adjustment available, but not as much as can be achieved with the removal of the torsion bar. The bolt that is farthest to the rear of the car is the rear camber adjustment (white arrow). The bolt next to it adjusts the rear toe-in setting for the car (yellow arrow).

Make sure that you don't loosen the screw so much that it doesn't press against the edge of the torsion bar end. If you find that you can't get the correct adjustment that you need, you may have to remove and adjust the location of the torsion bar adjustment lever that fits on the end of the bar.

The lowering of the rear suspension is a bit more complicated. In a similar manner to the front of the car, the factory measurements are based on the difference from the center of the torsion bar to the center of the road wheel. To arrive at this number, measure the height of the bottom of the torsion bar cover from the ground, and then add half the diameter of the torsion bar cover. Then subtract the height of the center of the wheel. For the European 911SC, this measurement should be 16 millimeters ±5 millimeters (U.S. measurement 37 millimeters ±5 millimeters). On the earlier cars, this distance was 12 millimeters. The maximum difference between the right and the left should be no more than 8 millimeters. Check the *Porsche Technical Specifications Booklet* for your year car for the exact specifications.

The rear suspension uses a rear trailing arm that is sprung using a torsion bar. This torsion bar is connected to the rear of the trailing arm via a long radius arm. Adjusting the position of this radius arm with

respect to the torsion bar is what changes the height of the car.

In order to adjust this height, you need to remove and reset the splines on the rear torsion bars. For more information on removing the torsion bars, see Project 64. The inside end of the torsion bar has 40 splines, and the outer end of the torsion bar has 44 splines. This clever arrangement allows you to make incremental changes in the torsion bar height. Simply move the inner spline clockwise one position, and the radius arm counterclockwise, and you will lower the radium arm by about 5/6 of a degree. Repeat this adjustment procedure until you have achieved the desired ride height, and both sides are equal in height.

James Bricken of Pelican Parts offers the following tip on achieving the rear height and balance that you are looking for:

Often one end of the torsion bar, or the other, will stick in place causing a loss of base line (which means you have to start from scratch). The way I do it (and I do it often), is to remove the lower-rearward bolt on the torsion bar cover and the lower shock bolt. This allows you to fully drop the rear suspension. Then I use a Smart Tool (but a simple leveling protractor works as well) and measure the inclination of the spring plate. Next, I scribe a line on the trailing arm where the spring plate meets it. This gives me a good approximation of where it should be when I reassemble it. Then I take the whole thing apart, generously lube the new torsion bars and install them. I then install the spring plates on the torsion bars just slightly and take measurements with the Smart Tool, adjusting them until I get the least amount of change from the original setting. Once I am satisfied that I am close, I put the rest of the suspension together, without fully tightening anything except for the camber and toe bolts. Once the car is on the ground, and I am happy with the results, everything else is then tightened down.

An excellent method for synchronizing the settings of the left and right rear torsion bars is to use a level to determine the amount of adjustment required. Aside from measuring the total height of the rear suspension, you can also measure the angle that the rear radius arm makes with the horizontal. Place the car on a flat and level surface, and then place a bubble level tool on the radius arm. You can adjust the height of the bubble level tool by placing small spacers underneath each end of the level. Once the level is adjusted, compare the angle to the opposite side by taking the level and the spacers and placing them on the opposite radius arm. Adjust the setting of the torsion bars as needed to make sure that the level of the left and right suspension are exactly equal.

If you have a later-model 911, you're in luck, as you don't have to remove the torsion bar covers and radius arms to get at least some degree of adjustment. On these cars, the radius arms were equipped with an adjustment screw. To raise or lower the rear of the car, simply loosen the large nut and bolt closest to the torsion bar. Then rotate the other bolt located next to it. This bolt is eccentric, and will cause the rear of the car to be raised or lowered as you turn it. Adjust the height as described previously, and then tighten the bolt located nearest to the torsion bar. Make sure that you don't touch the two nuts located toward the rear of the car—these adjust the toe-in and the camber for the rear suspension, and should only be adjusted by a trained professional using an alignment rack.

A third method of adjusting your rear suspension is to use an aftermarket radius arm. These arms, available for about $400 a pair, have a built-in adjustment

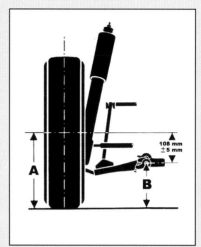

3 **Top:** As determined by the factory, the measurement for determining the front ride height is calculated by subtracting the height of the center of the road wheel from the height of the center of the torsion bar. The larger the number, the lower the car sits to the ground.
Bottom: The rear height measurement is similar to the front end measurement. The specification for the rear height is determined by the difference in the height from the center of the torsion bar (B) to the height of the center road wheel (A).

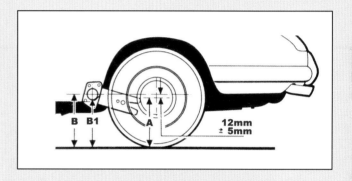

screw that works similarly to the adjustment screw for the front suspension. This radius arm allows you to quickly make adjustments and is designed more for racers than the casual everyday driver. They also allow for quick and easy change of the torsion bars.

After you've made all these adjustments to the ride height of the car, it's a wise idea to have an alignment expert check and align the car, especially if you have had to remove the rear radius arm. Make sure that you have the ride height set before you take the car in, as subsequent adjustments will alter the alignment specifications. Drive the car for a few miles, and then double-check all your measurements. Make sure that the left-to-right height of the car is the same after driving. When adjusting your 911 ride height, it's smart to consider the weight balance of the car. With the correct alignment dialed in, a properly set up 911 will have approximately 40 percent of the weight on the front wheels and 60 percent on the rear, with the chassis riding very slightly lower in the front.

SUSPENSION
PROJECT 56 • INSTALLING THE BUMP STEER KIT

 Time: 1 hour

 Tools: Rachet set

 Talent:

 Applicable Years: All

 Tab: $25

 Tinware: Bump steer spacer Kit

 Tip: Make sure that you loosen the steering rack before you install the kit

 PERFORMANCE GAIN: Tighten control over your steering after lowering your front suspension

COMPLEMENTARY MODIFICATION: Lowering the front suspension, and aligning the car, install turbo tie rod kit

If you decide to lower the front end of your 911, there is a good chance that your steering will develop what is commonly known as a bump steer problem. When traveling over a bump in the road, the steering wheel will jerk in your hands. This problem occurs when the tie rods are no longer at the proper elevation for stiff, sure steering. The solution is to install a bump steer kit. This kit raises the steering rack up to the proper level and minimizes the effect.

Installation is quite easy, and takes only about an hour. As your first step, it's a wise idea to jack up the front of the car. Make sure that you place the jack stands in secure locations (see Project 1). The next step is to remove the belly pan from underneath the steering rack. This pan protects the rack, fuel pump, and brake lines from rocks and debris on the road. The pan is held on with four bolts. On later cars, the bolts also fasten the mounts for the front sway bars.

Now, move to the front trunk of the car. Right behind the gas tank there is a small trap door that covers one of the front blower motors and the steering rack connections to the steering column. With the

1 In the front luggage compartment, there is a small trap door that covers the front blower motor, and also the steering rack connections. Before attempting to raise the rack, make sure that you loosen the connection of the rack to the steering column. This will allow it room to move upward.

2 The spacers fit between the rack and the cross-bar that holds the entire front suspension. Make sure that you use the proper-length bolts when reattaching the rack to the bar.

trap door open, reach down with two 13-millimeter wrenches and loosen the rack at the point where it mounts to the steering column. This will allow you to raise the rack slightly.

Back under the car with the pan removed, remove the two lower bolts that attach the steering rack to the suspension cross bar. Once these are removed, take a long screwdriver and pry up the rack until enough space exists between the rack and the cross bar to insert the spacer. Place the spacer in position, and then repeat the operation for the opposite side. It's normal for there to be significant resistance against raising the rack.

Once the spacers are in place, insert the new mounting bolts that were included with the bump steer kit. Make sure that you compare the new bolts to the old ones, and use the new ones that are about 1 centimeter longer than the original bolts. In addition, on some of the older cars, there may be a clearance problem, and the rack may not be able to be raised up the full recommended amount. Make sure that you watch for potential conflicts, and shave some of the material off the spacers if there is any interference.

Once you have the spacers installed, turn the wheel back and forth several times to ease the rack into its new position. Tighten down the steering rack connection point in the front trunk, and replace the belly pan underneath the rack. It's also a very wise idea to have your front-end alignment checked, as the installation of the spacers will alter your front toe-in adjustment.

SUSPENSION
PROJECT 57 • REPLACING THE BALL JOINTS

 Time: 4 hours

 Tools: Ball-joint nut removal tool, very large hammer and punch

 Talent:

 Applicable Years: All

 Tab: $150

 Tinware: Ball joints, new ball joint retaining pin

 Tip: You may have to use a Dremel tool to remove the large castellated nut off of the bottom of the ball-joint.

PERFORMANCE GAIN: Tighter steering and suspension

COMPLEMENTARY MODIFICATION: Replace the tie rods ends, replace shocks

The ball joint, located at the bottom of the strut, helps the entire assembly pivot and rotate as the steering turns and the suspension rides up and down. This critical component wears out over time, and should be replaced every 100,000 miles or so or if the front suspension is begins to feel wobbly.

Step one is to remove the pin that holds the ball joint in place. This pin is inserted in the strut and needs to be pounded out with a large hammer. If the pin is completely rusted in, you may have to drill out its center. This probably won't be necessary, but with rusty cars expect the worst. When hammering on the the pin, be careful not to damage the threads, or it might need to be replaced. Place a nut over the threads to protect them from the hammer. I would use a punch or extension to hammer on, to avoid hitting your caliper or your strut. Make sure to drive the pin out before you remove the castellated nut from the bottom of the joint, or the strut will hang loose and be difficult to keep steady.

The next step is to remove the small locking washer attached to the bottom of the ball joint. Take

1 After removing the spring clip, you can attach the tool to the bottom of the ball joint for removal. Make sure to use a very long breaker bar, as these nuts tend to rust in place and are often very difficult to remove. The arrow points to the ball joint pin; removing these can also be a challenge. Use a large hammer and a punch to drive out the pin. If you damage it in the process, make sure to replace it.

some needle-nose pliers, pull out the cotter pin from the bottom of the ball joint, and remove the washer. Now, remove the large castellated nut that holds the ball joint to the bottom of the strut. There are a few ways to do this. The best method is to use a breaker bar or impact wrench and a ball joint nut removal tool, which is specially designed for this purpose. Another method is to use a large hammer and chisel, although you could damage the castellated nut. You can also try using a large pipe wrench to get a good grip on the nut. A fourth and more destructive method involves cutting it off with a Dremel tool; only attempt this if the first methods fail miserably.

After the pin and castellated nut are out, tap the ball joint out of the strut with a hammer. Make sure to clean out any rust or debris from the inside of the holes where the pin and ball joint are inserted. Spray some WD-40 in there to help things along.

The new ball joint should be positioned so that the cutout wedge in the shaft is facing the hole for the pin. Gently tap the ball joint up into the strut, making sure that the wedge is somewhat aligned with the hole. Now, tap the pin into the strut. It should go in smoothly, and align with the ball joint wedge as it goes in. Replace the nut and washer on the opposite side of the pin, and tighten the nut until the back of the pin is almost flush with the strut. Replace the large castellated nut on the bottom of the ball joint if it was damaged. Reinstall this nut and torque to 250 N-m (184 ft-lb). Make sure to replace the locking washer and retaining pin at the bottom of the ball joint.

I recommend that you perform the replacement on one side, complete the job, and then move and do the replacement on the opposite side. In this manner, you can check your work and refer to the side of the strut that you haven't disassembled for reference.

SUSPENSION
PROJECT 58 • TIE ROD END REPLACEMENT

Time: 2 hours

Tools: Tie rod removal fork, wrench set

Talent:

Applicable Years: All

Tab: $50

Tinware: Tie rod ends, cotter pins

Tip: Measure the length of the tie rod before you remove it.

PERFORMANCE GAIN: Tighter steering and front suspension

COMPLEMENTARY MODIFICATION: Upgrade to the Turbo tie rod kit.

1 Removal of the tie rod end is very difficult without the proper tool. This pitchfork tool applies pressure to the rod end and separates it from the control arm. A substantial amount of hammering on the tool is usually required, as the rod ends have a tapered fit that is designed to fit snugly in the control arm.

2 Installation of the new rod end is the easiest part of the process. The rod end is simply placed into the control arm and the top nut is tightened. Don't forget to insert the safety cotter pin (not shown) into the nut to prevent it from backing out.

It's very important to keep the front suspension of your 911 tight and firm. The system's moving parts have a tendency to wear out and become loose after years of use. A steering wheel that can be turned a few degrees in each direction without impacting the wheels' direction can indicate that one or more suspension components are worn beyond their useful life.

Among the most common parts to replace are the tie rod ends. These universal joints are located on the end of each tie rod and control the angular position of each front wheel when the car is steered. If the tie rod end is worn, then precise steering is an impossibility, and the car will also have wobbly front wheels and a possible alignment problem. Worn-out tie rods can cause vibrations in the steering wheel.

Replacing the tie rod end is relatively simple—if you have the proper tools. Each tie rod is attached to the spindle arm with a beveled fit. This means that the tie rod is securely pressed into the spindle arm and cannot be removed without a special tool. The best tool for removal is an angled pitchfork tool that is designed specifically for this task. Do not hit the top of the rod end with a large hammer, as this will only serve to bend your entire spindle arm.

Pull out the small cotter pin from the castellated nut and remove the nut with a socket wrench. Place the pitchfork tool in between the spindle arm and the rod end and then hit the tool repeatedly with a large hammer. The wedge in the pitchfork tool will drive the rod end out of the arm. You may have to hit the pitchfork tool quite a few times before the rod end will pop.

Before removing the rod end from the tie rod, make sure to measure and mark their location in relation to each other. The length of the entire tie rod must remain exactly the same; otherwise the toe-in adjustment on your front-end alignment will be significantly skewed. A good practice is to mark the tie rod end on the threads where it was screwed into the tie rod and then screw the new one into the exact same location.

Once the rod end is separated from the arm, you should be able to simply unscrew it from the tie rod. It is important to note that the standard tie rods have two adjustment points, one near the rod end and one near the rack. Make sure that you hold the tie rod steady with a wrench while you unscrew the rod end, or you may accidentally change the length of the rod.

The new rod end is attached by tightening the new castellated nut down on the top threads. Align the hole for the cotter pin with the tops of the nut. Insert the cotter pin and bend the ends to make sure that it won't fall out. It's wise to have your front-end alignment checked, because the replacement of the tie rod ends can change the toe adjustment.

While you're replacing your rod ends, it's also a good time to install the Turbo tie rod kit (see Project 59). This kit makes the entire steering mechanism a lot stiffer, reduces bump steer, and it also includes two brand-new tie rod ends.

SUSPENSION
PROJECT 59 • INSTALLING THE TURBO TIE ROD KIT

Time: 4 hours

Tools: Tie rod end removal fork, socket set

Talent:

Applicable Years: All

Tab: $150

Tinware: Turbo tie rod kit

Tip: Install the kit when you need to replace the tie rod ends.

PERFORMANCE GAIN: Tighter steering control

COMPLEMENTARY MODIFICATION: Lower your front end, replace your tie rod ends

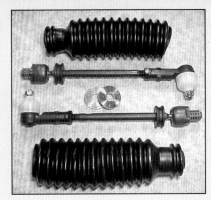

1 The complete Turbo tie rod kit contains everything you need to perform the conversion. The kit includes new tie rod ends, spacers, the tie rods, and new dust boots for the entire assembly. If you are planning to replace your tie rod ends anyway, it makes good sense to upgrade to the kit.

2 When you remove the old tie rod, make sure that you line it up with the new one, and set the lengths of the two rods to be equal. If they are not equal, your alignment will be significantly off. Make sure that the distance between the rod end and the mounting flange that mates with the rack is the same. Regardless of how precise your measurements are, you should have the car aligned after having the tie rods installed. Remember to account for the additional spacer (not shown).

One of the most popular upgrades for the 1969–1989 911 is the installation of the Turbo tie rod kit. The tie rods used on the normal 911 were designed so that they are flexible, and become looser with increased use. The tie rods designed for the 911 Turbo, on the other hand, use a different design that creates a much stiffer and secure steering feel, while increasing the overall life of the tie rods themselves.

The first step in installing the kit is to jack up the front of the car, and remove the two front wheels. Follow the procedures outlined in Project 1. After the front of the car is off the ground, remove the tie rod ends from their connection to the A-arm. For guidance on this process, see Project 58. Do not remove the rod ends from the tie rods, or rotate them or the tie rod. With this project, it's best to work on one side of the car and completely finish prior to moving on to the other side. This will make the job go a bit quicker, as you learn from your experience.

Once you have the rod ends disconnected, remove the spring retainers that attach and secure each end of the rubber bellows to the tie rod and the steering rack. To gain access to these retainers,

remove the belly pan on the bottom of the car that protects the steering rack from dirt and debris. This pan is held on with four bolts. Once the pan is removed you should be able to see the steering rack, the rubber boots, and the spring retainers that hold them onto the rack.

Using a small screwdriver, carefully pry off the spring retainer from the bellows. Be careful not to damage the inner one, as you will reuse it when you install the new boot that comes with the kit. You can let the spring retainer hang around the inside of the rack housing—you don't have to completely remove it.

Now, unscrew the old tie rod from the rack. This sounds easier than it really is. The old tie rod may be quite snugly secured to the rack, and could require significant force to remove it. The good news is that the tie rod acts as an excellent wrench for removing itself. Simply bend the tie rod all the way down, and rotate it counterclockwise. You may need to stick a long screwdriver or bar into the hollow end to gain addtional leverage, but with enough force, the tie rod should become separated.

Once you have the old tie rod off, remove the old rubber boot. You will see the exposed metal shaft of the steering rack. Make sure that you don't get any dirt or debris on the rack while you are work-

151

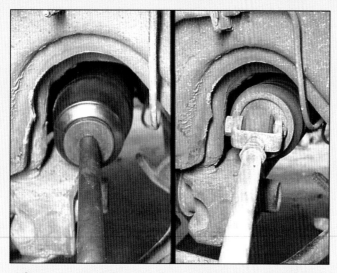

3 A comparison of the new and old tie rods, side by side, shows the difference in mounting the boot, and in the flange on the end of the rack. To remove the old tie rod, simply unscrew it from the rack.

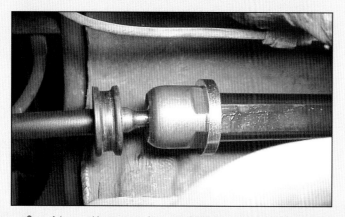

4 If the tie rod bottoms out when screwed into the steering rack, make sure that you use the spacer between the tie rod and the rack. Test fit the entire assembly beforehand and make sure that if you don't use the spacer, the tie rod is securely mounted to the end of the rack.

5 Don't forget to reattach the boot's spring retainer on the inner end of the rack. The boot protects the rack from dirt and debris that can clog and wear out the inner gears. Make sure when you are installing the boot that you don't get any dirt on the rack.

ing on it. The new tie rods will require the use of the large spacer that fits between the rack and the tie rod. Don't forget this spacer when installing the new tie rods, or they might not seat properly against the steering rack.

Before the final installation of the new tie rod, place the new one and the old one side by side on a workbench, and adjust the new tie rod so that the length from the rod end to the rack-mating surface is the same. You want to set the two lengths of the tie rods to be equal so that you can minimize the change in alignment of the car. You will have to get the car realigned regardless, but it's good practice to get the alignment close so that you can safely drive to the alignment shop. Don't forget to include the thickness of the spacers in your calculations of the lengths of the two tie rods. Mark the final position of the tie rod end on the new tie rod, and then remove it.

Before you screw the tie rod into the rack, make sure that you spread a few drops of Loctite onto the threads. After you insert the tie rod into the rack, use a pair of large Vise-Grips or Channel Locks to tighten it down. There really isn't too much to grab onto with a regular wrench, and chances are you won't have the special thin Porsche wrench that is required to tighten the tie rod.

Once the tie rod is tight, place the rubber boot over the tie rod and onto the steering rack. You will need to have the rod end on the end of the tie rod removed in order to make the boot fit. Getting the boot to cooperate and properly cover the rack and the tie rod may be the most difficult part of this process. Use pliers and screwdrivers to stretch the boot over each end. This may take a few tries, but it is possible. Once the boot is in position, replace the inner spring over the boot to secure it to the rack housing.

After the boot is installed, reattach the tie rod end. Make sure that the length of the tie rod is the same as the measurement of the old one. Adjust the position of the rod end to match up with the mark that you previously made when you compared it to the original tie rod.

To complete the job, install the new rod end into the front control arm (Project 58). Perform the same procedure for the opposite side. Reattach the belly pan, the wheels, and lower the car to the ground. The car should be taken straight to an alignment shop, as it is very easy to mess up the toe-in of the front suspension when you are replacing the tie rods. If you are planning to perform any other front suspension work that might affect the alignment, it would be advisable to do it now, since you will have to realign the car anyway.

SUSPENSION

PROJECT 60 • ALIGNMENT ON YOUR 911

Time: 2 hours

Tools: Alignment rack

Talent:

Applicable Years: All

Tab: $100

Tinware: —

Tip: Have a professional perform this job

PERFORMANCE GAIN: Better handling and better tracking of your front suspension

COMPLEMENTARY MODIFICATION: Replace shocks, wheel bearings, tie rod ends, ball joints, lower front end, upgrade to Turbo tie rods

The 911 is known for its good handling and excellent suspension system. Of course, precise handling and cornering are nonexistent if the car is not aligned properly. There are five different alignment specifications that must be set to properly align the 911. These are front-end caster, camber, toe, and rear-end camber and toe. All of these may be set to the factory specifications, or tweaked slightly to give better performance when setting your car up for racing. If the alignment of the suspension is slightly off, then you might get some significant tire wear and a loss of power and fuel economy. The most common sign of a misaligned front suspension is the car pulling to one side of the road when driving straight.

Although the home mechanic can perform the basic front-end toe-in setting, it is suggested that you allow a trained professional with an alignment rack make the other adjustments. It's nearly impossible to determine the correct angles and settings for your car without the use of an alignment rack.

Camber refers to the tilt of the wheel, as measured in degrees of variation between the tire centerline and the vertical plane of the car. If the top of the

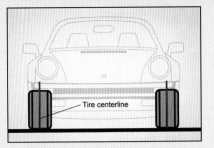

1 **Zero Camber.** When the car is aligned with zero camber, it means that the wheels are directly perpendicular to the ground. The tires make even contact with the road, and exhibit a minimal amount of wear and friction when turning. The weight of the car is distributed evenly across the tire tread, but the steering control can be a bit heavy. Tire sizes are shown smaller than scale and camber angles are exaggerated for ease of illustration in these diagrams.

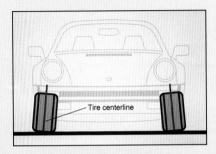

2 **Negative Camber.** The lower parts of the tires are angled outward, causing tires to wear more on the inside edges. The 911 has an independent front suspension, which creates a slight negative camber when traveling over bumps. As the suspension compresses upward, the wheel tilts in slightly to avoid changing the track (distance between left and right wheels). Although this momentarily changes the camber of the wheel, it prevents the tires from scrubbing and wearing every time that the car travels over a bump.

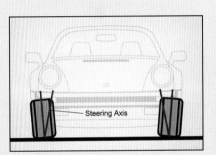

3 **Positive Camber.** This can cause the outer edges of the tires to wear more quickly than the inside. At factory settings, the 911 should have a slight positive camber (about 1/6 of a degree). This is designed into the suspension to provide increased stability when traveling over bumpy roads, or through turns on the typical high-crowned roads.

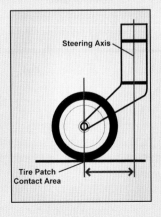

4 **Positive Caster.** The concept of positive caster is best demonstrated by the wheels of a shopping cart. The steering axis of each wheel is located in front of the point where the wheel touches the ground. The load of the cart is in front of the wheels, and as the cart moves forward, the wheels rotate on their axis to follow the cart's direction. This creates an inherent stability that tends to keep the wheels straight, unless they are forcibly steered in a different direction.

wheel tilts inwards, the camber is negative. If the top of the wheel tilts outwards, the camber is positive. On the 911, the camber should always be set as close to neutral as possible, with a slight positive emphasis (about 1/6 of a degree). On some of the older 911s,

5 **Positive Caster.** The 911 has slight positive caster, which creates an inherent stability when the car is moving in a straight line. With the angle of the strut tilted back, it places the steering axis and the load in front of the contact patch where the tire meets the pavement. Like the shopping cart example in the previous illustration, the 911 tends to move forward in a stable, straight line until the wheels are turned in a different direction. The rear trailing arm of the 911, by its design, has extensive positive caster built in.

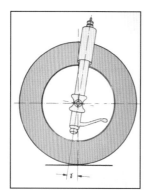

6 **Toe-In and Toe-out.** The toe of the front suspension refers to the angle of the two wheels with respect to each other. Significant toe-in or toe-out will cause extreme tire wear, as the wheels constantly try to move toward each other (toe-in), or move away from each other (toe-out). The result is that severe friction is created on the tires, and at highway speeds, the tires will wear significantly and power/fuel economy will suffer.

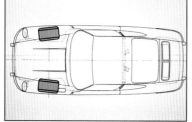

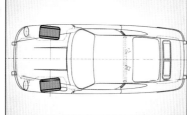

7 **Toe-out through Turns.** When going around a turn, the inner wheels will turn at a tighter radius than the outer ones. This is so that both wheels will be able to turn around the same point without any tire wear. The outer wheel turns at an angle less sharp than the inner wheel. This minimizes the amount of "scrub" of the tires on the pavement as the car turns.

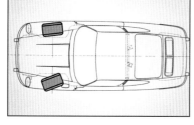

8 The only way to get the proper measurements for aligning your car is to have it professionally done on an alignment rack. The one shown here is owned by Alex Wong of Precision Tech Motorsports and costs in excess of $18,000. The proper alignment of your 911 is not something the home mechanic can reliably perform. There are even many incompetent shops out there who are unfamiliar with the intricacies of this task. It's best to find a shop that can properly perform the job according to factory procedures and settings. When purchasing new tires, don't necessarily settle for the tire shop's default alignment—it may be less than you pay for. The extra time and money spent taking your car to a professional will pay off in the long run.

the chassis can sag due to rust and age, and it is sometimes difficult to get all of the negative camber out using the normal adjustments. The installation of a camber strut brace (Project 54) can help prevent sagging shock towers, but unfortunately it cannot help to undo damage that has already taken place.

On the rear suspension, the camber is set using an eccentric bolt that is rotated to change the angle of inclination (see Project 55). The rear wheels should be set for a slight negative camber (about 1 degree), as the trailing arms tend to bend slightly outward as the car accelerates under power. Since one half of the wheel is mounted firmly on the ground, the top of the wheel has a tendency to twist outward. Setting the rear wheels to have a slight negative camber means that under power they will be mostly neutral.

Caster is the angle that the steering axis is offset from the vertical plane. On the 911, the strut points toward the rear of the car, resulting in a positive caster angle. This angle is typically set at about 6 1/2 degrees. The amount of caster in the suspension directly influences the control and stability of the wheels when traveling in a straight line. Since the 911 rear suspension utilizes a trailing arm design, which has a tremendous amount of built-in caster, there is no adjustment for the rear caster.

Toe refers to the angle of the two wheels with respect to each other. If a car has toe-in, it means that the front edges of the wheels are closer to each other than the rear edges. With rear-wheel-drive cars like the 911, sometimes the front wheels try to move toward a toe-out position under power. Setting the wheels to have very slight toe-in can help neutralize this effect. Toe-out occurs when the front edges of the wheels are farther apart than the inner edges. Some toe-out is necessary when turning, since the angle of inclination of the inner wheel must be tighter than the outer wheel. The rear wheels also have a toe setting, and this should be set as close to neutral as possible.

So how should your 911 be set up? It all depends upon what you are going to be using it for. If you are planning to race your car, then you will probably want as much negative camber as allowed by the racing rules. This is because the car will have a tendency to straighten out in turns, and you want the maximum tire patch on the road when you are cornering. Setting the camber to a negative value means that when the camber starts to change to slightly positive through turns, the negative setting will help neutralize this effect. Seek professional help for alignment specifications and any answers to questions that you might have.

SUSPENSION
PROJECT 61 • INSTALLING A FRONT SWAY BAR

Time: 3 hours

Tools: Hole saw, hand drill, Dremel tool (if required)

Talent:

Applicable Years: 1965-1973

Tab: $350

Tinware: Front sway bar, front sway bar mounts

Tip: Proceed carefully and check your measurements before you cut metal.

PERFORMANCE GAIN: Better handling, better suspension

COMPLEMENTARY MODIFICATION: Adjust/replace your torsion bars

1 This photo shows the inside fenderwell and the stock early 911 sway bar installed. Use a new bushing at the bulkhead, and also new drop link bushings when you are installing the bar. Also make sure that the nearby brake lines and shocks don't have any opportunity to make contact with sway bar mechanism. Check the bar for clearance when the car is elevated, and when it's resting on the ground.

2 This is what the inside of the fender looks like opposite to the sway bar mount. The nuts shown here are welded in from the factory. If your car doesn't have these mounting nuts and bracket already installed, you will need to install the aftermarket bracket, which has these nuts integrated into its construction.

It's almost unbelievable that the early 911s did not ship with a stock front-mounted sway bar. The front sway bar is probably the best suspension improvement that you can perform on your 911. The sway bar adds stiffness to the suspension by coupling the spring effects of one side with the other. The sway bar acts as a torsion bar that resists suspension displacement across the width of the car. When one side of the car starts to dip, the sway bar (connected to the other side) acts to pull it back up. Through this coupling effect, the car maintains an increased stiffness and reduces side-to-side sway.

Up until 1973, almost all 911s appear to have shipped from the factory with the mounting tabs for the bulkhead-mounted sway bar. In 1974, the sway bar was mounted below the body and integrated into the front suspension (see Project 62). Some racers prefer the through-body setup that was used on the early cars. You can install this through-body bar on the later cars with a set of aftermarket mounting brackets.

For 911s with the mounting tabs already installed, the attachment of the sway bar is a snap. For those without these mounting tabs, you will have to drill the holes required for the installation of the aftermarket bracket. You may also have to install the U-tabs onto the A-arms of your car if it didn't come with them installed. Most cars will have a cover attached to the sway bar mount on the inside of the fender. If your car has this cover, then simply remove it and the sway bar installation becomes a bolt-in process.

The first step in installing the sway bar is to obtain all the parts that you need. For this installation, you will need a sway bar kit with drop links, a U-tab mounting kit, the sway bar mounting kit for the bulkhead, and new bushings for both the bar and the drop links. You will also need a 1-inch hole saw to drill the hole for the sway bar in the bulkhead, if your car doesn't already have this hole.

You can choose to install the stock 19-millimeter Porsche sway bar setup, or you can opt for an aftermarket setup. The stock original Porsche sway bar kits are still available, although they can be quite expensive. A good aftermarket kit is the Weltmeister sway bar kit. Available in 16-, 19-, and 22-millimeter the right sway bar for your task can easily be fitted to your car. I suggest that you use the stock 19-millimeter-size sway bar if you are planning to drive the car on the street, or the thicker 22-millimeter sway bar if you plan to do some racing. The Weltmeister bars also offer adjustability along the torque-arm of the bar, which means that you can lower or increase the rate of stiffness in only a few minutes.

INSTALLING A FRONT SWAY BAR

3 Shown here are the U-tab kit and the aftermarket inner bulkhead mount from Weltmeister. The U-tab kit contains the necessary hardware to mount the tabs to the 911 A-arm. The bulkhead bracket consists of heavy-gauge sheet metal with three encapsulated nuts on the rear.

4 On the left is a picture of a factory 911 A-arm with the U-tab already installed by the factory. If your A-arms are missing this U-tab, then you will need to install the kit onto the A-arms, as shown on the right. Install the sway bar into the car first, so that you can double-check the location required for the U-tabs. Make sure that they are in the same location on both sides of the car.

The first step is to install the U-tab kit on your 911 front suspension arms. Jack up the front of the car and remove both the left and right wheels. Most 911s without sway bars did not come with these tabs installed. Check your A-arms before you order the kit, though, as some did sneak out of the factory with the tabs attached. Drill a hole in the A-arms exactly perpendicular to the top surface of the A-arm. This hole should be located 5 1/8 inches from the center of the ball joint, or directly below the droplinks. Check your sway bar's location before drilling. Make sure that this distance is equal on both sides of the car. Fasten the U-tab kit to the A-arm using the hardware supplied in the kit. If you have access to a welder, then these tabs can be welded instead of bolted on.

The next step is to create the holes required for the sway bar to fit through the chassis. I recommend that you use the improved sway bar mounting bracket available from Weltmeister (Part Number SB-1955). This bracket mimics the factory-welded plate that was installed on cars outfitted with factory sway bars. The kit includes a template for drilling

the holes in the sides of your chassis. Make two photocopies of the template and tape it onto the inside fenders of your car, according to the directions in the kit. There should already be a depression in your chassis where the mount is to be located, so you shouldn't have too much trouble placing it in the correct position.

Drill two of the three small holes that are used to mount the adapter. Once these two holes are drilled, you will want to bolt the adapter plate to the car to use it as a template for drilling the remaining holes. For ease of drilling, mount the adapter plate to the outside surface of the fender well. You will have to reach around into the inside of the front trunk of the car in order to fit two bolts into the plate. With the adapter plate mounted to the outside face of the inner fender, you can now use the adapter to guide your drill for the large center hole and the remaining mounting hole.

Once you have the adapter mounted to the outside of the fender, use the third hole in the adapter plate to guide yourself, and drill through the chassis. Then, using the 1-inch hole saw, drill the large center hole through the chassis. Repeat the same procedure for the opposite side.

After you have all of the holes drilled, the sway bar can be assembled on the car. File down any of the edges that might stick out of the chassis sheet metal from the holes that you drilled. Make sure that you use new bushings at the mounting points near the fender well, and also use new drop link bushings. Remove the adapter plates from the outside of the fender, and place them on the inside of the car, using some masking tape to temporarily hold them in place. Then insert the sway bar into the chassis. Place the bushings onto the bar, and then attach the outside mounting plates to the sway bar on each side. Finally, bolt the arms to the ends of the sway bar, and attach the drop links to the U-tabs on the A-arms. Make sure that the drop link clears the brake line and the strut before you reattach the wheel.

If you are going to be using your car for racing, then a wise upgrade might be a set of adjustable drop links. These allow you to dial your front suspension for greater balance, or to adjust the sway bar in case the track on which you are racing only banks in one direction.

When you put your car back on the road, you will feel a remarkable difference, particularly during quick turns. You will wonder why the factory never installed sway bars as stock equipment in the first place.

PROJECT 62 • REPLACEMENT OF SWAY BAR BUSHINGS AND BRACKETS

 Time: 3 hours

 Tools: –

 Talent:

 Applicable Years: 1965-1973 with sway bars, all 1974

 Tab: $85

 Tinware: Complete set of sway bar bushings

 Tip: Try removing the front bar without taking out the A-arm. On some 1974+cars, this may work.

PERFORMANCE GAIN: Stiffer suspension

COMPLEMENTARY MODIFICATION: Weld new rear sway bar bracket, replace front torsion bars

1 The front sway bar bushings are mounted on the A-arms and a bracket that attaches to the mounting points for the rear belly pan. The A-arm sway bar bushings are inserted into a metal bracket that is welded onto the top of the A-arm. The arrow points to the bolt that attaches the A-arm to the cross-member. This is one of the bolts that needs to be removed to gain enough maneuverability to remove the sway bar from the A-arm bushing.

As the 911s age, the tendency is to find them with worn-out bushings, particularly the sway bar bushings. On the 1974 and later cars, the front and rear sway bars were mounted to the suspension and ran underneath the body of the car. Replacing of the rear bushings is a relatively simply process, but replacing the front bushings requires a bit more effort.

The first step in replacing your bushings is to figure out if they need to be replaced. Carefully inspect them for cracking, and also check to make sure that their inner diameter hugs the sway bar tightly. If they do not appear to be worn, then simply apply a little bit of lithium grease inside the bushing. If they are worn, then they will need to be replaced.

Begin the process of replacing the front bushings by jacking up the car, and removing the lower belly pan that covers the steering rack (see Project 59). The two rear brackets that hold the center front sway bar bushings (1974 and later) should come off when you remove the belly pan. Use the sheet metal seam of the car as a point for placing the jack stand—you will need full access to the A-arm and cross-member.

Now, remove the bolts that anchor the front of the A-arm to the chassis. Refer to Project 64 for more details. Once you have the front of the A-arm disconnected, loosen and remove the torsion bar adjuster screw. Remove the adjuster lever as detailed in Project 64 as well. Now, loosen and remove the large bolt that holds the cross-member to the chassis. Make sure that you are not using the cross-member as a support with your jack stand. Removing the bolt in this condition may make the car unstable.

When this bolt is loose, you should be able to pull the A-arm out of the cross-member. Let it hang from the ball joint underneath the shock. You should now have enough leeway to maneuver the A-arm so that you can slide the sway bar out of the bushing. Slide the other end of the sway bar out as well once you have one side clear.

The new replacement bushings are split down the middle, so they should easily slide onto the bar and into the bracket that is welded onto the A-arm. Remove the old bushings and insert the new ones, making sure that you coat the bushings with some white lithium grease on the inside. Place the sway bar into the A-arm on one side, and then into the A-arm on the other side. Reattach the A-arm and torsion bar lever according to the directions in Project 64. Bolt up

REPLACEMENT OF SWAY BAR BUSHINGS AND BRACKETS

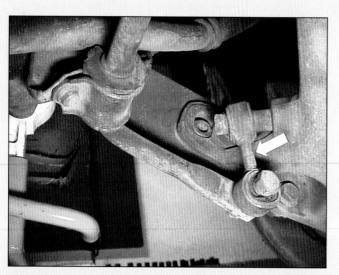

2 The rear sway bar is attached to the car chassis with a large bracket that has a tendency to break. The drop links (shown by the arrow) for the sway bar contain two rubber bushings that wrap around two mounting bolts. Replacing these bushings simply involves removing the bolts and substituting the new bushings for the old ones. Depending on your year 911, you may have to replace the entire droplink in order to replace the bushings.

involves the removal of the bar and drop links. Remove the bar and install the new drop link bushings by pressing them in with a vise. The center bushings for the bar should be sandwiched between the mounting brackets for the sway bar and the inner fender wall. See Project 61 for some additional information on the early sway bars.

The rear bar is much simpler. Starting in 1978 cars, all six of the rear bushings are held in with bolts that can be easily removed. To replace the bushings, simply unbolt the brackets that hold them in. The small rear drop links are held in with bolts too, and can be removed simply by removing the bolts.

The earlier cars didn't have bolts, but instead had drop links that pushed onto large balls on each end. Removing these drop links sometimes requires quite a bit of force to pull them off. Use a pair of Vise-Grips or Channel Locks on the drop links for more leverage. Remove the older, worn-out bushings and replace them with brand-new ones. Remember to spread some grease on the inside of them.

The rear sway bar bracket on the later cars is notorious for cracking and breaking. If you experience an annoying rattle from your rear suspension, you might want to check this bracket. Shake the rear sway bar, and see if the bracket is loose. An upgraded factory bracket for the rear sway bar can easily be welded into the original mounting spot on the chassis, and should be significantly stronger than the original mount.

the belly pan underneath the car, and you are done with the front bar.

On the early cars manufactured before 1974, the sway bar runs through the center of the car, not underneath. The replacement of the bushings simply

SUSPENSION

PROJECT 63 • SHOCK REPLACEMENT

 Time: 3 hours

 Tools: Drill/press for roll pin (Bilstein shocks only), Allen socket set

 Talent: ††

 Applicable Years: All

 Tab: Up to $500

 Tinware: Front and rear shock absorbers

 Tip: Match front shock absorbers to the struts on your car.

 PERFORMANCE GAIN: Better handling and performance

COMPLEMENTARY MODIFICATION: Installation of a camber bar, replacement of ball-joints, and tie rod ends

One of the most popular projects to perform is the replacement of the front and rear shocks on the 911. It is usually recommended that you replace both the front and the rear at the same time, as they take roughly similar abuse over their lifetime. The front and rear shocks are not likely to wear out unevenly. As a rule, the shocks should always be replaced in pairs.

I recommend that you replace your shocks every 50,000 miles or so, or if they start to show signs of fading or wearing out. If you push down on a corner of the car, it should spring back with almost no oscillation up and down. If the car bounces up and down, then you probably need new shocks. Different driving patterns may also affect the life of shock absorbers. Cars that are raced or often driven on windy roads may need to have their shocks replaced more often than street cars.

The first step in replacing your shocks is to determine what type of front strut you have in your car. The front strut is the part of the front suspension that pivots on the ball joint that the brakes, wheels, and tires are mounted to. Certain types of shocks will only fit

1 The top set of shocks are Bilstein front shocks, original equipment on some 911s. It is important to make sure that you match the front suspension struts to the type of shocks that you purchase. The lower two shocks are Boge rear shocks, and were also original equipment on the 911s. Unlike the front, the rear shocks do not have to be matched to the original struts sold with the car.

2 The front strut pulls away after the top fastening nut is removed. At this point, the dust shield can be removed, and the shock insert can be removed. For the Bilstein inserts, make sure that you remove the roll pin that is installed at the bottom of the strut. For all other shock types (Koni, Boge, etc.) the shock should simply lift out of the strut. These are Bilstein struts, most easily determined by their green color. Koni inserts are usually red, Boge inserts are typically black, and yellow inserts can be either Bilstein or Koni. All the struts should be appropriately labeled by their manufacturer as well.

3 The roll pin that holds in the Bilstein shock must be installed properly, or it will break under normal driving conditions. The roll pin must be installed with the slit facing away from the center of the shock. If not, the shock will flex the roll pin, and over time this will cause the metal to yield and break.

certain types of 911 front struts. If your 911 has Bilstein struts, then you must replace them with new Bilstein shocks. If you car has Koni struts, then likewise, you must use Koni shock inserts as replacements. You cannot use another shock, as it will not fit inside your 911's front strut.

The easiest and most basic method of determining which front strut you have is to take a look at the color of the strut. Green struts are almost always Bilstein struts, red is almost always Koni, black is Boge, and yellow struts can be either Bilstein or Koni. One sure method of checking for Bilstein struts is to look for

SHOCK REPLACEMENT

4 The rear shocks are much easier to replace than the front ones. Support the rear trailing arm, and then unbolt the rear shock mount located in the back of the engine compartment, toward the front of the car (shown by the arrow). Make sure that you keep the top of the shock from turning as you remove the retaining nut.

5 Down below, the shock is simply bolted into the rear trailing arm. With the trailing arm supported by a jack, unbolt and pull out the shock from the chassis. The installation of the new shock is quite a straightforward, bolt-in process.

you remove the small roll pin from the bottom of the strut prior to removing the large nut. This will keep the shock secured in place while you hammer or drill out the roll pin. Open the trunk and you will see the large nut located in the center of the shock tower mount. For pictures of this nut, see Project 54, Installing a Camber Strut Brace. After you remove the nut from the top of the strut, you should be able to take the entire strut and pull it out from under the fenderwell. You will need to push down on the shock in order to gain enough clearance to do this.

After the strut has cleared the fender, remove the dust shield from the top of the shock. The insert should now pull out of the strut. Check the rubber O-ring at the top of the insert for damage, and replace it if necessary. Make sure that you don't let the shock hang from the rubber brake line. Doing so will almost certainly damage your brake lines.

Installation of the new shocks is easy. Simply place the new insert into the strut and reattach it to the shock towers with the large nut. For Boge, Koni, and other shocks, simply insert the shock in the strut and reattach it. If you have Bilstein inserts, install the roll pin in the lower part of the strut. A very important part of the installation is assuring that the roll pin is installed correctly. The roll pin must be installed with the groove facing away from the center of the insert. If the roll pin is installed backward, or at some angle in between, the vibration of the shock will cause the roll pin to break after repeated up and down motions. Make sure that you install the roll pin as shown in the photos that accompany this project.

The rear shocks are much simpler. They are basically a bolt-in replacement. You can install any type of shock (Boge, Bilstein, Koni, etc.) on the rear suspension regardless of what the car originally shipped with. Before you begin the replacement of the rear shocks, jack up the rear of the car. You don't need to remove the rear wheels.

To remove the rear shock, place a jack under the rear trailing arm and lift it up slightly. The shocks support the weight of the trailing arm when the car is suspended in air, so you need to remove this tension from the shock prior to removal. Inside the engine compartment, all the way toward the front, is the mount for the rear shocks. Remove this large nut while keeping the top "tab" of the shock from turning. Under the car, simply remove the large bolt that mounts the rear shock to the trailing arm.

Install the new shock by inserting it up into the car, and replacing the rear trailing arm bolt. Back inside the engine compartment, reinstall the retaining nut on the top of the shock.

the roll pin that is installed at the bottom of the shock (see Photo 3). The Bilstein inserts are installed "upside down" as compared to the typical method of mounting the cylinder on the bottom. The shock extension therefore must be constrained in the bottom of the strut. The roll pin accomplishes this by securing the insert in the strut. If your strut has this roll pin installed in the bottom of the strut, it is a Bilstein strut.

When you order your new front shocks, make sure that you order replacements that will match your strut type. If you wish to change to a different type or manufacturer, and you have Koni or Bilstein struts, then you will have to change out your inserts, which is not exactly a simple job. The Boge inserts can accept shock absorber inserts from a variety of manufacturers. When you order rear shocks, it doesn't matter which brand you order—they should all fit your 911.

Before you begin, jack up the front of the car and remove the road wheels from both sides. Now might be a good time to inspect your tie rod ends, brake discs, and pads.

The first step in removing your front shocks is to remove the large nut that holds the insert to the top of the car. If you have Bilstein struts, I recommend that

SUSPENSION
PROJECT 64 • REPLACING/ UPGRADING TORSION BARS

Time: 2-4 hours

Tools: –

Talent:

Applicable Years: All

Tab: $125 per torsion bar

Tinware: Torsion bars

Tip: Always replace bars in pairs.

PERFORMANCE GAIN: More responsive suspension

COMPLEMENTARY MODIFICATION: Upgrade to thicker torsion bars, lower your 911

The 911 suspension uses both front and rear torsion bars to spring the weight of the car. While many lesser cars use coil springs, the 911 suspension uses the torsional stiffness of the metal bars in order to provide the necessary spring. Like traditional coil springs, as the cars age the torsion bars have a tendency to become weak, or even snap and break. The replacement procedure for the front bars is quite easy, and can be carried out by the home mechanic.

The front torsion bars are mounted parallel to the direction that the car travels; spring the A-arm using an adjustable stop that is mounted on the end of the bar (see Project 55). To remove the front torsion bars, begin by jacking up the front of the car and removing the front wheels. Remove the bottom belly pan cover that protects the steering rack and fuel pump. Do not support the car using the front torsion bar covers, as you will have to remove these in order to access the torsion bars. Instead, support the car from the bottom of the car, near the seams of the sheet metal. Also, place an emergency floor jack under the cross-member, near the torsion bar adjusting screw, after you have the car in the air.

Now, unscrew and remove the torsion bar adjustment screw (see Project 55). The torsion bar adjusting lever that the screws mate with should be able to be pried off of the end of the torsion bar. If you cannot remove the adjusting lever because it is still under pressure from the weight of the A-arm, place the jack underneath the A-arm and lift it up slightly. When the pressure is relieved, and the adjusting lever is free, it should pull off relatively easily. Remove the foam gasket that is behind the adjusting lever.

At this point, you should be able to see the torsion bar sticking out of the A-arm. Try to remove the torsion bar by pulling on it. If necessary, use a cloth rag and a pair of Vise-Grips to get a better grip on the bar. Make sure that you don't damage the splines on the end, or scratch the paint on the bar. Twist and wiggle the bar back and forth. If it will not come out, then you need to tap it out from the opposite end. If your torsion bar is broken, then you will have to tap out the other half from the opposite end anyway.

To tap the torsion bar out, move to the very front of the car and remove the front cover bracket from the front of the A-arm. On later cars, this cover is integrated into the mount, so you may have to remove the A-arm mount. Check again to make sure that you did not place the jack stand that supports the front of the car under this A-arm. Once this bracket is removed, you should be able to see the small dust cap on the end of the A-arm. To remove this dust cap, drill a small hole into the center, and then use a punch to pull it out. You can also hammer out the bar from the other end, knocking the plug out in the process. After the dust cap is removed, tap out the torsion bar with an appropriate punch. Make sure that you do not damage the torsion bar splines as you tap it out.

After you tap the bar out, you should reinstall the front dust cap and reattach the A-arm to the chassis. It's a wise idea to weld up the small hole in the dust cap, or fill it with a little bit of epoxy or silicone. If the

1 This is the view after removing the torsion bar adjustment screw, the adjustment lever, and the foam seal. Sometimes it will be easy at this point to pull the torsion bar out of the A-arm. Make sure that you don't damage the splines as you pull the bar out. Also note that in the background, you can see the jack stand supporting the weight of the car underneath the cross-member, not the A-arm. It's not safe to disconnect the A-arm mounting point while the car's weight is supported on it.

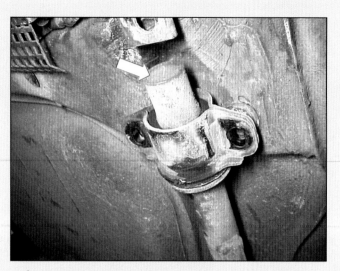

2 This photo shows the front of the A-arm when the cover/bracket are removed. The small arrow points to the dust cover that is pressed into the end of the torsion bar. This cover is about the same size as a quarter, and is made out of thin sheet metal. The plug is pressed into the end of the torsion bar cover, and needs to have a hole drilled in the center of it to gain enough leverage to pull it out. Be careful not to damage the torsion bar when you are drilling the hole.

3 Here the brake caliper bolts (red arrows) and disc have been removed to access the radius arm bolts. The trailing arm is lowered to the point where the radius arm bolts (yellow arrows) can be removed, the arm can be pried off with a few large screwdrivers, and the torsion bar no longer twists in either direction. You can find this point by raising or lowering the rear trailing arm with the jack. The green arrows indicate the toe-in and camber adjustments for the rear trailing arm.

cap has become damaged, then it will be necessary to replace it with a new one. On the older cars, it is common for the splines to be dry and rusted. You may also find damage to the female splines, necessitating replacement of the A-arm or adjuster.

When you have the bar removed, inspect it for any corrosion or damage to the bar or the end

splines. If such damage exists, then the bar should be replaced.

Reinstallation is straightforward. Simply reinstall the bar after liberally coating it with some white lithium grease. The bars are pre-stressed from the manufacturer, so don't mix up the left and right sides. The bars are marked L and R on their ends.

When fitting the torsion bar back into the car, make sure that the suspension A-arm is hanging as far downward as possible. Insert the bar into the A-arm, and install a new foam seal over the torsion bar if the old one was worn. Now, place the adjustment lever back onto the end of the torsion bar. Make sure that you leave as little clearance as possible between the adjusting arm and the inside top of the cross-member. Thread the adjustment screw into the adjustment lever, and then follow the adjustment guidelines explained in Project 55.

While the front torsion bars are mounted along the length of the 911, the rear bars run across the width of the car. The bars provide the spring for the suspension of the rear trailing arms. A large spring radius arm, or spring plate, connects the end of the torsion bar to the trailing arm, and provides adjustment for ride height, and balance from left to right.

The first step in removing the rear torsion bars is to jack up and remove the rear road wheels. Do not place jack stands under the torsion bar covers, as you will need to remove these. Instead, support the car from under the engine and the transmission, taking care not to place the jack stands in any location that may cause damage to the engine case. You can also place the jack stands under the torsion bar tube that runs the width of the car.

Now, place the jack under the rear trailing arms and raise them up slightly, so that the shock absorber is compressed about an inch from its maximum travel. Make sure that you don't jack up the shock absorber too much, as this will tend to raise the car off of the jack stands. Remove the lower bolt from the shock and let it hang there next to the trailing arm. Now, remove the four bolts that hold on the torsion bar cover and the spacers that go underneath it. Use two large screwdrivers to pry off the cover.

Unfortunately, removing the torsion bar requires that you remove the radius arm as well—particularly if you want to save your original suspension bushings. You will need to remove the rear caliper and brake disc in order to access the bolts that hold on the radius arm. See Project 47 for more details on this procedure. You will also need to remove the small torsion bar access cover on the outside skin of the car. This cover is painted the same color as the car, and on early cars may require the removal of some rocker trim below the door.

The rear suspension bushing is molded into the radius arm itself, and the two together are considered a single part by the factory. You can cut or burn away the older bushing, but then you will have to replace it with a newer bushing. The replacement bushings are a different style from the original ones—they are not molded into the radius arm, but instead wrap around the inner torsion bar cover. Although the original bushings twist as the car moves up and down, the replacement bushings don't—they rotate instead. This means that the replacement bushings have a tendency to squeak. Needless to say, I recommend that you remove the entire radius arm and save your original bushings.

Before you remove any of the bolts that hold the radius arm to the trailing arm, lower the trailing arm until the tension from the torsion bar exerted on the radius arm decreases. You should be able to lower the radius arm to a point where the torsion bar will not exert any force on it. At this point, all of the spring will be taken out of the torsion bar, so that there is no tension at all on the trailing arm/radius arm assembly. You may have to use trial and error, and raise and lower the rear trailing arm a few times to find the right height where there will be no tension from the torsion bar. It's important to relieve any tension on the radius arm before you disconnect the bolts that attach it to the trailing arm. Otherwise, the radius arm may spring back violently when you remove the last bolt that attaches it to the trailing arm.

On the older cars, four bolts attach the radius arm to the trailing arm. Two of these are the camber and toe adjustments, and the other two attach the radius arm firmly to the trailing arm. On the later-style cars with the right height adjustment screws (see Project 55), you will need to remove the large adjustment bolt and the locking bolt as well. When there is no more tension on the radius arm, and all the bolts have been removed, you should be able to pry off the radius arm with two large screwdrivers.

Pull out the old torsion bar, being careful not to scratch the protective paint. Make sure that you mark the location of the torsion bar with respect to the radius arm, if you are planning to reinstall it in the car again, and would like to keep the car at the same ride height. The paint plays an important role, as it prevents rust and scratches in the bar. If the bar is allowed to rust, or is scratched, this will create a stress concentration in the bar that will decrease its strength.

If the torsion bar has broken, then the other half of the bar will be trapped in the center tube. To

4 With the radius arm removed, the torsion bar can be pulled out of the torsion bar tube. Make sure that you remove the small outer access cover on the car before you try to remove the bar from the tube. You may have to remove some of the lower rocker trim on the early cars in order to remove the access cover.

5 This is what the radius arm looks like, removed from the car. The arm has a vulcanized rubber bushing that is molded into the metal piece. The inner torsion bar cover (what you place the jack stands on) is pressed into the inside of the round bushing. Replacement bushings are not as good as the original ones, and should only be installed if the original bushing is deteriorated.

remove the broken half, simply remove the torsion bar on the other side of the car, and poke a long rod through the tunnel. You should be able to push the broken bar end out of the tunnel.

If you are planning to reuse the torsion bar, then carefully inspect it once you have it out of the car. Repaint any damaged paint with primer. The bar should be replaced if there are any splines on the ends that are damaged. Check the bar for rust and corrosion—you should replace it if you find either.

Reinstallation is straightforward. Make sure that you place the correct bar in the correct side of the car. Although the left side will fit the right side, the bars are pre-stressed from the factory to be installed on a specific side of the car. The bars are marked L or R on the ends of them, corresponding to the left and right side of the car.

Coat the bar and the splines with some lithium grease and reinstall them into the car. The bar should be appropriately adjusted according to the procedures detailed in Project 55. Make sure that you have the bar balanced against the opposite side to ensure that the car sits level. You should also have your suspension alignment realigned and adjusted after you replace your torsion bars.

SECTION EIGHT
INTERIOR

You spend a lot of time inside your car, so why not have it look good on the inside as well as the outside? This section deals primarily with the restoration of some of the 911's interior components. A great looking interior improves the overall appearance of your 911, and also makes it more fun to drive.

INTERIOR
PROJECT 65 • ENGINE SOUND PAD INSTALLATION

 Time: 2 hours

 Tools: –

 Talent:

 Applicable Years: All

 Tab: $75

 Tinware: New engine compartment sound pad, 3M Super Weatherstrip Adhesive 08001

 Tip: Best time to replace this pad is when the engine is out of the car.

! PERFORMANCE GAIN: Sharper looking engine compartment, quieter engine

COMPLEMENTARY MODIFICATION: Replace rear deck lid shocks

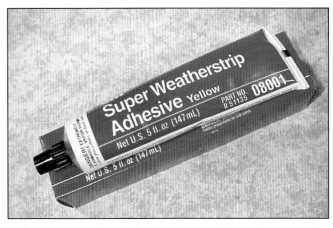

1 3M Super Weatherstrip Adhesive 08001 is one of those modern miracles of science. By far one of the best glues out there, its primary advantage is that it requires only a minute or two of holding before it adheres. It dries incredibly quickly, and it is easy to use. The only drawback is the fumes, which are not very healthy to breathe.

2 The newly installed sound pad significantly cleans up your engine compartment. Make sure that while the glue is drying, you keep pressing the pad against the back wall. Porsche has since superceded the sound pads to a later-style that is lighter yet just as effective at blocking sound. Don't be alarmed when your replacement weighs half as much as your original one.

It's common for the engine compartment sound mat to deteriorate after years of use. Porsche's mat is made of a spongy material which often falls apart, leaving sponge remains all over the inside of the engine compartment. Replacement is easy, and made easier by removing the engine from the car.

The first step in replacing the mat is removing the old one. In most cases, this won't be difficult. The older mats tend to easily pull away from the glue that originally held them to the rear of the engine compartment. If you don't have the engine or fuel injection removed, this task will be more difficult. First remove your air filter housing for better access. It's OK to rip the mat as you are taking it out. Just make sure that you cover the parts of your fuel system (intakes on carburetors, for example) that are open and susceptible to foam chunks falling inside.

Installing the new mat is straightforward. The key is 3M Super Weatherstrip Adhesive, easily among the best glues ever created. Glue anything with this stuff, and it sticks right away. Lay the mat on the ground and apply the glue to the back. Creating a crisscross pattern on the back of the mat works well. Make sure

to apply the cement to all the mat's edges so they will stick to the rear of the engine compartment. If you're planning to replace your rear deck lid shocks (Project 81), I would do that before installing the new pad.

The 3M Super Weatherstrip Adhesive is fantastic, but noxious. I recommend using a filtered gas mask when applying it. Working in the engine compartment doesn't aid in the ventilation process. The $30 gas masks available at most hardware stores do an excellent job of filtering out the glue fumes, and it seems a low price to pay to avoid getting cancer later on.

For 10 to 20 minutes after you place the new pad, press on it to ensure that it makes contact with the rear of the engine compartment. The adhesive will do the rest. After about 12 hours of final curing, the glue should be quite strong.

INTERIOR
PROJECT 66 • RE-DYEING INTERIOR LEATHER AND VINYL

 Time: 3 hours

 Tools: –

 Talent: ▮

 Applicable Years: All

 Tab: $5

 Tinware: Black leather/vinyl dye

 Tip: Test a small portion of the dye on an inconspicuous spot before you do the whole seat.

 PERFORMANCE GAIN: Nicer looking leather/vinyl interior

COMPLEMENTARY MODIFICATION: Replace the interior carpet

1 This seat cushion shows before and after results. Its front has been treated, while the rear has not. The leather dye won't remove cracks and wear from the seat, but it sure goes far to disguise them. Re-dyeing the seats is an excellent way to give your interior new life, without spending a fortune on recovering kits.

Whether your 911 was equipped originally with leather or vinyl seats, chances are they are showing their age. Probably more than any interior item on the car, other than the steering wheel, the driver's seat takes the most abuse and wear throughout the years. After more than a decade of use, the seats certainly can look worn.

One of the most expensive restoration projects you can perform is recovering your seats, especially if they are made out of leather. Recovering kits can cost almost $500 just for the material alone. You can count on spending several hundred dollars more to get the kits installed, if you don't do it yourself. If you're a master seamstress, then perhaps you have the talent and patience to perform a really good job, but for most of us the recovering job is way beyond our skill set.

There is, however, a "dirty" little secret that a lot of used car dealers use to replenish worn and cracked leather. Using a leather dye, the look of the seats and associated leather parts on the car can be significantly improved. The good news is that this dye can be the same type that you use to redye leather shoes.

There are several different brands out there, but the one that I have personally used is the Kiwi leather dye. This is readily available from most supermarkets and department stores.

It is important to note that you should try out the dye on a small section of your seats prior to using it on all of the leather. You want to make sure that the leather will soak up the dye, and that it won't bleed or rub out when you sit on it. Take a small section of the seat (preferably the side), and apply the dye liberally. The Kiwi brand has a small sponge incorporated into the bottle, so that it spreads the dye evenly across the fabric. Be careful not to use too much, or it will create drips that will run down the side of the seat.

After you have applied the dye to a test area, let it dry for about a half-hour or so. Take an old white sock or handkerchief and vigorously rub the area that you applied the dye to. The white cloth should show no signs of any black dye. If it does, then your seats might have been treated with some type of leather protectant that is not allowing the dye to adhere properly. Again, it is very important to check to make sure that the dye will not rub off or you may never be able to wear anything white in your Porsche again. Make sure that you wet the seat a bit too, to see if it will come off when the seats get wet.

If your car has black seats, then you should have no problem finding a dye that is a good color match for your car. If you have a tan or brown interior, you might have to search out different colors from various sources. Try a shoe repair store for odd colors. They might even be able to mix up a dye that would be color-matched to the original fabric that is in your car (they often dye women's shoes to match certain-color dresses).

If your car is equipped with vinyl seats, the same process can be used, but it would be wise to search out a dye that is formulated specifically for vinyl. Again, make sure that you test the dye on a noncritical section of fabric prior to applying it to the whole seat. And again, you might want to toss a little water on the test area to make sure that the dye doesn't run if it happens to get wet.

INTERIOR

PROJECT 67 • INSTALLING A NEW DASH PAD

 Time: 12 hours

 Tools: –

 Talent: ᛟᛟᛟ

 Applicable Years: All

 Tab: $500

 Tinware: New dash pad, and new front windshield seal

 Tip: Take your time, and have plenty of patience with the windshield.

! PERFORMANCE GAIN: Much nicer looking interior

COMPLEMENTARY MODIFICATION: Replace your front windshield and seal.

One of the most common problems with the older Porsches is that the dash pad cracks, fades, and separates after years of exposure to the sun. There are a few ways to prevent this, but few original owners thought to keep the dash pad protected from the sun.

Replacement of the dash pad is not cheap, nor is it easy. New dash pads (if still available for your year 911) typically cost around $600 or more. Used ones in decent condition are very difficult to find, and still fetch prices of $300–$450 depending upon the year or color. The best bet is to find one of these used ones, install it, and then take care of it by keeping it out of the sun.

The first step in replacing your dash pad, unfortunately, is to remove the front windshield. The dash pad cannot be replaced with the windshield in place. The lower part of the windshield seal tucks over the edge of the dash pad. It's nearly impossible to get the dash in and out without removing this seal, which means removing the windshield. For more information on removing the windshield from your car, refer to Project 79.

Once you have the windshield out, things get a bit easier. The dash pad is attached to the chassis of the car using two different types of fasteners. The rear of the dash pad is held in using small plastic clips, similar to the ones that hold the door panel to the door. The other fastener is an embedded stud, which protrudes through the sheet metal of the chassis and is secured with either a metal or plastic nut.

The layout of the mounting studs and plastic clips on the dash pads has varied over the years. Sometimes, even if you order the correct dash pad for your year 911, you might find that the studs and clips are located in the wrong places. The dash pads for the very early cars (1965–1968) are no longer available. From 1969 through 1975 the dash pads all had a center speaker vent that was separate from the dash pad. In 1976 the speaker grille disappeared from the top of the dash pad. In 1977 a center air vent was added and remained there until 1986, when the dash pad was redesigned again, this time without the small plastic clips that attach it to the top of the dashboard.

The difficult part of removing the dash pad is that the fasteners can be difficult to locate, and it's also hard to tell if they are the snap-in type or the embedded-stud type. Early dashes up to 1985 had these plastic snap-in retainers, but the later-style ones used on the Carreras (1986 and up) used a dash pad that only had studs. Refer to the photo in this project for the locations of the different types of fasteners.

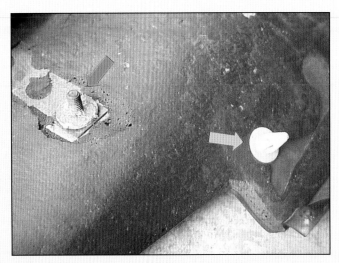

1 The dash pad is held on with two different types of fasteners. One type simply presses into the top of the metal support (shown by the yellow arrow), whereas the other is actually an embedded stud in the pad itself (green arrow). If you are performing this for the first time, the most difficult part of the job is figuring out which fastener mates to which hole.

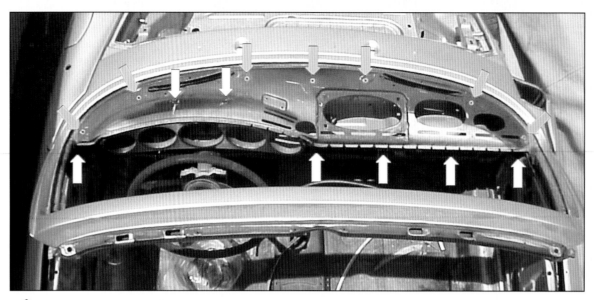

2 This photo shows the location of the studs (shown in white) and the plastic press-in fasteners (shown in yellow) on a 1973 dash board. Various changes occurred throughout the years, but for the most part, most of the fasteners have remained in the same place. Use this photo as a guideline for where to look for the studs that hold your dash pad onto your car.

Access to the nuts that hold the dash pad can also be difficult. You will need to remove most of the gauges from their holders (see Project 88 for details on removing gauges). You also might have to remove the glove box and the radio. Depending upon how big your hands are (no kidding) you may have to remove a few more items as well, such as vents or hoses.

The good news is that the nuts that secure the dash pad to the chassis are usually not on very tight, and in most case can be removed simply using your hand. This, of course, will be the case for all of the nuts except for the one that is the most difficult to reach (Murphy's Law).

Another thing in your favor is that if you are removing the dash pad from your car, chances are it's already in less than acceptable condition, and a little bit more wear and tear from the removal process won't really matter. There is a good chance that you will mess up or damage the dash pad when removing it, so beware if you are planning to reuse it. During the process of removal, you will most likely learn where all the difficult-to-reach fasteners go, and the particular tricks to reach them. Make sure that you don't accidentally unplug or pull on any wires or hoses located behind the dash—it can be a huge pain to troubleshoot dashboard electrical problems.

To detach the small plastic clips that hold the rear of the dash pad, gently pry up or pull on them. The clips should pop out of their mating holes in the top of the dashboard. Don't be too concerned if one or two of the clips become separated from the dash—it's easy to reglue them back on later.

Installation of the new pad is pretty easy, compared to the removal process. Simply take the new one, and line it up properly with all of the holes for the embedded studs. Then snap down the rear of the pad, making sure that all of the plastic clips seat properly into the top of the dashboard. Attach the nuts to the ends of the embedded studs. In most cases, finger tight is usually tight enough. If you overtighten the nuts on the dash pad studs, then you might pull them out of the dash pad, or worse, deform the pad itself.

After all of the clips are attached, and the studs are tightened, then it's time to reinstall your windshield—not one of your easiest jobs. For more information, see Project 80, and remember to have patience during the install.

The best method to shield the dash pad from the sun is by using a prefabricated cover that is fitted to the dash pad. There are several different types, but my personal favorite is the one manufactured out of velour. It looks slick, and it does an excellent job of insulating against the heat of the sun. There are a few other types of covers available as well, and which one you use is subject to your individual taste. The important thing to remember is to make sure that you use the cover to protect your new investment from the heat of the sun.

PROJECT 68 • HEADLINER REPLACEMENT

 Time: 10–12 hours

 Tools: –

 Talent: 👤👤👤👤👤

 Applicable Years: All coupe cars

 Tab: $100–$500

 Tinware: Headliner, 3M Super Weatherstrip 08001, headliner clips, window seals, tensioning stays

 Tip: Take your time

 PERFORMANCE GAIN: Much more attractive interior

COMPLEMENTARY MODIFICATION: Replace dash pad, replace weather stripping, repair sunroof

Replacing the 911 headliner is one of the most difficult and complex projects in this book. However, if you work slowly and carefully, you should be able to perform the job within a weekend or two with minimal damage and downtime to your car.

What makes the process so difficult is the fact that you need to remove a large portion of the interior, the front and rear windshields, and both side windows. You also need to remove the rear back panel that fits behind the rear seats. To make the job easier, it's also recommended that you remove the seats and the sunroof. While you have all of these parts taken out, it's also a wise idea to fix and repair some other items that need attention, like the sunroof (Project 85) or a cracked dash pad (Project 67). Needless to say, replacing the headliner can incorporate quite a few more projects that will slow down the process of getting your car on the road again.

The first step is the removal of the window glass from the front, rear, and sides of the car. For more information on the procedure for this, see Project 79. The glass removal is a tricky process that requires plenty of patience.

I also recommend that you remove the seats so that you can move around inside the car. The seats are simply bolted down to the chassis of the car with four bolts. You can access the bolts in the front by moving the seat back all the way. The bolts in the rear are removed by moving the seat all the way to the front. Once the bolts are removed, the seat can simply be lifted out. While you have both seats out, you might want to recondition them with some leather dye (see Project 66).

With the glass out of the car, it's time to remove the old headliner. Start with the front of the car, and remove the tensioning clips that hold the headliner to the car. Then carefully remove the old headliner by tearing it off of the points where it is glued onto the car. Pull out the interior lamps, and remove the sun visor brackets and interior coat hooks. Make sure you keep the old headliner, as it makes a useful guide for installing the new one. As you remove the old headliner, make a note of where the lights, coat hooks, and other fixtures were located so that you can reinstall them later. Where the headliner disappears under the vinyl trim on the roof pillars, peel back the trim until you can remove the old headliner.

If you are going to be replacing the door seals, then remove them from the edge of the car. They should simply be glued in place. If you are planning to reuse them, then you only need to pull out the top

1 The rear section of the headliner is by far the trickiest. When reinstalling the window seals, make sure that they don't dislodge the headliner from its position. When reinstalling fixtures like the rear pop-out window latch, make sure that you carefully mark the holes with a permanent marker before you cut them with a knife. It's very easy to make a major mistake at this point in the game. Make sure that you don't cut too much area out of the fabric.

2 The alignment and location of the zipper are important so that you can gain access to the sunroof motor. Make a note of the location of the zipper before you remove your old headliner. Don't forget to install your coat hooks and the interior lamps, as they actually help to keep the headliner tight. When installing the headliner, unplug and remove the interior lamp, then thread the wires through the headliner soon after you install it. Don't forget, or you will have to fish around for the wires, and you could end up damaging your headliner.

3 When you are removing the old headliner, take careful note of how it was originally installed on your car. You will want to follow the cuts and curves that were part of the original headliner. Take a few pictures to remind yourself later on. On curves and tight edges, cut the headliner and feather it as shown on this original headliner. This will allow the headliner to reach around corners, and maintain a tightness that avoids wrinkles. Use glue on each feathered finger, because the installation of the new glass seal will have a tendency to pull them off.

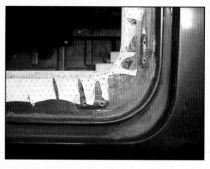

portion of the seal. Door seal replacement is covered in Project 77.

After you have the old headliner removed, it's time to prepare the new one for installation. On dark-colored cars, I prefer to install a black headliner. The black headliner holds up better against dirt and grime. The black headliner, however, makes it a bit darker inside the car at night because the white has a tendency to reflect light. You also may need to dye your sun visors to match the headliner when you are finished.

Cars without sunroofs have tensioning wires that keep the headliner intact and straight as it traverses the car. This headliner is a different kit from the one for cars equipped with sunroofs, so make sure that you purchase the correct kit. Prior to the installation, make sure that these stays are inserted into the loops in the headliner. If the tensioning stays are looking a bit ragged, make sure that you replace them with new ones.

The headliner itself comes folded in a package when delivered. This will make for some nice wrinkles in the fabric. I recommend that you let the headliner hang for a couple of days on a wall, as this will help some of the wrinkles. Don't iron the fabric—it's vinyl, and can easily melt or become distorted. If too much heat is applied to one section, then that section will expand or contract and create a permanent wrinkle that will not be able to be tensioned out.

Start the installation by clipping the headliner to the door openings on each side. For setting up the

headliner, I recommend using office supply binder clips. They are very strong, and they will help hold the headliner in place while you wait for the glue to hold. Stretch the headliner back to the rear of the car and clip it to the top of the rear window. Do not cut or glue any of the headliner just yet. Make sure that you have the zipper lined up with the sunroof motor in the rear.

Once you have the headliner in place, remove each side individually and tension out each side until you are happy with the results. The headliner shouldn't have any wrinkles in it at this point. If it does, then retension the headliner until all the wrinkles are gone. At this point, you can make some broad general cuts to fit the headliner so that you can tension it. These cuts will need to be made near the door pillars and windows.

If your car is a sunroof model, only make the cutout for the sunroof after the headliner has been completely placed and tensioned. Make sure that you don't cut too much material out for the sunroof—start with plenty of extra as you can always trim more later on. The procedure is largely the same as with the regular roofs, except that there are no traverse stays to tension the roof.

With the headliner appropriately tensioned, begin by gluing the front edge of the headliner. Glue the headliner over the edge of the pinch-weld that grips the window seals. Make sure that you don't use too much glue, and place the glue evenly around the edge so that no sections of the headliner are left unglued. A small disposable paintbrush can help you to spread the glue without making a mess. Be careful not to get any glue on the outer surface of the headliner.

Unglued sections will make the installation of the window seals difficult. I prefer to use the 3M Super Weatherstrip 08001 discussed in Project 65, although some installers use a general-purpose spray-on adhesive instead. Although this adhesive is very quick to dry, make sure that it is completely dry before moving on to another section. Use the small tensioner clips to hold the headliner to the front windshield recess once the glue is set. Again, make sure that the glue is dry and the headliner is tight before moving on.

Working toward the rear of the car, keep tensioning and gluing small sections at a time. Don't worry about the sun visor and interior lamps at this time—they will be cut out later on. Make sure that you work slowly; glue and tension each small section at a time. Perform the gluing process in a well-ventilated area, as the glue can be quite noxious over time.

When encountering round corners, as on the sunroof and rear window, carefully cut the headliner into small strips that you can place around the radius of the window. When you reach the rear window, make sure that you use the rear tensioning clips to secure the headliner to the edge. This is so the headliner will not be pushed off of the recess by the installation of the window seal.

On some headliners, there may be a small metal tensioning stay at the very rear of the headliner. Insert the tensioning stay into the loop at the end of the headliner and tuck it into the metal hooks located on the rear shelf. This will help to tension the rear of the headliner.

Once you have the headliner installed around all the edges, trim the edges around the door and front pillars. Make sure that you leave enough material to cover the pillar to the point where the leather/vinyl trim is located. Use a small pair of scissors, or a sharp hobby knife to carefully trim the edges.

Once the headliner is installed and clipped, use your knife to cut out the small openings for the interior lamp, the clothes hook, and the sun visor mounts.

4 There is perhaps nothing that can spruce up your interior better than a new headliner. Old, water-stained headliners show the age of the car all too well. It also helps to clean your sun visors with a bit of bleach or grease remover. Just make sure that they match the headliner when you're finished.

Use the old headliner as a guide for the locations that you need to cut out. Pull the electrical leads through the interior lamp hole, and reattach the lamp. Insert the lamp into its clip, making sure that the lamp is appropriately grounded to the chassis, and not accidentally insulated by a flap of the headliner.

Final tensioning can be done by pulling out the fabric and reapplying glue in small increments. Additionally, a hair dryer or heat gun can be used to tension the headliner a bit further, but be careful as a large amount of heat can destroy the fabric. Also, don't expect the hair dryer to perform miracles—only small folds will be reduced by its use.

Once you have completed the installation of the headliner, reinstall the door seals, and the window glass. Be careful when installing the seals for the glass—they can accidentally pull off poorly glued sections of the headliner. The seals are designed to help keep the headliner in place, so make sure that they don't get caught on any folds of extra fabric when you are installing them.

SECTION NINE
BODY

This section is a grab bag of projects that deal with everything from headlamp upgrades to door equipment repair. Whether you are planning on replacing your hood shocks or installing a rear "Whale Tail" spoiler on your car, the projects in this section will help you improve the overall performance and exterior appearance of your 911.

BODY
PROJECT 69 • WIPER REVERSAL

 Time: 3 hours

 Tools: Socket set

 Talent:

 Applicable Years: 1968–

 Tab: –

 Tinware: –

 Tip: Inspect your master cylinder while you are in the front trunk.

 PERFORMANCE GAIN: Increased visibility through the front windshield

COMPLEMENTARY MODIFICATION: Replace the front heater blower motor and hoses.

The procedure for reversing the wipers is actually quite easy—the hardest part is gaining access to the wiper motor assembly in the front trunk. You need to remove the front blower motor cover, and then pull away the blower motor assembly. Make sure that you disconnect the blower motor hoses before pulling out the blower motor. The control cables that are connected to the motor and the air vents do not need to be disconnected.

The wiper motor is protected by a U-shaped bracket that is integrated into the wiper motor assembly. Before you start the disassembly of the wipers, make sure that the wiper motor is parked properly in its home position. It's wise to spray some water on the windshield and turn on the wipers (never run them dry, as this can scratch the windshield) just to see how the entire assembly works. Be careful of your hands, as this assembly is quite powerful, and could easily break some of your fingers if they are in the wrong spot at the wrong time.

The key to reversing the wipers is to park the wiper motor in its home position, remove the small arm that is attached to the wiper mechanism, rotate

1 After removing the carpet and the access panel in the rear of the front trunk, disconnect the blower hoses from the blower motor and front air vents. Pull out the blower motor so that you can gain access to the wiper arm assembly underneath the dashboard.

2 Locate the small arm that rotates and drives the wiper arm assembly, hidden behind the U-shaped protective bracket. Remove the nut (shown by the yellow arrow), and pry the lever arm off of the shaft that is connected to the wiper motor. Rotate the wiper arms so that they are all the way on the right side of the windshield. The motor shaft should not turn at all while the wipers are being moved. When they are parked all the way on the other side, reconnect the arm and tighten the nut on the shaft. Spray some water on the windshield, then flip on the wiper motors and test to make sure that they are working properly.

the wipers to the right side, and reattach the arm. It is also just as easy to switch back if you are restoring the original factory location that a previous owner of your car had moved.

Make sure that you test the wipers before you replace the blower motor assembly and hoses. If you are having problems with the intermittent wiper function, then the relay is a prime candidate for cleaning or replacement. The wiper motor relay should be located near the wiper motor in the front trunk. Location varied a bit from year to year, but most of the later cars had the relay attached to the firewall. Try removing the relay and cleaning the contacts. If that doesn't work, then it's probably time for a new relay.

When reinstalling the blower motor assembly, be careful to make sure that no cables, wires, or hoses get in the path of the wiper motor assembly. On some of the early cars, if the wiper motor gets stuck, the resulting current overload can burn out the wiper switch.

With the wipers parked on the right side, the straight wiper on the left sticks up into the area of the windshield. For a cleaner-looking windshield, swap the left and right wiper arms. Then, take the bent wiper arm, place it in a vise, heat it up with a torch, and bend it slightly in the opposite direction. An alternative is to replace the angled wiper with another good used straight one.

While you have the blower motor out and accessible, make sure that you inspect your hoses, master cylinder and the surrounding area. If you see brake fluid leaking from around this general area, it's probably time for some replacement or repair work. See Project 52 for more details.

BODY

PROJECT 70 • LENS REPLACEMENT

 Time: 30 minutes

 Tools: Screwdriver

 Talent: ⚫

 Applicable Years: All

 Tab: $50–300

 Tinware: Front and rear turn signal lenses, fog lamp lenses, side marker lenses

 Tip: New lenses can improve the looks of your car more than you would think.

PERFORMANCE GAIN: Sharper looking exterior, and brighter illumination

COMPLEMENTARY MODIFICATION: Higher wattage bulbs, Halogen kit, Euro lenses

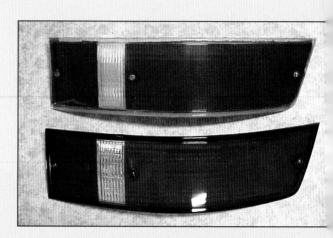

1 New lenses can make a remarkable improvement on the exterior looks of your car. Most often, owners don't realize that their lenses have deteriorated significantly. The most obvious sign of age is cracking, but fading and scratching of the lenses also degrades the appearance of the car. The installation of new lenses is probably the easiest way to instantly improve the looks of your 911.

Few projects are as easy as lens replacement, yet improve the looks of your car so significantly. Replacing old faded lenses not only improves the overall look of your car, it also increases its safety as well. Faded lenses tend to block much more light than brand-new ones.

For many years, it was very difficult to obtain replacement lenses for the very early 1965–1968 911s. These lenses were manufactured out of non-removable plastic that was actually melted into the turn signal housing. When they were available, replacement lenses could only be purchased with the entire turn signal assembly, and were several hundred dollars each. Replicas of the original lenses have been surfacing recently. These replicas have the original markings on them, and are virtually indistinguishable from the original ones. The availability of these lenses is a great gift to the owners of early 911s attempting to restore their cars back to original form.

In 1969, Porsche changed the body design of the 911, and also changed the lenses. A removable lens design was implemented, and this basic removable type of design was incorporated into 911s up to and including 1989 models.

The design of the front lenses changed again in 1974, and remained constant through 1989. The rear lenses remained the same as the ones from 1969, with the exception of the use of black trim instead of chrome, starting in 1973. The European cars had the addition of plugs that covered the U.S.-spec side marker lenses. They also had the addition of a small marker light on each side of the car, just in front of the door. Performing an upgrade to a European spec car involves the addition of these two features.

All rear turn signals from all years came in at least two forms, U.S. and European spec. The U.S.-spec lenses were all red with the clear back-up lens in the middle. The Euro-spec lenses were amber

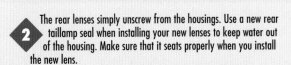

2 ▶ The rear lenses simply unscrew from the housings. Use a new rear taillamp seal when installing your new lenses to keep water out of the housing. Make sure that it seats properly when you install the new lens.

3 ▶ The front turn signals and side markers also easily unscrew from the housing. Make sure that you clean out the inside of the housing before replacing the lens. Doing so will increase the reflectivity of the mirror-type surface on the inside, and make your light glow more brightly and more uniformly.

toward the outside of the car, clear for the back-up light, and red on the inner red brake lens. On the earlier cars, a rare French-spec lens incorporated amber lenses where the back-up clear lens was located. Both types of lenses are interchangeable, and you may want to use Euro lenses in the rear if you prefer the look to the U.S.-spec lenses.

On 1986 and later cars, the brake lamp system incorporated the DOT-required third brake lamp. The lens in this light is also replaceable, and will look out of place if the two rear lenses are replaced without touching this one.

The replacement process is quite simple. The lenses unscrew from the housing, and the new ones take their place. When installing the lenses, you should make sure that you use a new seal to ensure that the inside of the housing doesn't get wet. When replacing the lenses, check all your bulbs to make sure that they are operating properly. For some models of cars, higher-wattage or

even halogen bulbs are available to make your lenses shine even brighter. Also make sure that you don't overtighten the screws, or you might crack your new lenses.

Often overlooked are the fog lamp lenses. Rocks and debris have a habit of scratching and marring the surface of the lens, reducing the light output from the bulbs. Replacing these lenses is easy. Simply unscrew the housings, remove the retaining rings, and replace the lens. Clear lenses were standard in the United States, while yellow lenses were available for other countries. As with the other lenses on the car, the U.S and European versions are interchangeable.

Another neat addition is the European rear fog lamp. Mounted on the lower valance, this small fog lamp was an option through 1989. The rear fog lamp was activated by pulling the fog lamp switch, and rotating it clockwise. (See photo in Project 97.)

BODY
PROJECT 71 • H4 HEADLAMP UPGRADE

Time: 1 hour

Tools: Screwdriver

Talent:

Applicable Years: 1965-1989

Tab: $275

Tinware: H4 headlamp assemblies, headlamp seals

Tip: Be careful not to strip out the mounting screw.

! PERFORMANCE GAIN: Brighter and better focused lights while driving

COMPLEMENTARY MODIFICATION: Replace the fog lamp lenses, install headlamp lens protector film

The standard U.S.-spec headlamps that the 911s ship with leave much to be desired. Somewhat outdated U.S. specifications for headlamps means the stock 911 has a somewhat weak pair of headlamps. Combine that with the 911's need for speed, and you may have a dangerous combination on the road at night.

One of the most popular and easiest upgrades for your 911 is the installation of the H4 headlamps originally used in the European cars. In Europe, most driving is done on country roads, where the high beams are used normally, and the low (or meeting beams as they are often called), are only used when meeting another car on the road. These headlamps have a better-focused beam, and also a much brighter bulb. The bulb for the H4s is also replaceable, unlike the U.S. units, which have sealed-beam assemblies. Be aware that in some states, the H4s are indeed illegal. However, most states have been very lax in enforcing the regulations, since newer technology such as the Litronic headlamp kits are slowly changing the specifications.

The reason that the U.S.-spec headlamps are required to be a sealed-beam unit dates back to a specification from the 1930s. This law mandated that all cars must have the sealed-beam unit because it was thought that water could get within the assembly and corrode the reflective backing surface, making the light less bright. Obviously, this is somewhat outdated, but has only been changed recently to reflect changes in technology. Also, the H4 is not legal because the DOT adjusting knobs are missing and the glass is not fluted per DOT regulation.

The H5 headlamps were also a semi-sealed-beam unit that was used on the 911 in the late 1980s. Despite the fact that the number five is greater than four, these are not considered to be superior to the H4s. The H4 is still hands down the best headlamp that will fit your 1965–1989 911.

All 911s through 1989 can use the H4 headlamps; however, the 1987–1989 911s require a wire harness adapter that will mate with the bulb. The headlamp bucket and fender that hold the housing are identical across all these years. You can also use a higher wattage bulb, but doing so may require the installation of heavier-duty wiring and a high-power relay.

The first step in installing the H4s is to remove the older, sealed-beam units. The headlamp ring that covers the headlamp unit is attached with a single screw at the bottom of the unit. Remove this screw, and the cover should simply slide off. The sealed-beam assembly is attached to the car by four screws. As you remove each one, be careful that they don't fall down into the bucket, as they can easily escape into the drain hole at the bottom.

Once you have the headlamp bucket removed, unplug the harness from the bulb. The new H4 assembly fits inside the fender opening without any modifications. Place the halogen bulb in the new assembly, and make sure that it is attached firmly with the two metal spring clips. Be careful not to touch the bulb with your fingers, as there are oils in your hands that will create hot spots on the glass, and make the bulb burn out much more quickly than normal. Use a paper towel or tissue when handling the bulb.

The assembly itself is attached to the fender by the one screw at the bottom that used to hold on the headlamp ring. Place the assembly into the fender, and make sure that the wire harness is folded out of the way. There should be a slight edge at the top of the fender that the top of the H4 assembly will "clip" into when tightened. Make sure that the assembly is properly installed onto this clip when you tighten the screw at the bottom. You should be able to pull on the top of the assembly without having it move. Also make sure that you install a new headlamp seal around the interface between the assembly and the fender.

When you have completed the installation, adjust your headlamps so that they point the light in the right direction. Park the car on a flat surface about 25 feet from a garage door or wall. Then adjust the vertical adjustment until the beam hits the wall at about the same height as the lightbulb on the car. Then adjust the horizontal pointing of the beams so that they are skewed just slightly to the right. To make these adjustments, turn the two screws embedded in the rim of the headlamp assembly.

The H4 assemblies change the outer appearance of your 911. Some people don't care for the look of the H4s once installed, so make sure that you appreciate the new look of the lamps before you install them. Also be aware that the H4 assemblies are specific to right- or left-hand drive 911s. Make sure that you purchase the correct one for your car. A USA left-hand drive H4 assembly will not work properly in a UK right-hand drive car—the light will focus into oncoming traffic!

1 This photo shows an H4 unit, headlamp seal and a halogen bulb. Sometimes the bulb will come with the unit, and other times you might have to purchase it separately. It's also a wise idea to replace your headlamp seal when you install the new assembly. These assemblies are available with trim in either chrome (shown in the picture) or black. The black trim can be painted to match your car for a smoother look. The chrome units usually look better on the 1973 and earlier cars because they will match the chrome trim on the rest of the car a little better.

2 Installation is pretty much a snap. Simply remove the old sealed unit and assembly, and place in the new H4s. The harness plugs directly into the bulb, which is supported within the assembly. Make sure not to touch the glass surface of the bulb with your fingers.

3 This photo shows the final H4 assembly installed. Although you get much better lighting from the H4s, some people don't like assembly's look on the front of the car. The older sealed-beams have a distinctive classic look that you may not wish to part with. It's wise to check out a variety of cars with and without the H4 headlamp, to make sure that you want to make the switch.

BODY
PROJECT 72 • INSTALLING A ROLL CAGE

 Time: 8 hours

 Tools: Drill, tape measure

 Talent:

 Applicable Years: All

 Tab: $350

 Tinware: Roll cage kit with mounting hardware

 Tip: Make sure that you align everything properly before you start drilling holes in your 911.

 PERFORMANCE GAIN: Added protection from roll-overs

COMPLEMENTARY MODIFICATION: Install five-point racing harnesses

1 Most roll cages are very similar and relatively easy to install. Removing the seats is a must, and you should make sure that everything fits before you start drilling holes in your chassis. Make sure that you really want to install one before you jump into the process. Removing and reinstalling the roll cage can be a pain. This photo shows a competition roll bar with the crossbrace installed.

2 The roll cage is mounted to the floor of the car. Backing plates on the floorpan under the car are usually a wise idea, to prevent the floor from buckling under a significant load. The good news is that you probably won't care too much about damaging your floorpan if there is a load on the roll cage—your car will be upside down with the roof completely crushed! (Let's hope not . . .)

If you ever want to step up to the next level in weekend racing, you will most likely have to install a roll cage in your car. Depending upon the class and rules that you are racing under, you may be required to have the roll cage and associated five-point harness installed before your car hits the track.

Installing the roll cage is really not too difficult, and most can be installed with without any major alterations to the chassis. They are usually mounted to the floor of the car, and to the rear shelves, just outside of the rear seats.

There are several different types of roll bars available, but most can be put into two different categories—street and competition. The competition bars have a crossbrace that extends about shoulder height across the width of the car. The street roll cages usually don't have this crossbrace. The competition crossbrace strengthens the roll cage, and provides a very convenient spot to tie your five-point harness to.

The roll cage can be installed in an afternoon, but it's important to work carefully, as you don't want to accidentally drill holes in the wrong spots. Both of the front seats need to be removed, and you will have to carefully maneuver the roll cage a bit in order to insert it into the rear of your car.

When you are ready to mount the roll cage to the car, make sure that you follow the manufacturer's directions very carefully. Improper installation can affect the safety and structural integrity of the entire setup. Before you decide to drill any holes in your car, carefully measure the bar to make sure that your holes will be symmetrical on both sides. You may want to remove some of the fabric from where the rear mounts attach before you start drilling into the car.

Most roll cages have pretty large mounting flanges, but you may want to reinforce them with plates underneath the chassis floorboard. This will help prevent the floorboards from tearing from any unforeseen stresses placed on them. I recommend reinforcing any attachments to the floorboards, whether you are bolting in a roll cage, or adding seat belts to your car. The floor of the car can be surprisingly weak.

Roll cages not only make the car safer, but they look cooler too. The addition of the roll cage also allows you to easily attach your five-point racing harness. One of the more popular additions to the roll cage is the addition of a camera mount so that you can videotape your driving performance for evaluation later.

BODY

PROJECT 73 • INSTALLING A NEW HOOD CREST

 Time: 1/2 hour

 Tools: –

 Talent:

 Applicable Years: All

 Tab: $35

 Tinware: Hood crest, seal, two speed nuts

 Tip: Don't tighten the nuts on the crest too much, or you might crack the gels on the front.

 PERFORMANCE GAIN: Sharper looking hood

COMPLEMENTARY MODIFICATION: Install a car bra

1 This before-and-after photo really shows the difference that a new crest can make. As with the lenses on the car, it is difficult to tell how tarnished and old the hood crest has become without looking at a brand-new one. With such an easy installation, it is perhaps the quickest method of instantly improving the exterior looks of your 911. The new crest is so shiny, it's hard to take a good picture of it!

2 The inside of the hood is manufactured with access holes so that you can remove and replace the crest. Make sure that you don't overtighten the two speed nuts, or you can crack some of the plastic gels embedded into the front of the crest, or damage your hood.

Over many years, the Porsche crest located on your front hood can take a beating. Rocks, gravel, soot, rain, snow, sleet, and other debris can scratch and dull the finish of the crest so that it no longer shines the way it should. The good news is that replacing the crest is one of the easiest projects that you can do, and it significantly improves the looks of your car.

It is important to note that you should only use the original Porsche crests manufactured under license from Porsche. In past years, there have been some counterfeit crests available for about half the cost, but the OEM crests from Porsche are of a much higher quality.

There are two different styles of the crest—one for the early cars (up to 1989), and one for the later cars. Make sure when you order yours, that you get the proper one for your car. Small changes in the crest have occurred over the years as well, so if you are looking for 100 percent originality, you may want to look for a crest that is new old stock (NOS). It is also important to replace the rubber seal that mates the crest flush with the hood.

The crest is attached using two small self-threading nuts that Porsche calls "speed-nuts." These nuts are designed to be used both with the crest and the other emblems used on the car. The speed-nut is a small aluminum disc with a puttylike insert that allows it to hold the emblem snug without the danger of denting or damaging the hood of the car. The speed-nut also stops water from leaking into the inside of the sheet metal.

The crest is attached to the car and held on with the speed-nuts on the inside of the hood. To remove the old crest, simply open the hood, and unscrew the nuts using a small 8-millimeter socket and an extension. Be careful that the speed clips don't fall into the recesses of the hood. When installing the new crest, place the rubber gasket around the crest and test fit it against the hood. Sometimes the small prongs on the crest may need to be bent slightly in order to make them fit the holes. Be sure not to bend them too much, or they will break off.

It's also a wise idea to get a small piece of masking tape, and tape the crest and seal to the hood before you install it. The speed-nuts are meant to be attached once, and removing and reinstalling them can damage the small studs on the crest. Use a small dental pick to fit the gasket around the crest before it's completely tightened down. Tape the crest to the hood to make sure that the rubber seal doesn't slip out of position while you are tightening the speed-nuts. Proceed slowly, and check the seal before you tighten up the nuts. This is a very simple job that can be messed up if you don't keep a watch on the seal.

BODY

PROJECT 74 • DOOR STAY REPLACEMENT AND REINFORCEMENT

 Time: 3 hours

 Tools: Needle nose pliers, socket set, hex socket set

 Talent:

 Applicable Years: All

 Tab: $85

 Tinware: Door stay reinforcement kit, new door stay mechanism

 Tip: Make sure that you flatten the damaged metal on the door before installing the kit.

PERFORMANCE GAIN: Doors that don't fly open

COMPLEMENTARY MODIFICATION: Replace speakers, door panels, window switches, mirror switches, window regulators, door handles

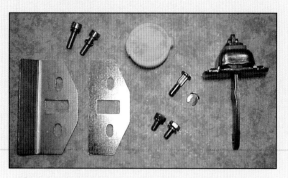

1 The complete door stay reinforcement kit includes two sandwich plates, lithium grease, a new door stay, and the connecting pins and screws. Weltmeister manufactures this particular kit. Even if your door doesn't show signs of wear, I recommend that you install the reinforcement kit as a precautionary measure. Years of opening and closing the door can damage it almost beyond repair. It's better to invest a little bit of money and time up front than replace your entire door later on.

One of the weaker parts designed on the Porsche 911 is the door and its door stay. The door and the door stay mechanism have a tendency to tear and rip the sheet metal inside the door. Luckily, there is a reinforcement kit that will save the door most of the time, although some 911 doors can get pretty beat up in the process.

After seeing the damage done to the door on my 911SC, I would recommend that everyone install the door stay reinforcement kit on both the passenger- and driver-side door. If the door becomes severely damaged, it may be unrepairable it. The internal piece of supporting metal that holds the door stay together is welded inside the door. The process of welding deep inside the door is not an easy one, and if the damage is severe, nothing can be done to fix it. The best solution might be to scrap the door. Considering that, I think that the reinforcement kits are good insurance.

The first step in fixing your door is to remove your door panel. Refer to Project 75 for more information on this particular procedure. Once you have the door panel removed, remove the front door-mounted speaker and peer inside of the door to assess the damage. If the door stay has been in bad condition for quite a while, chances are high that the sheet metal inside your door is torn. Hopefully the reinforcement kit will be strong enough to support the weakened metal.

To remove the doorstop, tap out the small pin that holds the door to the chassis. On some models, a small clip was used to secure the pin. On other models, the pin simply can be tapped out with a hammer. Remove the door stay by loosening the two nuts or bolts that hold the door stay to the door. The door stay will fall to the bottom of the door, where you can reach in and pull it out.

If your sheet metal is severely damaged, it may be wise to remove your door—not an easy task. Removing the door is beyond the scope of this project, but it involves disconnecting and removing all of the harnesses from the door, and having a helper support the door while the fastening bolts are removed.

In order to make sure that the reinforcement kit works best, you should tap out the damaged sheet metal on the mounting surfaces with a hammer until they are flat. Try to bend and tap the metal back to its original shape as much as possible. If there are any ridges or grooves, the "sandwich" effect of the rein-

forcement kit may not work effectively. After the sheet metal has been flattened, assemble the door stay parts together within arm's reach of the door. Feed the outer supporting plate through the hole in the door, making sure that it doesn't drop down in the recesses of the door. If it does fall, it may be very difficult to retrieve without taking the door off. Use a piece of string and tie it to the support plate, just in case you drop it.

With the outer plate in place, mount the door stay and the inner plate using the two bolts supplied with the kit. In order to use the kit, you must use the style of door stay that does not have embedded studs, but threaded holes instead.

After you have the assembly sandwiched together, moderately tighten down the door stay. Reattach the "tongue" of the door stay to the chassis of the car. Make sure that the door opens and closes properly, and that the door stay is aligned for proper operation. Loosen the bolts and adjust the door stay if necessary.

When you've found the right position, tighten the bolts as much as you can without stripping them. Make sure that the damaged metal is sandwiched tightly between the heavy-gauge steel reinforcement plates. If all goes well, the reinforcement kit should prevent further damage to your door.

2 This is what the damaged door stay looks like from the outside. The nuts have been pulled away completely from the door, and the sheet metal has been completely torn and ripped. Make sure that you flatten these pieces before you install the reinforcement kit.

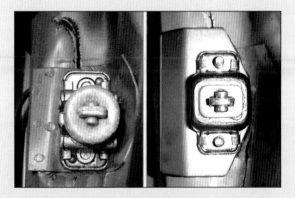

3 The picture on the left, from inside the door, affords us a look at more internal damage. Repeated opening and closing of the door has caused the sheet metal to tear and begin ripping. You should attempt to weld and repair tears like these before you install the kit. Unfortunately, this tear is deep inside the door, and is very difficult to get to with a welder. The newly installed reinforcement plate does much to support the metal and prevent tears. Only time will tell if it will be enough to recover from this much damage. Note the two different types of doorstops.

4 The outer door stay reinforcement plate fits between the door and the inner mounting plate. Some creative negotiating may be required to get it to fit inside the door. Depending upon how damaged your door is, you may have to loosen and adjust the doorstop, once you reattach the tongue to the frame of the car.

PROJECT 75 • DOOR HANDLE REPLACEMENT

Time: 4 hours

Tools: Hex key set

Talent:

Applicable Years: All

Tab: $20 for inner handle, $300 for outer handle

Tinware: New outer or inner door handle

Tip: There are lots of things that go wrong with the doors—fix them while you have the door apart.

PERFORMANCE GAIN: You can get into or out of your car!

COMPLEMENTARY MODIFICATION: Replace window/mirror switches, upgrade to metal interior door handles, check/replace window regulator, recover/replace door panel, fix door stay, fix/replace mirrors

If you are not the original owner of your 911, chances are that there are quite a few things wrong with your car, and you wonder how they got broken. There probably isn't a place on the car with more gadgets and devices that break than on the door. Not only do you have window glass and seals that leak water, but you have door handles, mirror and window switches, window regulators, door stays, and door panels—all of which are very susceptible to damage and breakage. Even if you work on your car only moderately, there is a very high chance that you will need to dive into the door to fix something that has broken. This project specifically targets the replacement of the outer door handle, but because there are so many moving parts on the door, we'll discuss just about everything else as well.

The first step in fixing anything with the door is to disconnect the battery. There are live electrical connections in the door that can short out if you don't remove the negative ground from the battery. Next, you need to remove the door panel. There are quite a few fasteners and clips holding the panel onto the

door—many of them hidden out of view. Door panels changed over the years, and yours may vary slightly from those in the photographs, but if you work slowly and don't pull too hard on the panel, you should be able to figure out how to remove it. This project will concentrate primarily on the 911SC door panels, although the removal procedure for the other year door panels is similar in nature.

Start by removing the top interior trim piece that runs along the length of the door. This is held on by a few screws, and is also secured by the mirror switch plastic retainer. Remove the retainer and the screws, and the top trim piece should lift off. This would be a good time to replace the mirror switch, if you have been experiencing problems with it.

The bottom pocket that runs along the door also needs to be removed. This is held on with a few screws that go through the door panel. On some models, they can be slightly hidden, so you might have to hunt for them. Once you have the bottom pocket removed, gently pry off the speaker panel, if your 911 is equipped with door-mounted speakers.

Now, remove the large handle that is attached to the door. This is held on with two bolts on the top, and two on the bottom. The two on the top are clearly visible once you remove the top strip; however, the ones on the bottom are covered by the door handle on later-model cars. The door latch handle is attached to the door mechanism by a small rod. Release the door latch handle from the rod to gain access to the bolts that hold on the larger door handle. Once you remove these bolts, the large handle should pull off of the door.

This would be a good time to upgrade to the aftermarket inner door latch handles. The original Porsche ones are manufactured out of plastic, and they have a tendency to bend and break after many years of opening the door. The aftermarket door latch handles are manufactured out of anodized or black-painted aluminum, and are a lot tougher than the plastic ones. To replace the handles, simply remove the small pin that holds them to the large door handle. A small circlip keeps the pin in place, and should be removed with a pair of needle-nose pliers. You may also want to spread just a small bit of white lithium grease on the points where the pin makes contact with the door handle. Be careful not to smear it anywhere near where you might grab the handle with your fingers. I also recommend that you replace the small plastic clips on the door handle rod with new ones—they have a tendency to wear and break from use.

On later models, one overlooked fastener is the door lock knob. Behind a small cap lies a hidden screw that must be removed in order to remove the door panel. Remove this screw and pull off the knob and its corresponding plastic surround. On the early cars, the screw that attaches the window crank arm needs to be removed. Simply pry back the plastic covering and underneath you will find the screw.

The door panel itself is also held onto the door with plastic clips similar to those used to hold on the dash pad (Project 67). To remove the door panel, simply pry it out from the door. It's a smart idea to use a large screwdriver, and pry right near the spot where the plastic clips are attached to the door. This will minimize the chance that the plastic clips will accidentally pull out of the door panel. It's not a big deal if they do pull out of the door panel—you can always glue them back on later.

After you pull the panel off of the door, be aware that the window switches are still attached to the panel. They can be removed by bending back the small tabs that attach them to the door. Pull them out of the panel toward you, and then disconnect them from the wires. Make sure that you label the wires clearly before you remove them from the switches. This would be an excellent time to replace the window switches if they have been giving you trouble.

Once you have the door panel off, put it in a very safe place, where it won't accidentally get crushed. The inside of the door should now be easily accessible. There should also be a thin layer of plastic lightly glued in back of the door. Carefully remove this plastic and place it with the door panel.

Now, you should have full access to the door. If you are planning to replace just about anything inside the door (window motor, regulator, door stop) you will need to remove the door-mounted speaker. Lots of 911s have had aftermarket speakers added to them over the years, so the mounting configuration of the speakers is likely to vary from car to car. In most cases, though, it's easy to figure out the best method to remove the speaker simply by taking a close look at it.

If you are planning to replace your broken doorstop, make sure that you look at Project 74. If you are planning to replace your window regulator or window glass, Project 78 covers this in detail. For now, we'll assume that you're planning to replace or rekey your door handle.

Access to the door handle can be made through one of the large holes in the inside of the door. Make sure that you have the window rolled all the way up, or you won't be able to get at the nuts that secure the door handle to the door. Using a small socket, remove the two nuts that hold the door handle onto the out-

1 Removing the 911SC door panel requires removing lots of small little parts. In the upper left corner, you will see the mirror switch and a single mounting screw for the front of the door panel. The mirror switch can be removed by unscrewing the small plastic disc around the switch. Use a small screwdriver inserted into one of the holes for this task. In the upper right is the mount for the top of the handle. This is only visible after you remove the top inner trim piece on the inside of the door. The lower right photo shows a few bolts hidden by the door handle and the door latch. The latch is connected to a small rod that exits out of the door. The photo in the lower left shows the lock knob that hides another screw that holds the door panel on. Early-model doors are much simpler and require less effort to remove the door panel.

2 Once you have the door panel off, it's a good time to replace some electrical switches. The mirror switch and the window switches are both very prone to failure. It's a wise idea to replace them while you have the door apart.

side of the door. Be careful not to let the nuts fall into the recesses of the door, and also be careful not to let the door handle fall on the ground.

If you are replacing the door handle, installing the new one is straightforward. Simply install it onto the door and secure it with the two nuts on the inside of the door. I recommend replacing the two door handle seals with new ones when reinstalling the door handle. If you are replacing an old door handle, it might be possible to switch your old lock tumbler with the new one, and avoid adding a new key to your set for the car. If your old door handle didn't match the rest of your car, it is a good time to rekey the lock. See Project 76 for more details on the lock rekeying procedure.

Reassembling the door is basically the task of reattaching all the parts that you have previously removed. Make sure that you didn't drop anything in the door or leave any tools in there (you've heard of surgeons leaving tools in patients' bodies, right?) or the door will develop an annoying rattle. When reattaching the lower door pocket, make sure that the screws line up with the holes in the door. Make sure that you don't force anything, or you might rip and damage your door panel.

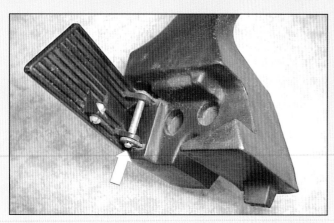

3 The inner door handle is held in with a small pin that is secured by a small circlip. Remove the circlip, and the pin should slide out. The aftermarket door handles, made out of aluminum, are a great improvement to the flimsy original plastic ones.

4 Inside the door, two nuts fasten the door handle to the door. When you remove these nuts, make sure that your door handle doesn't fall to the ground and become scratched. Access is tight, so a small socket wrench is your best bet here.

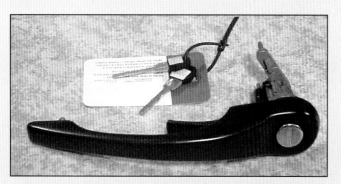

5 Brand-new door handles typically are supplied with a new tumbler and a new set of keys. Before you install the door handle, it's a wise idea to rekey it to the rest of your car (see Project 76). Even easier, you can switch the tumbler out of your old door handle and place it in the new one.

BODY

PROJECT 76 • REKEYING PORSCHE LOCKS

 Time: 3 hours

 Tools: Depends on the lock

 Talent:

Applicable Years: All

 Tab: $35

 Tinware: Lock rekeying kit

 Tip: File down the edges of the lock cylinder when you are finished for a smoother turning lock.

PERFORMANCE GAIN: Only one key on your keychain

COMPLEMENTARY MODIFICATION: Replace your door handles, or ignition locks

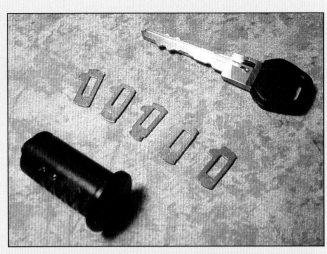

1 The lock cylinder basically consists of the tumbler, the tumbler pins, and the small springs that push out the tumbler pins. There are five different types of tumbler pins, labeled with a small stamp on each one. The lock rekeying kit contains an ample supply of these tumbler pins, so that you can find the configuration that is needed to rekey your particular lock.

One of the most common problems with older Porsches is that somewhere along the line, one or more of the door handles, glove box, ignition, or hood locks has broken. Broken locks are often replaced with a good used lock that has its own key, making the owner of a classic Porsche sometimes look like a high school janitor carrying a hunk of keys around. Most people don't know how to rekey their own locks, and are loathe to go to an expensive locksmith. It's really not that difficult—all you need is a little time and patience.

Another common scenario exists when you purchase a car, and the glove box or hood lock uses a particular key that has been lost a long time ago. It's possible to rekey any Porsche lock to fit just about any Porsche key—even if you don't have the original key for that lock. However, difficulty will arise if the lock is locked. The only practical method of getting the lock open would be to have a locksmith come out and pick the lock.

The first thing that you need to do is get the lock cylinder out of the car. That can be a project all by itself, and it varies greatly with different years and dif-

ferent types of locks. Most locks, however, can be removed by disassembling the parts around the lock. For more information on the door locks and the ignition locks, see Projects 75 and 91.

Once you have the lock cylinder out, you need to disassemble it. Most lock assemblies have a retaining screw that holds in the inner cylinder. Remove this screw, and you should be able to pull the cylinder out. Some other locks are not meant to be taken apart, and thus are very difficult to rekey. The 1974–1989 glove box lock is one example. These locks require you to drill out a tiny roll pin that holds the assembly together.

Before you disassemble and remove the lock cylinder, make sure that you insert a key—any Porsche key—into the lock. This will prevent the small tumbler pins from flying out when you pull the cylinder out. It is very important that you don't remove the key until you place the cylinder (sometimes called the lock tumbler) on a workbench, where you can catch the tumbler pins before they fly out of the lock.

When you pull the key out of the lock cylinder, make sure that you wrap your hand around the tiny brass tumbler pins. These are spring-loaded, and will fly out if you are not careful. Take the key and insert it back into the lock cylinder and get a feel for how the lock works. When the key is inserted, the tumbler pins are pulled down into the grooves of the key and become flush with the outer surface of the cylinder. This allows the lock to rotate within its housing, and

185

2 When the lock is properly configured for a particular key, the tumbler pins will line up perfectly with the housing edge. This allows the tumbler to rotate in the housing without getting caught in one of the grooves. When you remove the key, the tumbler pins are pushed out by small internal springs, and will not allow the cylinder to rotate.

A typical lock rekeying kit will contain 25 tumbler pins, or five of each type. With this kit, you can usually rekey three or four locks easily.

The procedure for rekeying the lock is very simple at this point. Simply remove a tumbler pin that does not meet flush with the cylinder when the key is inserted, and replace it with a different one. If you try all five pins, then one should definitely work and fit flush with the housing. Repeat the procedure, substituting the pins one by one until the all the tumbler pins are flush with the cylinder when the key is inserted.

If the lock cylinder or key is very worn or the key is wobbly in the housing, the tumbler pins might not easily become flush with the housing. At this point, you might need to perform a little trick to get them to fit better. With the key inserted into the cylinder, take a file or some sandpaper and file down the tips of the pins that are sticking out until they are flush with the housing. "Helping" the tumbler pins in this manner will make sure that your lock turns smoothly, and doesn't stick when the key is inserted. In general, it's a wise idea to file down the surfaces of the tumbler pins even if they appear to fit perfectly. This technique can also be used if you run out of the correct-sized tumbler pins. Simply file down the ones that you have until they are flush with the housing. One downside, though, is that this makes it slightly easier to pick the lock.

Once you have figured out the correct configuration for the lock, reassemble the cylinder. Make sure that you use a little bit of white lithium grease on all the joints and the tumbler pins. It's also a wise idea to record the number sequence of tumbler pins that you used, in case you need to rekey another lock.

the lock to be opened. If one or more of the tumbler pins don't match the pattern on the key, then the lock will not be able to rotate freely.

There are five different types of tumbler pins, all of them slightly different. In the typical glove-box lock, there are five tumbler slots. The number of different combinations for this lock is 625, or 5x5x5x5x5. In other words, the chances of two keys fitting the same lock would be one in 625. Each tumbler pin should have a number stamped on it, from 1 to 5. On some of the early cars, the tumbler pins don't have any numbers stamped on them, so the process of rekeying involves a bit more guesswork.

PROJECT 77 • REPLACING WEATHERSTRIPPING

Time: 3 hours

Tools: –

Talent:

Applicable Years: All

Tab: $40-$350

Tinware: New weather stripping seals, 3M Super Weatherstripping glue

Tip: Make sure that a seal needs to be replaced before purchasing a new one.

PERFORMANCE GAIN: Quieter, dryer car

COMPLEMENTARY MODIFICATION: Rebuild sunroof, replace windshield

1 Replacing the door seal is an easy job. Simply pull out the old one from the door frame. Then make sure that all the leftover glue and seal pieces have been removed from the channel. The new seal simply glues in place inside the channel. Shut the door and leave the windows open when you let the glue dry.

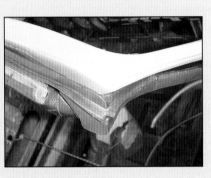

2 The front and rear targa seals are similar to the door seals, in that they fit inside a wide channel. Remove the old seal in a similar fashion— pull it out from the car. Then install the new seal using the 3M Super Weatherstrip. Make sure that you start on the side and glue the seal in the groove as it goes around the top. Test fit the seal first to ensure the fit before you start gluing.

As the 911s get older, one of the most irritating things that can happen is that they begin to leak water. Although most Porsche owners don't drive their car in the rain, the occasional unexpected downpour can considerably soak up one's interior carpet. The solution, of course, is to replace the seals that are leaking.

Two of the most common seals to leak water are the sunroof seal and the front windshield seal. The sunroof seal replacement is easiest when the sunroof has been removed. See Project 85 for more details. The front windshield seal that mates the glass to the car can only be replaced with the removal of the windshield. See Project 79 for more information on this removal process. The installation of new seals in the front, rear, and side windows is documented in Project 80. The door seals on the coupes have a tendency to leak after many years. On the targa and cabriolet cars, there are quite a few more seals that can leak, such as the windshield frame-to-roof seal, front targa bar seal, and the two side targa top seals.

The first step in solving water problems is to determine where they are coming from. Have an assistant sit inside the car as you spray water on it with a hose. Aim the water at specific areas of the car, starting with the lowest points first. Make sure that you wait a few minutes before moving to a new position. If you have patience, this method will pay off, and you will be able to figure out where the leak is coming from.

If the door seals appear to be leaking, this is an easy fix. New coupe door seals are relatively inexpensive, at about $40 each. To remove your old door seal, simply take the seal and pull on it. It should be lightly glued into the frame of the door, and should only require a moderate amount of force to remove it from the doorframe. Then test fit the new seal to the door, making sure that it fits well and is the proper one for your car. For installation, the new seal should have a very light coat of 3M Super Weatherstrip 80001 (see Project 65) applied to the edge that meets the doorframe. Insert the seal all the way and make sure that it makes appropriate contact with the metal inner groove. Close the door and let the glue dry as the door compresses against the seal. You probably want to keep all your windows open, as the smell from the glue can be pretty powerful.

Targa and cabriolet owners have a significant disadvantage when it comes to keeping water out of the

REPLACING WEATHERSTRIPPING

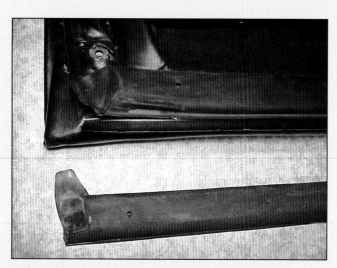

2 The targa side seals are also a common place for leaks to start. The seal itself is a complex part, consisting of both metal and rubber pieces. Sometimes water leaks into the older seals and can cause the embedded metal to rust. Replacement is quite easy as the old seal is simply unscrewed from the roof, and the new seal installed in its place.

Move to the top of the windshield and carefully place a bead of glue in the upper channel, as well as down the opposite side. Be careful that you don't spill any in your interior. The glue has a tendency to become stringy and can leave long strands that can drop down into your interior. Stretch the seal all the way across the windshield frame and make sure that it fits into the other side before you push it against the glue in the metal track on top. When you have finished gluing in the seal, place the top on the car, and also close all the doors so that the glue can dry while the seal is in its proper position.

The front targa bar seal at the rear of the roof is similar to the windshield frame-to-roof seal, with a few caveats. In addition to the glue, small plastic rivets hold the seal in place. These rivets contain small serrations that lock the rivet in and keep it from popping out. Four plastic rivets help to keep the seal firmly mounted to the targa bar. In addition, you must make sure that the two large holes that locate and accept the pins on the targa roof are lined up with the receptors in the targa bar. Glue the front targa bar seal in a similar manner to the windshield frame-to-roof seal, working from one side to the other.

An additional problem for Targa owners is that Porsche has recently superceded the Targa roof seal to one used on later cars. The problem is that these seals do not fit properly on the early cars, and need to be trimmed to fit. The trimming process is somewhat difficult, so I recommend that you keep your old seal for as long as possible before you decide to replace it. One tip: the later style Targa side seals work better with the new seal. I recommend replacing all three seals at the same time so that you can cut and trim them to fit together.

The side seals on the targa-top roof are also another source of major leaks. The good news is that these are very easy to replace. They are simply attached with four small screws to the sides of the roof. Remove the screws from the old seal, and attach the new one. You shouldn't have to use any glue or sealing compound on the new seals.

Well, these are the major problems with water leakage in the 911. There are other seals that might also leak after many years, but if you replace the ones shown here, you will probably have a 95 percent chance of staying dry.

car. Because of the design of the roof, several more places need to mate properly to keep water out. First and foremost are the windshield frame-to-roof seal, and the front targa bar seal. These seals have a tendency to become dried out, brittle, and cracked over many years of exposure to the sun.

Replacing the windshield frame-to-roof seal is an easy task. Simply remove the old seal from the metal channel in the car by pulling on it. You may have to cut and slice a few pieces out of the channel, but if the seal is old, it should come right out. Make sure that the channel is free of any remaining rubber pieces and glue before you start installing the new seal.

Test fit the new seal in the channel to make sure that it will fit properly. You may have to stretch the seal a bit to make it fit entirely across the car. This is normal, as there shouldn't be any slack in the seal. Start with one side of the car and prepare to glue the seal by placing a bead of 3M Super Weatherstrip along the side channel. Slide the seal into the channel and make sure that it is fully seated against the metal and the glue. Press the seal into the channel, and close the door to let it seal. Wait about 5 to 10 minutes for the glue to dry before you start on the top.

PROJECT 78 • REPLACING YOUR WINDOW REGULATOR AND MOTOR

 Time: 3 hours

 Tools: Hex key set

 Talent:

 Applicable Years: All

 Tab: $75-$200

 Tinware: New regulator, new window motor, white lithium grease

 Tip: Be careful not to scratch the window or the paint on your door.

PERFORMANCE GAIN: A window that works

COMPLEMENTARY MODIFICATION: Door handle replacement, door stop replacement, window switch replacement, speaker upgrades, door panel replacement, channel seats, window slot seals.

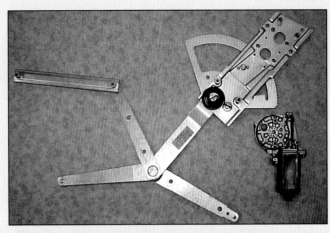

The window regulator is one of the more common items to break on the 911. Plastic wheels on the regulator combined with regular wear causes them to break and the window to stop working. The motors seldom fail, but when they do, they can be expensive to replace.

Are you tired of having to open your door and get out to retrieve your burger at the drive-through? Perhaps it's time to replace your window regulator, or power window motor. The difficulty of this project varies with the year of your car, but the results are immediate and quite rewarding. Not much is better than driving in your 911 with the sunroof open and the windows down on a nice sunny day. Having a broken window regulator can surely put a damper on that.

The first step in replacing either the regulator or the power window motor is to remove the door panel. For cars equipped with power windows, disconnect the battery as well before you start. Make sure that you eliminate the power window motor as a potential problem before you start tearing into your door. Double-check all the fuses that control the power windows, and swap out the relays to make sure that there isn't a problem with them. If one of the windows works and the other doesn't, then chances are that it's the window motor or the window switch.

For details on removing the door panel, see Project 75. When you have the door panel removed, check the window switch to make sure that it's working properly. Try swapping the two switches, or plug in a new one. If there still is no response from the window, then the motor probably needs replacing. Check to see if power is getting to the motor when you press the switch. Of course, if there is plenty of noise coming from the door and the window isn't moving, then it's quite obvious that the motor is fine, but the regulator needs to be replaced.

Make sure that you remove the door's speakers as well, if your 911 is so equipped, and that the window is rolled down (if possible). Reach down into the door through one of the access holes and remove the power connections from the motor. Make a note of which connection goes where.

Now remove the bolts that hold the window regulator inside of the door. These will require a hex key set. Although the entire process can be done with the door attached to the car, gravity has a tendency to make the job a bit more difficult. While removing the door is not an easy job, if for some reason you plan to remove the door at a later date, this would be a good time.

After you remove the bolts that hold the regulator and motor assembly to the door, you should be able to move the regulator around inside the door. Be careful not to scratch the glass when you are moving items inside the door. Maneuver the regulator so that

2 This photo distinguishes the six bolts that fasten the regulator to the door from the other bolts that hold on the window channel and the door lock mechanism on a 911SC. After you remove these bolts, you should be able to rotate the regulator so that you can access and remove the window motor. Changes in regulators over the years result in different mounting and adjustment methods. The general procedure is the same for late-model cars.

3 These three bolts fasten the window motor to the regulator. Be careful when you remove the motor, as the spring on the regulator will snap back, and the resulting movement can damage either the window glass or the door lock mechanism.

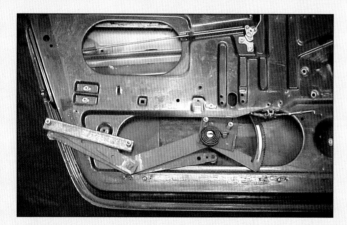

4 With much negotiation, the window regulator can be removed from the lower part of the door. Rotate some of the arms into the correct position in order to pull the regulator out of the door. Make sure that you have the window pushed up all the way before you try to remove the regulator.

you can see the three bolts that attach the motor to the regulator. Unbolt these three, and remove the motor from the regulator. Be careful when you remove the motor, as the window spring may make the regulator spring around a bit inside the door, and you want to make sure that it doesn't scratch any of the window glass. The motor can be tested on a

bench by applying 12 volts DC to the two terminals. If it doesn't turn, then chances are that you have a broken window motor.

After the motor is removed, you should be able to slide the bottom part of the regulator off the track that is attached to the window glass. Push the glass up to the top, and tape it to the top channel of the door. After the regulator is free, it should be relatively easy to pull it out of the door.

Inspect the regulator for wear. It should be relatively easy to figure out if the regulator is broken. The usual points of failure are the plastic rollers, and also the points where the regulator pivots and is riveted to itself. If you have a new regulator on hand, compare it to the damaged one, and you should be able to see the problem.

Installation of the new regulator is straightforward. You might have to negotiate the alignment of the window and the attachment of the motor inside the door. It make take one or more tries to get it right. The regulator spring is designed to be compressed when the window is lowered, so it might be easier to reinstall if the window is raised about halfway up the channel. Lubricate all moving parts of the regulator with white lithium grease prior to the installation. Make sure that you also spread plenty of grease on the plastic wheels and inside the track at the bottom of the glass.

Before you reinstall the regulator, it's probably a wise idea to inspect and replace the window channel guides if they are worn. These are the two channels that guide the window as it is raised and lowered by the regulator. They can be removed from inside of the door. Also worth replacing are the window slot seals. These inner and outer "window scrapers" keep water from dripping down into the recesses of the door.

Before you close everything up inside your door, it's probably a wise idea to test the proper operation of the window. Hook up the power connections to the window motor, and try to raise and lower the window. Or, if you have manual windows, install the crank and see if the motion is smooth and uniform. Also make sure that you adjust the stop positions of the window once you have reinstalled the regulator. There are screws located on the regulator that control these stop positions.

Unfortunately, this procedure works best for the 1974–1989 911s. On the earlier cars, the opening in the door is not large enough to remove the regulator. Instead, the entire window frame and glass must be removed as well, and the regulator must be pulled out through the top of the door.

BODY
PROJECT 79 • GLASS REMOVAL

 Time: 30 minutes to 1 hour per pane

 Tools: Sharp X-acto knife

 Talent:

 Applicable Years: All

 Tab: $0, unless you are careless

 Tinware: –

 Tip: Cut all seals all the way around several times, and don't rush this job.

PERFORMANCE GAIN: Allows you to perform other projects

COMPLEMENTARY MODIFICATION: Replace seals, replace glass, install new dash pad, install new headliner

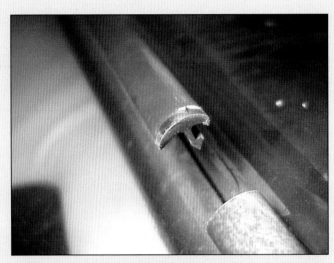

1 The window trim has a small hook that fits nicely into the seal. When you are prying the window trim off, make sure that you don't bend the aluminum too much, or it may be unusable when you try to reinstall the windshield. To get started, slide back the middle joining piece and start prying back the aluminum trim.

One of the most perplexing tasks to perform on the 911 is the removal of the window glass, whether it's the front or rear window, or either of the side quarter windows. The process is not easy if you don't know what you are doing. However, with a few tips and step-by-step instructions, the process is made much easier.

A few of the projects in this book require removing and replacing the window glass—replacing the windshield seal (Project 80), installing a new dash pad (Project 67), and replacing the interior headliner (Project 68). The process of removal can be quite tricky, so I've dedicated an entire project to it.

All four major pieces of glass on the 911 coupe are attached in a similar manner. The front windshield as well as the rear and two side quarter windows are held in primarily by a rubber seal that grabs both the glass and the chassis of the car. It's a very similar system to the one used on the 356. The 911 cabriolet and targa have the same system for mounting the windshield, and the targa uses the same method for mounting and securing the rear window. The rear targa window installation is very difficult, and you

should probably enlist the help of someone who has done it previously. On earlier 911s with rear pop-out windows, the process becomes even easier, as the glass and frame are simply unscrewed from the car.

The first step in removing the glass is to carefully remove the window molding from the car. The early cars were equipped with chrome window molding that actually inserts into the glass seals. On the later cars, this trim was anodized aluminum. In either case, it is very easy to damage and destroy the molding when you are removing it.

For the windshield, start by taking a medium-sized screwdriver and sliding the little molding joining clips that are located on the top and bottom to the side. Don't scratch the molding with the screwdriver. Now, carefully gently pry up one part of the molding with the screwdriver. Work carefully, and make sure not to bend the metal trim as you are removing it. If the trim is bent significantly, then it will be nearly impossible to reinstall when you try to replace the windshield.

Gently move around the perimeter of the molding using the screwdriver to pry it up. Never take one end of the molding and pull on it, as this can bend it beyond recovery. Just carefully inch the screwdriver around the molding, being very careful not to bend it significantly. If you need any encouragement on having patience, just keep in mind that if you damage them, these two pieces are about $75 each to replace. The rear window and side window pieces are even more expensive to replace, so the key word here

191

2 After the seal is cut or scored, the part that attaches the windshield to the chassis can be torn away. Pulling on the end of the seal should make it separate from the rest of the seal. After this section of the seal has been removed, the entire piece of glass should be loose and ready for removal.

is patience. If your trim is fading or damaged already, then this would be an opportune time to replace it.

After you have removed all of the molding from your car, I recommend hanging it from the ceiling. Replacing the windshield or glass is not a one-day task, and you don't want this very fragile molding just sitting around where things will pile on it. Make sure that it is tucked away in a very safe spot.

Now, the process of removing the glass can begin. Take a razor blade or an X-acto knife, and begin cutting through the seal where it mounts to the car. The point is to cut away the part of the seal that is holding the glass onto the frame of the car. You want to cut down the distinct groove in the middle of the seal that normally holds on the window trim. Don't worry about hitting anything underneath, as there isn't anything under the seal to worry about, with the exception of the rear window. Make sure that you cut deeply through the seal, as it won't separate from the car if it's not completely separated.

The process of cutting the seal takes a bit of patience, and there is a tendency to want to rush the job. However, you should make sure that you proceed carefully, as the old windshields are often very brittle and break much more easily than new ones. When you get to a point where the seal starts to separate completely and you can grab it with your hands, you can usually tear the seal out of the groove after scoring it with the knife. Gently pull on the seal, and it should rip itself and tear away from the car. Refer to the second photo in this project for more details.

The rear window may contain the defroster mechanism embedded into the glass. It's a wise idea to be more careful about cutting into the seal, because there are wires actually running through the seal. However, these wires in most cases don't run though the area that you are cutting. To be on the safe side, try to score the seal without cutting all the way through, and then tear it by pulling on an end that is loose (similar to the second photo in this project). This should help you remove the glass without damaging the wires.

After the seal has been cut in half, there should be nothing really holding in the windshield. Try wiggling it to see if it's loose. There is a chance that the rubber on the seal may be sticking to the windshield, in which case you may have to apply slight pressure using your hands (no tools!) on the inside of the windshield. If the seal is significantly stuck on the inside, use a plastic putty scraper to separate the seal from the glass on the inside. Don't worry about the glass falling out or sliding—gravity will keep it in its original spot.

When the windshield is finally loose, you can rock it up on its bottom and remove it from the car. Depending upon how long your arms are, you might want to have an assistant help you. It's not heavy, but it's not too light either. Make sure that you store your windshield in a very safe spot where it won't get damaged or stepped on.

The removal process for the side glass is very similar. On 911s with the pop-out rear side windows, you can simply unbolt the entire glass, and then worry about the seal without the concern of breaking the glass. On 911s without the pop-out rear side windows, the removal process is almost exactly the same as the windshield. Be very careful not to use any tools to pry the window out.

For the rear, the process is a made a bit trickier by the addition of the defroster. After you cut and remove the inside part of the seal, you should be able to see the electrical connections that are attached to the glass. It's very important to remove these connections before you remove the glass, as they can bend and break if you don't. Simply unplug the wires from the glass. There should be four in total. With the plugs disconnected, you should be able to remove the rear glass just like the front windshield.

If by some chance you do break your windshield, replacements are somewhat common, and easy to find. Most windshield shops will come and install a new windshield in your car for about $150 (here in Southern California). Other locations may charge a bit more, but the general price range shouldn't vary too much from this figure.

PROJECT 80 • INSTALLING WINDOW GLASS

Time: 1 hour per pane

Tools: Thick sturdy cord

Talent: 4

Applicable Years: All

Tab: Depends on which window you are installing

Tinware: New rubber for the window

Tip: Proceed very, very carefully, and don't rush this important job.

PERFORMANCE GAIN: No more wind in your face

COMPLEMENTARY MODIFICATION: Replace window seal, replace front dash pad

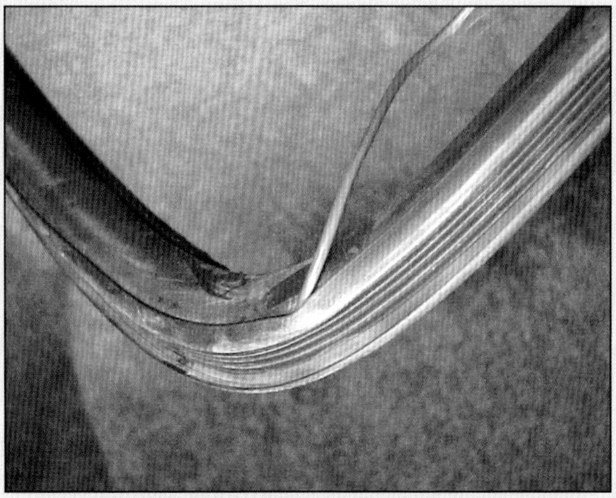

1 Prepare the window glass by placing it on a tire or soft, flat surface. Attach the seal all the way around the outside of the glass. You may have to stretch and pull the seal to get it to fit. Once the seal is in place and the bezel installed, insert the cord into the groove that mates with the edge on the body. Make sure that you have about 6 to 8 inches of overlap when the cord is inserted completely around the entire window.

Make no mistake about it, reinstalling glass into your car is not an easy task. There probably isn't a Porsche shop out there that won't admit to breaking at least one windshield trying to install it. The trick is to have plenty of patience, and to make sure that you don't put any excess pressure or loads on the glass. However, the process of installation requires that you push slightly on at least part of the glass. As the glass ages, it can become very brittle, and may crack a lot easier than a new windshield. Unfortunately, you may end up doing everything right and still break your windshield.

The procedure for the installation of the front windshield is similar for the other panes of glass in the car. The main difference is that the front windshield is very large, and has an increased tendency to crack because it's much longer. The length of the glass may actually magnify stresses and forces placed on the windshield. The side windows and rear glass are less susceptible to cracking. However, the rear window needs special consideration because of the defroster wire that is running through the seal. For the remainder of this project, we'll concentrate mostly on the front windshield, and then give hints and tips on how the other panes are different.

The first step in installation is to attach your rubber seal to the edges of the glass. It's really not a wise idea to recycle an old seal, as these were probably damaged in the glass removal process, and will not seat properly. Always use a new seal. I also recommend that you only use OEM German rubber when replacing your seals. I've found that most of the cheaper reproduction seals are of an inferior quality. It's not worth it to save a couple of bucks, only to have the seal leak on you at a later date.

Before you install the seal on the glass, make sure that you place the windshield on a scratch-free surface. An old rubber tire with a blanket tossed over it makes an ideal candidate. When you fit the seal to the glass, make sure that the orientation of the seal is correct. The groove for the aluminum bezel always faces toward the outside of the windshield. Using a bit of soapy water on the edges of the windshield may help with the installation of the seal.

When the windshield is to be installed into the car, a strong cord is used to properly pull the edges of the seal inward. The cord must be inserted into the inner ridge of the seal prior to placing the window on the car. After the seal is properly mounted on the windshield, thread the cord into the channel groove of the seal. Refer to the diagram that accompanies

2 This diagram shows how the seal holds the glass to the edge of the window frame. The installation cord is inserted into the seal where the lip of the chassis is located, as indicated by circle number four on the diagram. As the seal and glass are pushed against the lip on the body and the cord is pulled out, the edge of the seal (indicated by the dotted lines) is pulled over the lip into its final position. Make sure that the seal is firmly in place all the way around the edge of the window after the cord has been completely pulled out.

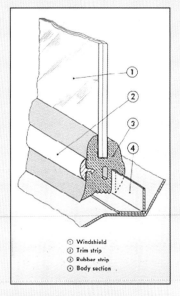

① Windshield
② Trim strip
③ Rubber strip
④ Body section

3 Installation of the glass can be a tricky process, especially with older glass. While an assistant applies pressure from the outside, pull the cord out on the inside, forcing the seal to the inside of the pinch weld lip on the body. If the seal doesn't properly seat against the body, carefully try to refit the seal using a small screwdriver or appropriate plastic tool. If you can't pull the seal over the lip, remove the window and try again.

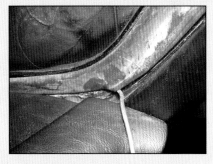

this project for a better indication of where it's supposed to go. When the cord is completely wrapped around the outside perimeter, make sure that it overlaps itself by about 8 inches.

Now, attach the aluminum trim bezel to the seal. This is not an easy task. The trim actually helps hold the seal to the glass. If the aluminum trim becomes bent or dented, straighten it as you install it. It will be much easier to fix any dents or waves in the aluminum trim now than when it is installed. If the trim is damaged, or bent too far out of proportion, it will be nearly impossible to reinstall it, and you will probably have to purchase a new one. Install the upper and lower clips that cover the gap between the two trim pieces.

Once you have the trim and the two clips installed, it's time to place the windshield onto the car. Before doing this, make sure that all remains of the previous rubber seal have been removed from the lip of the mounting surface. Sand and paint any rusted areas that you find. Water has a tendency to seep into the windshield area, and once in there the water may become trapped and corrode the metal.

Before placing the windshield, coat the seam/recess where the seal is about to mount with some dishwashing soap to ease the installation seal's installation. You can wash the soap off later with water. Place the glass into the car, with the lower edge going in first. Center it in its recess, then push the top of the windshield into place. Remember not to use too much force, lest you crack and break the glass. Patience is a required virtue here.

Move the glass around and check the gaps on all sides to ensure that it is properly positioned. Now, from inside the car, start to pull the cord out, while an assistant applies pressure on the outside of the glass. The trick is to make sure the seal is pulled over the lip by the cord that you are pulling from the inside. If the cord doesn't pull the seal over the lip, then the windshield won't seat, and you'll have to start over and rethread the cord. Make sure not to damage the headliner when you pull the cord out. (It's easy to do.)

The pressure your assistant applies on the windshield is most important for the bottom edge of the glass; the weight of the glass makes pulling the cord out just a little bit more difficult. It should be apparent that a weak cord for pulling would not suffice in this situation. Nylon cords like the ones used for starting lawnmowers are excellent for this task, or even thin electrical wire. Once the cord is completely pulled out, the windshield should be completely seated.

Once the glass is in place, make sure that the aluminum trim is properly seated. Press it in or tap it lightly with a plastic hammer if it is not. Double check that the seal is properly seated all the way around the windshield. If it isn't, you might be able to use a small screwdriver to pry the seal into its correct orientation. This could damage the seal and glass, so exercise extreme caution. Check the headliner inside the car, and tuck any excess back under the seal.

The installation of the rear window is a little different from the front. The rear defogger wires should be threaded into the seal prior to attaching it to the car. Be careful not to damage the fragile contacts on the rear defogger window. Make sure that you place the glass into the car with the top lip first, and then the bottom lip. With the installation of the rear window, there are more sections of headliner to potentially damage. The side windows are installed in a similar manner to the front and rear glass.

Proceed with caution at every step, and make sure that you have a patient assistant. If you do break any glass, vacuum it out of your vents before you turn them on. Use appropriate gloves when handling the glass. Even thick-edged glass like the windshield can cut you if there is a small chip on it.

BODY
PROJECT 81 • REPLACING HOOD SHOCKS

 Time: 1 hour

 Tools: Needle nose pliers

 Talent:

 Applicable Years: All

 Tab: $45

 Tinware: Pair of front hood shocks, single for the rear

 Tip: It may be easier to use bolts and lock washers instead of the little clips that hold the shocks in.

 PERFORMANCE GAIN: No more lids falling on your head

COMPLEMENTARY MODIFICATION: Upgrade to rear dual shock kit

1 Each shock is held in place by a small pin and clip. Make sure that you are careful not to lose the clip or the pin in the recesses of your engine compartment or front trunk. The new shocks should last you several years.

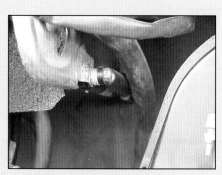

2 The dual shock kit for the rear deck lids is shown here. A spacer separates the outer shock from the inner one, while allowing them both to use the same mounting points. A long bolt with a nylon-insert washer keeps the entire assembly together. Install the dual shock kit if you are installing a rear spoiler on your 911.

Are you getting tired of having your deck lids fall on your head? It's probably time to replace your hood shocks. These are among the most disposable parts on the 911. They will fail—it's just a matter of when. Replacing them is an easy task, made even easier with small hands that can reach into tight places. With a little bit of patience, this task can be completed in about an hour.

The front hood uses two gas-pressurized shocks that hold up its weight. Start by lifting up the front hood, and securing it using a long stick or a baseball bat. Make sure that this support is securely affixed, as the hood will hurt if it falls on your head. Starting with the right side, remove the small clip on the pin that connects the hood shock to the hood itself. Remove the same pin from the mount that connects the shock to the floor of the front trunk.

Position the new shock in the same place and orientation that the old was in. Refasten the clips to the pins, and make sure that they are securely fastened. Repeat the procedure for the left side. This is a bit trickier, since the bottom of the shock is surrounded

with hoses, brake lines, and electrical cables. It is very easy to drop both the pin and the clip down into the recesses of the front trunk. In this case, it may be easier to replace the pin with a bolt and a nylon lock nut to prevent it from coming loose. If you do decide to use the bolt and washer approach, make sure that you don't clamp down too tightly on the bolt, as it will compress the shock against the mount, and may damage the mount.

The rear shocks are very similar in their replacement process. If your car has a factory-installed tail on the rear deck lid you probably have a shock on either side of the car. Replace these in a similar fashion to the ones in the front, being careful again not to drop the clip or the pin into the engine compartment.

If you recently installed a Carrera or Turbo tail onto the rear of your car, you will probably need an extra hood shock to support the extra weight. There is a special kit for dealing with this problem. The kit contains a couple of spacers and an extra hood shock that is placed directly alongside the other shock, on the same side of the car. This extra shock is more than enough to hold up the extra weight of the deck lid. The kit is installed pretty easily and takes about 10 minutes to complete. Simply take the clips and pins out and install the new pins, the spacers, and the extra hood shock alongside the original one.

PROJECT 82 • UPDATING TO THE TURBO LOOK

Time: 40 hours

Tools: Expert body shop

Talent: 🔧🔧🔧🔧

Applicable Years: All

Tab: $4,000

Tinware: Turbo Look update kit and accessories

Tip: If you are having your car painted, this is the time to do the update!

PERFORMANCE GAIN: An awesome looking 911

COMPLEMENTARY MODIFICATION: Paint your car.

With the introduction of the 911 Turbo (internally called the 930), Porsche refined the looks and beauty of the 911 silhouette even further than it had done before. The original 911 Turbos had front and rear flared fenders, a large "whale-tail" spoiler mounted to the rear deck lid, and a front spoiler that was mounted below the front bumper. This advanced, 911-on-steroids look is highly desired by many owners of normally aspirated 911s. As a result, the 911 Turbo Look conversion is very popular.

It is important to note that in the late 1980s, Porsche introduced an option on the normally aspirated 911 Carrera called the "Factory Turbo Look." While containing all of the visual enhancements that accented the lines of the regular 930, the Factory Turbo Look cars also contained all of the advanced suspension components that were originally installed on the 930s. In other words, the Factory Turbo Look Carreras were essentially 911 Turbo cars without the Turbo engine. Everything else was basically the same, including the suspension and brakes.

It is important to note this distinction, because many people selling their cars advertise them as Factory Turbo Look cars even though they are not. All

of these cars should have the 911 Turbo brake calipers and full suspension on them. If they don't, then that is a clear indication that the car is a conversion and not the genuine article. That's not to say that these conversions should be avoided—they are just worth less than the original Factory Turbo Looks because they are missing the highly sought-after 930 brakes and suspension.

Another popular option for racers was to start with the 911 Carrera Factory Turbo Look cars, and turbocharge the 3.2-liter engine with an aftermarket turbo kit. This afforded the cars the benefits of all the turbo brakes and suspension with the addition of a five-speed transmission (until 1989, the 930s were shipped with a four-speed transmission) and the extra Turbo power. Needless to say, there are plenty of cars out there whose lineage has been significantly altered from the original. This is not necessarily a bad thing—as long as the changes have been well documented and the work performed professionally.

Ironically, the Factory Turbo Look cars do not fetch prices that are significantly more than the standard 911 Carreras. In most cases, the cost of performing a Turbo Look conversion on a normal 911 will not increase the value of the car by a corresponding amount. However, this is mostly true of any upgrade or conversion that you might do to your car.

For those of us not lucky enough to own a 930 or even a 911 Carrera Factory Turbo Look, there is the option of performing the Turbo Look conversion. It is probably best to consider this conversion when you are painting your car, since a large amount of bodywork will be involved. It's also a wise idea to find someone who has performed this conversion before, because bodywork of this nature is more of an art than a science. Practice and patience are important here. Someone being the cheapest doesn't mean that he or she will perform a good job.

OK, so you're interested in upgrading your car to the Turbo Look. There certainly isn't enough room here to go into details about how to do it yourself, so we'll just discuss what you need to have done and the costs involved. The following list summarizes what you need to perform the Turbo Look upgrade:

• **Front Fender Flares.** Sometimes you can find original Turbo or Turbo Look fenders with the flares already installed. If you can, then the process becomes a lot easier, as the front fenders can simply be bolted on in place of the older fenders.
• **Rear Fender Flares.** Unlike the front fenders, the rear ones are welded on, and they are a pretty significant part of the rear body. There's not much you

can do to get out of welding on the flares to the rear of your car.

• Rear Bumper Extensions. In order to meet up with the rear fender flares, the rear bumper must have these flared extensions attached.

• Rocker Arm Extensions (front and rear). The rocker panels underneath the doors need to meet the front and rear flares. Extensions that curve outward to meet the flares are welded to the rocker panels. There are aftermarket kits containing all the flares and extensions that you need to perform the upgrade. The typical cost of this kit is about $850.

• Turbo Tail. You will also need the distinctive 930 Turbo tail. There were two different types produced. The early one, used only on the 1976–1977 Turbos, and the later-style "Tea Tray" Turbo tail. Good used factory Turbo tails can be hard to find, but good aftermarket ones exist. The used factory tails usually go for around $500 each, and the aftermarket ones can be found in good condition for about $350. You will also need to make sure you have good outer rubber on the tail, and a new seal for the seam where the tail meets the deck lid. See Project 83 for more information.

• Front Chin Spoiler. If you already have a chin spoiler on your car, you will need to replace it with the Turbo front spoiler. The spoiler extends farther up the car than the regular one, and actually meets the flared fenders.

• Wider Wheels. At least 7 inches in the front, and either 8 or 9 inches in the rear. Don't forget new tires if the wheels that you find are bare. The 7-inch wheels are quite common, running about $300 for the pair. However, the 8- and 9-inch wheels are very difficult to find, and can sometimes run about $1,000 for the pair in good used condition.

• Wheel Spacers. Since the suspensions between the 930 and the 911 are different, you will need wheel spacers in both the front and the rear. Usually the front wheels require about 1-inch spacers, and the rear wheels require anywhere from 1- to 2-inch spacers, depending on how the flares were attached. The wheel spacers can cost up to $500 if purchased brand new.

As you can see, the costs for the parts alone can add up. The bodywork costs from the body shop will also cost several hundreds of dollars too. Not to mention that you will have to paint the car as well. For some owners, it's a bit too much to swallow. However, if you want to upgrade the looks of your car to the awesome silhouette of the Porsche 930, there really isn't any other way to go.

1 The rear fenders of the Turbo are really monstrous! Here you can see the rear extensions attached to the bumper. The 9-inch wheels fit quite nicely under the extra-wide fenders, and give that "I mean business" look.

2 As shown in this photo, the front bumper doesn't need any extensions attached to it. The rubber chin spoiler accounts for the extra flare in the fender. The 7-inch wheels fill out the fenders nicely, when combined with the 1-inch spacers. On the opposite side of the wheel from the spoiler is the rocker panel, which needs to have the rocker extensions welded on in order to line up with the new profile from the larger fenders. It's important to install the chin spoiler, as this will help to aerodynamically balance the large rear spoiler.

3 The 1974–1989 911 is in its best form with the addition of the Turbo Look. Many people feel that the tea-tray tail is obnoxiously large, except when accompanied by the fatter tires and flared look of the Turbo. There is definitely something to be said about the beauty of the entire package. The 911 owner who wants the look of the Turbo without the expense of the 930 should seriously consider either a Factory Turbo Look or a conversion.

BODY
PROJECT 83 • REAR SPOILER/TAIL INSTALL

Time: 6 hours

Tools: hand drill

Talent: ♟♟♟

Applicable Years: All

Tab: $500-$1,000 including painting

Tinware: Tail, tail seal, rear deck lid, dual shock kit, tail rubber

Tip: Find a used rear deck lid to mount the tail to so that you can always remove it at a later date.

PERFORMANCE GAIN: Better downforce on the rear wheels

COMPLEMENTARY MODIFICATION: Install the chin spoiler to balance the car aerodynamically.

The installation of a rear spoiler, or tail, is one of the more popular additions to the 911. Not counting the fiberglass aftermarket spoilers or tails, there are four different factory tails that were installed on the production 911. The first spoiler was called the "duck tail," because of its relatively short upward stroke on the rear of the car. This tail was originally fitted to the 1973 911RS Carrera and was later adapted for production cars.

In 1976, Porsche introduced the 911 Turbo, with a wider body supported by flares and a large spoiler that was immediately dubbed the "whale tail." This spoiler kept the style and flair of the original engine grille, while incorporating a large flowing wing on the rear. These tails are not very common, and were only installed for two years, 1976 and 1977. This tail has a smaller square grille section.

In addition to the Turbo tail, there is an uncommon early Carrera tail. This tail is very similar to the first Turbo tails, but doesn't have the additional square engine grille of the Turbo.

In 1978, Porsche introduced another version of the Turbo whale tail. This later-style whale tail is by far

the most popular of all the tails. The tail consists of a large fiberglass enclosure that bolts onto the rear deck lid. The engine grille is parallel to the ground, and the rubber of the tail surrounds the outside with an upper lip that resembles a tea tray.

In 1984, Porsche introduced the 911 Carrera, and with it another version of the tail. This Carrera tail is similar to the late-model Turbo tail, except that it's a bit smaller and more subtle. The fiberglass enclosure is less expansive than the Turbo tail, and the rubber is contoured more toward the horizontal. To the unsuspecting eye, the late-model Turbo tail and Carrera tails look very similar. It is important to note, however, that because of the different sizes of the enclosures, the mounting holes for these two tails are different.

So which one should you put on your car? It all depends upon your individual taste. For the early cars, it's most common to fit a duck tail or an early whale tail. For the later cars, either the late-model Carrera or Turbo tail will be an appropriate match. You may even opt for an aftermarket tail that was never originally installed on a factory car. The choice is yours.

The first step in installing the tail is to find the parts. New aftermarket fiberglass late-model Turbo tails can run about $400 for just the fiberglass enclosure. The rubber lip can sometimes cost just as much, bringing the total to about $700. A good reproduction duck tail can run about $300, and usually replaces the entire rear deck lid. Carrera tails are the most expensive, running about $700 for a good aftermarket package, or around $900 for a Porsche original tail.

With the high price of tails, buying a used one at a swap meet is a good idea. The factory original tails can be determined by the word "PORSCHE" cast into the center outer rear of the fiberglass, just under the rubber lip. The rubber lips can also be OEM or aftermarket, with the former having a Porsche crest molded into the rear of the rubber. Either way, inspect both the tail and the rubber for damage. Most of the damage that occurs to the tails happens on the way to the swap meets, and not when they are installed on the back of the car. Make sure that there are no scratches in the rubber, and that it's not torn or pitted in any manner. Check the fiberglass enclosure for cracks and breaks—these will have to be repaired at a later date. Good used aftermarket tea tray tails with OEM rubber can be found for about $400. Used OEM tails sell for around $550.

In addition to obtaining your tail and rubber, I recommend that you purchase a used rear deck lid to mount the tail on. This will increase the value of your car, because not everyone who might purchase your car will want the rear tail installed. Having the original deck lid is a huge bonus, because it can easily be removed and reinstalled at any time. You will need to have the tail painted to match your car anyway— painting the new deck lid will not increase the cost too much. Sometimes you can find a deck lid that previously had a tail attached. Since these are already drilled, their value is usually less than a normal deck lid. You can sometimes find one of these less expensive lids, and save yourself some drilling time.

Once you have your tail and rubber, you need to line it up with the deck lid and drill the mounting holes. The late-model Turbo tail and the Carrera tails did not have the same mounting holes. Therefore, if you do purchase a predrilled deck lid, make sure that it is drilled properly for the tail that you would like to install. Note that a deck lid drilled for the late-model Turbo tail will not work for a late-model Carrera tail.

To drill the holes for the tail, take the grille off the engine lid (it's simply bolted on), and line up the fiberglass enclosure with the tail. Depending upon the tail, there might be at least one hole on the tail that will correspond with a hole on the deck lid. Slip a bolt through this hole, and then make sure that the tail is aligned properly with the sides of the deck lid. Reaching through the fiberglass enclosure, carefully mark the hole on the surface of the deck lid with a permanent marker. Remove the enclosure, and drill the holes in the deck lid.

Drill the holes in the deck lid to be the same size as the ones in the fiberglass enclosure. Make sure that you use a very sharp drill bit, and don't press down on the deck lid too much, or you might dent it.

Now, take the fiberglass enclosure, the deck lid, and your gas flap cover to your local body shop. The gas flap cover is for matching the color of the paint used on the tail to the color of your car. The flap is easily removed using an Allen key wrench. Have the shop repaint the entire tail, including the top black grille. Sometimes if you bring a six-pack of beer with you to the shop, your stuff will get done surprisingly quickly.

When you get the tail back from the shop, it's time to bolt the whole assembly together. Take the fiberglass enclosure, and bolt it to the deck lid with the rubber lip attached. The Turbo tail base seal should be appropriately placed in between the tail and the deck lid. Make sure that you use new mounting hardware and nuts with nylon inserts. When you are bolting the tail and the deck lid together, don't use too much force, or you might break the fiberglass on the tail, or dent the deck lid.

1 Here are some examples of tails that have been installed on 911s over the years. In the upper left is the duck tail, first seen in 1973 on the Carrera RS, and then later adapted to street models. The upper right shows the tea tray Turbo tail, probably the most common tail for owners to add to their car. The lower left shows the late-model Carrera tail, which is basically a modified version of the Turbo tail with a sleeker rubber trim. The Carrera tail also doesn't extend as far back on the engine grille as the traditional tea tray Turbo tail. In the lower right is a very early Carrera tail, similar to the early 911 Turbo tail. This tail was used on some of the early Carrera cars in the 1970s.

2 Here are all the parts required for installing the tail. Shown here is the tail, the deck lid, and the gas flap that is used for color matching. These parts are about to be shipped off to the body shop for painting. Make sure that you repaint the black inner portion of the tail. Otherwise the paint job on the outside will look sharp and fresh, and the inside will look worn and tired.

After the tail is attached to the deck lid, it's time to install it on the car. Carefully remove the bolts that hold the old deck lid to the car. If you have an A/C evaporator attached to the rear grille, carefully remove it and place it on top of the engine. With the help of an assistant, install the new deck lid/tail assembly onto the car. Reconnect the A/C evaporator to the rear of the deck lid, using longer bolts if necessary.

At this point, it's a wise idea to install the dual hood shock kit required to keep the extra weight of the tail up in the air. Refer to Project 81 for more information on this procedure.

If you install a rear spoiler on your car, the factory literature says that you must also install a front-mounted spoiler to aerodynamically balance the car (Project 84). Failure to do so may make the car handle poorly.

BODY
PROJECT 84 • INSTALLATION OF A CHIN SPOILER

 Time: 2 hours

 Tools: Hand drill

 Talent:

 Applicable Years: 1974-1989

 Tab: $280

 Tinware: Chin spoiler and hardware mounting kit

 Tip: Be careful of speed bumps and driveways after installation.

! PERFORMANCE GAIN: Better aerodynamically balanced car

COMPLEMENTARY MODIFICATION: Insallation of a rear spoiler

Another popular addition to the 911 is the installation of a chin spoiler. The chin spoiler is attached to the front valance panel, and is usually used in conjunction with the installation of the rear whale tail spoiler. You should not install a rear spoiler on your car without mounting a front spoiler as well. The rear spoiler changes the profile of the car in such a fashion that the car becomes aerodynamically unstable without the front chin spoiler. That's not to say that the car will suddenly flip upside down if you are driving along, but the forces on the car will be unbalanced. You can,

however, install a front-mounted spoiler without the installation of the rear spoiler.

Probably the most difficult part of installing the chin spoiler is figuring out where and how it is attached to the car. Figuring out the mounting hardware that comes with the kit is similar to putting together a jigsaw puzzle without seeing the picture on the box. The photo that accompanies this project should help save you a lot of time by actually showing you where each fastener is located.

The chin spoiler is made out of rubber and is attached to the lower lip of the front valance of the car. Most cars will not have the holes drilled in the front valance, so you will most likely have to drill them yourself. If you work slowly and carefully, the entire spoiler can be mounted beautifully within a couple of hours.

The first step for installation is to jack up the front of the car. Although you can perform the install with the car on the ground, it will be easier to maneuver with a bit more room between the valance and the ground. Then, test fit the spoiler to the car. It is important to note that the cars with 911 Turbo flares on the front use a different chin spoiler that extends all the way up the side of the car to meet the front fender. See Project 82 for a photo of this spoiler.

If you so desire, you can remove the entire lower valance panel from the car and place it on your bench. While this will be more convenient for drilling the holes, it may take a while to remove and reattach the valance—adding to your total install time. It's easy enough to drill the holes in the valance panel while it's mounted to the car. Remove the valance panel only if you need to, or if you feel more comfortable drilling the holes on your workbench.

The first holes you drill in your valance panel should be the ones all the way on the side of the car, nearest to the wheel. The spoiler has two embedded studs inside the rubber that mount the spoiler to the side of the valance panel. Carefully hold up the spoiler to the valance panel, and mark the locations of these holes. Rotate the wheel of the car out of the way

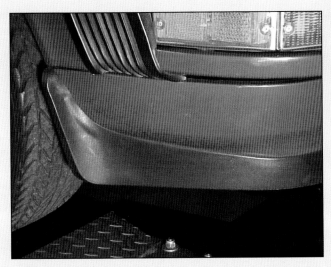

1 The chin spoiler is installed on the lower part of the valance panel as shown here. Start with each end of the spoiler and work your way across. You may need to stretch the spoiler across the bottom of the valance panel to make it fit appropriately.

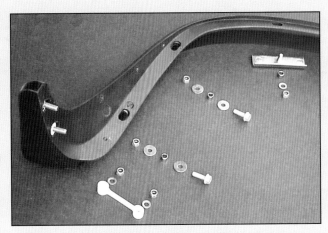

2 The mounting kit for the chin spoiler can be very confusing to sort out. Seven plates with embedded studs are used to mount the front lip of the spoiler. Small spacers fit over the studs to make sure that the rubber part of the spoiler is not crushed when it is assembled. Two bolts and spacers on each side attach the spoiler to the sides of the valance panel. Finally, the upper lip of the spoiler is attached to the upper side of the valance panel and secured on the opposite side with two nuts. A white "dog-bone" spacer is used to keep the nuts off of the back of the valance panel.

if you need a bit more room to negotiate. Double- and triple-check the proper location of these holes, as they will be the most visible if you mess up. Repeat the procedure for the other side of the car. You may have to stretch the spoiler to reach the other side.

Once you have the four side holes drilled, mount up the spoiler to each side of the car. The small "dog-bone" spacer is used on the inside of the valance panel, to offset the mounting nuts from the panel. When mounted, the center of the spoiler will hang and sag down. Tape it up under the valance panel into its final position with some masking tape.

Now, using the spoiler as a guide, carefully drill the holes in the valance panel. It's important to note that the mounting plates for the spoiler are not a perfect fit, and the embedded stud in the plate will hug the inside of the hole on the spoiler. In other words,

double-check where you are drilling your holes in the valance panel. The holes in the rubber spoiler are much bigger than the hole that you will drill in the valance panel. Make sure that the hole in the valance panel is centered in the hole in the spoiler, and also oriented toward the inside of the car.

Each time that you drill a hole, use the mounting hardware to fasten it loosely to the valance panel. When you have finished drilling all the holes, tighten up the hardware and make sure that the spoiler is tightly fastened to the front valance panel.

Remember when driving that your spoiler decreases the clearance of your 911. If you have already lowered your car, you will not have much room for going over speed bumps. Make sure that you are aware of the new height clearance before you accidentally knock your new spoiler off of the valance panel.

BODY
PROJECT 85 • SUNROOF REPAIR

 Time: 5 hours

 Tools: —

 Talent: ﾔ ﾔ ﾔ

 Applicable Years: All coupe cars

 Tab: $100–$200

 Tinware: New sunroof cables, seals, plastic guides

 Tip: Make sure to grease the rails liberally upon reassembly

 PERFORMANCE GAIN: More sun!

COMPLEMENTARY MODIFICATION: Replace/replenish the sunroof headliner

A sunroof is extremely confusing if you've never worked on one before. In reality, it is simple and easy to repair. The motor drives two cables that move the roof forward and backward in a track mounted to the car. The primary problems with the sunroof involve the cables breaking or the roof leaking. This project will go over the details associated with complete sunroof removal and renewal of the cables, the motor, and the sunroof seals.

The first step in repair is to access the sunroof motor. The coupe cars have a zipper that runs along the width of the headliner in the rear of the car. Unzip this, and behind the headliner you'll find several panels with foam sound insulation on them. Remove the panels, and above them you will see the sunroof motor and transport mechanism. Be careful removing these panels, as the foam is sometimes quite old and easily flakes off.

Release the mechanism from the sunroof cables by removing the two screws that hold it to the motor bracket. The mechanism should remain attached to the sunroof motor, and can hang by the small flexi-

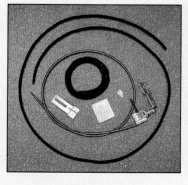

1 Shown here are some of the pieces that you need to effectively repair and renew most sunroofs. The velvet/felt seal on the outside mounts to the inside edge of the chassis in the front and sides of the sunroof opening. Inward in the photo are the sunroof cable (two required) and transport mechanism. The cable and the mechanism are integrated and have to be replaced at the same time. In the inner circle are the rear sunroof seal (top), the rear sunroof guide with plastic insert (left), a front lifting pad (center, four required), and the triangular plastic lift piece that helps push the sunroof into its home position when closed (right, two required). Not shown is the flat rubber seal that mates the rear of the sunroof to the car. Note that the sunroof cables are asymmetrical. If you look at the left and right replacement cables, you might think one was incorrectly manufactured. This is not the case. Compare the new cables to the older ones, and it should be apparent how they fit into the guides.

ble coupler that connects it to the motor. The edge of the cables should be clearly visible where the gear mates to them. Now that the cables are loose, you can remove the sunroof.

At the front of the passenger compartment, examine the headliner installed into the sunroof. This piece is simply pressed into place by spring clips, and it covers all the mounting hardware for the sunroof. Remove it by pulling down on its edges. Remember to only pull down on the piece that is attached to the sunroof, and be careful not to damage the rest of your headliner. After you get a good grip on the headliner, it should just pop out of the sunroof. The clips that hold it in place are similar to the ones that hold the door panel to the door. If you need to slide open the roof to gain more leverage, you should be able to simply push it, now that the cables are disconnected.

Once this headliner piece is loose, slide it back toward the rear of the car. At this point, the attachment points for the sunroof should be clearly visible. On each side, there is a guide piece attached to the sunroof toward the rear of the car, and also a guide piece that is attached to the sunroof cable. Remove the bolts that attach the sunroof at these four points, and you should be able to lift the sunroof out. Make sure that you place the roof in a safe location.

Once you have the roof removed, it should be apparent how the track assembly works. The cable is attached to a guide that runs inside the aluminum channel. The motor pushes this guide forward and backward to open and close the sunroof. At this point, it's advisable to completely remove all aluminum channels from the top of the sunroof and

2 Removal of the sunroof begins with pulling out the headliner piece that is snapped onto the roof. Grab an edge and pull downward, and the metal snaps should disengage. Once the headliner is loose, push it back out of the way toward the rear of the car. The sunroof attachment bolts can now be reached and removed.

3 The sunroof motor is located near the rear of the car, and can be reached by unzipping the headliner and removing some of the sound-deadening panels. Be careful when unzipping the headliner, as the fabric can get old and may rip when you pull on it.

4 The motor mechanism must be disconnected for you to remove and install new cables. This will allow the cables to be inserted into their channels. Once the roof is installed and in the closed position, reconnect the mechanism, mating the brass drive gear with the sunroof cable.

5 In order to install the new cable and travel mechanism, you need to remove the channel that holds it in. Simply unscrew the main aluminum channel and any others that may block it from the sunroof top. Pull out the old cable and mechanism. Make sure that you clean the channels completely prior to their reinstallation.

6 New sunroof seals help finish the job correctly. There are a total of three seals: two that go on the sunroof and one that goes on the body. The right side of this picture shows the seal that is mounted to the sunroof. This seal is glued onto the roof itself and winds its way around three-quarters of

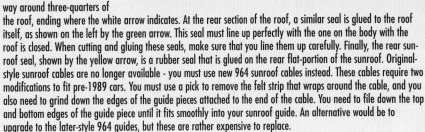

the roof, ending where the white arrow indicates. At the rear section of the roof, a similar seal is glued to the roof itself, as shown on the left by the green arrow. This seal must line up perfectly with the one on the body with the roof is closed. When cutting and gluing these seals, make sure that you line them up carefully. Finally, the rear sunroof seal, shown by the yellow arrow, is a rubber seal that is glued on the rear flat-portion of the sunroof. Original-style sunroof cables are no longer available - you must use new 964 sunroof cables instead. These cables require two modifications to fit pre-1989 cars. You must use a pick to remove the felt strip that wraps around the cable, and you also need to grind down the edges of the guide pieces attached to the end of the cable. You need to file down the top and bottom edges of the guide piece until it fits smoothly into your sunroof guide. An alternative would be to upgrade to the later-style 964 guides, but these are rather expensive to replace.

clean them. You should also clean the air deflector plates at the front of the sunroof. Make sure to clean all sections of the track and also the air deflector plates, and don't use any grease on the cable or chanels. The heat from the sun tends to melt the grease and make it drip inside the car. Also, the grease attracts dirt and debris. The sunroof channels will be open to the air and wind when you are driving along; dirt and debris will find its way in there. On the roof itself, you will want to replace the two rear channel guides that have plastic inserts, and also the small triangular plastic pieces that help to lift the roof up into its closed position. I also recommend replacing the sunroof seals. With the aluminum guide channels removed, place the seal onto the body and glue it in place, using 3M Super Weatherstrip 80001 (see Project 65). On the sunroof, glue the rear strip and the remainder of the sunroof seal to the roof itself. Refer to the photo accompanying this project for a clearer understanding.

After the seals have been replaced and the guide rails installed, the roof can then be reinstalled back into the car. Make sure that the rear guides are fed into the sunroof channel, and the front of the roof is mounted to the guides that are attached to the sunroof cables. The front height of the sunroof can be adjusted by rotating the small nuts that are located under the front channel guides, while the fastening screws are loose. These guides also lock in the left/right position of the roof as well. The rear height of the roof can be adjusted by altering the location of the screws that mount the rear guides.

Once the roof is installed and properly adjusted, reconnect the motor to the cables. Simply bolt the drive mechanism together—there shouldn't be any adjustment involved. Test the sunroof motor for proper operation. If all goes well, reinstall the soundproofing material, zip up your headliner, and dig out the suntan lotion.

SECTION TEN
ELECTRICAL

On the older 911s, electrical gremlins have a tendency to sneak into their wiring. This section covers a wide variety of projects aimed at reducing the amount of electrical and gauge-related problems in the car—whether it has a broken odometer or has trouble turning over the starter, the projects in this section will help you troubleshoot and repair these nagging problems.

ELECTRICAL

PROJECT 86 • FUEL LEVEL SENDER REPLACEMENT

 Time: 30 minutes

 Tools: Socket set

 Talent:

Applicable Years: All

 Tab: $75

 Tinware: New gas tank sending unit and gasket

 Tip: Perform the replacement in a well-ventilated area.

PERFORMANCE GAIN: Accurate fuel gauge readings

COMPLEMENTARY MODIFICATION: Inspect the gas tank for debris

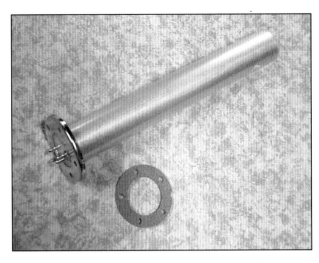

1 The brand-new gas tank sending unit is an aluminum tube with a small float that rides up and down the center. Make sure that you remove the small retaining pin that protects the sender during transport before you install it.

2 Removal and installation is very straightforward. Simply unbolt the old one and attach the new one in its place. Make sure that you use a new gasket to avoid fuel odor seeping out of the top of the sender.

Have you ever run out of gas because your fuel tank wasn't working? Chances are if you have, you've already replaced your sender, because running out of gas is indeed irritating. However, if you've been putting it off, don't worry—it's an easy procedure.

The fuel tank is located in the front trunk, under the trunk carpeting. Access couldn't be easier, as the sender is located right on top of the tank. The sender itself is a long aluminum tube that has a little float that rides up and down in the center.

To replace this unit, simply remove the five nuts that hold the sender down, and pull it up out of the tank. It's wise to perform this task in a well-ventilated area, as there is no way to avoid spilling some gas or breathing some fumes. Also, be sure to run the tank down as low as possible before making the replacement. Don't let the pump run dry, however, as this might damage it. You also might want a fire extinguisher handy just in case "something goes wrong."

The old sender should simply pull out of the tank. Take a small flashlight and look down the inside of the tank to see if there is any debris. Hold the flashlight a long way away from the entrance of the tank—you

don't want any fuel to ignite. You might want to empty the tank and clean it out if you see a lot of junk inside.

Installation of the new sender is straightforward. Use a new gasket when installing the new sender, and make sure that you remove the safety pin from the bottom of the sending unit before you install it.

Following the installation of the new sender, if your gauge is still not reading correctly, check the connections to the gauge itself. If the connections are fine, then you will probably have to replace the gauge. For more information on replacing the gauge, see Project 90.

205

ELECTRICAL
PROJECT 87 • STARTER SYSTEM TROUBLESHOOTING

 Time: 4–10 hours

 Tools: Voltmeter/Ammeter

 Talent:

 Applicable Years: All

 Tab: $120–$250

 Tinware: High-torque starter, transmission ground strap

 Tip: Most starting problems are caused by bad grounding

 PERFORMANCE GAIN: Easier, quicker starting

COMPLEMENTARY MODIFICATION: Upgrade to a high-torque starter

At one time or another, everyone will have problems starting their 911. The first place to look for trouble in your starting system is your battery. The battery is perhaps the most important electrical component on the car, and due to its design and nature, is perhaps one of the most troublesome. Before doing anything drastic like replacing your starter, you should make sure that your battery is in good condition.

Begin by checking the voltage on the battery posts using a voltmeter. Place the meter's probes on the posts of the battery, not the clamps. This will give the most accurate indication of the voltage in the battery. A normal battery should read a voltage slightly above 12 volts with the car sitting still, and no electrical devices on. (The small trunk light in the front trunk shouldn't make a difference in this reading.) A typical reading would be in the 12.6-volt range when the battery is fully charged. If the reading is 12 volts or less, then the battery needs charging or needs to be replaced with a new one. To be certain, you can take your battery to your local auto parts store for testing.

When the car is running, the alternator should be outputting anywhere from about 12.5 volts to about 14 volts. If you don't see any significant change in the voltage after you start up the car, then your alternator or voltage regulator could be faulty. If the voltage is high at the battery (around 17 volts or higher), then the regulator is most likely faulty and needs to be replaced. Overcharging the battery at these higher levels will cause it to overflow and leak acid all over the inside of your car.

Once you have determined that your battery is fine, you should make sure that your transmission ground strap is properly installed. The engine and transmission are mounted to the chassis using rubber mounts. While great for the suspension, the rubber mounts make lousy electrical conductors. To compensate for this, there is a transmission ground strap that electrically connects the transmission and engine assembly to the chassis. To accurately assess the condition of the ground strap, you need to crawl underneath the car after it's been jacked up, and take a look at the bottom of the transmission. If the strap is corroded or damaged, it might be best to install a new one. Make sure that you clean both ends of the strap and the areas that it mounts to on the chassis. With all electrical connections, it's a good idea to clean the area that you are mounting to with rubbing alcohol, and also to sand the area lightly with some fine-grit sandpaper. Doing so will remove any dirt, grime, surface rust, or other corrosion that may interfere with creating a good electrical connection.

Another problem area for starting is the starter, of course. The starter is a somewhat complex device for what would seem to be a simple task. A solenoid on the starter both actuates the small gear that turns the flywheel and switches on the main starter motor. It is important to throw in a note of caution here. The starter motor is connected directly at all times to the positive terminal of the battery. If you accidentally touch the terminals of the starter with a metal object that is grounded, you will quickly generate a lot of sparks, heat, and enough current to fry your alternator and a large chunk of your electrical system. I have heard of two separate occasions where a person was working on his car, and his watch touched the terminals of the starter and the chassis ground. This literally caused the watch to become welded to the chassis of the car! The lesson—exercise caution in this area. Don't wear any jewelry when working on the car, and always disconnect the negative terminal from the battery.

Another potential problem is the starter teeth on the flywheel or ring gear. If the starter seems to engage and spin up with a high-pitched whirring sound, then it is likely that the starter is not fully engaging the flywheel. This is especially prevalent with intermittent problems, in which sometimes the starter will work fine and then other times it will spin freely. The fix for this is to inspect the flywheel teeth, and to replace the flywheel or ring gear when the engine is out of the car. A bad solenoid can cause similar problems.

When 911s have trouble turning the engine over with the starter motor, it is often because there isn't enough current to fully trigger the solenoid on the starter. A number of factors can cause this. The most common reason is old wiring. As the car ages, the wiring has a tendency to lose some of its electrical conductiveness. This can be caused by the wires getting bent or crimped, or it can also be triggered by the constant heating and cooling of the wires. This tempering of the metal within the wires can directly affect their conductivity. With age often comes corrosion, and as we can see simply by looking at the Statue of Liberty, copper corrodes quite easily, leaving a light green layer that doesn't conduct very well.

The solution is to track down the problem in the wiring and fix it. Very often, tracing back the electrical connections from the starter and carefully cleaning all the contacts will improve the situation significantly. While this can be a time-consuming process, it's really the only way to track down these electrical gremlins. Chances are if you are having wiring conductivity problems with your starting system, it's probably affecting other electrical systems as well.

The primary method of tracking down bad connections is to test them with an electrical multitester. Test the resistance across lengths of wires and connections in your car and look for any that are significantly higher than others. Chances are with a little cleaning of both the wires and the contacts, the system will improve.

The electrical portion of the ignition switch is another source of trouble. This small part often wears out and fails after many years. One symptom of this problem is an ignition switch that requires a lot of force to start the car. Another symptom is headlamps that flicker on and off when you wiggle the key. For the replacement of this switch, see Project 91.

If you cannot find the problem causing your starting woes, there is a potential solution called a hot start relay kit. While this solution will work by bypassing some of the faulty wiring, it is basically a Band-Aid put on a much bigger problem. The hot start relay kit takes the power from the starter cable that is connected to the battery and uses it to activate the solenoid. The relay is powered by the electricity that travels through the "faulty" wiring. Since the hot start relay only requires a few milliamps of

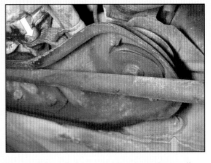

1 The infamous transmission ground strap is one of the easiest parts on the car to overlook, yet can cause so many electrical troubles. Since the transmission and engine mounts are insulated by rubber, the ground strap is the only significant ground to the engine. If the ground strap is disconnected or missing, then the current that turns the starter must travel through the engine harness or other small points of contact. Needless to say, this situation usually doesn't provide enough current to start the car. The white arrow points to the location where the transmission ground strap attaches to the transmission. The yellow arrow shows the chassis mounting point.

2 While upgrading to a high-torque starter shouldn't be your first step in troubleshooting a difficult-starting 911, it can be a worthy upgrade to a starter motor that has genuinely worn out. The aftermarket starter motors offer higher horsepower, and are also significantly lighter than their factory counterparts.

electrical current to operate, it fixes the problem of starting the car. However, as mentioned previously, if you have electrical starting problems you probably have additional electrical problems elsewhere. These are best tracked down and fixed, instead of glossed over.

Finally, if you have determined that the problem lies with your starter, you should replace it. The starter is relatively easy to replace—simply disconnect the electrical terminals and unbolt it from the transmission. See Project 7, Engine Removal, for a few more details on the removal of the starter.

You can replace your unit with a genuine Bosch rebuilt unit, or, for about the same cost, you can opt for a quality aftermarket unit. The aftermarket starters are higher-torque starters, weigh less, use newer technology, and are generally a really good bet for placement in your car. In most cases, the cost between the OEM and aftermarket starters is negligible. Compare the two before you make a decision. If you want to go with a completely stock 911, then stick with the Bosch unit. Otherwise upgrade to the aftermarket starter.

Another popular option for upgrading your starter is to install a 1.5-horsepower Bosch unit. The early 911s shipped with the Bosch 17X starter, which is rated at only 3/4 horsepower. The later-style Bosch 68X unit is a bolt-in replacement and offers much better cranking than the original 17X starter. New Bosch units are not available, but rebuilt ones can be found if you have a good used core.

ELECTRICAL

PROJECT 88 • SPEEDOMETER REMOVAL

 Time: 30 minutes

 Tools: –

 Talent: ★

 Applicable Years: All

 Tab: $150

 Tinware: New speedometer

 Tip: Make sure you mark where all the wires go before you disconnect them

 PERFORMANCE GAIN: Better reading of actual speed

COMPLEMENTARY MODIFICATION: Upgrade to 150-mile-per-hour speedometer

1 The speedometer is held into the dash using a rubber seal. Pulling on the outside of the speedometer should remove it from the dashboard. Make sure that you disconnect the speedometer cable if the unit isn't electronic. Some of the wires attached to the rear of the unit may not be too long, so be careful when pulling on them.

In the early 1980s, the United States mandated that all cars sold would have their speedometers limited to 85 miles per hour. While fine for the standard Buick or Toyota, this limitation is somewhat of a pain for Porsche owners. The good news is that this law was changed a few years later, and Porsches were again equipped with a speedometer that could more accurately reflect their performance.

More good news exists for cars equipped with the paltry 85-mile-per-hour speedometer. The speedometer can be replaced with either an earlier- or later-model unit with the higher speed markings. In the same manner, a mile-per-hour speedometer can be replaced with a kilometer-per-hour speedometer.

The first step is to find yourself the proper speedometer. There have been different faces and different-type styles used on a few of the 911 speedometers, so you should probably take a look at one you are buying very carefully to make sure that it matches the rest of your gauges. Also, the gauges manufactured by VDO for Porsche have a less-than-desirable life for the odometer (see Project 89, Odometer Repair), so make sure that any used gauge you purchase is fully tested

and working. Otherwise you may have to pay an additional $100 or so to have the gauge repaired.

Replacing the speedometer couldn't be easier. Like the rest of the gauges, the speedometer is held into the dash with a rubber seal. You should be able to grab onto the speedometer and pull it out from the dash. Gently pry on the rim of the speedometer with a stiff putty knife if it doesn't want to come out easily. Work carefully so that you don't ding anything. You can also reach around underneath the dashboard and push it out from behind. Be aware of the wires that are attached to the rear of the unit as you are pulling on it.

Replacement is easy—simply remove the wires from the old one, and plug in the new one. Make sure that you make a note of which wire goes where, as it is easy to get confused, and the speedometers are not well marked. Also make sure that you don't damage any of the small light bulbs or their fixtures when removing them from the rear of the gauge. An additional concern is scratching the glass or plastic face of the gauge.

On the very early cars, the gauges were held in place using two small clamps behind the gauge. In order to remove the speedometer, you need to remove the two clamps and pull out the gauge. On cars equipped with cable-driven speedometers, you need to unscrew the cable from the back of the unit before you remove it from the dash.

Getting your speedometer out of the dash is the first step in a few projects. Once you have the speedometer out, you can send it in for recalibration, have the odometer repaired, or simply have it cleaned and a new faceplate installed.

ELECTRICAL
PROJECT 89 • ODOMETER REPAIR

 Time: 4 hours

 Tools: Small screwdriver set

 Talent: ![talent icons]

 Applicable Years: All

 Tab: $10–$100

 Tinware: Spare used gauge

 Tip: Exercise extreme care when removing the outer ring of the gauge—it can be damaged very easily

! PERFORMANCE GAIN: Working odometer and speedometer

COMPLEMENTARY MODIFICATION: Calibrate speedometer, upgrade to 150-mile-per-hour model, install glass gauge faces

One of the items on the 911 almost guaranteed to fail is the odometer. Perhaps the most predictable failure on the entire car, the odometer is also one of the most visible. Two distinct design flaws with the odometer, coupled with the fact that many 911s have passed the 100,000-mile mark, add up to a lot of broken odometers.

The good news is that they can be fixed. The bad news is that the parts to fix them are not readily available. There are some things that you can do to fix them, however, with a few tools and a couple of hours to spare.

The VDO odometer used in all 911s, and many other German cars, has two distinct flaws in its design that can cause its premature failure. One of the problems with the odometer is that some of the important internal gears are made of plastic. With age, the odometer can stick, and if it does, these plastic gears will grind and become destroyed. The other design flaw involves a pot-metal gear that is pressed onto the main odometer shaft. After many years, this gear often comes loose on the shaft, refusing to turn the odometer.

1 Removing the outer sealing ring can be a very tricky process. Use a small screwdriver and carefully push out the edge of the outer ring. Try to minimize the amount of damage that you do to the ring—these are not available as separate parts, and are easily destroyed. One good thing to remember regarding the process of removing the ring is that the edge that is dented and marred is not visible at all when the gauge is installed.

If your odometer has stopped working, yet your speedometer still works, the cause is probably one of the two faults described above. The first step in repairing the unit is to remove it from the car. Follow the procedure described in Project 88 (Replacing the Speedometer) to remove it from your dash.

Take the unit and place it on a workbench where you will have plenty of room. The first step is to remove the outer retaining ring that secures the face of the gauge. This removal procedure must be performed very carefully, or the edge of your gauge will look as if your dog has chewed on it. To remove the outer ring, place a small screwdriver between the side of the gauge and the retaining ring. Gently push out with the screwdriver and pry a small section of the ring away from the wall. Repeat this process until you have pushed the retaining ring out from a little more than half of the gauge. At this point, you should be able to remove this retaining ring by pulling on the ring, or by prying it off with a screwdriver. Remember to do this carefully or you will damage the retaining ring. When the ring is loose, it will slide off of the gauge face. Even if you deform the rim slightly, it doesn't really matter because the rim is hidden from view when the gauge is installed in the car.

Now remove the two small screws on the back of the speedometer that hold the entire assembly to the housing. With a little bit of coaxing, the internals should slide right out. Be careful from this point on not to scratch the delicate faceplate, or tap, bend, or break the speedometer needle.

A main failure point within the odometer is the pot-metal gear that is pressed onto the odometer drive shaft. The shaft holds all of the numbered wheels together and is connected by a plasticworm gear. If the pot-metal gear is loose, it needs to either be glued or deformed enough to be pressed back onto the

2 The often fickle odometer mechanism can fail at two different points. The plastic worm gear indicated by the arrow on the left can become chewed up and worn if the odometer sticks. The only way to fix this is to replace the gear. Unfortunately, these gears are not available as separate parts. The other point of failure involves the small pot-metal gear indicated by the arrow on the right. This gear is pressed onto the main shaft, and often becomes loose after many years of operation. The repair is performed by removing and repressing this gear back onto the shaft.

3 A large assortment of rings and seals hold the top glass to the gauge. Make sure that you don't damage these when you are removing and handling them. A good fix for spots and fading on these rings is to use a black permanent marker to touch them up. Such an easy technique can improve the looks of your dash by a surprising amount.

odometer shaft. To remove the shaft, simply pull on the small gear that is on the opposite end of the pot-metal gear. To prevent the number wheels from coming loose and falling out everywhere, stick a small piece of tape across the assembly. This way, the entire taped assembly can be removed and easily replaced later on.

It can be difficult to remove the gears without taking the faceplate off. Be aware that if you remove the needle, you will have to have the gauge recalibrated. The best thing to do to gain more clearance is to remove the small screws that hold the face on, and then rotate the face so that you can get the wheels out. Again, be careful not to break off the speedometer needle.

After you remove the odometer drive shaft, you have a few options to make the repair. You can try gluing the gear onto the shaft, but this is difficult as there isn't too much clearance and working room when the unit is finally assembled. You can place some glue on the inside of the gear, and hope that it will be enough to hold the gear. You can also roughen up the shaft a bit with some sandpaper or a grinding wheel. My recommendation is to actually deform the wheel by compressing it with a pair of Vise-Grips or some other applicable tool. Carefully squeeze the wheel at its mounting point until the inside becomes slightly oval. This should be enough to make the gear adhere to the shaft.

If the wheels are still together, and they haven't become separated from the tape, reassembly is a bit

easier. If the wheels have become jumbled, reposition them in their proper order. Make sure that the trip meter wheel with the extra white attachment is placed all the way on the right, and that the wheel with the copper metal insert is placed next to it. Refer to the photo accompanying this project if there is any confusion. To reassemble the odometer shaft, place all of the numbered wheels into the housing and insert the shaft through the wheels, making sure that the numbers stay aligned.

At this point in time, you can set your odometer to any mileage amount that you would like, although it is difficult to put the unit back together without messing up the specific number that you want. Push the odometer driveshaft back into the housing and through the pot-metal gear. Depending upon how you decided to deform the wheel, this may take some force. Make sure that all your numbers are lined up before pushing the shaft back into the pot-metal gear. Check it by looking carefully at the face on the mechanism. It is possible to have numbers that are half-turned and not even with the other numbers. Getting this right may take more than one try.

The other major problem with the odometer stems from the plastic worm gears getting worn out. Unfortunately, these gears are not available as separate parts that can be ordered. In most cases, however, you can head to your own local junkyard and pick up an old VW or BMW gauge made by VDO, and chances are that it will have the exact same gears inside. It's recommended to gather 3-4 of these (they usually cost about $3–$5) at a time to make sure that you get some decent used parts inside. Replacement of the gear is straightforward—simply loosen up the assembly and swap out the gear. It is important to keep in mind the reasons why the plastic worm gears may have been chewed up. If the odometer doesn't spin freely, then your speedometer cable will turn the gear and chew it up again. Make sure that the odometer gears turn freely before installing your new worm gear.

Place the odometer/speedometer mechanism back into the housing and mount it with the two screws you removed earlier. It is possible to test the operation of a mechanical speedometer using a hand drill hooked up to the rear of the housing, but in most cases, it's just easier to reinstall it back into the car. Replace the gauge face and reattach the outer ring by pressing down the ring around the outside of the gauge. Make sure that you clean the inside of the gauge and the glass before you reassemble everything. With your repair complete, your gauge should work well for years to come!

ELECTRICAL
PROJECT 90 • OIL TEMPERATURE GAUGE UPGRADE

Time: 1 Hour

Tools: –

Talent:

Applicable Years: 1978-89

Tab: $100

Tinware: Temperature sender, and gauge module

Tip: Blow compressed air onto the face of the gauge prior to installing it.

PERFORMANCE GAIN: More accurate temperature readings

COMPLEMENTARY MODIFICATION: Upgrade/fix your other gauges and senders

1 The numbered oil temperature sender module is what you need to start with. This particular module is from a 1977 911 and is numbered up to 340 degrees Fahrenheit. Earlier cars had different variations in the numbering scheme. These gauges are often available at swap meets, or modules themselves can be purchased new individually.

2 Make sure that you replace your oil temperature sender (shown by the arrow) when you upgrade your gauge. There are several different types of senders, and each one must be matched specifically to the gauge, or you will get false readings. The switch is located in the rear of the engine compartment, just to the lower right of the fan, facing the rear of the car.

In 1978, Porsche switched from using a numbered temperature gauge to one that only has white and red ranges. Fortunately, it's easy to replace your plain range gauge with one that has accurate numbers. The only catch is that you must match the sender to the gauge. Each sender is calibrated for a certain gauge within a specified range. If you use the wrong gauge with the wrong sender, you won't get accurate readings.

The first step in performing this upgrade is to obtain the small gauge module that has the numbered oil temperature on it. You can usually find older gauges with these modules in them at local swap meets, or the module itself is still available new for about $70. Once you have the module, make sure that you order the correct sending unit for it. The most common sending unit is the one that originally came with the 1969–1977 911s.

The module can be easily installed into the rear of the gauge. To start, disconnect the battery and simply pull the gauge out of the dashboard (see Project 88). The gauges are held in with only a thick rubber gasket, so they should just pull out. Once you have the gauge out, carefully mark the wires that connect to the oil temperature module on the right. You don't need to disconnect the wires that are connected to the oil pressure module. There should be three wires, plus two lightbulbs that you need to remove. The lightbulbs simply pull out of their sockets—don't be afraid to pull on the wires, or use a screwdriver to pry the lightbulbs out of their fixtures.

Now, remove the four small screws that hold the module into the gauge. These screws are sometimes reinforced with a little glob of glue on the outside, so make sure that you use an appropriately sized screwdriver, and be careful not to strip them. Once you remove the four screws, the module can be easily removed. Replace it with the new one and tighten down the four screws. Make sure that you blow off the face of the module with compressed air to clean it before you place it back inside the gauge. Reconnect the wires, and press the gauge back into the dashboard.

Now proceed to your engine compartment, where you will find the oil temperature sending unit to the lower right of the fan, facing the rear of the car. Simply unbolt the unit and remove it. A little bit of oil may spill out, so have some paper towels handy. Install the new sender, making sure that you use a new metal gasket between the sender and its mount. Tighten the sender down tight, but don't apply too much torque (maximum 25 N-m/18.4 ft-lb).

When you're finished, start up the car and check to make sure that everything is working OK. While the car is warming up, check the temperature sender in the engine compartment to ensure that it is not leaking. Tighten it up a bit if it's wet with oil.

PROJECT 91 • REPLACING YOUR IGNITION SWITCH

 Time: 2 hours

 Tools: Dremel tool or die grinder

 Talent: 🏃🏃🏃

 Applicable Years: All

 Tab: $55-$300

 Tinware: New ignition switch (full switch, or electrical only), new break-off bolts for ignition switch

 Tip: Removing the steering wheel might make the job a bit easier.

⚠ **PERFORMANCE GAIN:** More reliable starting and electrical systemss

COMPLEMENTARY MODIFICATION: Relay ignition switch

1 From the factory, the ignition switch is bolted into the dashboard with break-away bolts. If you're lucky, the previous owner has already replaced the ignition switch at least once, and the bolts have already been removed. When placing the switch back into the dashboard, you can attach it with four break-off bolts. This photo shows the four original bolts replaced with two regular ones.

One of the most common electrical items to fail on the older 911s is the ignition switch. This failure shows up in a number of ways. The car can refuse to start some of the time, the key may not turn easily in the ignition, or strange electrical problems like the headlamps flickering on and off may appear. The correct solution for all of these is to replace all or part of the ignition switch.

Probably the most difficult part of the whole procedure is removing the switch from the dashboard. On later cars, the it is hidden behind a large plastic disc, which you can simply unscrew it from the dash. On the earlier cars, there is a small plastic ring that needs to be unscrewed in a similar manner. Once the ring is removed, you can see the ignition switch assembly.

The switch itself comprises two separate sections, one that holds the key and the lock mechanism, and another that contains a somewhat complicated electrical switch that controls the starter and the other elec-

trical systems of the car. The good news is that the electrical portion of the ignition switch can easily be replaced on 1970–1989 911s. The typical cost of this part is about $55. Earlier cars will have to make do with finding a good used switch, as new ones are no longer available. If your key doesn't turn too well in the ignition, chances are you have a worn-out tumbler. You can attempt to rekey and refurbish the tumbler yourself (see Project 76 on lock rekeying for more details), but the process can be quite difficult. It requires that you drill out a pin that has been pressed into the housing. If you make a mistake, you can damage the entire assembly. In other words, the ignition switch assembly wasn't really designed to be taken apart.

Once you can see the ignition switch, you can probably figure out why the next step is the hardest. The switch is bolted to the frame of the car with what's known as a break-off bolt. This may deter thieves, but it also makes your task a lot more difficult. To remove these bolts, take a die grinder or Dremel tool and grind off the top of the head. Once the heads of the bolts are gone, you should be able to pull out the switch. In some cases, you can also grind a slot into the top of the bolt, and use a large screwdriver to remove

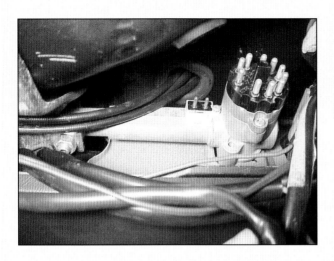

2 The view from under the dashboard affords us a look at the ignition switch and its electrical connections. It's nearly impossible to remove the electrical portion of the switch without removing the entire assembly. Make sure that you loosen the steering wheel lock bolt on the left before you attempt to remove the switch.

3 Shown here is the electrical portion of the switch removed from the remainder of the assembly. After many years, the electrical portion is usually what wears out, resulting in intermittent starting problems with the ignition key.

the bolts. Removing the steering wheel will probably give you a bit more room to work (see Project 92).

Once you have the bolts removed, you can crawl under your dashboard and remove the switch. Begin by loosening up the nut that holds the ignition switch onto the steering wheel lock. On some cars, you may not need to loosen this nut up, as the switch may just slide out of position. Disconnect the large 1.5-inch electrical plug from the ignition switch. You should be able to remove the entire assembly from the car now. You may have to negotiate a path through the maze of wires and cables that runs underneath the dash.

Once you have the switch out, it's very easy to replace the electrical portion. Simply remove the two screws that hold it to the back of the switch, and replace it with a new one. The switch has a locating pin cast into the housing, so there is only one way that it can be put back together.

Replacing the electrical portion will most likely solve some ignition and starting problems. Electrical systems flickering on and off as you turn the key is a good clue that your switch is worn. Also, a bad switch sometimes causes unexplainable starting problems, when the starter coil doesn't even click. I even had one

car that wouldn't shut off the starter after the engine kicked over. Both the engine and the starter kept running together—even after I had removed the key!

If you are planning to rekey your ignition key, get ready for a very difficult job. In order to remove the tumbler assembly, you need to carefully drill out the small pin that is located on the side of the tumbler housing. Make sure that you use a sharp drill bit, and be prepared to spend some money for a new ignition switch if you happen to mess up.

The replacement process for the ignition switch is straightforward, except for the final installation of the switch into the rear of the dashboard. You should use new original equipment break-off bolts that are commonly available from your local parts dealer. The heads of the bolts will break off automatically when you torque them down. Or, if you think that you are going to remove the switch again, use regular bolts.

As an addendum, I have heard from various sources that you can remove the electrical portion of the switch without grinding away the breakaway bolts. Although I can't reach the two electrical portion screws on my 911SC, a few mechanics have told me that it is possible. It's worth a try to save time.

ELECTRICAL
PROJECT 92 • REPLACEMENT OF STEERING WHEEL SWITCHES

 Time: 1 hour

 Tools: 27-millimeter deep socket and bar, steering wheel lock device, impact wrench (if you have one)

 Talent:

 Applicable Years: All

 Tab: $140–$250

 Tinware: Replacement turn signal switch, wiper switch, or cruise control switch

 Tip: Some sloppy switches may have just come loose in the housing. Check the switch before purchasing a replacement

 PERFORMANCE GAIN: Switches that work

COMPLEMENTARY MODIFICATION: Replace/recover steering wheel, replace steering wheel bearing

1 An excellent method for removing the steering wheel involves the use of a steering wheel locking device. These locks are excellent for being able to grab onto the wheel, and they give you a tremendous amount of leverage when removing the center nut. In this configuration, simply squeeze the two levers together, and the nut should easily loosen up. Make sure that you don't turn the steering wheel until it stops and then try to remove the nut. This can most certainly damage your steering rack.

With many older 911s, there is a tendency for the steering column switches to become worn out. The replacement procedure for these switches is relatively easy. The hardest part, in some cases, may be finding a replacement switch if you have an older car. The older turn signal and wiper switches have become increasingly difficult to find in either new or used condition.

The first step in replacing your switch is to remove your steering wheel. If the wheel has never been off of the car, this might be the most difficult part of the job. The wheel is mounted on a spline and fastened with a 27-millimeter nut. To remove this nut you need a 27-millimeter deep socket and an impact wrench.

The horn pad covers the steering wheel. On late-model cars, the horn pad simply snaps onto the wheel, and can be removed by pulling on it. On the earlier cars, the horn pad must be rotated counterclockwise in order to remove it. Hold the steering wheel in one hand and rotate the center horn pad with the other. When the horn pad is free, reach around to the back and carefully disconnect the wire that connects to the horn. Disconnect the battery before attempting this, or your horn might sound repeatedly during the process.

If you don't own an impact wrench, there is another neat trick that I developed for removing the steering wheel. First, take one of those obnoxiously large, red steering wheel locks and clamp it onto the steering wheel. The long handle on the lock will allow you to gain a significant amount of leverage on the wheel. Then insert the deep socket onto the nut. Compressing together the steering wheel lock handle and the long handle attached to the socket will enable you to loosen the steering wheel nut. Under no circumstances should you ever turn the steering wheel all the way to the end of the rack and use the end stop to hold the wheel while you remove the nut. The steering wheel has a lot of leverage, and you can easily damage your rack and pinion if you apply a large amount of torque to the wheel.

2 The black plastic housing under the steering wheel has eight screws holding it on. The two yellow arrows indicate the horn contact piece that needs to be removed. The white arrows point to the four small screws that hold the housing to the steering column. (The fourth one is hidden underneath the horn contact strip.) There are two more screws on each side of the plastic housing that also need to be unscrewed before the upper and lower black plastic housings can be removed.

3 Removing the black plastic housing shows the switches underneath. Removing the switches is easy—they are simply bolted onto the steering column. The wires that connect them to the chassis wiring harness are threaded down into the steering column. Replacement is an easy task from here.

Once you have the nut off of the wheel, simply pull the wheel off of the steering column. If the wheel is stuck on the splines and doesn't want to come off, then take a rubber mallet and gently tap the rear of the wheel until it begins to move.

Now, remove the black enclosuresth that surround the steering column. There are eight screws to be removed in order to gain access to the switches. Start by removing the two screws that hold on the horn contact piece. Then remove the four screws contained in the recess of the black enclosures. Finally, don't forget the two screws on either side of the enclosure. These screws can only be seen from the sides of the steering column. Once you have all eight of these screws removed, you should be able to remove the upper and lower black surround.

Once the enclosure is removed, then you should have easy access to the switches. These can be removed by unscrewing them from the steering column. If you trace back the wires from the switches, you will easily see where they are plugged in underneath the dash. If you unplug them, the wires can be fed through the steering column.

Installing new switch simply involves threading the new wires through the steering column, fastening the new switch, and plugging it in underneath the dashboard. When reinstalling the steering wheel, make sure that you tighten up the 27-millimeter nut firmly, but don't use too much force. The steering wheel is not going to fall off by itself.

Sometimes, depending upon what is broken inside the switch, the individual switches can be repaired using parts from another broken one. Carefully inspect the switch for broken parts, and compare it to a new one if necessary. The switch itself can be taken apart, but make sure that you take a few photos of how it is put together before you attempt a disassembly.

While you have the steering wheel partially disassembled, you might want to replace the steering wheel bearings. This however, requires that the entire steering column assembly be removed and disassembled—not an easy job to accomplish in an afternoon.

ELECTRICAL

PROJECT 93 • INSTALLING A NEW STEREO

Time: 3-6 hours

Tools: Wire clippers, wire strippers

Talent:

Applicable Years: All

Tab: $300

Tinware: New stereo and mounting kit

Tip: Proceed slowly, as some installation components are designed to be installed only once (no chance to fix mistakes).

PERFORMANCE GAIN: Great sounding tunes

COMPLEMENTARY MODIFICATION: Upgrade your speakers

Drivin' a swank Porsche ain't nothin' if you don't got no tunes! 'Nuff said. There comes a time when most people want to upgrade the stereo that came in their 911. If your car and radio are really old, then no doubt you are torn between leaving the factory radio installed, and installing a new top-of-the-line CD player. It's always been my contention that the car should be for enjoyment while you're driving—thus install the new stereo. On the other hand, you can opt to do what I did in my 356—leave the original Blaupunkt radio installed in the dash, and place a new model hidden away inside the glove box.

Designing and implementing a new stereo system in your 911 can be a daunting task, if not an art. For the purpose of simplicity, we'll assume that you only want to replace the head unit in your car. Any car audio aficionado will let you know there are hundreds of options that you can install, including the addition of amplifiers, bridges, subwoofers, tweeters, and CD changers. Most people reading this project would probably be happy with a newer CD player in their car, so we'll stick to that.

The first step in this procedure is, of course, to obtain the stereo. The Porsche 911 has always used the standard car stereo form factor that has pretty much become commonplace for the last few decades. Most units nowadays support four speakers, and don't need external amplifiers, so any basic off-the-shelf unit should suffice.

There are two main parts to the installation of the stereo: the physical installation of the unit inside the car, and the electrical hookup of all the connections. Either one of these tasks may be made easier or harder by the stereo that you have in your car right now. If the unit that is currently installed is properly connected and is easy to remove, then the new installation shouldn't be too difficult. Make sure that you disconnect the battery from the car before you start working on the electrical connections.

The old stereo obviously needs to be removed before the new one can be installed. Depending upon how it was originally installed, this could be the most difficult step of the entire process. In general, car stereos are designed to be very difficult to remove, in order to discourage theft. If the unit that is installed is a pull-out unit, one in which the entire machine can be removed from the dash, the task will be easy, as you can access all of the mounting points simply by removing the stereo. However, if the unit doesn't pull out by itself, it may require several hours of work to try to remove it.

Car stereos usually ship with a mounting sleeve that you mount securely inside the car, and then slide the stereo into. These sleeves have special angled metal tabs that you bend and twist to make sure that the sleeve or bracket is securely installed in the dash. The sleeves usually have a minimal number of screws and bolts, and instead rely mostly on these tabs to secure the main unit.

Once the mounting sleeve is properly installed and secured in the dash, the main unit is slid into the sleeve. Small, spring-loaded locks usually snap the main unit into place. It is these snaps that make the unit very difficult to remove. It is almost impossible to access the mounting points for the sleeve with the main unit installed. It's also nearly impossible to remove the main unit once it is installed into the dash. Hence the difficulty for both the potential stereo thief, and the fellow trying to install the new radio.

One rule of thumb to follow is to make sure that you double-check your work, and don't accidentally install the stereo incorrectly. Because of the nature of the sleeve-mount design, fixing your mistakes will be very difficult. Unfortunately, a lot of damage can occur to the both the stereo and the mounting hardware when you are removing it, so if you mess up, you might end up destroying your brackets. Make sure that you follow the instructions that came with the stereo—there aren't really any specific mounting instructions that pertain only to the 911.

If your car has the original stereo installed in it from a long time ago, it may be easier to remove. Some of the very early stereos were simply bolted into the dashboard, without much thought as to theft-prevention. A quick look under the dashboard should confirm this.

The second part of the installation involves the wiring of the stereo. Each 911 has been wired slightly different from year to year, so the best method for figuring out what each wire connects to is to check where the wires to the previous unit were connected, by trial and error, or by checking the electrical diagram for your year car.

In general, new stereos will have the following connections that will need to be hooked up to your 911:

- Left and Right Front Speakers. Very often, previous owners will install speakers in the doors, or additional pairs of speakers throughout the car. The best bet is to look at how the previous speakers were connected, and then tap into those lines. For early 911s with the large center speaker, you should connect both the left and right speaker channels together and connect them to the speaker. Check the stereo manual to make sure that this will not create an impedance imbalance and damage the stereo. Make sure that your speaker connections (positive/negative) are connected properly. In most cases, it won't make a difference, but with some stereos it does matter.
- Left and Right Rear Speakers. Again, the best bet for wiring these speakers is to check how they were connected previously.
- Continuous Power. This is the lead from the starter switch that is always turned on. This power lead is considered "hot" 100 percent of the time, even when the car is sitting in the garage. The power supplied by this line makes sure that the clock and any memory functions of the stereo are retained when the ignition is off. On most 911s, this line exits out of the ignition switch and is colored yellow. Double-check this with a multitester before tapping into it.
- Switched Power. This power line is "hot" only when the ignition is turned on. If you wish to have your radio operational even when the ignition is off, connect this line to the continuous power line. This line also exits out of the ignition switch and is usually colored red. Again, double-check before you tap the line.

1 Most new stereos come with a mounting bracket that is to be installed into the dashboard of the car, and secured with mounting tabs. The stereo then slides into this bracket, and can't be easily removed. This, of course, is to prevent theft, but can be a huge pain if you make a mistake while installing the unit.

2 The newly installed stereo will not only sound better, but it will give your car an updated look that brings it into the twenty-first century. No more AM/FM radios or 8-tracks here!

- Antenna Connection. The antenna should have an RF connector on it that plugs into the back of the radio. This is a standard connector, and every car and radio should have matching connectors and receptacles.
- Power Antenna Switch. If your car has a power antenna, then it will need a signal from the radio to indicate that the radio has indeed been turned on. If your radio doesn't have one of these switches, then you can connect the power line for the antenna to the switched power line. This, of course, means that your antenna will be up anytime that your ignition is on.
- Ground. Make sure that you connect this to a nearby spot on the chassis. It's wise to use one of the nuts or bolts that mount the radio to the chassis.

It's also a wise idea to place a small fuse in the lines that power the radio. For the most part, either the continuous power or switched power line will carry most of the current. Find out which from the stereo installation instructions and install a small fuse in this line, if the stereo didn't come with one already.

ELECTRICAL

PROJECT 94
• TROUBLESHOOTING
ELECTRICAL PROBLEMS

 Time: As long as it takes

 Tools: Multitester

 Talent:

 Applicable Years: All

 Tab: –

 Tinware: New fuses

 Tip: Do some preliminary checks first, and then make a battle plan for isolating the problem.

 PERFORMANCE GAIN: No more electrical gremlins

COMPLEMENTARY MODIFICATION: Install/replace light bulbs, fuses, relays

Intermittent and annoying electrical problems are common with older cars. Example: A dashboard light goes on when you hit the brake, but only when the rear defogger is on, or the radio only works when you are in reverse. As bizarre as it sounds, electrical problems like these are very common on older cars, and unfortunately they can be quite difficult to fix.

What typically goes wrong with the wiring on these cars? Several things can happen. First and foremost, every time the car is sold, there is a high chance the new owner will do some modification to the wiring that only he or she will know about. The installation of a new stereo, power mirrors, a radar detector, or the worst of all, an alarm system, can seriously mess up your wiring configuration, if not performed correctly. You're left holding the mess, armed with only a few sporadic clues as to what is causing the problem. Troubleshooting electrical problems is a tough chore, and one that most automotive repair shops will not perform without telling you they will charge you their $80-an-hour diagnostic fee.

This project will give you some tips for troubleshooting your electrical system, but it's not meant to be a step-by-step guide for fixing all of your problems. That would take almost as many pages as are contained in this book!

The first step in troubleshooting is to make sure that you are armed with all the information that you can get. Namely, the most important item you need to get your hands on is a copy of the electrical diagrams for your year car. At the time of this writing, they are available from a few sources. Check the information sources section in the back of this book for more details. These diagrams are essential for troubleshooting electrical problems.

One of the most common problems is the continuous drain on the battery. One example would be a situation where you leave the car sitting for a week or two, and the battery becomes completely drained. This means that something is "on" inside the car, bleeding the battery of power. Start by disconnecting your battery ground, and connecting an ammeter to the battery negative and to the chassis. The ammeter will show the amount of current that your electrical system is draining from the battery. When you hook the meter up, it will most likely show that there is some small current flowing through the system. Don't start the car or turn on any electrical accessories, because this might blow up your meter. Disconnect the front luggage compartment light before beginning any testing.

Now, move to the fuse box in the front trunk, and start removing fuses. See Project 26 for a picture of the fuse box located in the front trunk. Carefully watch the ammeter to see if the current drops to zero when a particular fuse is pulled. If it does, then you have successfully isolated the electrical circuit with the problem. You are more than halfway to solving your problem. Look at the electrical diagrams and you should be able to tell what components are located on that circuit. Try disconnecting each one, while watching the ammeter, and you should find the culprit.

If pulling fuses doesn't reveal anything, try pulling out the various relays. Sometimes a relay will be powered on, but the device it controls will be disconnected. This may lead to gradual battery drain. One example of this is the heater levers between the seats that control the blower motor in the engine compartment. If the blower motor is disconnected, but the levers are pulled up, the relay will be activated, and the battery will slowly drain down.

While we're on the subject of wiring diagrams, in 1975 Porsche switched from using typical voltage wiring diagrams to using a current flow diagram. How do you read a current flow diagram? It took me a little time to figure it out. Imagine that you are looking at a diagram that shows waterfalls emptying into a lake. At the bottom of the page (electrical ground), is similar to a large lake that the waterfalls empty into. At the top of the page (high-voltage potential) is similar to the top of the cliff, right before the water falls off the edge. Each path that the current diagram shows can be interpreted as a separate waterfall that turns a small turbine and generator as it falls down into the lake. The electrical accessory can be seen as the generator. The battery of the car is similar to a pump that pumps water from the lake back up to the cliff.

After you get used to them, you will undoubtedly find that the current flow diagrams are much easier to read, primarily because they separate circuits from one another. You don't need to look at one circuit that you don't care about, just to find an electrical fault in another. The current flow diagram can tell you everything that you need to know right away.

Another common electrical problem is the device that just won't work. If you carefully look at the electrical diagrams, you will notice that there are actually six points of failure for most electrical devices on the 911. For lack of a better example, we'll use a blower motor to explain and demonstrate the electrical troubleshooting process.

Starting from the rear of the electrical chain, the first point to be concerned about is the actual device itself. You can start the troubleshooting process by testing the motor. Unplug it and apply 12V DC to the blower motor to see if it will turn. It if doesn't then you have a problem with your blower motor.

While the motor is unplugged, another excellent test to perform is to check the electricity in the wires leading to the blower motor. If all the switches are on, and there is no power going to the blower motor, then the problem lies somewhere else.

The next spot to check would be the relay for the blower motor. Consult the electrical diagrams to determine which one is the correct relay. When the switch is pulled for the blower motor, the relay should make a slight clicking noise on and off. Swapping out relays with one that is known to work is a good method of checking the proper operation of the relay as well.

If the relay checks out, then you want to make sure that the fuse is still good. Identify the proper fuse, and check to make sure that it has not blown. Also, the long tubular fuses that the 911 uses are susceptible to corrosion building up on the terminals. Make sure that the fuses are clean and securely seated. If necessary, check the continuity across the two points that hold and mount the fuse. Photo five in Project 26 shows the location of the fuse box in the front trunk, on the left side.

Many electrical components on the car are also switched through the ignition switch—allowing them to be turned on and off with the ignition. If your blower motor doesn't work along with a host of other equipment, then you might have a faulty electrical ignition switch. One clear symptom of this is the blower motor turning on and off as you jiggle the key back and forth. For ignition switch replacement procedures, see Project 91.

The switch for the device itself may be faulty. In the case of the rear blower motor, the switch is connected to the red handles on the floor of the car. Check the switch with a continuity tester to make sure that it is working properly.

Finally, if all the other tests fail to locate the problem, the wiring may be at fault. Especially on older cars, the wires have a tendency to become brittle, and sometimes break, even if the outer insulation is intact. Using a continuity tester, check each of the wires in the harness that powers the blower motor to see if any have lost continuity.

If all of these steps fail to pinpoint the problem, then you probably made a mistake somewhere along the line, or there might be a short circuit somewhere in the switch or the wiring of the car. Only painstaking testing using a continuity tester will be able to locate such a problem.

SECTION ELEVEN
MISCELLANEOUS

This section contains all the projects that didn't quite fit into any of the other predefined categories. Take a look at the Personal Touches project for my pick of the most interesting and unique additions that various owners have made to their 911s. Car bras, bolt removal, wheel selection and car care are also detailed in the projects within this section.

MISCELLANEOUS
PROJECT 95 • EDM BROKEN BOLT AND STUD REMOVAL

 Time: As long as it takes

 Tools: EDM type removal machine

 Talent: –

 Applicable Years: All

 Tab: $100-$300

 Tinware: New studs

 Tip: Some tasks should be left to a professional.

PERFORMANCE GAIN: Getting your engine back on the road

COMPLEMENTARY MODIFICATION: Clean and/or bead blast your engine parts

There is a sinking feeling that you get when you break off a stud in your very expensive Porsche 911 engine case. Or transmission case, or the rear calipers—that aren't made anymore and took six months to find. Never fear, these problems have a solution, one that most people haven't even heard of.

My own personal dilemma occurred when I was removing the engineering marvels called Dilavar studs from my 3.0-liter engine case. See Project 12, Engine Teardown, for a more detailed description of this laborious process, which involved several specialized tools, including a blowtorch! However it happened, I was left with a broken stud in my engine case. Repeated attempts to grip it with a pair of Vise-Grips proved fruitless. An attempt at welding a nut to the Dilavar studs also resulted in failure and a string of shouted obscenities.

All was not well in my world when I phoned Alex Wong of Precision Tech Motorsports for advice. His solution was to take the case to Tap-Ex, a company I had never heard of, but which I will now never forget.

Tap-Ex is owned by John Blackwell, who is probably one of the country's premier experts at removing

1 Your worst nightmare! This head stud has been broken off in the case. This particular stud was a Dilavar stud, which cannot be easily welded to, and has a real tendency to break. The 911 exhaust studs located in the cylinder heads in particular tend to shatter and break because they have been tempered repeatedly by the heat from the engine's exhaust system.

2 As with any precision machining process, the setup process must be performed very carefully. The engine block must be placed exactly square to the disintegration tool, or the electrode might wear away the inside threads of the hole instead of the broken stud.

3 The electrode is a hollow copper tube that is positioned carefully with respect to the broken stud. The electrode must be positioned square to the case, or it might damage the threads as it wanders off course.

4 The engine block is covered with plastic to keep the coolant and lubricant from spraying around the shop. The coolant serves a dual purpose: to cool the area that is being disintegrated, and to carry away bits of metal from the area. In this case, we attempted to cover up the case so that the fine particles of metal wouldn't find their way into the recesses of the engine. To put it mildly, we were not successful, and the engine case had to come apart to be cleaned.

broken studs from just about anything. The tools in his arsenal involve a set of machines called electrical discharge machines, or EDM. EDM pass a large electrical current through metal, literally zapping away bits of material until nothing remains. The process is a rare sight and is utterly fascinating to watch.

The beauty of John's process is that it is only destructive to the bolt or stud being removed. A small

5 Sparks fly from the stud as it is slowly disintegrated. As the machine automatically drives the electrode deeper into the case, the operator must be careful to watch for the point where the electrode hits the bottom of the stud. The machine will pause for a brief moment when the electrode is not contacting any metal, and then start eating into the case when the electrode hits the bottom of the hole.

6 The hollow electrode burns away the middle of the stud, leaving both the center core, and the outer threads in the case. When the electrode reaches the bottom of the case, the center core can be easily removed.

7 The outer threads that remain are now significantly weaker, and can be simply removed using a beveled tool inserted into the inner section of the threads. The hollowed-out stud is then easily backed out of the case with an extractor tool.

8 The usefulness of this process is clearly shown by this photo that John had in his collection. Anyone who has worked extensively on older 911s knows that the machine is set up to remove an old broken exhaust stud. A job that would have been nearly impossible to do without removing and tearing down the engine is now completed in under an hour. $200 versus a complete engine rebuild? Kind of puts things in perspective.

electrode is used to literally burn away the stud, making it increasingly easier to remove with an extractor tool. With my 3.0-liter aluminum case, the Dilavar stud had broken off on one of the cylinders, and was very difficult to reach with normal tools. I could have opted for the traditional approach of having my machine shop drill out the hole, but if something went wrong,

then the case might be permanently damaged. In addition, the Dilavar studs don't make the best candidates for drilling.

The first step is to mount the case flat on the tool bed. It's important to have a straight line down the hole for the machine to burn away the stud. A hollow copper tube that is smaller in diameter than the stud was used as the electrode in this case. The electrode burned away the middle part of the stud, leaving a core and the outer threads. Because the electrode is disintegrated along with the stud, it's quite difficult to figure out when the electrode has reached the bottom of the case. When operating the machine, John needs to be attentive for the one- to two-second delay that occurs as the tool pauses at the end of the hole.

The process begins literally with sparks flying. As the electrical current burns away the middle of the stud, sparks and small bits of metal are thrown out of the case. The coolant that is sprayed on the whole process serves a dual purpose—to cool the area and also to remove the little bits of metal that are burned off. John covered the case with a clear plastic sheet so that we could observe what was happening without getting hit by any flying debris or coolant.

When the electrode reaches the bottom of the case and the machine is stopped, the center core of the stud can easily be picked out of the hole using a pair of needle-nose pliers. At this point, only the thin outer edge of the stud remains in the case, and it can be easily removed with a simple extractor tool.

While a lifesaver, this process did have one major drawback. It was impossible to keep the coolant out of the inside of the case. Since the coolant was used to wash away all the small bits of metal from the process, the entire inside of the case became contaminated with a fine grit that you could feel with your fingers. That, of course, meant that the entire bottom end of the motor needed to be rebuilt—something I had hoped to avoid.

When I went back to pick up the case, John had a whole stack of cylinder heads from a manufacturer that he was working on. He routinely takes on jobs that are shipped from all around the country. If you have a tough job that needs the help of such a process, John is your man. The tab for the process was about $160 for both the broken Dilavar stud and a small sheet metal screw that had been broken off as well in my engine case.

Contact:
Tap-Ex /(310)323-3834
1940 W. Rosecrans Ave.
Gardena, CA 90249

MISCELLANEOUS

PROJECT 96 • STUBBORN BOLT/STUD REMOVAL

 Time: Many hours

 Tools: Stud remover, angle grinder, Dremel tool, WD-40

 Talent:

 Applicable Years: All

 Tab: Could be big bucks if you destroy the part

 Tinware: New bolt/stud

 Tip: This project is full of tips.

 PERFORMANCE GAIN: Getting the bolt out and getting the job done

COMPLEMENTARY MODIFICATION: –

If you are planning to restore a car that is even slightly old, then you will undoubtedly come across the old nut, bolt, or stud that is rusted solid and won't come off. This project will expose you to some of the methods used by several of the "experts" in the field.

The first step in getting rusty or stuck fasteners off is to perform a preemptive strike. It is often the case that you find a nut or stud will not come off after you have already stripped or damaged it. If you think that the nut might give you problems, it's far better to tackle the removal process carefully, rather than end up destroying one of your precious parts.

If you are planning to remove an old rusty bolt in a day or two, it's a wise idea to soak the area with a good lubricant like WD-40. The lubricant will eventually soak down and penetrate into the joint, making it easier to remove and break apart. This seeping process takes time, however, and the bolt should be soaked the night before you attempt to remove it at the very least. This will place you a step ahead in the battle to remove it.

When removing these old bolts, it's very important to have the right tools for the job. A properly fitting wrench is essential. Many people often use the

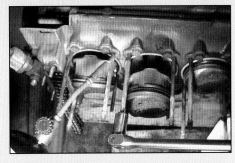

1 The propane torch is one of my personal favorite tools. Make sure that you heat the case and not the stud. You will notice that it may take a long time for the case to warm up. Keep the torch focused on the area and don't let it stray onto the stud. The white inner portion of the flame is the hottest—the blue part indicates a cooler region. Make sure that you only use the torch in a well-ventilated area, as the propane will create harmful carbon monoxide gas.

wrong tool for the wrong bolt. The 12-point star bolts on the CV joints of some Porsches are an excellent example. A simple hex Allen key tool will fit into the bolts, and will probably be able to remove most of them, but chances are that one of the bolts will become stripped. Using the right-sized tool to remove a fastener means that you are increasing the odds that it will come off easily.

For pulling studs, Snap-On offers an excellent collet-based stud-removal tool that does the job very well without damaging the stud. This tool latches onto and compresses around the threads of the stud, and then squeezes them tight. Then the tool and the stud can be removed. If you are removing head studs out of an engine case, an extra Vise-Grip or two might be useful as well to get an extra bit of torque on the studs.

Exhaust studs are notoriously difficult to remove from the heads, and they also have a tendency to snap when removing heat exchangers. Make sure that the area is lubricated heavily before even attempting to remove a rusty heat exchanger. Unfortunately, if the stud snaps off, there really isn't too much that you can do. Since the studs are heated by the heads, they become very brittle over time. Basically the only way to remove a broken head stud is to have it drilled out or removed using an EDM process (see Project 95).

A tool that may help you out when you need to remove bolts is a common propane torch, or even better, an oxy-acetylene torch. Propane torches are available at most hardware stores, and are useful beyond belief. Particularly on bolts and studs that have had Loctite used on them, the torch can give you an extra advantage in removal.

Take the torch, and heat up the surrounding metal that the stud is embedded into. This will help to melt any Loctite on the threads, and will also help to expand the metal that is surrounding the stud. Do not apply heat directly to the stud, as this will make the stud heat up and become even more stuck in the hole. If you are removing a head stud from an engine case, you will find that it will take a surprisingly long time to heat up the case. Aluminum and magnesium

2 The tools of destruction and mayhem are shown here. The Dremel rotary tool (upper right) with flexible attachment (not shown) is best suited for cutting off small nuts, bolts, or studs. These will account for about 95 percent of your problems. The angle grinder (left) is for more serious tasks when rusted nuts must be completely ground down. WD-40 is an excellent penetrant for removing rusted and stuck bolts. The Snap-On stud remover (lower-middle-left) is a hard-to-find tool, yet is very useful for removing those troublesome studs. Finally, the electric impact wrench is a useful tool for removing nuts that are mounted with a lot of torque.

conduct heat very well, so make sure that you focus the torch on the case for a while before you try to remove any studs. Also make sure to use the torch only in a well-ventilated area.

On the opposite side of the equation, you can sometimes use coolant to help remove a stuck bolt. One of the best-kept secrets is the "compressed air in a can" that your local office supply store sells specifically for blowing dust out of old computer equipment. If you hold the can upside down, the gas inside (which is not really ordinary air) will drip out as a very cold liquid. You can drip this liquid onto bolts and into areas that you might be having trouble with. Be careful though, as the cold will have a tendency to make the metal increasingly brittle and prone to breaking. Use eye and skin protection when using coolants—they can be deceptively dangerous.

The application of heat and cold together can be a powerful combination. As the joint heats up, and then is cooled again, rust and Loctite may break free from the rapid expansion and contraction. There is no real exact science for this, so trial and error is the rule of thumb.

Another important point to remember is to make sure that a nut or bolt that you are trying to remove can actually be removed. It is often the case that someone will try to remove an embedded stud or a nut that has been welded on, only to find that this is an impossible task. The long starter bolt on the 914 and the welded nut on the inner fender strut of the 911 are two examples of this type of fastener. Before you dig out the angle grinder, check and double-check to make sure you aren't missing something that's not too obvious.

Sometimes it makes sense to take a nut and have it welded to a stud that is stuck. This will allow you to place a wrench on the nut and hopefully remove the stud. Make sure that you clean all of the rust, debris, oil, and anything else that might be on the stud before you attempt to weld to it. Sometimes the stud will be old and brittle, and may not take well to welding. This

is usually the case with the exhaust studs. Also, most studs can only be effectively welded to if they are made of steel. The alloy Dilavar head studs of the later 911 engines cannot have nuts welded to them—the nuts just break right off as soon as you try to turn them.

Another useful tool is the impact wrench. This is most helpful when you are trying to remove a nut that turns on a bearing, or one that is attached with a great amount of force. The steering wheel nut is an example of one that turns. The impact wrench "hits" the nut with repeated blows, knocking it loose. It's a very useful tool, and will save you plenty of time when you need to remove one of these specialty bolts.

The weapon of choice when all else fails is the Dremel tool or its big brother, the angle grinder. These two tools of destruction really don't stop at anything when it comes to cutting through metal. The Dremel tool is my personal favorite because it is so small and can be positioned and placed in so many different positions. Adding to its versatility is the fact that you can add a flexible shaft to the tool that allows you to place the rotating blade just about anywhere you can reach.

The Dremel, or rotary tool, spins at about 50,000 rpm and uses small ceramic-like discs to cut and grind through steel. There are small carbon-fiber reinforced discs available that are more expensive than the regular discs, but they last longer, and are more effective at cutting through steel quicker. I recommend using these discs—particularly if you can buy a large bag of them at a swap meet or other venue. Make sure that you don't ever use the Dremel tool without eye protection.

The angle grinder makes no apologies for being the most destructive of all tools. The grinding wheel can grind, wear, cut, and melt away steel much faster than any other tool. It's especially useful for grinding off nuts and studs that are so badly rusted that there is no way to get a tool on them. Make sure that you use appropriate eye, ear, and nose/throat protection when using the grinder, as this tool kicks up a lot of small metal particles into the air.

When all else fails, you can sometimes use a hand drill to drill out an embedded or broken stud. While not the prettiest solution, the hand drill is still an effective method of removal. Make sure that you start drilling with a very small drill bit and gradually increase the diameter of the bit. Also make sure that you use plenty of lubricant. When the hole that you have drilled gets to be about the size of the stud, try to remove the remains of the stud using a pick. Be careful not to damage the threads of the hole by drilling too large of a hole. When you are finished, chase a tap down the hole to clear out the threads, or if it's damaged, thread the hole to a larger diameter.

MISCELLANEOUS
PROJECT 97 • PERSONAL TOUCHES

 Time: infinite

 Tools: Unlimited

 Talent:

Applicable Years: All

Tab: $1-$5,000

 Tinware: Just about everything in the catalog

 Tip: Keep an eye out at swap meets for cool additions that can add to your 911.

 PERFORMANCE GAIN: The sky is the limit.

COMPLEMENTARY MODIFICATION: Wash your car.

As principal photographer for the internet-based Porsche parts company Pelican Parts, I've had the opportunity to photograph a lot of different modifications that people have made on their 911s over the years. While not all of them improve the looks of the car in my opinion, it can certainly be said that Porsche owners like to modify their cars more than most people. Whether it's the addition of Turbo flares and body panels or the complete installation of a Chevy V-8 engine, if you can think of it, it's likely that some passionate 911 owner has spent hundreds of hours and thousands of dollars to do it. This project is designed to give you some ideas for projects for your 911.

1 In the 1980s, Porsche shipped an anniversary edition of the 911 that had painted wheels that matched the color of the car. This is a popular modification for all 911s. Painting your wheels to match the color of the car is not a difficult job, and depending on the look of your car, it may improve the appearance significantly.

2 An uncommon sight is the rear fog lamp. This fog lamp was only sold on European cars. The addition of the rear fog lamp adds a unique European look to the car. The car in this picture is somewhat of a mismatch—the rear bumper guards are the larger U.S. type, and the rear fog lamp and turn signal lenses are European.

3 The addition of an original Porsche wooden wheel is almost always a nice touch. Originally shipped as an option on some early 911s and 912s, the wooden wheel stands out as a great addition to an already classy car. The after-market Nardi wheels from the 1960s and 1970s are also very popular among collectors. Depending upon your style, you may want to change your steering wheel to something increasingly classic, or a style more tuned toward the racing motif.

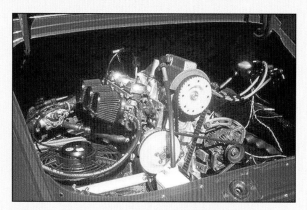

4 Perhaps the most popular upgrade to the 911 is the addition of a much higher-horsepower motor. While most owners choose this path, Wayne Sievers decided to reduce the weight of the car with a much smaller engine. He installed a 993-cc Geo Metro engine and radiator, complete with custom sheet metal and engine mounts into his 1972 911 coupe. The 3-cylinder engine uses Mikuni carburetors, a custom-made crankfire ignition unit, and requires no modifications to the chassis of the car. The smaller engine reduces the entire weight of the car down to 2,009 pounds, and makes the performance of the car similar to that of the 912.

5 Almost exactly the opposite of the 3-cylinder motor, here is an example of a Chevy V-8 motor installed into a Porsche 911. While often frowned upon by 911 owners, the Chevy engine is a source of good, cheap power, and can create a well-balanced 911 that takes off like a rocket. In this case, the engine was also moved forward into a midengined position, in order to better balance the car. This engine is literally sitting in the back seat of this 911.

6 Little graphics and decals that were anything but stock can dress up and improve the overall look of your car. While it may make concours judges cringe, the average Joe on the street will appreciate

the creative intent and the improved look. Tom Sharpes of the Orange County PCA (Porsche Club of America) Region came up with this snazzy way to dress up the top of the cooling fan.

7 On early 911s, the grille-mounted fog lamps are a semiunique addition. These slick-looking lamps were an option, and are very hard to find nowadays. However, aftermarket reproduction kits are available. A

kit that contains all the parts to perform this conversion costs around $300. Original fog lamps are extremely difficult to find.

8 One of the most popular styles for the 911 is the RS Replica. The 1973 911RS is one of the most-sought-after and most-replicated cars around. The conversions can range from the simple addition of the fiberglass bodywork and famous lettering to the more complex task of installing a 2.7 RS-spec engine. Either way, replicating the look of the 911RS is a very popular project for early 911 owners.

9 White gauge faces are another neat option for giving your interior a unique look. The faces can be installed by painstakingly removing each front glass from all of the gauges. Replacing the faces usually requires that you have your tachometer and speedometer recalibrated.

MISCELLANEOUS
PROJECT 98
• THE PORSCHE 912

 Time: A lifetime

 Tools: All of them

 Talent:

 Applicable Years: 1965-1969, 1976

 Tab: About $8-$10K for a good car

 Tinware: A Porsche 912

 Tip: 912s carry a mystique all their own—buy one for its handling and appearance, not its power.

 PERFORMANCE GAIN: Better handling than the 911

COMPLEMENTARY MODIFICATION: –

OK, admittedly, this is not a project. However, I felt it is necessary to dedicate some space to what is perhaps the most overlooked Porsche model, the 912. A rather simplistic explanation of the 912 is that the 912 is actually a 911 with a 356 engine installed in it. While that glosses over some of the important distinguishing characteristics between the 911 and the 912, for the most part the technical information on the 911 can be very easily applied to the 912 chassis. For engine information, the 912 owners can look for resources pertaining to the time-honored Porsche 356 line.

When Porsche introduced the 911 to succeed the popular 356, it quickly realized that it was lacking an affordable model to offer the buyers who had been purchasing 356s. While a 1600 SC coupe cost 16,450 marks at the time, the new 911 cost a whopping 22,900 marks. The demand for a lower-cost Porsche based on the 911 was met when the European 912 was released in 1965. A year later, the 912 was introduced to America, and quickly became a bestseller.

The 912 was discontinued after 1969, and was replaced with the 911T, a lower-cost version of the 911. The 912 model made a return to the United States again in 1976 with the introduction of the 912E. The 912E was based on the 1976 911 chassis, but incorporated the motor from the Porsche 914 2.0-liter. While the engine components were nearly identical to the 914, the 912E incorporated a L-Jetronic fuel injection system specific to that model year car. Unfortunately, since the car was only made for a single year, replacement fuel injection and exhaust parts are very difficult to find. The 912E indeed is an interesting and somewhat rare car, as there were only a little more than 2,000 ever made. However, because of their relatively low-powered engine and the difficulty in finding spare parts, they are not highly sought after.

The original early 912 was met with much enthusiasm for buyers who were looking for an affordable Porsche. The 912 received almost all of the updates and benefits of the 911 without the high price tag. The price of an early 912 with a four-speed transmission was 16,250 marks.

The primary difference between the 911 and the 912 is in the drivetrain. The 912 uses a four-speed gearbox (five-speed optional), and a four-cylinder 1,600-cc engine that is derived from the 356SC engine. Although virtually similar to the 356SC engine, the 912 engine was detuned from 95 to 90 horsepower. The comparable 1965 911 has 130 horsepower.

Despite the 912's absence of horsepower when compared to the 911, the 912 proved very popular, particularly for club racing events, in which speed and power are not necessarily the most important factors in reducing lap times. The 912, with its smaller, lighter engine, is much nimbler than the heavier 911. The 912, with a weight of 970 kilograms (2,134 pounds), is a full 10 percent lighter than the 1,080-kilogram (2,376-pound) 911. Almost all of the 911's extra weight is located in the larger, heavier engine in the rear of the car.

The extra weight of the 911 meant that it is a bit "tail happy" and tends to exhibit a bit of oversteer, especially around tight corners. In an attempt to compensate for this, the factory placed two 25-pound weights inside the bumpers of the 1967 and 1968 911s. Needless to say, the nimbler 912 didn't need this extra weight, because it was much better balanced.

The motor mounts in the 912 were also different from those in the 911, which led to better weight distribution. The 912 engine was much shorter than the 911 engine, and thus was mounted farther forward than its 911 counterpart. In

1 The engine compartment of a typical 912. The engine is basically the major difference between the 911 and the 912. The 912 engine is a four-cylinder motor with dual carburetors on each cylinder bank. The engine shared almost all of its parts with the 356, and used special sheet metal and motor mounts to fit inside the 911. The 912 engine with its stronger crank is a sought-after item for placement in older 356s.

order to adjust for a lighter car, the 912 incorporated suspension components that were specifically tuned for the lighter weight and better balance of the car.

Other than the engine and slight suspension modifications, there were very few differences between the 911 and the 912. Some of the early 912s had three-gauge clusters instead of the five-gauge clusters used on the 911. The 912 engine compartment had a rain deflector plate that was fitted over the engine grille to prevent water from leaking down onto the generator. Slight variations also existed in the some of the welded chassis components, and various interior trim options were slightly different throughout the years. For more information on the specific minute variations,

consult *The 911 & 912 Porsche—A Restorer's Guide to Authenticity* by Dr. B. Johnson. This book is a great reference for restoring both 911s and 912s and concentrates mostly on the interior and exterior trim of the cars.

So where can 912 owners turn for information? Most 911 reference books (including this one) are applicable to most areas of the 912, with the exception of the engine. The interior, exterior, brakes, suspension, and chassis are so similar that any technical information written about the early 911 will usually apply to the 912 as well. For technical information on the 912 engine, most owners can reference one of the many 356 repair manuals available. In some ways, 912 owners can be said to have the best of both worlds!

MISCELLANEOUS
PROJECT 99 • USING CAR BRAS

 Time: 30 minutes

 Tools: —

 Talent: 👤

 Applicable Years: All

 Tab: $125

 Tinware: Front car bra, mirror bras

 Tip: Make sure that the bra is tight—flapping bras can do more damage to your paint than rocks from the road

 PERFORMANCE GAIN: Protection of your paint job

COMPLEMENTARY MODIFICATION: Mirror bras

1 **Left:** When installing the bra on your 911, make sure it's tight and properly attached. Poorly installed bras can do more damage than rocks on the road. There are a few different types of bras, depending upon your 911's year. Some allow you to easily open the hood, and others use the hood as an attachment point.
Right: The MagBra is an interesting alternative to the cloth bra. It is made of a material that is similar to the one used for refrigerator magnets. Although it does not offer as complete coverage as the traditional bra, the MagBra is less likely to damage your paint if it gets wet, and won't do damage by flapping in the wind.

Many hazards exist on just about every road in the world. None can be as damaging to your paint as the gravel, rocks, and other debris kicked up by cars in front of you.

Without a doubt, the most effective method of protection is to use a front cover, comically named a "car bra." Many people feel that the look of the car bra detracts from the overall lines of the car. However, there isn't much else available to protect the front surface of your car. Most of the bras are made out of a stretchy type of black vinyl that has a leathery feel to it. The bra is attached to the front of the car and protects the bumper, hood, and sides of the fenders from rocks and gravel. The bottom side of the bra is lined with a feltlike material. Not only does the bra protect your car from scratches, but it will reduce the amount of damage flying rocks inflict. Expensive paint chips can be minimized by the use of a front-mounted bra.

There are basically two types of bras for the 911s. There's the one-piece unit that covers the entire front of the car. This one doesn't allow you to open the hood without removing the bra. The other type is a two-piece unit that separately covers the fenders and the hood. This type allows you to open the hood when the bra is attached. All the bras must be ordered specifically for your year car. The 1965–1973 911s typically use the same bra. The 1974–1989 cars used a later-style bra. The bras typically have openings for the U.S. fog lamps. Some bras can be specially tailored to your specific car. For example, you can eliminate the license plate opening, front bumper guard openings, fog lamp openings, or add holes for the headlamp washers. Either way, it's smart to get a bra that fits your car well.

Without a doubt, bras can be unwieldy and cumbersome, and it's wise to follow a few rules of thumb when using one. The first rule is to never leave the bra on the car when it's wet. This will create an environment for condensation and steam to build up underneath the bra. This resulting water vapor can seriously damage the paint underneath, either by cracking the clear coat or altering the shade of the paint. It's a good idea to get in the habit of removing the bra immediately from the car whenever it gets wet. You would hate to have to put the bra on the car just to cover up damage that it was supposed to prevent!

Watch the seams of the bra. Beverly Frohm of the Orange Coast Region of the Porsche Club of America recommends that you use soft felt squares on any point where there is a seam touching metal. She recommends using a minimum of six of these squares—one for each of the headlight openings, one each for the top of the fenders, and two side by side on the hood. Body flex during routine driving may cause the chassis to flex enough to cause substantial rubbing damage, especially on the hood. Adding these felt squares reduces the likelihood of damage.

Finally, the most important thing to do is to keep the bra clean. It won't help your car if dirt is trapped between the bra and the paint—it will only result in scratches It's usually not wise to purchase a used bra for your car, because it will probably be too dirty to amply protect your car from damage.

MISCELLANEOUS
PROJECT 100 • POLISHING ALLOY WHEELS

Time: 2-10 hours per wheel

Tools: Hand drill, electric sander, sanding block

Talent:

Applicable Years: All

Tab: $25

Tinware: Sandpaper, polishing compound, buffing wheels

Tip: Plan on spending a long time polishing your wheels for a great shine.

PERFORMANCE GAIN: Better looking wheels

COMPLEMENTARY MODIFICATION: Polish wheel center caps, install new tires

One of the most popular cosmetic upgrades that Porsche owners perform on their cars is to polish their alloy wheels. This is a task that is not to be entered into lightly, and requires quite a bit of effort and elbow grease to get it right. Proper preparation and meticulous attention to detail are necessary to avoid creating a sloppy-looking job.

Preparing the wheels for polishing is probably the most difficult aspect of the job. Most of the factory alloy wheels have been anodized with a hard protective covering. On top of the anodized coating, the factory often applied black paint. In order to perform a good job of polishing your alloy wheels, you will have to remove both the paint and the anodized coating. Keep in mind that the coatings on your wheels may be different from what you might expect because the previous owner of your car might have already had them refinished. The process of polishing and painting works best if the tires are removed from the wheel.

Paint Removal

Assuming that your wheels have black paint on them, the first step that you need to do is strip the paint. Purchase some brush-on paint remover and apply a coat to the paint that is on the wheels. Don't continue to brush the remover, as this will only make it evaporate. Make sure that you use thick chemical-proof gloves and wear old clothes—paint remover will burn right through your skin if given the chance! Make sure that you do this in a well-ventilated area.

After you apply the remover, leave it there for 5 to 10 minutes. You should be able to see the paint begin to bubble off of the surface. Using a piece of steel wool, scrub and scrape the paint off of the surface of the wheel. Using a plastic paint scraper may help remove chunks of paint as well. Apply another coat of remover when no more paint will come off, and repeat the process until the wheel is free of paint.

Anodization Removal

Once your wheel is free of paint, you will need to remove the hard, silver-colored anodized coating. Remember that not all wheels came with this coating, so yours may not require this step. Simply put, you need to sand down the anodized coating until it is no longer on the wheel. You can do this by hand, but it will probably take many, many hours, and you will probably need a new hand when you are done.

You can also use an electric sander or a buffing wheel on a hand-held buffer or hand drill. For the electric sander, use 180-grit sandpaper, and make sure that you change it often, as the coating will easily wear out the sandpaper. Follow up your initial sanding with a finer 240 grit.

If you are using a buffing wheel, start out with 80-grit grinding paste. When you apply the paste to the wheel, make sure that you let it dry out a bit before you use it. The wet paste will not work as well because the water will actually act as a lubricant. After a few minutes of buffing the wheel, you will see the anodized coating begin to come off. Make sure that you keep applying new paste to the wheel as it wears out. Clean the coating out of the buffing wheel with a small buff rake, as this will help the overall process. Again, patience is a virtue here. Turn on the radio and make sure that you take your time.

Another trick that I heard about but did not have enough time to actually try out before writing this book was to use lye on the surface of the wheel to remove the anodized coating. Lye is one of the most caustic and poisonous substances around, so exercise extreme caution when handling and disposing of it. Lye mixed with water is supposed to instantly dissolve the anodized coating.

Mirror Polishing

Once both the paint and the anodized coatings have been removed, then it's time to mirror polish the wheels. Beverly Frohm from the Orange County Region of the Porsche Club of America suggests using Mother's Wheel Polish, and cautions against using standard rubbing compound, as it can scratch your rims. Using a slightly damp rag, scoop out about two fingers' worth of polish. If you haven't done this before, I recommend that you use a flat part of the wheel to start with.

Using a circular motion, apply the polish in a similar manner to the application of car wax. Press down on the rag, but don't use too much force. Keep rubbing until the compound begins to disappear. At this point the rag will turn black, but don't worry, as this is a normal occurrence. Wipe off the wheel with a clean, dry cloth, and you will begin to see the shine coming out of the wheels. Again, patience and perseverance are key to doing a good job. Repeat the process of applying and rubbing down the wheel until you get the finish that you are looking for. Plan on spending a few hours on each wheel—any less, and it's probably not worth your starting the job.

Another good product worth mentioning is Wenol. This polishing compound reduces the amount of elbow grease that you need to produce a really good-quality shine. Wenol makes a line of products that work on the metal in a similar manner to the polishing compound, except that there is a type of chemical reaction as well, which helps to give a good shine with a minimal amount of work.

Don Haney of Pelican Parts has a special tip to offer for polishing wheels. Known for his immaculately polished Porsche wheel clocks, Don recommends spreading a little bit of baby powder on the surface of the wheel. When you blow away the baby powder it will reveal scratches in the surface of the wheel that are very hard to see with the naked eye. Go over these areas again with the polishing compound to remove the scratches.

Fixing Deep Scratches

Really deep scratches are best fixed by a wheel polishing professional, but there are some tips to hide and remove scratches from your wheel. Take some 1,500-grit sandpaper and wet it down with water. Using an even motion, carefully sand the area that is scratched, blending it into the surrounding area. This technique will be similar to color sanding paint on a car. To assist you with the sanding job, you can pur-

1 One of the most important aspects of paint application or removal is the proper masking of the wheel. With this particular wheel, it was desired to protect the outer rim of the wheel from the paint remover. The circular shape has been carefully masked off with blue plastic tape, and then covered with masking tape. The blue plastic tape bends and stretches much more easily than the masking tape and thus can be made to fit to curves a lot more smoothly.

2 Two options for your wheels are silver paint and full polishing. Without a doubt, the silver paint is the easiest option and is sometimes preferred by 911 owners. While full polishing may take several hours per wheel, silver paint can be applied to your wheels in an afternoon. These wheels were damaged in accidents. They are shown here sliced in half, in preparation to be turned into wall clocks.

chase special rubber pads at most automotive parts stores. These pads can help you sand more evenly than your fingers normally can.

Once the area where the scratch is located feels as smooth as the surrounding area, take some wet 2,000-grit sandpaper and go over the area again using the same motion and technique as previously used. Make sure that you keep the sandpaper wet—when you rinse it off, you are washing away tiny metal

3 Wenol polishing compounds and formulations give a really good mirror finish without a lot of elbow grease. The two varieties shown here reflect the coarse (red) formulation that is used to polish surfaces that are very dull. The milder compound (blue) both polishes to a mirror shine and protects the surface as well. Wenol can be used on just about any metallic surface, plated or polished.

particles that can ruin your sanding job. Once the area is smooth, simply repeat the steps previously described to polish the wheel.

Painting the Wheels

Painting is the easiest of the jobs described here. Start by elevating the wheels on a bench or table so that you can have good access to them. Again, remember to only work in a well-ventilated area. Start by carefully masking off any area of the wheel that you do not wish to have painted. This is not an easy job, as there are many curves and valleys in the typical 911 Fuchs wheels. Avoid using newspaper to mask your wheels as it is a bit too thin, and can bleed paint onto the aluminum finish. I prefer using pages from old magazines, as they are much thicker and will protect the unpainted areas much better.

The masking job needs to be almost perfect. Spend time making sure that straight lines are indeed straight, and not wavy. A poor masking job will make the wheels look very cheap and amateurish. Also make sure that you spend some time carefully masking the curves of the petals on the wheels.

When painting the wheels, it's wise to apply a thin layer of self-etching primer. This will help the paint adhere to the aluminum surface. When the primer has dried, take some 1,000-grit sandpaper and wet-sand the primer to make sure that it is perfectly smooth. Remember to keep the sandpaper wet all the time.

Now, apply a thin coat of the satin black aerosol paint. You will have to use trial and error to find the brand of paint you prefer—most garden-variety aerosol paints will be fine. Wait for the paint to dry and then apply another layer. If you would like a really smooth finish, wet-sand each layer of paint with 1,000-grit sandpaper. This, of course, significantly adds to the total time for the project.

When the paint has completely dried, remove the masking tape and paper. You should have a fine set of polished and painted wheels, shiny enough to rival any good concours car.

Wheel Maintenance

Caring for your wheels is the final part of the equation. If you drive your car, you're going to have to accept that the wheels will get dirty or scratched. Remember that if you remove the protective anodized coating from the wheels, they will have a greater chance of being scratched by dust and road debris.

To clean the wheels, you should treat them like you would treat your paint. Use soft terry cloth towels, and some specialized wheel cleaner that won't cloud up or tarnish the aluminum surface. I recommend P21S wheel cleaner, which seems to be very popular with 911 owners.

If your wheels get some scratches, you can simply rework them a bit with the polishing compound. I usually go over the wheels at least once or twice a year with the compound to remove any scratches or embedded dirt.

You also might want to place brake dust shields on the inside of your alloy wheels. These metal discs help to keep the dust and debris from your brakes from getting all over the outside of your wheels. The only downside to using discs like these is that they reduce the amount of air that cools the brake rotors.

Curb damage or deeper scratches can be removed by a good wheel polishing shop. It's important to take the wheels to a shop that knows what it's doing, otherwise they might grind and polish the wheels to an uneven shape. Have them check to make sure that the wheel is still perfectly round after the polishing is done.

PROJECT 101 • TIRE AND WHEEL SIZING ON THE 911

Time: 4 hours at a tire shop, many more in research

Tools: –

Talent: ▮▮

Applicable Years: All

Tab: $300-$1,000

Tinware: New tires, valve stems

Tip: Find a tire shop that will allow you to try fitting certain sizes and types of tires on your car, or find a friend who has a tire/wheel combination you like and borrow them.

PERFORMANCE GAIN: Good tires can increase your handling and brakinng significantly.

COMPLEMENTARY MODIFICATION: Upgrade to larger wheels

For this project, I polled a number of people on the Internet mailing list, Rennlist.org, in an attempt to figure out what the best and most popular combinations of tire and wheel sizes were for the various models of 911. Unfortunately, I confirmed what is inherently true about almost all 911 owners—they love to modify and tweak their cars. Out of all the responses, no two were exactly alike. I've compiled and summarized the feedback here so that you can make an educated decision when equipping your 911.

Let's talk for a few moments of tires in general. Although you can write volumes on tire sizing and design, we'll try to cover the basics here. Early tires had inner tubes, much like common bicycle tires. It's very uncommon to find these tires still fitted to 911s these days; however, if you pick up an older car, it may indeed still have the original tires on it.

With the advent of new materials, the tubeless tire has basically become the tire of choice. The tubeless tire has a bead that seals itself automatically against the rim when inflated. Tubeless tires are easier to mount on wheels, deflate more slowly when

punctured, and can be temporarily repaired without removing the tire from the wheel rim.

Tires are sized using a system that takes into account the tire's aspect ratio. This aspect ratio is a function of the tire's height with respect to its width. An example of a common European tire size is 195/65R15. The number 195 refers to the width of the tire in millimeters. The second number, 65, refers to the height of the tire as a percentage of the width (this number is also the tire's aspect ratio). Therefore 65 percent of the 195-millimeter width would give a tire height of about 127 millimeters. The letter following the width and aspect ratio is the tire's maximum speed safety ratings:

Q=99 miles per hour,	160 kilometers per hour
S=112 miles per hour,	180 kilometers per hour
T=118 miles per hour,	190 kilometers per hour
U=124 miles per hour,	200 kilometers per hour
H=130 miles per hour,	210 kilometers per hour
V=149 miles per hour,	240 kilometers per hour
W=168 miles per hour,	270 kilometers per hour
Y=186 miles per hour,	300 kilometers per hour
Z=149 miles per hour,	240 kilometers per hour and over

Needless to say, a good Z-rated tire should be more than adequate for nonsuicidal driving! The last number in the tire size is the wheel diameter in inches. In this case, 15 refers to a 15-inch-diameter wheel.

Tread is another important consideration in selecting a tire. You should select your tire based upon what type of driving you plan to do. With the 911, it's usually a bit more complicated, because most people don't drive them in all types of weather. With a family sedan located in a snowy environment, an all-weather tire is a natural choice. However, most 911 owners do not drive their cars in the snow or the rain.

In an ideal setting, such as on the race track, flat-surfaced tires called racing slicks are best, because a maximum amount of tire rubber is laid down on the road surface. However, slicks have almost no traction in wet weather. The water has a tendency to get under the tire and cause it to hydroplane by elevating the wheel onto a wedge of water as it is moving forward.

The array of choices for tire tread is way beyond the scope of this project. One rule of thumb is to make sure that you purchase a tire that is appropriate for your climate. Using a snow tire or all-weather tire on a 911 that is rarely driven in the snow will significantly reduce the tire's contact patch area and reduce cornering performance on dry roads. However, not equipping your

1 Shown here is a slightly rolled fender with a 7-inch wheel under it. Under some circumstances, the tire and wheel will fit with an appropriate amount of clearance. Differences in tire sizes, and differences in the bodies and construction of the 911 may give different results for different combinations of wheels and tires. Have patience, do some research, and make sure that you take your car to a tire shop that will let you try out different sizes of tires.

car for bad weather can result in disastrous effects in an unforeseen storm. If you drive your car only during the dry summer months, look for a conventional performance tire with a maximum-contact patch area.

Another important consideration is the tread wear and traction. The tread wear refers to the average number of miles that can be put on the tires before they need to be replaced. A tread wear indicator of 100 means that the tires should last 30,000 miles. An indicator of 80 means that the tires will last 20 percent less, or 24,000 miles. Wear is different for each car, and each driver's personal driving habits, but the various ratings are good for comparisons among different brands and different types of tires. Traction is related to the type of materials used in the tire. The more hard rubber is used, the longer the tires will last, but the hard rubber provides much less traction. A rating of "A" for traction is best. These tires will grip the road well, but will generally wear out faster than the "B" or "C" traction-rated tires.

It is important to consider another factor in addition to tread wear when selecting a tire. Most tires have a shelf life based on the rubber's natural process of breaking down and becoming brittle. It doesn't pay to purchase a 30,000-mile tire if you are only going to be putting 3,000 miles a year on your car. After 10 years, the rubber may be cracked and deteriorated beyond safe use, even if there is plenty of tread left on the wheel. This is also an important consideration if you are purchasing a 911 that has been in storage for many years. Although the tires may have plenty of tread on them, they may actually be dried out and ready to fail. If the tires develop cracks in the sidewalls from aging, they can blow out when heated up from driving. A blowout is a very bad situation, and can cause you to lose control of your car very quickly.

So, what tires and wheels can you fit on your 911? The early 911s didn't have any fender flares on either the front or the rear of the car. As a result, it's difficult to fit anything other than a 6-inch-wide wheel under either the front or rear fenders without adjusting the fenders or the suspension. The very rare 911R 7-inch wheel will fit, but at last check, these wheels were about $1,000 each. Fifteen- or 16-inch-diameter wheels should fit fine, as long as they aren't wider than 6 inches. In order to accommodate a 7-inch wheel to these early cars, you can trim the inside of the lip on the fenderwell, or you can roll the fenders outward. Sometimes you can make a wider rim fit by installing a smaller-profile tire, but this defeats the purpose of the larger rim, and may also make the tire fit poorly.

Rolling the fender involves using a baseball bat or long piece of pipe on the inside lip of your fender to push it out slightly. Many people do this to get a larger wheel or a larger tire to fit. However, many people don't prefer the look of the rolled fender, and it could adversely affect the resale value of the car. If you give the car a bit of negative camber, you can also make the 7-inch rims fit in the rear.

The 1969–1973 cars had a slight fender flare both front and rear, as did the 1974–1977 cars. However, easily fitting a 7-inch wheel under these fenders is difficult. To complicate the situation even more, there are many different tire sizes available nowadays that weren't available back when the cars were new.

With many of the older cars, the tire sizes that you can fit on the car often depends on the condition of the car. Sometimes the chassis are perfectly balanced from left to right, and sometimes they are slightly off from being in an accident, or simply from body sag. It's best to find a tire shop that will allow you to try out several tires on your car in order to find the best fit. Go in the afternoon on a slow day and talk with your tire salesman to see if he will let you size the tires on your car. If he won't then go to a different shop—there are plenty of them out there willing to cater to you, especially if you are going to shell out some money for high-performance tires.

A 205/50/16 tire will fit nicely on the 6-inch wheels that came stock with the early 911s. For a bit more aggressive profile, try installing a 225/50/16 on either the 6-inch or the 7-inch rims. Unfortunately, tire sizes differ from each manufacturer, so one size from one company may fit better than another. This is another good reason to find a good tire shop that will tolerate fitting the tires specifically to your car. The factory owner's manual from 1974 recommends

165HR15, 185/70VR15, or 215/60VR15 for the stock 911. Unfortunately, good performance tires for 15-inch wheels are getting very difficult to find. The options are much greater for cars equipped with the 16-inch wheels.

In 1978, Porsche widened the flares on the rear of the 911SC, giving much better options for installing tires. The factory also increased the width of the rear wheel to 7 inches. The factory owner's manual for the 911SC indicates that the standard tires for the 911SC are 215/60VR16 for the front and 225/50VR16 for the rear. If you can't find the 215-sized tire, a good 205/55R16 will suffice.

With the wider wheels, the options for the installation of tires grow exponentially. As with the early cars, rolling the fender can help to accommodate a wider wheel and tire. The rear fenders on the 1978–1989 body can be rolled out to fit an 8- or even 9-inch wheel. The fronts can sometimes fit a stock 7-inch wheel combined with a 225/50/16 tire without modifications, but it depends on the car.

It's also possible to place some larger 17-inch wheels on the 1978–1989 chassis. The type of offset used on the wheel and the tire size will affect whether it will fit or not. The offset of a wheel is the distance of the center of the wheel from the edge of the mounting flange on the hub. Different wheels with varying offsets will affect tire sizing considerably, so make sure that you know which types of wheels and offsets you have before you attempt to mount tires to them.

So after reading this project are you still confused? You should be, and rightly so. It appears that there is a never-ending amount of options for tire sizing on the various 911 models. The best way to figure out what type of tires to place on your car is to inquire around. Check on the Internet at the various technical bulletin boards (www.pelicanparts.com) or on the Internet email list Rennlist.org. Bruce Anderson's book, *Porsche 911 Performance Handbook* also has a very handy table on recommended wheels and tire sizes for all year 911s. Nevertheless, you will find that every 911 owner has an opinion to share, and a wheel/tire option tried on his or her car.

PORSCHE 911
RESOURCE GUIDE

Without a doubt, information is the most valuable asset that you can have when working on your car. However, you probably already know that if you are reading this book. There are a few great resources in the world today that can offer you a tremendous amount of technical information and tips on fixing up your 911. Here is a brief list of them and some short descriptions.

Pelican Parts Website and CD-ROM (www.pelicanparts.com)

The Pelican Parts website is arguably the largest automotive website on the internet at the time this book was published. Dedicated primarily to Porsches, and containing more than 500 technical articles, 15,000 photos, technical diagrams, electrical diagrams, and a technical bulletin board, you can find an answer to just about any Porsche question. With a used parts classifieds section and a very complete and comprehensive on-line catalog, Pelican Parts is an excellent place to find both information and parts for your car. The entire Pelican Parts website and technical library is also available on CD-ROM, free of charge. See www.pelicanparts.com or call 1-888-280-7799 for more details.

Rennlist (www.rennlist.org)

With more than 40,000 members on its electronic mailing lists, the Rennlist is an excellent forum to trade information, ask questions, and communicate with other Porsche fans. Although the information available on the Rennlist is not always 100 percent correct (anyone with a computer can sign up), with a little bit of filtering and some common sense, a lot can be learned from this huge collective resource.

Porsche Factory Workshop Manuals

Arguably the best printed resource for repairing your 911. The factory manuals can get expensive—you need to purchase multiple sets that build on each other in order to cover all of the later cars. An inexpensive alternative is the factory parts diagrams on microfiche. Available at Pelican Parts and other parts houses, the microfiche costs less than one-tenth the cost of the printed manuals, with almost all the same pertinent information. It is highly recommended that you purchase either the printed manu-

als or the microfiche if you are planning to work on your 911. The high cost of the printed manuals can be more than worth the money saved by performing repair tasks yourself.

Porsche Technical Specifications Books

Another excellent resource is the factory technical specifications book. At the time of this writing, some of these are no longer being produced by Porsche, and thus are getting very difficult to find. The tech spec books contain specifications and tolerances that are not contained in the factory manuals. These books are published in a 4x3-inch format, and retail for about $13, when they can be found.

Bentley Porsche 911 Service Manual

An excellent alternative to the sometimes confusing and always expensive factory workshop manuals are the Bentley Service Manuals. The Bentley manuals are extremely comprehensive and clear to understand. Detailed pictures, procedures, and diagrams document just about every repair and replacement procedure on the 911. The manuals are well worth their $129 price tag. The only manuals currently available are for the 1984–1989 911 Carrera and 1978-1983 911SC, but others are currently under development.

Porsche Parts and Technical Reference Catalog

Not too many people even know that this book even exists. This 125-page book, printed by Porsche, has detailed diagrams and part number listings for all the major parts used on all models of the 911 from 1974 through 1989. This book was out of print for a while, but has recently resurfaced. The Porsche part number for this book is PNA 000 147, and it commonly retails for about $15.

Up-Fixen Der Porsche Series

The Porsche Club of America has compiled all of the technical articles and columns that have appeared in the Club's monthly magazine into a series of books that are tremendously valuable for technical content. The entire series consists of 11 volumes, and costs about $150, all of which is definitely worth it. Contact the PCA National Office at www.pca.org.

Haynes Workshop Manual

The Haynes Workshop Manual by Peter G. Strasman and Peter Ward is another good cost-effective resource for your 911. Much criticized for glossing over many procedures, the Haynes manual is nonetheless an excellent resource at a great price ($15) when compared to the factory manuals. The Haynes manual shouldn't be relied upon as your only resource, but it is indeed important to have one as a reference.

Haynes Guide to Purchase and D.I.Y. Restoration of the Porsche 911

This book is another excellent resource that contains some information that is difficult to find elsewhere. Concentrating primarily on the interior, bodywork, and engine, this book offers some great procedures and pictures of various projects. At the time of this writing, this book is out of print, but used copies can be found if you look for them. Written by authors Lindsay Porter and Peter Morgan.

The Reader's Digest Complete Car Care Manual

When I first picked up this book at a used book store, I had no idea from the cover that this would become the favorite book in my collection. This book contains about 500 pages of excellent information on just about every system in modern cars, and explains how they work. The text is written so that normal people can understand it, and it is also accompanied not by photos, but extremely detailed color hand-drawn diagrams. If you can find this book, I recommend that you add it to your collection.

Porsche 911 Performance Handbook

While not explicitly a hands-on book, this book by Bruce Anderson offers a unique set of technical information and tips for improving the performance of your 911. The book is chock-full of information on the his-tory of the 911 motor, along with suggestions for engine rebuilding and suspension/brake modifications.

Panorama (Porsche Club of America)

Panorama is the monthly magazine of the Porsche Club of America. If you are not a member already, I suggest that you become one. The glossy monthly magazine is worth the cost of membership alone, and you will find a lot of technical information, as well as advertisements for companies dealing solely with Porsches. Contact the PCA National Office at www.pca.org.

Excellence Magazine

A Porsche-only magazine, *Excellence* is a great resource for Porsche owners. It contains a vast amount of advertisements from Porsche parts companies, and also has good editorials on the cars themselves. It also includes a good tech forum each month, and also a good question-and-answer column. (415) 382-0580.

911 & Porsche World Magazine

This is a British magazine that has a slightly different flair from the other two featured above. Its focus seems to be more on some of the older cars, rather than the newer Porsches. The subscription cost is high because it has to be shipped from England, but the magazine is less commercial than others, and usually contains a lot of good content. See www.chpltd.com. Also sold in the U.S. at www.pelicanparts.com.

Grassroots Motorsports Magazine

This magazine, while not dealing exclusively with Porsches, concentrates on the types of tasks that the backyard mechanic might encounter while restoring and hot-rodding an older 911. The articles tend to focus more on the technical repair and upgrade aspects of owning the cars than other comparable magazines. See www.grassrootsmotorsports.com.

European Car Magazine

European Car has been around a long time, and has shifted through many phases in their magazine content. Fortunately, it is returning to hosting a lot of Porsche content including a recent series of technical articles on a 911S restoration. In addition to technical content on the 911, the magazine covers a lot of general Porsche and German car models.

PORSCHE 911 INDEX